THEN THIS HAPPENED:
AFTER TRANSPARENTLY

I HAVE NO
TOLERANCE FOR
White Supremacy
Racism
Islamophobia
Anti-Semitism
Transphobia
Homophobia
&
Patriarchy

Previously published as
TRANSPARENTLY:
Behind the Scenes of a Good Life

LISA S. SALAZAR

THEN THIS HAPPENED:
After Transparently

Previously published as Transparently:
Behind the Scenes of a Good Life

Scripture taken from the HOLY BIBLE, NEW INTERNATIONAL VERSION®. Copyright © 1973, 1978, 1984 Biblica. Used by permission of Zondervan. and from the NEW AMERICAN STANDARD BIBLE®, Copyright © 1960,1962,1963,1968,1971,1972,1973,1975,1977,1995 by The Lockman Foundation. Used by permission. All rights reserved.

IISBN-978-0-9869319-2-5 ; 2nd Edition ; Printed Book (6"x9")
ISBN-978-0-9869319-3-2 ; 2nd Edition; eBook
ISBN-978-0-9869319-4-9 ; 2nd Edition ; Audiobook

ISBN-978-0-9869319-0-1 ; 1st Edition ; Printed Book
ISBN-978-0-9869319-1-8 ; 1st Edition ; eBook

transparently.ca
contact@transparently.ca
Cover and book design by Lisa Salazar

Table of Contents

Foreword by Duncan Holmes

When I first met the Salazar brothers, Santiago and Enrique, they almost seemed like conjoined twins. That wasn't the case, of course, because while it seemed to work with a common, complementary creative brain, and occasionally finished each other's sentences, Enrique was older than Santiago, and, as I got to know them better, I discovered there were substantial differences in their personalities, in the way they did things, went about their lives—and how those lives would unfold.

Enrique and Santiago, we Anglicized the Spanish and called him Jim, were brothers who had put their wildly artistic talents together to form Salazar Graphics, a hot little firm that, with others in town, supported Vancouver's ad agency business in the Mad Men days of the Sixties and on into the more docile decades that followed. Salazar Graphics worked out of offices in the city's historic Gastown district, then in a period of rebirth. Along with cosmetic changes that brought old bricks back to life, Gastown became a gathering place for tie-dyed, flower-power kids and endless stores hung with psychedelic black light posters of the era.

I met Enrique and Santiago when I became marketing director for the new and burgeoning Keg Restaurants family. With ease and direction that seemed to come from their very hearts, they were able to chart a graphics course for the Keg in its early, rapidly growing years. Again, the skills of one complemented the talents of the other. Not only were their images right, but the execution of the art was magnificent. Every piece, from typography to illustration, reflected superb training and a desire to take ever-bigger creative steps to make things work as they should.

Over the years, as we saw more of each other with the Keg and later with other clients, I learned more about the Salazars, even if we never really became social partners. As Enrique continued his bachelor life, Jim shared his family stories as I shared mine. His wife and three sons. My wife and four daughters. I met his siblings and his parents, who I always figured looked the part of comfortable Colombians, continuing always to converse in Spanish with their sons—as close-knit as a family could ever be. And as with Jim, I suspected that their Christian faith was strong, even if this course of personal belief never seemed to manifest itself in too much joy. My inclination on many occasions was to question why melancholy pervaded their collective lives. I never asked.

I can't recall exactly when these events happened, but somewhere in our relationship, there were two shockers. Out of the blue one day, Enrique blacked out and slammed into a parked car. He was diagnosed with brain cancer, and after a long downhill ride, a man who, in retrospect, I barely knew left us. It was a huge gap in this close-knit family, the loss for me of a friend. The second thing? Jim confided in me the details of an extraordinary life secret. As a child in California, he had been coaxed into a private setting and sexually molested by someone he believed he could trust.

I can't explain why, but it was difficult to understand how this incident affected him. As a child, for some inexplicable reason, I blackmailed the man involved in a similar sexual encounter, demanding money or exposure of his crime. Then I promptly thought no more about it. Judge me as you will.

Jim's admission opened the door to more profound exchanges between us, and in the years that followed, we shared much, even as I believe I sought more. My journalistic curiosity prompted an ongoing need to keep prying about Jim's life, the secrets that perhaps remained to be shared.

On Friday, October 15, 2007, again out of the blue, a much bigger message opened Santiago Salazar's life book in a spectacular way. On the previous Friday afternoon, Jim answered a question about what he was up to and was working on a biographical thing about himself. I said that I would love to read it when it was done, and he said that when it was finished, maybe I could. On Monday, after discussing an unrelated client thing, I asked about the progress of the bio, and if I could read it. Jim hesitated but agreed on the condition that partner Joyce and I read it jointly.

I don't remember how Jim's Big Message was first broached, but he said his life was about to change, and could I guess how? To me, it seemed obvious. He would enter the ministry. This guy could quote the bible chapter and verse, spent regular mornings in its study, and was a disciplined churchgoer and Sunday in-church performer. It seemed pretty logical that in this light-bulb moment, he would chuck commercial art for the ecclesiastical cloth. No, he said, not that.

It was a long e-mail—almost as long as my words to date. It told of a life of pain, where something physical, physiological, emotional, and more had been trapped inside his body. Inside him was a woman. And the time had come to free her. Santiago, Jim would become Lisa.

Regardless of the huge consequences that I knew would be forthcoming in Lisa's life, my immediate reaction was joy. The joy that this imprisoned person could break out and take a natural path to potential happiness. I said to myself that this had been the reason for all those years of sadness. A butterfly in whatever form would emerge awkwardly from a chrysalis and fly into an endless life of sunshine. Saints be praised!

Lisa would later say: "Our short conversation (on Monday) and the subsequent one ten minutes later when you called back became forever cast in my memory. My life didn't come to an end as I had feared. Instead, your words that day helped cut an opening for the path that would widen with time. I am so grateful to you and Joyce... "I will never forget the comment you made when you called me after reading the letter. You said that this explained why you wondered what made me so incredibly sad every time you walked away from one of those heavy conversations. You admitted how you had tried to pry open that very private door on more than one occasion, to which I replied that I sensed that—and would try to change the subject or deflect you away."

In the subsequent year, as the Santiago of yesterday disappeared quietly into the grey blur of history, we watched Lisa walk ever more confidently into a new world of womanhood. It was always a vision of pride, of bravery, and new-found happiness.

Foreword by kaitlyn Bogas

I met Lisa in the fall of 2009. I had written an article about my transition for a local Vancouver publication, and Lisa had responded online to support what she had read. As far as I know, it was the first time that she had really "outed" herself publicly. It was something that she really didn't have to do and hadn't planned to do, but I am ever so glad that she did. On that day, Lisa took a huge step in becoming who she is today, a wonderful woman of love and compassion who I'm quite certain will spend a lifetime helping others.

I'm not certain why many among us choose to make our stories public. Perhaps we are all too aware of the stigma that is attached to being trans. We believe that it's all so obvious that everyone will just "get it," even if we have to beat them over the head long enough with our stories of personal liberation. Perhaps, on the other hand, we feel so much like celebrating that we made it through our tormented pasts, and survived long enough to reach transition, that we feel like shouting through the streets.

Transitioning requires a tremendous leap of faith on the part of the individual. I believe that we must prepare ourselves to lose everyone and everything we hold dear. Our ability to care for ourselves and our families is compromised the second we come out. And all of this for what? There's no pink or blue light in your brain that shows up in a CT scan, no blood test, no genetic tests, and no tattoo behind your left ear. All you have is that persistent feeling that you are not whom you appear to be, and that thought never leaves.

I would ask of you, then, that you share this leap of faith that Lisa felt compelled to follow. Open your mind to her story; she has no reason to lie to you. Keep compassion in your heart, and allow Lisa to take you through an amazing life story!

Section 1 Preface

Just before New Year's 2010, I began corresponding with a friend who asked me some insightful questions. She challenged me to think deeply about my life, experiences, and identity in just a few emails. I found myself pouring my heart out to her, and before I knew it, we had exchanged several lengthy emails.

During one of our exchanges, I mentioned to her that I may have a good start on a book thanks to her questioning. I had never written anything longer than a college term paper, but something about her questions sparked a fire. My friend encouraged me to keep writing and said the more I answered her questions, the more she wanted to know.

By the end of February, I found writing to be therapeutic. I would laugh and cry as I wrote, amazed at how quickly my story came together. I had never felt so compelled to write, and I knew I was onto something special.

As I wrote, I pondered on a title for my book. I knew I didn't want to add to the growing list of stories about trans people, and I didn't want readers to expect this book to be a testament to "the cause." Most of all, I wanted to emphasize that my life has not been a tragedy, and I don't wish or deserve pity or admiration.

I have had a blessed and happy life, despite my gender identity crisis that took me more than 40 years to understand and another 16 years to reconcile and accept. Ultimately, I chose a title that best describes this book: a look behind the scenes of my good life and the process of becoming transparent about who I am. Despite my private and confusing struggle, I have had a busy and happy life full of healthy distractions, but I couldn't avoid the inevitable tension.

Dedicating this book to just one person was impossible for

me. I have been blessed with amazing parents and siblings, and I am most grateful for my wife, who has known me as her husband and the father of her children. I am also fortunate to be surrounded by an amazing group of friends. To my family and friends, thank you for allowing me to journey with you in the past and for the amazing gift of continuing our journey together.

I also acknowledge that, despite my wavering faith, Christ is the thread woven into my life that kept me from unraveling. Or, if you prefer a less religious way, the Higher Power that has kept me from losing it crazy and harming myself. This book is not just about my journey of self-discovery but also a tribute to the love and support I have received from those around me.

The Preface for Section 2 follows Chapter 12.

Chapter 1: Trip to the Moon & Beyond

The anticipation and excitement of my first airplane trip on a Braniff Airlines DC-7 from Bogotá to Miami via Panama City were beyond words. Even now, over six decades later, I still remember it like it was yesterday. For a 10-year-old, it was akin to traveling to the moon. My family of eight, including five children aged 2 to 16, my parents, and my grandmother, were finally realizing our two-year dream of moving to the U.S. on October 6, 1960.

As we arrived at El Dorado airport in Bogotá, I recall the chaos and commotion. Our extended family, aunts, uncles, cousins, and close family friends had gathered to bid us farewell. Some were crying, while others cheered us on. The moment was overwhelming, and I was unsure if I should be happy or sad. We were the first of our extended family to migrate, it was hard to fully grasp the significance of the moment.

Today, only a handful of my numerous first cousins remain in Colombia, with many having become grandparents and great-grandparents and now scattered across Florida and Texas.

For me, as a fourth-grader, moving to the United States was a dream come true. My classmates were envious, and they thought I was lucky to be going to America, especially to California. Although I couldn't fully comprehend the excitement at the time, I now understand the universal appeal for life in the United States went deeper than just moving to a new place.

The political climate of the time played a significant role. With Castro's takeover in Cuba, the possibility of leftist guerrillas succeeding in Colombia and other South American countries loomed large. Perhaps this influenced my parents' decision to make a change. However, there were other reasons as well, which I will delve into later.

I imagined California as a giant Disneyland, with sunny beaches, blue jeans, and Milky Way candy bars—images forged from movies, the Wonderful World of Disney that aired every Sunday night on Bogotá's one television station, and from the stories of those who had gone to "paradise" and returned with LevI's and chocolate bars and Bazooka bubble gum.

Bogotá has a constant climate all year round, being close to the Equator and high in the Andes, with warm days and cool nights—very different from the hot and muggy climate in Florida when we arrived. As we stepped off the plane on the tarmac in Miami, we were hit with a blast of hot air mixed with the smell of diesel fuel and a noticeable humid muskiness that lasted until we entered the air-conditioned terminal.

We had a mountain of suitcases with us, and it took us ages to clear immigration and customs. Only my father and older sister could speak English. My dad would take turns with my mom holding my baby brother, while the rest of us waited quietly while dad dealt with the officials, and presented our customs declarations, visas and passports.

We landed with what my mom felt we would need to survive our first month in the U.S. My parents had sold off many of our belongings in a couple of garage sales that were organized by a gringa who had experience in such matters. Some of the larger things were put in storage in case we returned after a few years, and the rest was shipped through the Panama Canal to San Francisco.

We had only lived three years in our new house, which sat on two large lots in a new suburb in the north of Bogotá. One half of the property was yard, and my dad, who along with my mom was a golf enthusiast, placed a very short par three hole on it, complete with green and bunkers. The house had marble floors and huge plate glass windows, which ran the whole length of the house facing the yard. Dad and my uncles owned a marble mill and contracting company; this explains the marble floors. (Dad was the firm's administrator, and his two oldest brothers were both civil engineers and the founding senior partners.)

My parents chose not to sell the house in Bogotá since they wanted to keep the door open in case we returned to Colombia.

Instead, the house was leased to the American Embassy for a U.S. Air Force colonel, part of the American mission in Colombia. The lease was for three years. This set the clock for our possible return.

As a family, we embarked on what felt like the longest vacation we had ever taken: two weeks in the U.S. at the Golden Nugget Motel in Miami Beach. The motel's swimming pool and beach entertained us kids as we soaked up the sun and played. Our taste buds were introduced to the delicious Wonder Bread and sliced processed cheese that became our go-to meal for the duration of our stay.

During our time at the motel, my parents went out to look for a car that would be suitable for our upcoming road trip across the United States. They returned with a shiny, brand new, pale green 1960 Buick Le Sabre two-door hardtop with air-conditioning. It was a large car with a huge trunk, but packing and arranging all our luggage was no easy task. Nevertheless, we managed to fit everything in, and the car was laden with so much baggage that it sat low to the ground like an ocean freighter.

We arranged ourselves in a way that would be considered illegal today. Dad drove, and Mom and my grandmother took turns sitting in the front passenger seat with one of us kids sitting between them. The backseat was even more cramped, with four of us squished in and the two-year-old on someone's lap.

Dad insisted that the air-conditioning would only work if all the windows were rolled up. Unfortunately, he and my grandmother were heavy smokers, with my mom occasionally smoking. We were held captive for hours at a time in a cramped space filled with second-hand smoke. We would fall out of the car every time we stopped, gasping for fresh air and feeling green.

Dad regretted exposing us to so much second-hand smoke, and in 1963, he quit smoking cold turkey when he learned that one of his older brothers had died from emphysema caused by smoking.

As we made our way up the coast, we eventually had to say goodbye to the beach and head north through central Florida. It was my first time seeing and experiencing the ocean, and I was sad to leave. We had a cousin who lived in South Carolina, and before heading west, we drove up to see him and his wife. I'll never forget the amazing deep apple pies his wife baked when we arrived. They were the epitome of American food.

Driving through Alabama and Mississippi, we were always on the lookout for Howard Johnson's restaurants. My older sister Carmen was addicted to their strawberry milkshakes, and we all loved their cheeseburgers. I was still learning English, but with Carmen's help, I was able to order what I wanted and say "thank you very much." As a ten-year-old, I was unsure of how to act and often looked to my older siblings for guidance. I tried to emulate Enrique, my older brother, by liking what he liked and speaking like he spoke.

On top of the cultural adjustments, I also struggled with being a bedwetter. It was not an easy problem to have on a trip like this, and I couldn't help but wonder how many motel mattresses I had ruined. It certainly didn't help my already low self-esteem. I was constantly weighing myself against others and looking for similarities and differences. Bedwetting was a difference that made me feel inferior, especially since no one else in my family seemed to struggle with it.

1.1: California, Here We Come

As I look back on the fall of 1960, I realize it was a pivotal moment for my family. It was also when I came face to face with my vulnerabilities, compounded by the fact that I could not speak the language. Moving to a new country can be daunting, but for the most part, my experience was anything but traumatic. Yet there were moments of sheer panic that, in retrospect, are funny to me now.

One such moment occurred when we visited the subterranean caves in Carlsbad, New Mexico, en route to California. I needed to use the restroom, and my dad pointed me toward a sign that ended with "MEN." I entered confidently, only to find myself smack in the middle of the ladies' washroom, with all of them staring at me like an interloper. After what seemed like an eternity of stunned silence, I dashed back out of there but stopped to examine the sign one more time. "WOMEN," I concluded, must mean the other sex. Across the passageway, I saw another sign that only said "MEN" and entered cautiously.

Though it's a cute story now, at the time, I just wanted the earth to open up and swallow me whole. I've always been hypersensitive and had a well-developed sense of guilt and shame, making me the person who sees a cop and automatically sticks his hands out to be handcuffed. I was pretty hard on myself and had a tendency to overthink things, which led to a constant sense of inadequacy and insecurity that overshadowed any success or praise I might receive.

I stayed close to my brother Enrique during our journey across the Southern states. This was especially true when we went to Disneyland in California. He was my protector, charged with keeping an eye on me and taking the same rides, including the Matterhorn. Though later on, when I was a freshman in high school and a junior, he despised being tasked with caring for his little brother. "Yes, you can borrow the car to go to the basketball game, but take your brother with you," my mom would say. Those words were a bitter pill to him, and at times he resented me.

At an early age, I recognized that though I tried to be just like Enrique, there were things he did or said or things he liked that did not seem to fit me. Too introspective and insecure to realize it was natural to feel this way, I forced myself to try harder to be like him. Without realizing it, I was developing the skill that served me well all my life: the suppression of who I am.

In the larger scheme of things, there was nothing extraordinary about the uprooting and transplanting of our family. No generation, tribe, or nationality has been immune to a yearning to live in a different land, in a better place, regardless of the cost. If there was a price to be paid for our relocation, it was paid in large part by my grandmother and my mom. They lost their social and family standings and were cut off from everything that defined them. By comparison, we kids were a bit more resilient and adaptable. Consequently, our sense of isolation and detachment was short-lived, but it was not so for them.

My Dad was always the visionary and the driving force behind everything we did. He had always dreamed of moving to the U.S. since the day he got married, despite his business ties with his brothers back in Colombia. When he was just eighteen, he left on a steamship and arrived in New York City with only twenty dollars in his pocket. Unlike his two older brothers, my grandfather refused to pay for my dad's education because he wasn't a straight-A student like his siblings. Dad decided to do it on his own and left on bad terms with his father.

In New York, Dad had slept at the YMCA when he could afford it and survived doing all kinds of low-paying jobs. Over time, he learned to type, write shorthand, and do general office work. Eventually, he became the secretary to an executive in Dayton, Ohio.

One day, he received a telegram from one of his brothers with news that their father was dying and imploring him to come home to make peace with him. So, he returned to Colombia a few months before the Japanese attacked Pearl Harbor in December 1941. There, he met my mom at his brother's birthday party in mid-November. For now, his dream of going back to the U.S. had to wait. There was a war on, and he had fallen in love.

As for why we ended up in San Jose, California, it all had to do with my parents' friendship with the Sisters of Marymount. They ran a handful of all-girl schools in the U.S., including one in Bogotá, where my older sister Carmen had been enrolled. So, my parents decided to live in America, where the sisters had one of their schools. They ruled out most of the schools on the East Coast because of their cold, snowy winters.

The choice was then between their two schools in California: one in Palos Verdes near Long Beach, and the other in San Jose, south of San Francisco. San Jose won out because it was close to San Francisco, and the weather was milder than that of Los Angeles.

When we arrived in San Jose, we pulled into a motel on US 101. It was a far cry from the resort-like motel we had stayed in Miami. We planned to stay there until my parents found us a house. For two weeks, we endured the boring little corner of San Jose. The motel was coincidentally downwind of an Accent plant, and we breathed in copious amounts of MSG-laden stinky air. We watched TV from the moment we awoke until we went to sleep at night.

As a young language learner, I quickly learned the value of repetition when trying to master a new language. Fortunately, the repetitious nature of daytime television was a welcome resource for me. I eagerly absorbed every word and phrase that I heard, even if they were initially meaningless in isolation. However, when combined with the moving images and facial expressions on the screen, these words and phrases suddenly came to life and became comprehensible.

Day after day, I eagerly tuned in to shows like *The Price is Right, Captain Kangaroo, Andy Griffith, Route 66, My Three Sons, Surfside 6,* and *I Love Lucy,* eager to learn more and improve my language skills.

When my parents bought our new house, it was in one of the many subdivisions that were popping up all over the Santa Clara Valley. The valley was once filled with picturesque orchards, but now these new developments were starting to consume the land. There was a social divide between the East and West Valley at the time. The East was where the Mexicans, Chicanos and Black people lived, and it was the older half of the city that was not enjoying the rapid development of the West.

Our new subdivision was called Primrose Lane, and it was in Phase I, which was almost sold out. Phase II was already under construction, and the sound of hammers and electric saws was a constant for almost a year after we moved in. Most of the new homeowners were aerospace workers at massive facilities for companies like Lockheed and General Electric; Silicon Valley was not yet a reality.

Our family was a perfect fit for the neighborhood since most families had two or more kids. However, most of the newly occupied houses had barren adobe-like dirt lots with no landscaping. The houses were sold this way, and it was up to the homeowners to seed their lawns, plant their trees and shrubs, and do their own landscaping. But not us. My parents bought one of the four display homes on Camellia Way, which boasted a fully landscaped designer yard. We did not have to lift a finger; we had the complete turnkey package.

With the house purchase complete, my parents' next task was to acquire all the furnishings and household items we would need. As delivery trucks arrived with mattresses, bureaus, chairs, tables, sofas, and linen, we "made do" for the first few days. Curiosity drew kids from up and down the block, and little by little, we began to recognize our neighbors and exchanged friendly gestures since we could not communicate any other way. It was a new beginning, and we were excited to start this new chapter of our lives in our brand-new home.

1.2: Growing Roots

As my family settled into our new home, reality hit me hard: I was starting school in a foreign country. Angela and I were enrolled in a public elementary school, and I was placed in Mr. Bennett's fifth-grade class. My older siblings attended different schools, and we were all transported by yellow school buses. At Moreland Elementary School, I was the only foreign national and English as Second Language (ESL) student, making me a novelty to my new classmates.

Mr. Bennett, who reminded me of Perry Mason, was my teacher. He spoke Spanish, which made the principal, Mrs. Anderson, believe he best fit me. During my first day, I was introduced to the class and seated at the back of the room. I felt a bit overwhelmed during recess when my curious classmates bombarded me with questions that I didn't understand.

But one boy, John, took me under his wing. He was a friendly freckle-faced strawberry-blonde boy whose father was a captain in the fire department. John gently pulled me aside during the first week of school to explain that running in the hallways was forbidden and I would get in trouble if I continued to do so. I was grateful for his help and thought to myself, "I don't want to get in trouble."

As I navigated the new school environment, I learned about other rules, such as an invisible line separating the playground for the first to fourth graders from the fifth and sixth graders. I discovered this line the hard way when I ventured into the wrong area and was surrounded by fourth-grade boys who taunted and bullied me. They pushed and poked me while yelling incomprehensible words. I could only understand one phrase, "Stupid Mexican!" Thankfully, John came to my rescue, pulling me to safety beyond the invisible line.

Starting school in a new country wasn't easy, but I was grateful for John's kindness and guidance during those early days.

As the days passed, our family settled into our new life in San Jose. I watched my parents and grandmother transform our house into a home, unpacking boxes and adding their personal touches. The scent of mothballs lingered in the air for days, but it was worth it to finally have our belongings with us.

As the primary breadwinner, my dad was under pressure to find work and support our family. He decided to enroll in night school to study for his real estate license believing it was a booming industry in San Jose. After all, San Jose was a boomtown and houses were being built at breakneck speed. What better industry to focus on?

Once Dad had his license, encouraged by his conversations with the agents who worked at Primrose Lane, he approached Stone and Schulte Realty, whose signs seemed everywhere.

They signed him up and assigned him to their office in East San Jose, serving the Chicano and Mexican community. This seemed like the perfect fit for my dad. Since he spoke Spanish, he was soon fielding leads left and right.

But success did not come easily. For every five offers he processed, only one would qualify. The majority of his time was spent on deals that ultimately fell through, leaving him with a disproportionate amount of work compared to his English-only colleagues. Despite this, he remained determined to provide for our family in this new country.

Meanwhile, life was changing in other ways too. My upcoming tenth birthday would be the first one celebrated without our extended family in Colombia. It was a reminder that from now on, things would be different. But as the days passed, we were slowly finding our way in this new place we called home.

The romance of life in America was beginning to lose some of its luster and magic for my mom, who had enjoyed having maids in Colombia who did the cooking, house cleaning and laundry. Now she was doing it all without complaining.

My grandmother was no slouch either. She pitched in and watched over us whenever my parents went out. I remember looking at her with admiration and sensing that she was lonely. We were the only social contact she had, yet she was always lovingly positive and reassuring. Because she didn't speak English, her isolation was total. Her only contact with the outside world was a Realistic transistor shortwave radio. She liked to listen to Spanish broadcasts of her favorite novellas (soaps). Aside from that, even watching TV with us was not as enjoyable for her, except for the variety shows with music and dancing such as Lawrence Welk and *The Ed Sullivan Show*.

However, this is what she wanted for us. Mom had been reluctant to leave Colombia, but my grandmother told her she should think about the future of her children in Colombia, especially in view of the events in Cuba. She added that she was willing to give up everything for her grandchildren so they could have the opportunity of a lifetime. For my parents, that helped to tip the scale in favor of coming to the U.S. They had agonized about how our move would affect my grandmother; mom was an only child, and leaving her mother alone in Colombia was not an option.

Wanting so badly to fit in motivated us to learn English. In those days, there were no ESL classes; it was sink or swim for Enrique, my younger sister Angela, and me. Carmen had a good command of English, thanks to her many years in school with the American Sisters in Bogotá. In class, Mr. Bennett allowed me to take part in math and science since, as it turned out, in fourth grade, I had already studied what was being taught in fifth grade in California. Mr. Bennet also included me in the vocabulary and spelling quizzes he gave every week.

The rest of the time, he had me sit at one of the art tables in the back of the classroom with a stack of old Sears catalogs and magazines, a pair of scissors, a bottle of glue and large newsprint scrapbooks. My assignment was to cut out objects, paste them into the book, and write down their names: toaster, tire, dress, hat, pants, glove, rake, vacuum cleaner, etc. I got to draw pictures of objects too. Since I am artistic, I had lots of fun at the back of the class.

My classmates were always surprised at how well I did on the spelling tests. My secret was that I was learning the words phonetically and pronounced them as if they were Spanish words. When Mr. Bennett would call out the words, I would sound them out in my head in Spanish, and that was it—it worked almost one hundred percent of the time. The vocabulary tests were usually multiple-choice, but I gradually began to understand and pick out the correct definitions.

1.3: A New Awareness

The fifth grade for me was a year full of new experiences. Among them was being in a coed class for the first time. The schools I attended in Colombia separated the boys from the girls. My last school even had different bus schedules, start times, and lunch periods for boys and girls. We never saw each other. For each, it was as if the other sex didn't exist. Now I realized things about myself that were very confusing, and I didn't know how to make sense of these conflicting feelings, thoughts, and questions.

This puzzle was all the more overwhelming when combined with all the other issues of being new in a foreign country and not knowing the language. Insecure and introspective, I never said anything to anyone, not just out of embarrassment but because I couldn't explain myself in a way that would make sense. It was as if there was yet another language I still had to learn.

These were not new feelings or questions. I had felt them for as long as I could remember, and however confusing and puzzling they were, I had no words to describe them. My new proximity to girls was both fascinating and scary. Though I had many female first cousins and had been around them whenever our extended family celebrated all manner of occasions, there was very little interaction between the boys and the girls. Boys were put together to play with boys and girls with girls. I was far enough in age from both of my sisters that, even at home, there was not that much interaction between us. With the move to the States, I was suddenly exposed to girls my age five days a week; I was unprepared.

There was one little girl in my class whose name was Marsha. I don't know why I found myself transfixed by her. She was fearless, always hanging upside down from the monkey bars in her capris, not caring if her skirt flew up.

That was the first time I experienced an awareness that I wished I were a girl. This thought was quickly doused with a bucket full of self-recrimination and self-ridicule. How could I be so silly? And what if anyone found out I had this crazy notion in my head?

Marsha's dad was either laid off or transferred, and her family moved away halfway through the school year, and I never saw her again. But she was the one who caused me to ask myself, why was I not a girl? It made more sense to me; I felt more comfortable with that idea than that of being a boy.

This puzzle I was trying to solve felt like a million-dollar question, but it was also the start of my journey to understand the disconnection I had with my body. From my earliest memories, I had a sense that something wasn't quite right. As a toddler, I vividly remember glancing down at my genitals while playing in the bathtub and feeling uncomfortable, grabbing the washcloth to cover myself up. This behavior continued as I got older, avoiding looking at or acknowledging that part of my body.

Parents of trans individuals are often asked if they noticed anything different or unusual about their child, but there were no obvious red flags in my case. My parents were loving and attentive but unaware of my internal struggles. I learned to hide my feelings and blend in with societal expectations.

The pressure to conform and hide my true self increased as I grew older. I learned to be stealthy and deceptive not out of malice but as a survival mechanism. I constantly worried about being discovered and feared accidentally letting my secret slip out. Although I wasn't engaging in any strange or secretive behavior, it was the turmoil in my head that I couldn't resolve.

There was one incident, however, that stands out in my memory. My parents surprised us during our first summer in California by purchasing an above-ground swimming pool. A neighbor had installed one in a day—it was an instant swimming pool! What a great idea, especially since summers in San Jose were much hotter than anything we were used to.

One afternoon, I found myself alone in the backyard near the swimming pool, mesmerized as I watched trails of tiny black ants make their way across the hot cement patio. As I played with them by putting obstacles in their way, I spotted Carmen's one-piece swimsuit hanging on one of the rungs of the pool ladder. I went up to it and touched it as if to see if it would bite. Suddenly I had this crazy idea to put it on.

Without thinking twice, I grabbed the swimsuit, stepped

behind some waist-high shrubs under my parent's bedroom window, quickly stripped off my clothes, and slipped into the one-piece swimsuit. It was way too big on me, and hung down unceremoniously. But no sooner had I put it on than I heard a loud knocking on the window above me. My mom shook her head and signaled, "No! No!" with her index finger.

I don't think Superman ever changed as fast as I did then. I rehung the suit on the ladder and was expecting my mom to come out to yell at me. But she didn't. That anticipation was probably worse, and I agonized like crazy. After a while, thinking my life was over and feeling overcome with embarrassment, I sneaked back into the house and into my room to wait for the world to end. I knew that Dad would be home soon, and I figured Mom would delegate justice to him as she had done many times before.

But nothing happened. I guess Mom just shrugged it off as an ordinary boy's curiosity. That was my first experience wearing a girl's clothing, and the guilt, shame, and embarrassment I felt went off the charts.

By the time sixth grade began (1961), we had been in the U.S. for under a year. My new teacher, Mrs. Lewin, lived directly across the street from us. Though my English was improving, there were still many things I misunderstood. At a neighborhood end of summer party, and Mrs. Lewin came up to me and bent down to tell me she was going to be my teacher that year. Honestly, I didn't fully understand everything she had said. I must have looked disappointed to her, so she asked if I was unhappy about being in her class.

I understood the word "happy" in her question, so I said "Yes!" With a worried look, she asked me one more time, and I gave her the same answer. Finally, she asked sadly, "You don't want to be in my class?" I finally understood what she was asking me, and I answered, "Yes, I want to be in your class." Then it dawned on me that "unhappy" was the opposite of "happy." Darn those compound English words!

"When I was in sixth and seventh grade, I attended Rogers Junior High School, which had just opened that year. It was a completely new experience for me. All the schools I had previously attended were old and had a distinctive smell of floor wax, old plywood desks, and a rubbery aroma. Rogers was different; everything smelled new and fresh.

The new junior high drew students from several elementary schools, so it took time to get to know everyone. I was still trying to find my place in this new country and felt insecure about myself. My desire to assimilate and fit in with everyone else fueled my doubts and feelings of inferiority. I couldn't shake the feeling that something was wrong with me, and my narrow view of the world and linear thinking caused me a lot of anguish.

As a boy, I often argued with myself about my body and what it meant. I didn't understand the biological differences between boys and girls until I was eleven. Before then, I only saw superficial differences between the two, such as how girls wore frilly dresses and ribbons in their hair while boys wore pants and dark colors. However, I wasn't particularly drawn to "girly" things, and my likes and interests were similar to my brother Enrique's.

It's hard for me to really describe what I went through during that time. I remember feeling like a broken record, constantly beating myself up for not knowing how to act. The easiest path for me seemed to be to mimic my brother, who didn't seem to have any anxiety about his body. I envied him for that, but at the same time, I grew repulsed at how comfortable he was with his own body. How could he not be turned off by it like I was with mine?

As time passed, I started to notice changes in my brother's body. He was well into puberty, and whiskers and body hair were beginning to appear on him. I was horrified for him, but at the same time, I couldn't help but feel envious.

When we lived in Colombia, we belonged to one of Bogotá's most exclusive golf and country clubs, known as "Los Lagartos" (The Lizards). Beyond compare, it was like an immense playground with a lagoon big enough for ski boats, two swimming pools, tennis courts, and acres of undeveloped property within its gates. We spent many weekends there, and I occasionally had to go with my dad into the men's locker room.

There, I saw men who were only covered by a towel around their waist, and I assumed women and girls probably did the same thing, but I didn't know how else they might be different. The only other impression I recall was the amount of body hair on some of those men; I found that very troubling for some reason.

When I was about five years old, I accidentally fell into the lagoon, fully dressed. As I was being taken back to my parents, I remembered when a boy my age had fallen into one of the swimming pools with his clothes on. His mother had rushed him into the women's changing room, and when they emerged, he was wearing a girl's swimsuit. He didn't seem to be worried about what anyone thought.

As I stood there dripping wet, I couldn't help but think about that boy. Why wasn't I allowed to wear a girl's swimsuit too? I was wrapped in towels while my clothes were wrung out and put back on me. I felt deprived, and I wondered why they didn't treat me the same way they had treated that boy. Years later, when my mom found me trying on my sister's swimsuit, I couldn't help but feel the same way—deprived.

Chapter 2: How American Can We Get

Back on the family front, the first two years in California were the most intense in terms of adjustments. Our new house was barely large enough for a family of eight. My mom and grandmother, bless their souls, had to recalibrate their recipes about cooking times. At the elevation of Bogotá—more than 8,300 feet above sea level—it takes twice as long to boil water. Consequently, there were many burnt meals in San Jose at first.

Most of our meals in Colombia would have been cooked from scratch. Though available in the market, such things as leafy greens were only used as a garnish and seldom consumed, as they were too commonly contaminated with salmonella and other nasty things. We ate plenty of rice, beans, and potatoes, along with some type of protein. Our meat was always well done, and our vegetables boiled to death.

Compared to the bounty of food and all the possibilities available in San Jose's supermarkets, our diet in Colombia didn't vary too much. The novel discovery for us in California was the frozen T.V. dinner and other packaged meals. These solved several problems since mom was tired of running a "hotel." Now we could pick the entree of our choosing. It was such a modern way to do things, but I don't think a single family member didn't put on additional pounds, and they came on quickly. Our bodies just soaked up all those calories.

So by the time seventh grade approached in the fall of 1962, I now had another problem—I was chubby and much more self-conscious than I had ever been. I was horrified to learn that, from seventh grade on up, one had to shower at the end of P.E. class, which was daily.

I was almost nauseous the first day we donned our P.E. clothes and showered at the end of the period. I did not want to face anyone when we showered in the locker room. I made my way from my locker to the closest six-headed shower pole with one arm folded against my jiggling chest and the other holding up the towel I had wrapped around my waist, just like I had seen the men in the country club do. It wasn't long before those in my stall started laughing at me. Then, to my horror, someone yanked the towel out of my hand. Someone else said, "Look at the tiny dick!" More laughter. If ever there was a moment when I wanted to vanish into thin air, this was it.

This was not a good way to start the school year. From that day on until my 21st birthday when California law exempted one from P.E. classes (even in college and university), I had to grin and bear it—pardon the pun. I'm not kidding; my heart was always in my throat, and to deal with it, I was determined to always run to the locker room to be one of the first in and out of the showers and into my clothes. If I was delayed for some reason, I would wait for as many to shower before I ventured in. Naturally, I never could talk to anyone about my little hang-up.

Today, post-traumatic stress is recognized as a serious medical condition, and there are support systems available to those who may be suffering from it. This wasn't necessarily the case in the early sixties. Would things be different for me if someone could have intervened? I'm not sure. Much of my confusion predated a couple of events in my life, which alone would qualify me for therapy today.

The first took place in the fall of 1962. Like Enrique, I too had started to deliver newspapers. His route was predominantly in our subdivision, whereas mine was across Williams Road, the main artery that fed our streets. Several blocks of two-story apartment buildings were on the south side of that busy street. I delivered the afternoon San Jose News to about eighty apartments.

At the end of every month, I would go door-to-door to collect three dollars from each customer. It often took several tries before finding my customers at home. One night, as I began my rounds, I knocked on one door, but there was no answer. I started down the stairs when I heard the door open behind me. A man called out,

"Who's there?"

I said I was the paperboy collecting for the subscription. He asked me to come back up. When I got to the door, I saw he was wrapped in a towel. He apologized and said he was just about to step into the shower. He invited me in and closed the door while he went to the bedroom to get his wallet.

Through all this, I kept thinking it was okay to see a man seminude and not to worry because he was covered in a towel, that I should take the cash, give him his receipt, and get out of there as fast as possible. Imagine my shock when he returned to the living room without the towel and sporting a raging erection. I didn't know where to look except down at the receipt book in my hands. He handed me the money, but as I went to take it, he grabbed my hand and pulled me into the bedroom, warning me to stay quiet. There he proceeded to masturbate with my hand wrapped around his penis. What resistance I offered was no match for his strength, and I could not pull away. I could not bear to look at what he was doing and just wished I had never been born. After he ejaculated and wiped his and my hand with a towel, he threatened me not to tell anyone. I left his apartment quickly and don't remember anything else about that night except washing my hands with soap for a very long time.

I was afraid to tell my parents and Enrique about what had happened to me, and I never did. The thought of telling them terrified me, as I was scared that my parents would take us back to Colombia if they found out. If the police were called, I was afraid that we could be deported, which would be a shameful outcome for my family. Moreover, I felt guilty and believed that what had happened was my fault.

The second incident occurred when I was fifteen, but before I share that experience, I need to fill you in on what happened between 1961 and 1965. Several events affected us as a family, including the Cuban missile crisis, which made us feel relieved to be in the U.S. We all feared what might happen to Colombia if the Cuban-inspired Communist guerrillas succeeded. I remember air raid drills, low-flying military jets, and the hysteria of those few weeks when things got a little intense.

By the summer of 1963, my parents had decided that we

needed a bigger house, and they chose to customize aspects and features of a six-bedroom, two-story home in the construction stage in a new subdivision. As a result, Angela and I had to change schools while Enrique would continue attending the same high school. Carmen was already enrolled at Foothill College in Los Altos.

I previously mentioned that our house in Bogotá was leased for three years, as the plan was that we might return to Colombia. There were intense discussions about this, and Enrique was quite vocal about not wanting to return to Bogotá, as he would lose a school year. He had calculated that because of his birth month and the different school year calendars, he would have to repeat the year he had just completed. He also argued that if Carmen had been allowed to graduate from the Marymount nun's school, he should be allowed to finish high school in California. My parents eventually decided to sell the house in Colombia.

Unfortunately, real estate prices are not tied to the exchange rate of the local currency, and as a result, my parents lost much of their personal worth when they exchanged the Colombian Pesos for U.S. dollars. They put that money into the purchase of the new house. The sale of the Camellia Way house in San Jose, which had been on the market for a long time, did not result in a significant capital gain, as there was a surplus of housing due to layoffs at Lockheed. It was a buyer's market.

We moved into the new house at the same time that school started in the fall of 1963. It was much better for living space, but I was upset to leave Rogers Junior High and all my friends behind. Being the new kid in school is always stressful, and it was doubly hard for me. Just as I was starting to feel comfortable with one group of people, I had to start over with a new group. I didn't like being an outsider.

I complained to Enrique about having to go to a different school, but he pointed out that I would get to be with my old friends again in ninth grade when I started at Blackford High School. He thought I was lucky since I would know twice as many people as those who had only attended one junior high school. He would have liked that for himself. He helped me see it in an entirely different light.

2.1: A Bit of a Sticky Situation

As an introverted and naive child, I was unaware of many things. My family moved to a new neighborhood with larger homes for larger families.

Across the street lived a family with several kids, and I became friends with the second youngest, who was a year younger than me. He was a bit overweight and reminded me of Beaver's chubby friend Gus from *Leave it to Beaver*. One day, he asked me if I wanted to "jack off" with him, but I didn't understand the question and shook my head. He got defensive and explained that his older brothers did it, but I still didn't comprehend. I sensed he was upset with me, and we never played together again.

As I grew older, I became more aware of the differences between boys and girls, but there were still many aspects of life that remained a mystery to me. I felt embarrassed by my chubby body, and my small, pointy breasts only added to my discomfort. Although I longed to be a girl, I knew deep down that I wasn't, and my body didn't resemble that of other boys. I was soft and plump, and I developed later than my peers. When I transferred to junior high school, I was relieved to find out that there were no showers in the locker room, sparing me from further embarrassment. However, I knew that I would have to confront this fear the following year when I started high school.

During my eighth grade, President JFK was assassinated, and the Beatles arrived from England. The girls were frenzied with excitement over the Beatles, and I too got swept up in their music. I was learning to play the guitar, and Beatles' songbooks with guitar chords. Although I wasn't very good, I spent hours playing their songs in my room and later with friends.

When we moved from Camelia Way to Lynn Oaks Drive, I had to give up my paper route. I managed to get a new route closer to home, but instead of delivering the afternoon edition of the San Jose News, I delivered the morning edition of the San Jose Mercury News. I had to wake up at 5:30 A.M. to finish delivering all the papers in time for school.

I had settled into a daily routine of being very quiet when I got up, so as not to wake anybody. To get to my bicycle, which was in the garage, I had to pass through the laundry room. One morning, I noticed a neatly folded stack of my sister's clothing, including several pairs of nylon underwear on top. I was overcome with curiosity, and knowing that no one else was up, I put them on to see if they fit. They did, but suddenly a pang of guilt ran through me, and I took them off and refolded them as I had found them before leaving as quickly as possible.

Seeing stacks of clothing like that did not happen very often, but now I was aware of their presence whenever they were there. I repeated this a few more times with the same kind of reaction, but in the process, I became aware of how I felt more comfortable with myself with them than I did wearing my own boy's undershorts.

One morning, I finally decided to wear them under my clothes when I went out to deliver the papers. However, when I got home, I realized I had a problem to solve. In my blinded indulgence, I had not realized that I had worn the only pair on that particular stack of folded laundry. Someone was going to notice them missing.

I had planned to take them off and place them with a pile of dirty clothes in the hamper, hoping that no one would be the wiser. People would start to get up soon, and I had to think quickly. Simply folding them and putting them back after having worn them for almost an hour and a half was not going to work. What to do? My solution was to take them to the bathroom, rinse them with some hand soap, towel dry them the best I could, and then place them over the heater vent in the bathroom floor. Fortunately, the furnace blew warm air, and the damp nylon fabric dried quickly.

I must emphasize that this curiosity of mine was not sexual. It was not a source of stimulation, and neither was it in any way a sexual fetish. As I mentioned, I was a late bloomer and had not yet started puberty; therefore, I was not aroused when I wore these items. I felt at peace and calm, transcending the disconnection I always felt with my body.

In my mind, I was facing a significant predicament. I knew that what I was doing was risky and the mere thought of getting caught terrified me. If anyone found out, I would become a laughingstock—ostracized and labeled forever. I had to be even more cautious and secretive than ever before.

The differences between me and my friends became even more apparent. Whenever they talked about girls, their conversations either went over my head or were insulting, which left me feeling insulted too. As a result, I found myself identifying more with girls than my male friends. This realization only increased the need for secrecy. I had to be careful not to act differently or say anything that might reveal my true thoughts, lest my friends reject me.

These differences with my brother Enrique were also noticeable. We no longer shared a bedroom in the new house, so we didn't spend much time together.

I was also naive in other ways. One night during Catechism class, our teacher handed us a paper and asked us to write down what we knew about the "facts of life." I had no idea what they were talking about and asked for clarification. My classmates snickered, and the teacher came up to me and said, "Tell us what you know about the birds and the bees." I still had no clue and wrote about birds and bees having wings and flying. The couple who were our teachers must have laughed when they read my answer. I'm still embarrassed thinking about it.   How can someone be so ignorant about sex at the age of thirteen? Well, lucky me, I was. There were times when I asked my dad specific questions, like when he picked me up from school in Bogotá and told me I had a baby brother. I was so surprised.

"Where did he come from?" I asked. I was almost eight years old, and his answer satisfied my curiosity.

"He was with the angels," my dad said, "and God sent him down to us." I had no idea my mom was pregnant, but I wasn't supposed to know. In those days, pregnant women had to hide their pregnancy, and sex was never discussed at home; we learned about it on the playground. Perhaps the language barrier contributed to my ignorance. I just never got the message.

2.2: On the Meaning of Words

Would things be different for me now if I had learned these things sooner? But before you conclude that sex education would have solved everything, know that I was already aware that I was different well before I could have understood sexuality. Sex education would not have helped my inner conflict about my identity; it probably would have only added to my distress by emphasizing that I didn't match the standard definition of male.

The summer between junior high and high school was a transition between schools. I took Algebra I in summer school, which helped me get acquainted with a few students and the campus. When school began in September, I felt less traumatized than I had at the other three schools I had attended since we arrived from Colombia. However, my biggest anxiety was P.E. and having to shower in public with boys who looked more like men than I did.

One day, I heard a group of older boys accusing someone of being a "homo." The only time I had ever heard that word was in connection to milk. Despite my private struggles with my identity, I was surviving life somehow and was generally a happy person. As the language around me became more sexual, I felt out of the loop. Something inside me told me to go with the flow and not ask questions.

Have you ever learned something new, only to discover that everybody has known about it for a long time? That's what happened to me with the word "homo." Puzzled by its pejorative use, I asked a friend what it meant. You should have seen the look on his face. He explained that a "homo" was a man who loved men and sucked their cocks.

That was a little too much information for me, and I was disgusted by the picture it put in my head. Swear words were still seldom heard in conversations, especially the f-word. Soon curiosity got the better of me, though, and I asked another person what "fuck" meant. If the friend who had explained "homo" to me was incredulous, this friend was shocked that I didn't know what the word meant. I had to be kidding; you could practically see him thinking. Betrayed by my naiveté, I quickly figured out it was best to pretend I knew what others were saying when they used these kinds of words.

One night in ninth-grade Catechism class at the church, I had a couple of painful hangnails that were snagging on everything.

I could not bite them off and thought a pair of fingernail clippers would do the trick. The problem was that I didn't know what they were called. I turned around to ask the friend sitting behind me whether he had one of the "click-click" things, "you know, for trimming fingernails," and proceeded to show him my hangnails.

Ed, my friend, was every bit as sinister as Eddy Haskell on Leave It to Beaver and took advantage of my lack of knowledge. He said he didn't have what I was after but told me to ask the girl sitting in front of me if she had a Kotex I could borrow. So I did. I could not figure out why she wilted forward on her desk. Ed could not contain his laughter. After class, I cornered him and insisted he tell me what a Kotex was, but his explanation did not help clear up the matter.

"It's what girls use on their cunts when they have a period, you moron!"

Okay, I thought, better not ask him to tell me what a "cunt" is—or what a "period" is, either.

Thankfully, she went to a different high school, so I only saw her at Catechism a few more times that year, and she kept her distance. That was okay, especially after I learned what those words meant.

Ed went to my high school, but fortunately, he was so busy being himself that he never brought up my stupidity. We had one thing in common: we both played the guitar. While he fancied himself as a lead singer and lead guitar player, I was content to be a rhythm guitarist, not wanting to be center stage. We formed a band with two other friends, one who played bass and one a drummer. We could play a few Beatles and Rolling Stones songs, maybe a repertoire of twenty in total, which was enough for roughly two sets.

On Christmas of 1964, Ed got us our first paying gig. We were paid twenty dollars to play at a college party in an apartment near our house. None of us was old enough to drive, so our parents dropped us off with all our stuff and picked us up afterward.

The band broke up around Easter because Ed's ego was too much for the rest of us. We weren't having any fun since he was always screaming at us. However, the drummer, bass player, and I remained hopeful of reuniting again without Ed.

One hot day in July, a college student who had hired us for

the Christmas party called me. He had learned about our band's breakup from the drummer and wondered if I was interested in joining another band looking for a rhythm guitar player. He told me they had a practice the following day, but I reminded him that I didn't drive and likely couldn't make it to the rehearsal. He responded that he would be happy to drive me, so I got permission from my mom.

The next day, as promised, he arrived at 3:00 p.m., and we loaded my guitar and amplifier into the back seat of his car. As we went down Winchester Avenue, he said he wanted to stop at his apartment for a minute. We pulled up in front of his place, and he said it was too hot to stay in the car, so he invited me to come in and cool off with a Coke. I was worried about leaving my stuff unattended in the car, but he said we would bring it inside.

However, once inside his apartment, he raped me. Though he didn't penetrate me, I felt horror as he thrust his penis between my buttocks and ejaculated. He threatened me not to tell anyone by saying he would tell my friends I was a "homo" if I spoke up. I was afraid to tell anyone for the same reasons as before, but now I was worried that this guy knew who I was and knew some of my friends. I buried this horrible episode deep into my subconscious and erected walls of protection and denial. I felt responsible for what had happened to me as if I was the cause.

I don't need to tell you how one erects these monumental walls of protection and denial. I buried this horrible episode deep into my subconscious; I would not allow myself to admit that any of this had happened. This event just added to my confusion. He groaned as he raped me and mumbled that I was just like a girl, soft and curvy. I can still remember, as if it was yesterday, his whiskers on the back of my neck and cheeks as he rubbed his chin on me as he lay on top of me. It sends chills down my back as I think about it.

What was I? Why was I different? Why did these men—first the paper route customer and now this guy—single me out? What did they see in me that I didn't see in myself? I felt responsible somehow, as if I was the cause of what had happened to me. The picture was very confusing.

Before the rape, I had my first wet dream. I thought I had wet the bed. I was devastated because I had not wet the bed for a long time and thought I had outgrown the problem. Fortunately, the mattress was dry; only my under-shorts were wet. I went to the bathroom and was surprised by the slimy moist substance. I had no idea what it was. It scared me. I washed up and went back to bed; this happened a few more times, but it was not until the college guy raped me that I put two and two together and realized what the fluid was. Then it also dawned on me that this was the stuff the man who masturbated had wiped off my hand that night. It was all too much for me. I wished this milky stuff didn't come out of me.

2.3: The Power of Advertising

Despite my terrible self-image and insecurities, I was elected class vice president in my junior and senior years of high school, which is quite ironic. It had nothing to do with my political savvy or self-confidence. In fact, I was horrified when I found out I had been elected. I couldn't believe it had happened to me.

I was on the ballot in the first place because I had designed and silk-screened campaign posters for myself as a joke. I thought the other candidates' posters were cheesy and made my own. Someone nominated me, and before I knew it, I was a candidate for class vice president. The morning after I attached my posters on the school's corridor walls, they were all gone! I was devastated, thinking someone had seen through my ruse and ripped them all down. However, the posters turned out to be collector's items, and students had stolen them to hang inside their lockers. I didn't even have a copy of the poster for myself! That experience taught me the power of advertising.

Art class became my sanctuary. Drawing was one thing I could do well, and Mrs. Lozano, my art teacher, was genuinely devoted to those of us who were serious and demonstrated some ability and talent. She provided direction for my life and instilled confidence in me as an artist. I was fortunate to have Mrs. Lozano as my teacher for two years, and she is solely responsible for my decision to pursue graphic design as a career. She recommended the graphic design program at San Jose State College, her alma mater.

As for my popularity, I'm not sure. I didn't like being in the spotlight and had huge fears whenever I had to speak in front of the classroom or any group. I was always afraid I'd mispronounce a word and sabotage my efforts to blend in and not be different. I remember once giving a book report and saying "shit" when I meant to say "sheet". The class howled, and I died a thousand deaths.

Academically, I was a "B" student. I could have done better if I had been able to focus more on my studies, but I had too much going on in my head. I thought life was confusing, and I was easily distracted. If only I could have turned off that inner voice!

By eleventh grade, many of my friends had girlfriends, and I felt the pressure to have one too. One day, I was hanging out with my friend Mike when he pointed out a girl who was two years younger than us. He described her as "hot." I observed her from afar to try and understand what he saw in her. She was undeniably very pretty. However, Mike was already in a relationship, so this girl was off-limits to him in some ways.

A few days later, he shared some interesting news with me. Apparently, the pretty girl had a crush on me. I was taken aback by this information, and it made me feel nervous and sweaty. These were new feelings for me, and I had no idea how to handle them. I didn't even know her name, so the thought of talking to her made me tongue-tied.

Whenever she was around, I would see her with a group of two or three friends at the cafeteria or in the school plaza during lunchtime. I noticed her stealing glances in my direction when I was close by, but I pretended not to notice. I greeted her with a simple "Hi," but then went silent when we came face to face. Despite my nervousness, we managed to have a brief conversation, and from that day on, we started to look for each other. Before long, we spent time together and walked home side by side. She was such a sweet and likable person, and I couldn't help but be completely smitten by her beauty.

When Sherry (that was her name) agreed to be my date for the Junior Ball, I was determined to learn how to act like a proper gentleman. I searched for information from all sources, including friends, and even eavesdropped on conversations to ensure I knew the proper protocols for social interactions, not sexual ones. I studied like an actor memorizing his part, desperate to ensure I did everything right.

Doing what was expected of me was a good way to fly below the radar, and I was getting better at it. However, I also had an insatiable desire to figure myself out. With a much better grasp of the English language, I secretly conducted research on myself. Unfortunately, everything I uncovered made me more uncertain about who I was. For instance, when I came across the word "transvestite" and looked it up in a psychology book at the public library, it said it was a person who derived sexual pleasure from dressing in clothes of the opposite sex. It went on to say that such people were fetishistic, and their behavior was deemed deviant. It also said that some people were treated successfully with electroshock therapy. Although this was interesting and terrifying at the same time, I felt that this description did not truly represent me since I did not cross-dress for sexual gratification. Nonetheless, I was intrigued by the concept, and it created a volatile mix of ideas in my mind.

I never fully cross-dressed; I only wore panties for the most part. Nor did I masturbate often since it produced too many strange feelings. From the first time I masturbated, I experienced both ecstasy and revulsion since it always reminded me of what that man had done years ago when my hand was wrapped around his penis. I did not enjoy handling myself, but there was no other way to make masturbation happen, so I learned to suppress my disgust.

Thanks to having a driver's license and later my own car, I was now more independent and able to buy the occasional "gift" for my imaginary girlfriend. I also occasionally took clothing from the items my mom would collect for the St. Vincent de Paul Society, figuring they would not be missed.

The need for secrecy and the fear of being caught was indescribable. I was certain that none of my friends engaged in such "deviant" behavior, and now I had another emotion to struggle with — overwhelming guilt and a sense of being an awful person. I wish I could make sense of it all. When I was younger, I prayed to God at night that I would wake up as a girl the next morning. Now, I wished He could make all of this disappear.

One Sunday, during church service, the Gospel reading

included a beautiful invitation made by Jesus, "Come to me, all you who are weary and heavy-laden, and I will give you rest." I remember thinking how much I wanted that to be true for me.

Chapter 3: From Teens to Busted

After graduating from high school, there was the usual reshuffling of relationships that happens among friends. This is when you realize you may never again see some people with whom you have spent years of your life.

Many people in my graduating class of nearly five hundred students would be going out of state to study or moving to other college towns or cities in California. Some stayed at home in San Jose to attend the local junior colleges, colleges, and universities. Only a handful of my classmates chose San Jose State; of those, I only knew three or four well enough to possibly have an ongoing friendship. But of those few, given that we all had different schedules, we still almost never saw each other.

Of course, what I've described is not unique. This happens to graduating classes everywhere. Most people are able to face relocation or take a new start like this in stride. Since I was unsure of who I was or what I was, the process for me was fraught with anxiety and trepidation. There was a sense of security in having what might be called a closed system, such as what is found from kindergarten through twelfth grade. That familiarity goes out the window upon graduating from high school. There is a period of adjustment while establishing new relationships and routines.

Perhaps the biggest adjustment for me was not the start of college and all the changes that entailed, but something quite different. A few weeks before the start of that fall semester in 1968, Enrique moved to Vancouver, BC, to work with our brother-in-law and his father, who were Canadians. Carmen had met her future husband at Foothill College, and they had been married in 1967.

Within the year, they moved to Canada. This was the start of our family's migration to yet another new country. When Enrique left San Jose, I lost my role model. He was the person to whom I looked for examples of how to act, what to say, and how to navigate through life. I can say all of this, and really only in retrospect because at the time, I didn't realize what a huge void his departure would create in my world.

Slowly, the temperature was rising in this pressure cooker that was my life. I desperately needed answers to my questions, but I did not know what exactly to ask or where to look for the answers. I felt so young, immature, and inexperienced—and I was, in fact, all of these. I was still seventeen years old when I graduated from high school and wouldn't turn eighteen until my first semester in college. As I looked around the classrooms, which included students of all ages, I was sure I was the youngest person in the room.

It was the beginning of my college journey, and life seemed like an endless maze of challenges and complexities. But amidst all the chaos, I stumbled upon an unexpected ally: Bruce. I still remember the way his calm and laid-back demeanor put me at ease, making me feel like I had found a true friend. And as fate would have it, we found ourselves in more than one class together, which gave us plenty of opportunities to get to know each other better.

Bruce was a veteran, a man of twenty-six with a sense of quiet confidence that I could only dream of. He seemed to have a certain wisdom about him that belied his age, and I couldn't help but envy him. Perhaps he sensed my vulnerability or simply took pity on me, but he was always kind and friendly toward me, and for that, I was grateful.

One day, as we chatted between classes, Bruce suggested I read a book called Siddhartha by Hermann Hesse. He told me I would find it in the college bookstore and highly recommended it. And so, I picked up the book, not knowing how much it would change my life. As I read it, I found myself drawn into a world of simplicity and inner peace, something I had never experienced before. It opened my mind to the possibility that I could overcome my problems by transcending them, and that idea gave me hope.

Life was far from simple, though. The war in Vietnam raged on, political unrest was rampant on campuses, and the anti-establishment mentality was everywhere. But somehow, the idea of simplicity in life and the quest for inner peace seemed to offer me a way out of the chaos.

As I delved deeper into Eastern philosophies, I found myself drawn to others who shared the same qualities I saw in Bruce. I had lost my faith in the Catholic Church and was searching for something to identify with, something that would give me a sense of purpose. And as I explored these new ideas, I began to question all my relationships, even those with my family.

Just as I was trying to navigate college life, tragedy struck our family. My beloved grandmother was diagnosed with cancer, and despite her brave fight, she passed away after a short and painful battle. Her loss left a gaping hole in our family, and I found myself struggling to cope with the enormity of it all. To make matters worse, my older siblings had moved away, leaving me as the oldest child at home.

I longed to break free from the bonds that held me back, but my parents couldn't understand my need for change. To them, I must have seemed like a self-righteous ingrate, blind to the love and support they offered. But my desire for independence went beyond just my relationships with my family. I was also struggling with my identity, unsure of who I was and where I belonged in the world.

For years, I had been collecting a few female garments, only to purge them from my life again and again. It was a pattern that had become all too familiar, but I couldn't seem to break free from it. And then, one day, my mom decided to reorganize my closet and found a jacket with its sleeves stuffed full of my secret collection.

As I walked into my room, I saw all the items piled on top of my bed, and my heart sank. I knew my life would never be the same again. My dad walked in behind me, and my mom demanded an explanation. I felt like my secret was finally out, and I was terrified of what would happen next.

In that moment, I heard a voice in my head begin to articulate a ridiculous story about a panty raid at one of the college dorms. I knew it was a long shot, but I had to try. I said that I had gotten stuck with the items after the raid and was only hiding them because I didn't know what else to do with them. I didn't want to throw them away because I thought it would be a waste and a crime.

I don't know how convincing I was, but both of them walked out of my bedroom, with my mom muttering something about placing the garments in a Goodwill box since it would now be impossible to return them to their proper owners. I had dodged another bullet, but I also knew I couldn't keep living a lie forever.

As I tried to come to terms with my identity, I knew I needed to move out and start my own life. But I couldn't afford to just yet. I needed to find a job that would allow me to pay rent and other living expenses. It was a daunting prospect, but I knew I had to keep moving forward. One step at a time.

There was a new craze for steak and lobster restaurants at the time, and one such restaurant had opened near home. I applied for a job and was hired as a busboy. Although it only paid less than three dollars an hour, once the tips were added, it provided me with enough money to pay for gas and car insurance but not enough to cover rent.

After about six months, there was an opening in the kitchen for a meat cutter. The head chef had been doing the meat cutting along with all his duties and responsibilities, and it was getting to be too much for him. He promoted and trained me to trim and cut the top sirloin butts and New York strip loins and tenderloins into various portion sizes with speed and accuracy. A quota had to be cut for each day of the week, but the great thing about the job was as long as it got done by 3:00 p.m., I could come in at any time to do it. Another great thing was I could grow my hair long, which was not permitted if working in the dining room. On most days, I would come in at 5:00 a.m., do my job, and be gone before 7:30 a.m.

Though I no longer qualified for tips, I was getting paid considerably more per hour than I had been as a busboy, and this finally afforded me the chance to move out. I was oblivious to how this was a very emotional day for my mom when I arrived with a friend's VW van to move my belongings.

Through Bruce, I had found a room in a house near the campus where the rent was very reasonable. When Bruce told me about this house, he warned me that one of the other tenants was a "Jesus freak." I remember thinking to myself that I was cool with it since I, too, was "spiritual," so I was unfazed.

The Jesus freak's name was Dennis, and his older brother, Roger, also lived in the house. Their father owned the property, which he had purchased as revenue property when Roger started as a student at San Jose State a few years earlier. Dennis was a year younger than me, but what bothered me about him wasn't that he was a Jesus freak, but that he seemed to exude a peace and confidence that I didn't possess. It wouldn't be long before I would experience his evangelistic fervor firsthand, which was always peppered with Bible verses. Some I recognized, but most were foreign to me. The fact was I had never picked up a Bible to read it for myself. Only what I had heard during the Catholic Mass formed my then-Christian understanding.

3.1: What Do I Know and What Do I Believe?

I saw more Jesus freaks than just Dennis around; it seemed like they were everywhere on campus. Their appearance was a mix of hippie and surfer, with long hair, beads, sandals, and tie-dyed T-shirts. Despite this, every encounter I had with them, or any chance I had to overhear their conversations, left me thinking that I wanted what they were talking about for myself.

One thing that impressed me about Dennis was that he was a Conscientious Objector (CO), which exempted him from the draft. I knew of several denominations and religions that automatically entitled one to be classified as a CO, but Dennis did not belong to any of these. This piqued my curiosity, and I asked him a lot of questions about it, because I knew at least three other people who had applied for this deferment and had been rejected. I needed to know what it was that Dennis had said that made the difference in his case.

His answer both puzzled and intrigued me. He claimed that he explained his beliefs based on several Bible verses to the panel interviewing him and that he had been able to defend his position to their satisfaction.

On one level, I felt that I was no less spiritual than Dennis, so I thought I, too, should have a CO deferment instead of the student deferment (2S) I had since turning eighteen. I sought out other friends of mine who had not qualified for the sort of deferment Dennis had obtained and asked them about their experiences. They all told me that it was not easy to convince the panel. I learned that the interview was designed to challenge you to defend your beliefs. It was very intimidating insofar as if you claimed that you were a Buddhist, they would have Buddhist priests and scholars doing the interview. If you claimed to be a Christian, they would have ministers or priests asking you questions. No matter your philosophy or religious affiliation, they had people well versed in whatever anyone claimed to be or believe. What chance could I possibly have?

Nevertheless, I drove to the Draft Board one day and walked in to apply for the CO deferment. The lady behind the counter explained that I needed to fill out some forms and bring them back. After that, I would receive the official application. Once that was accepted, I would be called in for an interview.

Later that night, I sat at my desk to fill out the form's top portion, including my name, address, selective service number, and other administrative questions. Afterward, there were four questions to answer. I decided to jot down my responses on binder paper before copying them onto the form.

The first question asked, "What is the basis for your belief that war is wrong?" The second question inquired about the books I had read or individuals who influenced me to form my beliefs. I was also asked to list pertinent references. Based on my beliefs, the third question sought to understand if I would be willing to participate in the military in a non-combatant capacity, such as a medic or materials and supplies handler or do clerical work.

The final question asked if I had ever publicly or privately expressed my views in written or oral form and requested that I provide the relevant places, dates, and times of such declarations.

I responded to the first question by writing almost two pages of my beliefs. However, upon reviewing the form, I realized that I was only allowed four lines to answer the question. I crumpled up my two sheets of paper and started over again.

I struggled to get beyond the words "the basis for my belief is..." as my beliefs unraveled before my eyes. It was like peeling back layer after layer of an onion as I questioned what I truly believed. Was I genuinely a conscientious objector, or was I doing this to appear spiritual? I could not confidently claim any one belief system, as I would not be able to defend such a position to anyone. In those candid moments, I confessed that the only reason I opposed war was that I did not want to die. And why didn't I want to die? Because I did not know if there was a God, heaven, or hell. Unfortunately, that type of answer would not have satisfied the Draft Board.

In my confusion about my identity and the distress it caused me, I often thought about death. Sometimes I felt like I couldn't go on, and that death would be better than continuing with my confusion and despair. However, the nagging thought of whether there was more to life than what I could see kept me from going there. What if there was a heaven or hell? I remember asking God to help me if he was responsible for the things I admired in others; I wanted what they had. I heard myself utter those words, but to whom was I saying them? I simultaneously mocked myself and hoped my prayer would be heard.

After all my frustration that night, it turned out I didn't need CO deferment after all; the war in Vietnam was winding down, and the U.S. Army reduced the number of young men it needed. And soon after, the draft was changed to a lottery system based on one's date of birth. My number was sufficiently high to spare me, which meant I was no longer in danger of being drafted.

In the days and weeks that followed, I noticed something different about my perspective on life. It was liberating yet scary at the same time. I felt a sense of tranquility that I had never experienced before. I didn't tell anyone what was going through my head, especially not wanting to be thought of as a Jesus freak. I could hear the mocking and ridicule that others subjected my friend Dennis to.

I noticed that I could have conversations with girls with ease, which was new to me. I had always felt tongue-tied and didn't know what to say. I felt pressure to befriend girls to get them into bed, but that wasn't how I felt. Suddenly I found myself having genuine and friendly conversations about class, events, and everything else, without any hidden agenda. Afterward, I would think, "Wow, I was just talking to a girl! And I wasn't at all choked up and tongue-tied!"

Finally, I noticed that I was shying away from drinking beer, wine, and the occasional joint. This had nothing to do with ideology or a legalistic outlook but because I just had no desire to get drunk or stoned anymore.

One Friday night, I arrived at a party with a six-pack of beer and joined some friends in the kitchen. They were passing a joint around, but whenever it came to me, I passed it to the next person without taking a hit. I was hardly sipping my beer, and after a while, one of the guys in the circle screamed at me.

"What the fuck is wrong with you, Salazar?" he said. "Did you get religion?" The others seemed to agree with him.

I denied it emphatically, but I was flabbergasted. I hadn't mentioned anything about what was going through my head lately. I kept my mouth shut; the last thing I wanted was to lose friends or be rejected. My new "unconscious" behavior had betrayed me. The internal changes I thought were private were somehow apparent to others after all.

Chapter 4: Spiritual War & the Works

I walked home from the party with my guitar and my remaining beers, dejected but also elated. I felt dejected because I thought these guys were my friends, but instead, they suspected me of "getting religion" and mocked me. I realized then that our friendship was solely based on getting stoned and drinking beer. They didn't care for me as a person. And to be honest, there were things I didn't like about them besides the partying. I felt elated because something liberating was taking place within me, which helped to overcome their rejection.

I kept my mouth shut for several weeks, but now there was no denying it. The words I overheard Dennis and the other Jesus freaks speaking resonated deep within me. I was comforted by their message and inspired by their faith. One night I finally found the courage to knock on Dennis' bedroom door. He was surprised to see me and asked what I wanted. Looking nervously around to ensure no one had seen me, I told him I needed to talk to him about something.

He invited me in and asked me to sit on one of the two chairs in his room as he sat on the other. Not knowing where to begin, I told him I had thought I might be losing my mind for several weeks. I shared with him about the night I realized I didn't want to die until I knew if Jesus was real and whether or not there was a heaven or hell. I then explained how I had noticed some new and different things in my life since then. Without saying anything about my secrets, I added that I was also aware of what I was like before noticing these changes.

The look on his face made me think I had said too much. He was pensive for a moment and then asked me if I could elaborate. I told him about the night of the party when I had been accused of being religious and how I felt embarrassed and unwanted but how I also felt elated and was genuinely happy about what had happened. I told him I had been trying to make sense of all of this, and how based on some of my recent lectures in psychology, the duality I was noticing in me seemed too much like schizophrenia. That was all I could say.

Dennis asked if he could read something to me from the Bible. I said yes, and he read this verse from Paul's second letter to the church in Corinth, chapter 5, and verse 17:

"Therefore, if anyone is in Christ, he is a new creature; the old things passed away; behold, new things have come. Now all these things are from God..."

I asked him to reread it, and this began to make sense. It helped explain the duality I was very aware of—how I felt like a new person. I asked him if what I had been going through meant I was 'in Christ?'

The next day, he presented me with an extra King James Bible he happened to have in his room. The pages had red edges and were yellowed. It must have been an old pew Bible from some church. I had never owned or seriously read a Bible in my life. He told me to read the Gospel of John and stick to the New Testament. I struggled with the archaic language and found reading the Bible difficult, but at that time I didn't know there were newer translations that used modern English.

It might have been later that day when Dennis asked if I'd like to attend one of the Bible studies he went to. It was all happening too fast, I thought. As it turned out, there was a scheduling conflict, and I couldn't participate in the study with him. That bought me some time. A few days later, Dennis asked if I wanted join him for church that Sunday, and I agreed to go.

Before this, I'd only been inside a Protestant church twice: once for a wedding and once for a funeral. Dennis and I attended a small Pentecostal church near the campus that Sunday morning. The whole experience was unsettling. I had never heard what they called "speaking in tongues" and was very self-conscious about raising my hands in the air with everyone else. However, I was impressed with how full the church was with people my age. There was a lot of singing, and it was loud. This was also new to me because singing at the Catholic Church where I grew up was subdued in comparison. I also found it interesting that this congregation was somehow affiliated with a Pentecostal church in Vancouver, where my sister Carmen and brother Enrique now lived.

Meeting new people and making fresh starts had always been difficult for me, and though it was no different that morning, I felt welcomed and was received warmly by complete and total strangers.

Back at the restaurant where I worked, I had developed a friendship with the chef, John. He often told me to come and hang out on the weekends in nearby Campbell, where he, his wife, and two young daughters lived in a rented farmhouse. John loaned me the VW van I had used for my move. He was a trained chef but was very hip, with longish hair and a short beard, and always wore leather sandals when not at work. I liked him a lot. I always had this sense he could read into my soul, that he knew about my gender confusion. He didn't, of course. He never knew or suspected anything. But John was the first person I ever came close to telling my secret. I felt very safe with him and his wife.

I was one of many people to whom John had given an open invitation to hang out at his house. Many people used to show up on the weekends, and it was common for musicians to bring their guitars and other instruments. We sang a lot of Joni Mitchell, Judy Collins, Gordon Lightfoot, and Bob Dylan songs. One talented person, who sometimes switched between playing bass and banjo, remarked he had heard a new band called "Love Song" and asked me if I'd ever heard of them. He was impressed by them. Not only were they good musicians, he said, but they also had beautiful harmonies. But what intrigued him the most was that they were a "Jesus" band. I had never heard of such a thing and was naturally curious. This "Jesus" thing seemed to be everywhere!

Within walking distance of San Jose State was the small campus of San Jose Bible College. We had heard about an open-air concert that would be held on an upcoming Saturday, which I attended with Dennis and some of his friends. When we arrived, the place was packed; there was music in the air and a very festive atmosphere. It was a real "love-in" without the drugs, alcohol, and "free love" I had seen in rock concerts at the county fairgrounds or on campus.

More importantly, through these first few weeks and months of my new Christian experience, I had come to believe and hope that I was going to be made normal, and that all my confusion and anxiety about my gender was going to be removed. In this new way of looking at things, I developed a fundamentalist view of life with very well-defined boundaries and codes of behavior. This zeal was stimulated by the sermons and devotionals I heard and several books that were very popular with Christians then. One of them was The Late Great Planet Earth by Hal Lindsey and his book that followed, Satan Is Alive And Well On The Planet Earth. Thus began my practice of spiritualizing and demonizing my condition and dealing with it as if it were a spiritual war with the devil.

4.1: Zealous, Immature & Stupid

As I mentioned earlier, the day I moved out of the house was emotionally difficult for my mom. Back then, I didn't appreciate what she was going through. Her mother had passed away, her oldest daughter and son were in a different country, and I was moving out, too. All the sacrifice and hard work that she and my father had done to improve our life must have tasted like ashes in her mouth that day. This six-bedroom house they had so lovingly purchased and customized for us, including the addition of a built-in backyard swimming pool, now seemed empty, with no one in three of its bedrooms.

By that time, my parents had invested in their own business and operated a dry-cleaning plant in one of the many malls in West San Jose. The idea was to be the owner-manager and have the qualified staff do all the work. Because of the laws governing dry cleaners, dad needed someone with a valid boiler license to operate the steam equipment. He found an older gentleman through the dry cleaners' union and a couple of women who could do the pressing. He and my mother took turns working the counter, and mom also offered her alteration services.

Things seemed to start well until the day the man hired to do the dry cleaning almost lost his hand when he failed to apply the brake to the large cleaning machine. He began to empty the drum when the load shifted, and his hand got caught between the opening and the door. Dad was forced to learn how to operate the equipment as quickly as possible and had to pass the test to be certified to operate the boiler.

Finding a replacement for this man was impossible, so this became my dad's full-time job instead of being just the owner-manager. I admire my dad and mom for what they had to do for us; they did it willingly and gladly.

It also pains me to admit that I failed to show them true love in my newfound excitement and zeal about my faith. In a self-righteous display of superiority, I came home one night to proclaim I had become a Christian. I walked in carrying the King James Bible that Dennis had given me and accused the Roman Catholic Church of hypocrisy and, by implication, my parents. They were hurt, and their reaction bizarrely validated me. I accused them of being like the self-righteous Pharisees Jesus often confronted when, in fact, I was the one being self-righteous! I was so wrong to have done that to them.

In defense, mom challenged me and said if what I had was real and if I felt the Roman Catholic Church was so wrong, then I had an obligation not to judge it but to come back to the Catholic Church and work from within to effect change. I scoffed at the idea. Why would I want to come back to such blatant bigotry? She pointed out how one's responsibility is always first to family and then to the world; by extension, the Catholic Church was my family.

I left the house angry that night. Instead of my parents having been excited for me, they were skeptical. They said they had seen me go through many phases in the last few years; perhaps this was just another one. Mom also wanted me to speak to a priest.

My new faith also caused me to do something about my small collection of girls' clothing. I felt guilty for having these things, so I purged them all. I saw them as tools of the devil to trap me. I was resolute on never purchasing girl's clothing again; to do so was sinful, and it was also depraved. All the horrible things I had read in those psychology textbooks added to my zeal and fervor. I was determined to become normal with God's help.

Returning to my brother Enrique, all the talk about graphic design excited him, and he became convinced that if I moved to Vancouver, we could form a small company to offer graphic design services. Initially, I thought he was crazy. Why would I want to go up to Vancouver? For one, on the two occasions I had visited him and Carmen, the weather had been cloudy and cold—in summer! Second, I had an aversion to new starts; honestly, this one frightened me.

But the truth was that if I wanted to pursue graphic design as a career, I would have to move to a larger, more commercial center. Graphic design jobs in San Jose were limited to working in newspapers or small printing companies, as there were few advertising agencies at the time. Silicon Valley, the computer revolution, and the creative services it would spawn were still years away. If I stayed in California, San Francisco was one option, and Los Angeles was another. Moving to a city where I knew no one was not a choice I was prepared to consider. Suddenly my brother's crazy idea of moving up to Vancouver seemed logical. So we were already planning and dreaming of how this would happen when I came into this new spiritual part of my journey.

One night, at the Bible study I was now attending near campus, the man who led the session asked anyone who had a prayer request to see him at the end. Nervously, I waited my turn, asked him to pray for my family, and explained how I had a confrontation with my parents, specifically my mother. I shared her comments and how she challenged me to return to the Catholic Church. She said this would prove to her that what I had was real and not just another phase I was going through.

His answer surprised me. He agreed with my mother and said if what I had was genuine, I should be willing to go back so she could see the changes were genuine. This was not what I wanted to hear. I wanted him to feel sorry for me and to agree with me, not with them. But I was also humbled and concluded that I wanted my mom to see my sincerity and that what I had found was true.

The night I argued with my mom about my new faith, one of the points I made had to do with music and how fervently and from the heart Jesus people sang at church. She had countered that

I needed to attend the new Sunday evening "Folk Mass" for young people. I felt admonished by what the Bible study leader said, so I attended this folk Mass that following Sunday.

4.2: Maybe Mom Was Right

What I can only describe as heartbreak is what I felt when I went to that Mass. Yes, there was singing, but the only people singing with conviction were the eight or so individuals leading at the front of the church. I wondered if the music was like the proverbial spoonful of sugar to help the medicine go down. I was moved and realized all these people just seemed to be going through the motions, but for whom their faith was simply something they did out of obligation and habit and not from the heart. It reminded me of how I had felt in church years earlier.

The priest who said the Mass that night had been at the parish for several years, and I recognized Father Maguire. At the end of the service, he came to the back of the church to greet people on their way out. I waited until the church was almost empty before I approached him. He remembered me after all these years. His sincerity was unquestionable. When I told him I had been "born again," his response was another surprise. He was very excited and happy for me. He thought it was great!

I was thinking of getting involved at the parish somehow. I considered helping with the high school group and offering music during Mass since I knew some Christian songs. Father Maguire was pleased to hear that and asked if I remembered the McLaughlins. I recalled them as the couple who taught catechism to junior high school students and prayed they didn't remember my ignorant answer about the facts of life.

Father Maguire said the McLaughlins ran the high school Catechism class, which met once a month at a local monastery for a one-day retreat. He announced that they, too, were "born-again" and would be happy to have my assistance.

Initially, I was confused, but the prospect excited me, and soon I met with the McLaughlins and other adult volunteers helping with the high school group. We attended our first retreat in November at a beautiful monastery near Stanford University. Deep in the woods, the setting was once a seminary but was now used for retreats and conferences since fewer young men were joining the priesthood.

At the high school retreats, students would meet at the church on Sundays at 1 P.M. and be driven to the monastery by volunteer parents and drivers. The retreat included activities, short devotionals, discussions, Mass, and a meal. By 6 P.M., they would return to the church to be picked up by their parents.

We planned something special for the upcoming December retreat during the students' Christmas vacation. A man from a local Protestant church led a non-denominational Bible study on Wednesday evenings, which I had investigated and found welcoming. The McLaughlins suggested inviting young Jesus People to share what Jesus meant to them, hoping to challenge the high school students. Stewart agreed to invite six people for that Sunday.

We all met at the church at the designated time, and I stayed behind, waiting for any latecomers. As I was driving away, I saw a young woman trying the church's locked doors. Assuming she might be one of the high school students or invited guests, I rolled down the window and asked if she was looking for the group. I told her they had already left, and I was designated to drive anybody who arrived late. I asked her if she wanted to ride with me to the monastery.

She accepted my offer, and we headed to Palo Alto. Along the way, we chatted about various things and how she knew Stewart. She told me that she was part of a group of Jesus People our age. Some of them attended Stewart's church, but the majority, including her, went to other churches in the area.

That December retreat felt like confirmation that God was working in my life. My indignation toward the Catholic Church had softened; I still had many unanswered questions, but I felt genuine love for the students and a deep bond with the McLaughlins and the priests at the parish.

Almost three months had passed since that night in Dennis' room when I had come to a deeper faith in Jesus. And for those three months, I had been free of identity torment. This is not to say I was unaware of my issues; it is just that I was so determined to be "victorious" in this spiritual battle that I spent my energy convincing myself that I was going to be healed. If I allowed myself to fail, it would signify my lack of faith. I had to prove to myself and others that I had unshakable faith, period.

The Wednesday night Bible study led by Stew became my primary source of spiritual sustenance and deep friendships for the following year until I moved to Canada.

4.3: Surprised to Meet Again

On Thursday of the following week, I went to the restaurant where I worked to pick up my paycheck and tips. When I arrived, the parking lot was full, so I had to park far from the entrance. As I approached the restaurant, four young women dressed in nurse's white uniforms exited, one of whom I recognized as the girl I had given a ride to from the church retreat. She seemed upset, and I could tell she was embarrassed for me to see her in that state. I asked if everything was okay.

It became apparent she didn't want to talk in front of her friends, so I offered to drive her back to her office. She accepted, and I quickly grabbed my check from the restaurant before returning to the car. Her name was Rachel, and I learned more about her on the way to her office. She worked for an oral surgeon and was upset because her coworkers had made fun of her "old-fashioned" views on marriage.

I dropped her off at work, and before saying goodbye, Rachel invited me to join her and some friends for spaghetti dinner at her apartment that Friday. She gave me directions to her apartment and told me what time to come.

Rachel lived with three other young Christian women, and I felt at home with all of them. They were part of a larger group of Christian youth who met for Bible study every Tuesday night. The study took place in a converted garage owned by a couple in their fifties known as the "Wallaces." Despite the age difference, the Wallaces, who were high school teachers, knew how to relate to young people with diverse backgrounds. It was a beautiful display of inclusion, and it reminded me of the early church.

There was genuine love and care for one another, and lives were being transformed before our eyes. People who had been struggling with addiction were finding their way, and reckless behavior was being replaced with something more positive. This was a stark contrast to the parties I had been attending, where getting drunk or high was the primary goal.

The most obvious change in my life has been my taste in music. It's funny how so many of the songs I used to love no longer gave me the same pleasure as before. They seemed so artificial and "carnal," making it difficult for me to sing them with any conviction or enjoyment. At the time, I was motivated to learn some of the new Christian songs I was hearing, which were starting to become popular and accepted in more progressive churches. I don't think this genre had been labeled as "contemporary Christian music" yet.

I began to lead singing at the least attended Sunday Mass at my parish, the twelve o'clock Mass. My previous fear of being in front of a large group had suddenly disappeared, at least when I was in church. I never imagined it would be so easy for me to do this.

Changes were also taking place within the Roman Catholic Church. The fact that a non-denominational Bible study led by a Protestant was allowed on its property was proof of this. In the spring of 1972, the McLaughlins told me that the parish council had approved a motion to send me to attend an international youth conference in Dallas sponsored by Campus Crusade for Christ called "Explo '72." I had not even heard of it when they told me. LIFE magazine would later report this event with a picture on the front cover, accompanied by the headline "The Great Jesus Rally in Dallas." I was overwhelmed and grateful for the honor, and the parish was covering my airfare and expenses since I would be going as the parish's delegate.

On the following Tuesday at the Wallace's Bible study, Rachel announced that her father lived in the Dallas-Fort Worth area and would welcome anyone who needed a place to stay if they were going to Explo '72. I spoke to her after the Bible study and told her I was going, and the church was paying for the airfare and registration, but we had not yet made arrangements for accommodations. Staying with her father would be most appreciated if it were possible. Rachel would be there herself, not just for this youth event, but to visit her sisters for a couple of weeks.

You've heard the phrase, "the higher they climb, the farther they fall." Well, that's what happened to me at that time. I had been so "good" about my secret for months and had resisted the temptation to give in to my "needs." Then one afternoon, it happened. My younger sister, Angela, discovered one of her bras in my room, stashed behind a box of LPs. She had come in to borrow a couple of records, which was perfectly okay with me. At the time, I was in the room, and she picked up the bra and asked me what it was doing there.

Not only was I busted by my sister, but I also felt like I had betrayed and insulted God, leaving me feeling horrible. Once again, my brain kicked into survival mode, and I made up a story about having been curious to see what the bra felt like, nothing more. I told her that I thought every guy on the planet had probably done something similar, and I made light of it. I begged her not to tell anyone, and she told me not to worry about it. She knew that guys did this stuff and left it at that.

Why was I still afflicted by whatever this? Why did I still feel and act this way? Why wasn't God fixing it? What was it going to take? Was my faith that weak?

Concerning my planned move to Canada, I concluded that my departure would be less emotionally difficult if I didn't draw too close to people. I had already experienced that when we left Colombia, and I knew I was not strong enough to go through that again. That is not to say my relationships with these new friends were cold and distant; it is just that I tried to keep them in perspective and did not allow myself to think of anyone in any other way than simply brothers and sisters in Christ. This way of looking at it was helpful when it came to my relationships with the girls in the group because I had no ulterior motives or hidden agendas; after all, they were my "sisters." The result was that I developed very platonic relationships, particularly with Rachel. So while we did things together, like going to the beach or driving into the Santa Cruz Mountains, we never perceived these outings as dates. Maybe we were fooling ourselves, but that is what it was — simply two friends enjoying each other's company with a common bond, which was our faith.

I finished my studies that year and graduated from San Jose State College. I was part of the first graduating class from the now-renamed San Jose State University. As Ronald Reagan was the governor then, his signature was on my diploma.

June came, and off I went to Dallas. Rachel and her father picked me up at the airport and drove me back to her dad's apartment. Rachel stayed with one of her two sisters. I got to meet her family that week. Little did I know that I would be getting married to Rachel two years later, but this was the furthest thing from my mind at that time. In retrospect, I have concluded that events in my life were being orchestrated on my behalf by God's hand. I could not have planned any of it.

As I grew slowly in my faith, a little humbler now, thanks to my indiscretion, I continued to believe that I would be normal someday. The process was not going to be overnight, and it was going to require my complete dedication, self-discipline, and a willingness to lay down my life on a moment-by-moment basis if I was ever going to get rid of this awful thing and win the battle.

I never shared my secret with anyone. I had come to embrace the promise that once we confess our sins, they are washed away, as far removed from us as the east is from the west, and God did not remember them anymore. How wonderful, I thought. If God was not holding them against me, I didn't need to tell anyone about them.

Chapter 5: Fundamentally Speaking

My knowledge of the Bible was growing slowly, and I was particularly interested in any verses or passages that might offer me the support I needed to maintain my "sobriety." I used these new tools and continually flogged myself with them to drive this demon out of my life. The relentless and persistent way I found myself thinking and dwelling on my issue made me feel all the more guilty and weak, but I zealously devoted myself to this uphill battle while keeping it to myself.

In conversations with Enrique in Vancouver, we had talked about my making a move in 1973. I wanted to take a year off before I started working full-time as a graphic designer.

The restaurant I worked for merged with several other restaurants, and this new company had plans to expand across the United States. I had a good relationship with the owners, and I was now working as a waiter. Thanks to the tips, I was making way more money than I had previously as a meat cutter. Additionally, they were hiring me to design menus and announcements for the company.

Because of my experience working on the floor and in the kitchen, and now with the marketing group, they offered me a full-time job if I went into their management training program. I declined since I planned to be in Canada within a year. Also, though I didn't say this, I did not want to live out of a suitcase all over the United States since the job entailed being part of an opening team at new locations. Nevertheless, the work I was doing for them as a waiter and graphic designer was right for me at the time since it gave me plenty of free time on my hands for church-related activities.

There was much talk among some of my Christian friends, including Stewart, who led the Bible study at the Catholic Church, about a Bible teacher who offered a one-week seminar known as Basic Youth Conflicts. Bill Gothard was a conservative and fundamentalist lay teacher who had developed a curriculum he employed in his work with young people in Chicago.

His work was touted as grounded in the Bible and much needed to counteract deteriorating family and social values. Many evangelical churches in the San Francisco Bay area planned to send large groups of members to attend an upcoming seminar in San Francisco's Cow Palace. It was a five-day event in the evenings, and I was among the group who attended the Wallace's Tuesday night Bible study who attend the seminar.

It was precisely the kind of teaching I felt I needed to be victorious and hoped that as my faith grew, so would my sense of being normal. Much of the seminar dealt with issues that constituted a positive self-image in light of God's truth, abstinence from premarital sex, God's ideal plan for marriage, Bible memorization, and many other such issues. I welcomed all of it with gusto.

Later, I became aware that not all church-going people felt Gothard's theology regarding the role of women in the church and society was acceptable. I want to give you a sense of the fundamentalist nature of what was taught. According to Gothard, women were to be subservient and submissive to men and should not be in leadership over men.

The problem with learning so many new rules and doctrines was that I had to apply them to derive any of their promised benefits. I approached all of this from a very cause-and-effect point of view. If I want to be like this, I must do that first. If I ever failed at something, I would go back to square one to see what I had missed so it would not happen again.

Nagging questions and feelings of inadequacy as a male were always there. The reminder that something unwanted was still part of me was no further than the bathroom. Assuming the average person empties their bladder a minimum of four or five times a day, each nature call was a visual and tactile reminder of so much that troubled me.

I have concluded that when God told Abraham he and his male descendants were to circumcise themselves as a sign of the covenant, He was asking them to do this for a reason. Knowing these people would need to have a constant reminder they were covenanted, He commanded them to be circumcised. In this way, they would be reminded of the covenant every time they handled themselves, an average of four or five times a day. Very clever of God, wouldn't you say?

I tried to deal with this tension by telling myself it was okay; God knew I was weak, and I just had to be patient because all this would go away one day.

Up in Vancouver, Enrique thought the large company he worked for might need a second graphic designer to help with the increasing workload. He put pressure on me to prepare my portfolio and send it to him as soon as it was ready. It took me several weeks to collect and mount a sufficient number of pieces to include.

I shipped the portfolio, and he received it within a few days and immediately took it to work to show his boss. His boss was very impressed with the portfolio but explained to Enrique that the company did not want to expand its marketing department. Enrique's plan for me to work there with him fizzled.

That same day, his boss had been invited to lunch by the president of a printing company. The printer explained that his company could not only look after their printing needs but would soon be able to assist with some of their creative needs because they were setting up an in-house graphic design office. When my brother's boss asked the printer if he had found a designer, he answered they were still looking for one. After lunch, they returned to the marketing department, and the two men asked Enrique to see my portfolio.

I got the phone call close to three in the afternoon. My brother was so excited he could hardly contain himself. He said I had a job, not where he worked, but at a print shop as an in-house designer. Furthermore, the printer was happy to know this arrangement would only be for one year, which is what my brother and I had been planning from the beginning: after one year of working for someone, we would find office space and start our own company.

One year was also the minimum time contract Immigration Canada required to qualify for a visa. Everything seemed to fall into place in my life, and I was very conscious that God was working on my behalf. To me, this was a sign of His blessing, which further made me want to believe that one day I would be normal.

5.1: Crossing the Line

On Tuesday, June 26, 1973, I left San Jose for Canada in my 1972 Dodge Colt, packed with my guitar, clothes, and as many belongings as I could fit. The remaining items, such as my bedroom suite, stereo, record collection, and other personal belongings, would come via Allied Van Lines a few days later. I spent the night at a rest stop north of Olympia, Washington, before arriving at the Canadian border the next day. After presenting my visa and immigration papers, I was processed and welcomed into Canada.

I called Enrique from the immigration office and told him I had just crossed the border and would meet him at his house. He had a bedroom reserved for me in the three-bedroom duplex he shared with a friend. I spent the rest of the day settling in and unpacking before celebrating with Carmen and her husband on Sunday. On Monday, I met my new boss at the printing company, and he gave me a tour and introduced me to his staff.

Although I was crestfallen when I arrived at the old building and saw the outdated office furnishings, I reminded myself that this was only for one year. Unfortunately, my office was not even in that building but in a grimy storefront around the corner on a hectic uphill portion of one of Vancouver's busiest streets. The traffic noise was almost deafening, and the constant hum of cars going by made it difficult to concentrate.

To prepare for my arrival, they had moved a couple of old wooden desks into the space and installed three phone lines connecting us to the main office and the outside world. I would be sharing the space with one or two sales representatives, but there were no drafting tables or art supplies anywhere to be seen. Fortunately, Enrique had established a relationship with a local graphic arts supplier. I spent my first day sourcing all the necessities for a graphic design office using the printing company's money.

Call it immaturity or naïveté, but I believed that the doors opening up for me were not simple coincidences; I believed they were God's confirmation for my life, which further bolstered my hope for you-know-what. All these little events were like God's "love notes."

I had not yet thought much about what church I would be attending. The only church I knew about was the Pentecostal church that was somehow associated with the one near San Jose State. On my second visit to Vancouver a year earlier, I had visited that church and had been confronted by one of its members on the way out. I was told that my long hair, which only came down to just below the collar of my shirt, was not suitable for men. He claimed they had a word of prophecy. This man saw it has his Christian duty to pass on God's instruction to me and was serious that I needed to correct my hairstyle as soon as possible. Consequently, his church was not even on the radar for me as a likely church to attend.

The printing company had recently hired two young sales representatives. One was a recent graduate from the British Columbia Institute of Technology's (BCIT) marketing program. I believe the other salesman, Vic, had attended the University of British Columbia (UBC), but I don't recall if he had a degree. In any case, the three of us were about the same age, and this was less intimidating for me. I soon learned that Vic was involved in a tiny church in South Vancouver on a residential street, and I thought perhaps I would attend church with him one day to check it out. Yet again, this seemed to be another love note from God.

The dizzying state I was in after I arrived in Vancouver lasted a few weeks. I was trying to orient myself and get used to a different pace of life. I was so used to driving on freeways—and long distances—for just about anything I had to do in California, but city life as I experienced it in Vancouver was undoubtedly different.

I won't dwell on the weather; let's just say I missed California's. However, my perspective on life had this eternal quality, and mere weather didn't matter as much. I would sing myself the words of an old Gospel song I learned along the way, "This world is not my home; I'm just a-passin' through."

Culturally, British Columbia was so different! I was surprised by how seemingly unfriendly people were the first time I walked downtown alone. I went to the Hudson's Bay department store for a few household items and parked my car a few blocks away. I was accustomed to smiling, acknowledging people as I walked past them, and even saying hello if I met somebody's eye. In California, if you said "Hi!" to a total stranger, they said "Hi!" back to you. I thought it was strange that now whenever I made eye contact with someone or said Hi! to them, whether male or female, they would immediately look away.

The experience was so startling that I thought maybe my pants were unzipped, but they were not. I discreetly checked while walking. When I told Enrique, he laughed and said, "Welcome to British Columbia!" He said it was a cultural norm and that I should get used to it. However, I found it odd that new people were not included socially at the printing company in Vancouver, unlike the restaurant company I worked for in California.

Even though I worked part-time for the California restaurant company, I was still invited out after work by different colleagues on more than one occasion. They often did things together on weekends, making camaraderie part of the company culture. I was surprised when Friday came without any of this kind of mingling at the printing company in Vancouver. I expected to be invited to do something with them after work or make some plans for the weekend.

I was acutely aware that in the past, I had always depended on Enrique to pave the way for me. But things were different now, partly because of my "religion" and his lack of it. Enrique laid down specific ground rules: no "proselytizing or evangelizing" him or any of his friends. He respected my beliefs, and I should respect his, even though they were not very evident. I told him he didn't have to worry and that I would keep it to myself.

Living at the house was uncomfortable because Enrique's roommate had a girlfriend who often spent the night with him. The seismic activity was constant, and it would have been less disturbing if their bedpost didn't thump the wall so loudly when they were in a romantic mood. It was hard not to feel awkward when I saw them the next day.

Although Enrique introduced me to many of his friends, I didn't have anything in common with them. They were all friendly and easy-going, and I was glad to meet them. However, I found it easier to be genuine with Vic, a stranger at work, than with my brother. It was sobering to realize this. On the other hand, my relationship with my older sister, Carmen, was different. We shared a common bond thanks to our faith. Although we were six years apart, and she was married with a young daughter, she went out of her way to make sure I wasn't alone on weekends or lacking anything.

Enrique and I no longer had many things in common except for our interest in graphic design. After a month, I decided to find an apartment. It was uncomfortable, not only for me, but also for my brother and his friend. Without me saying anything about Jesus or the Bible, they constantly apologized for swearing in front of me. They weren't cursing any more than before; they just became more aware of it.

I found a perfect one-bedroom basement suite in the house of an elderly Austrian couple. It was halfway between where I worked and where Enrique lived, making my commute shorter.

Work started slowly, but there was a steady stream of ongoing projects. The owner, Jack, paid me a straight hourly rate, regardless of the project. He didn't mind whether I was working on stationery or a complete rebranding for one of his customers. I'm convinced he gave away the graphic design service to get printing jobs. He undersold and missed opportunities to make the graphic design service a profit center. For example, logo designs, which most design firms and ad agencies charge good money for, were being expensed at my hourly rate, which was a fraction of what he could have charged. I had to keep reminding myself it was only for a year. It reduced the stress level to think of it that way.

Vic's congregation was a family church in the literal sense. Everybody was related in one way or another, and it had been the same size for a while. Unlike the growing churches I attended in California with weekly baptisms, this little chapel's growth seemed stunted, so I was noncommittal and didn't feel obliged to stay. I started looking for something closer to what I had experienced in California. Although I attended a Catholic parish in San Jose, I didn't consider myself Catholic and was free to attend any church, regardless of denomination. The churches I visited in California were large, attracting a lot of young people, such as Peninsula Bible

Church (PBC) in Palo Alto and Los Gatos Christian Church.

In the West End of Vancouver, one of North America's most densely populated neighborhoods and within walking distance of the downtown core, I discovered an intriguing Christian coffee house called the Hobbit House. My sister lived in the West End, and I would go and spend a lot of time with her on the weekends, returning to my basement suite around 10:30 or 11 p.m. Whenever I drove past the Hobbit House on my way home from Carmen's, I was always curious to check it out.

Curiosity got the better of me one night, so I pulled over and walked in just as it was closing for the night. A guy about my age was sweeping the floor and putting chairs upside down on top of the tables. He invited me to come back the following weekend. I told him I was new in town and was curious about what the Hobbit House was all about. He shared what went on in the coffee house. Then he asked me where I was from and what I was doing in Vancouver. When I mentioned that I was from San Jose, California, he got excited and introduced himself.

His name was Peter. He was from California, too, and had graduated from Stanford University. Now he and his wife, Corrine, were graduate students at the University of British Columbia and worked part-time for First Baptist Church, which owned Hobbit House. As caretakers and directors of the coffee house, Peter and Corrine lived upstairs. They became my closest friends in Vancouver, and since I played guitar and sang, I soon became one of the many people who provided entertainment at the Hobbit House on weekends.

I have mentioned that distractions were always a good thing for me. They allowed me to focus on things I enjoyed and, in a sense, helped numb the gender thing. Again, I saw this as another love note from God.

After now having lived here for most of my life, my initial impressions of people in Vancouver were very skewed and superficial. Contrary to my initial reaction, I have found the people in Vancouver as friendly as those in California. Admittedly, when I came to Canada, I was still very immature and superficial and saw things through a narrow lens.

Chapter 6: Is it Homesickness or Love?

I had been in Vancouver for about two months, mailing postcards to Rachel with short updates about once a week. She would reply a few days later, and we went back and forth like this throughout the rest of the summer. In the process, I was coming to realize something I had not allowed myself to see when I was living in San Jose. As I mentioned, I found Vancouver a difficult place to get to know people. I would have been lost if it hadn't been for Peter and Corinne, my brother Enrique, my sister Carmen.

I was consumed with anticipation for the next few days, and time seemed to move at a snail's pace. By the following Friday, I still hadn't heard from Rachel, and it was driving me insane. I gave her the benefit of the doubt, thinking that maybe the letter was delayed in transit. But after four long weeks, I still hadn't heard from her, and I didn't know what to do. Should I call her? Send another postcard? But what if she had already received my letter and was horrified by what I wrote? Perhaps she didn't share my feelings for her.

My self-confidence in front of my friends Peter and Corinne took a hit, and I almost didn't want to see them anymore. They were in on the plan, and every time they saw me, they asked if I had heard from Rachel yet. It wasn't supposed to be like this. I was climbing the walls with anxiety, and every time I returned home to my basement suite, I would check the mail slot to see if there was anything from Rachel. But there never was.

One Sunday after church, I decided to take action. I bought a postcard and wrote a short message to Rachel. I told her that I thought she was more mature than this and if I had said anything that made her uncomfortable, she should have told me. I added that I still wanted to hear from her and asked her to please write back. I dropped it into a mailbox, forgetting that it was the Sunday before

American Thanksgiving (Canada celebrates Thanksgiving in October).

The following Wednesday, I went to a Bible study at a local church and got home around ten o'clock at night. Just as I was unlocking my front door, my phone started ringing. I answered it just in time before the caller hung up. It was Rachel! I was completely caught off guard and stumbled over my words.

She asked, "Is this Jim?"

"Yes." My heart was racing.

Then she said, "Happy Thanksgiving!"

"Oh yeah, it's Thanksgiving tomorrow in the States—I had forgotten—Happy Thanksgiving to you!" I blurted out.

Quietly, almost inaudibly, she said she had received my latest postcard and was a little confused. She had gone through all our correspondence and wasn't sure what I was talking about on the postcard. I told her I had been climbing the walls for the last month and a half waiting for her to write me.

"I've been climbing the walls, too," she replied.

I couldn't believe what she had just said. I asked, "You have?"

"Yes," she answered.

I then told her I had come to realize how important she was to me, how I thought about her all the time and that I loved her. Rachel answered, "I love you, too!"

"You do?"

"Yes!" She admitted, "I love you, and I thought you had stopped writing because you had met someone else." Our communication breakdown resulted from her never receiving my four-page letter in the first place! The letter got lost in the mail between Vancouver and San Jose, so it made no sense when she got my tersely worded postcard.

I should have that first conversation memorized, but that is all I can remember about the phone call. We agreed to call each other once a week and would begin exploring the next steps if we got together. That was the plan.

I couldn't wait a whole week before talking to her again, so I called her the next day. We started calling each other daily, and I couldn't get enough of her! Our long-distance phone bills that first month would have paid for one of us to fly back and forth twice.

My parents celebrated Thanksgiving in San Jose with only Angela and John, the two children remaining at home. I'm not sure whose idea it was, Carmen's maybe, but the next thing I knew, our parents, with Angela and John, were coming up to Vancouver to celebrate Christmas. Previously, ever since Carmen and Enrique had moved to Vancouver, they had returned to California for the Christmas holiday. This would be the first Christmas in the thirteen years since we left Colombia that would be celebrated somewhere else besides San Jose.

Peter and Corinne went down to California to celebrate Christmas with their families and asked me if I would like to stay at the Hobbit House during their two weeks away. They were the same two weeks my parents would be coming to Vancouver. This gave me the idea to find out if Rachel could get time off so she could join us all for our first Christmas in Canada.

Once again, things were falling into place — yet another love note from God, I thought. Then I found out that my brother-in-law's younger brother and his wife, who lived only about a block away from the Hobbit House, would be going to Toronto to celebrate Christmas with her family, and their apartment would be vacant. Carmen inquired on our behalf, and they were more than happy to let Rachel stay in the apartment. This arrangement was perfect since Rachel and I were both mindful of our Christian views on marriage.

With all these details worked out, I called Rachel to suggest this crazy idea of her coming to Vancouver for Christmas. I first asked her if she would be taking any time off over the holidays. She said their office would be closed for two weeks because the doctor was taking his family on a ski vacation to Lake Tahoe. I couldn't believe my ears! I asked her if I sent her an airplane ticket, would she like to come up for Christmas, and then shared with her that my parents were coming up with Angela and John. (I had introduced her to my family when I still lived in San Jose.) She answered Yes! She would love to come up to Vancouver. Her alternative was to stay home in San Jose since she had decided not to go to Texas that year.

Peter and Corinne's departure overlapped Rachel's arrival by a couple of days. Since Peter sang in the choir, he invited us to

First Baptist Church's presentation of The Messiah. After the performance, there was a party for the choir at a house overlooking Vancouver in an area known as the British Properties. Rachel and I were a little nervous about crashing this party for church members only, but Peter insisted it would be okay.

What a fantastic house! It belonged to one of the wealthiest families in Vancouver, members of the church, with floor-to-ceiling picture windows and a panoramic view. On a clear day, one could see Vancouver Island to the west, the coastal mountains to the east, and as far south as the entrance to Puget Sound and the mountains of the Olympic Peninsula on the horizon.

Peter knew everyone and wanted us to meet some of the people there. The first time he introduced us, he said, "I would like you to meet Jim and his fiancée, Rachel." I saw the shock on Rachel's face as we both gasped. We had not even discussed engagement yet. Not wanting to embarrass Peter, we said nothing to him but gave each other this funny look.

She pulled me aside and nervously asked me, "Did you tell Peter that we were engaged?"

"No!" I stammered. "But how do you like the sound of it?"

"I like it a lot!" she smiled.

"I do, too!" I grinned.

And that was how we got engaged. Not the way I had expected it to happen; we had never dated officially, yet here we were, engaged, and it seemed so right. I was so grateful to God because I would be normal at last. He had answered my prayer.

6.1: The Countdown Begins

1973 was a Christmas to remember, although I don't remember much about it. There was so much to take in and so little time. It was a milestone: the first family Christmas in Canada, Rachel and I engaged, and my parents warming up to the idea of moving to Canada as well.

Rachel and I had our first official date in Vancouver. We laughed about being engaged before our first "romantic" date. It didn't take long for us to start thinking about a wedding day. She would return to California, which meant enduring a long-distance romance for several months. Spring and summer were out since it would have been too soon for Rachel to do all the necessary things to relocate to Canada.

As we looked at the calendar, we knew that whatever date we picked should be close to another important family date so those who had to travel could kill two birds with one stone. We didn't want to do it near Easter, Thanksgiving, or Christmas—and we wanted it to be on a Saturday. Since my mom's birthday is three days before my parents' anniversary in October, this seemed like the most convenient time of the year, and a fall wedding was also appealing to us. That year, Mom's birthday was on a Saturday. We concluded this would be a wonderful way to commemorate her birthday. So that's the day we chose—oblivious to the fact it was also her fiftieth birthday that year.

It was hard saying goodbye to Rachel at the airport for her flight back to California, but we were in love. The only thing that made it bearable for me was the knowledge that we would be together forever in just a few months. I was resolved more than ever to present myself to her on our wedding day as a transformed person, free from the curse of my gender confusion. I found the strength as I focused on my love for her.

In the meantime, she was busy planning with her friends. Our wedding would be simple and unpretentious, and the reception would be a potluck in the church hall—organized by her friends. We had agreed to keep phone calls to a minimum to avoid the large bills.

Since the wedding was going to be in San Jose, I would need to have the blood test done for the marriage license and finalize the arrangements with the minister. Several joint sessions with him were one of his prerequisites if he was to perform the wedding ceremony. I would need to be in San Jose for a couple of weeks to accomplish all of this, but first, I wanted to be free of my commitment to the printing company. My contract with them was ending in June, and I would need a few days, possibly a few weeks, to find office space with Enrique.

Enrique, being the business part of the equation, had gotten to know our bank manager on a first-name basis. I don't know how he did it, but the banker approved a company loan so Enrique and I could buy two identical, brand-new 1974 seven-seater VW vans. Rachel and I could then drive up after our wedding with all her belongings by removing the seats. I took delivery of the van, and a few weeks later, in mid-August, I drove down to California.

Rachel and I had not spent so many consecutive days together since the two weeks over Christmas. During this time, Rachel was living in a small one-bedroom cottage in Santa Clara. She had only lived there a few months and was sad to be leaving such a lovely place. Before I left to return to Vancouver, Rachel wanted to make me a special dinner. When I arrived, she had set up her tiny table with candles and flowers, and it looked amazing. We enjoyed roasted Cornish game hens, brown rice, and salad. It was all so lovely, as was Rachel.

After finishing our dinner and cleaning up, we sat on the couch and listened to soft music. Just then, the phone rang. Rachel answered, and her body language changed abruptly as if to prevent me from overhearing the conversation. She told the caller that she had not seen "him" for a while, and the last time she had seen "him," he had mentioned in a kidding sort of way that he was thinking of becoming a hairdresser. She then added that she had not spoken to "him" since.

Rachel was visibly shaken and uncomfortable as she hung up the phone. I asked her who had called and what the call was about. She explained that it was Stewart, the man who led the Bible study at the Catholic Church, who had also recruited her to be one of the people to come to the high school retreat. Rachel went on to explain that before moving to the cottage, she had lived in another house with Stewart's younger sister, Susan. A young man who had been part of the Wallace's Bible study group, had offered to come by once a week to mow their lawn as a favor. Rachel and her Susan had accepted his Christian charity. His name was Mark.

One Saturday, when Rachel was alone, Mark came by to discuss something with them. Rachel explained that her roommate was at work, but Mark asked if he could use the washroom. When he came out, he was wearing some of Rachel's roommate's clothing, taken from the laundry hamper, and had applied makeup to his face.

"This is what I wanted to talk to you about; I came to confess this is what I've been doing when I come to mow the lawn," Mark said.

Rachel and her roommate had given Mark the key to the house so he could go into the garage to get the lawnmower. He admitted to Rachel he had tried on some of her roommate's clothing, but they were too small for him, and he had been wearing Susan's clothing only since they were a better fit. Rachel told him that was something he would have to discuss with Susan; she told him to go back into the bathroom, take the makeup and clothing off and leave immediately. Rachel was very upset as she shared this with me.

Stewart was calling to find out if Rachel knew whether Mark had modified his behavior or if he had made further contact. Mark had applied at his church for some position and had confessed his misdeeds in an interview. Since Susan was Stewart's younger sister, I'm sure there was more than church business on Stewart's mind.

As Rachel talked to Stewart about Mark, I was faced with a difficult decision. Should I risk everything, confess my secret to her, or keep it to myself? The disgust in her voice sent chills down my spine — I feared she wouldn't want to marry me if she knew the truth. Was this a test from God? I was desperate and prayed for guidance, hoping to believe in His promise that all my sins were forgiven.

After a long silence, I mustered up the courage to tell Rachel that I had tried on my sister's clothing before out of curiosity. I tried to justify it as something that most guys had probably done, but Rachel knew this was different. I was overwhelmed with fear and sickness in my stomach, but I couldn't bring myself to make a full confession. Instead, I changed the subject and pretended it was no big deal, just a normal thing boys did.

My conscience has weighed heavily on me ever since that day. I often wonder how Rachel would have reacted if I had told her everything. At the time, I didn't even realize I was trans — I just knew that I wanted to be the best husband I could be for Rachel, no matter what it took.

Chapter 7: I Promise

Back in Vancouver, it was time to get serious about work. My brother and I found an office in the historic part of the city known as Gastown, which was enjoying a renaissance. Heritage buildings were being transformed into retail and office spaces, and the main street was repaved with red bricks.

Our office was in a funky triangular brick building that sat at the point of the triangular block. It housed a nightclub in the basement, some small shops on the main floor, and offices on the second and third floors. Ours was on the second floor at the point of the building. Almost all the other tenants in the building were creative types, so it was an excellent place for networking, camaraderie, and friendship.

As our graphic design company slowly gained traction, our big break came when the marketing director of the new restaurant chain, the Keg 'n Cleaver, saw the work we had done for a group of California restaurants. The Keg, with its steak and lobster offerings and all-you-can-eat salad bar, needed creative marketing materials, and we were the perfect fit.

Thanks to the Keg account, we established ourselves and covered our overheads. They became our primary client, providing us with consistent work that allowed us to grow our business. As our reputation spread, we began attracting more companies, leading to exciting new projects and collaborations.

Looking back, I realize that our success with the Keg was largely due to my experience working with California restaurants, which gave us an edge in understanding the industry. By showcasing our best work and demonstrating our expertise, we secured the account that proved to be a turning point for our business. The Keg not only provided a steady income but also helped establish us as a reliable and creative graphic design firm.

In the early days of our studio, before the Keg, we were like many freelance graphic designers working on contract for various advertising agencies. We thought introducing ourselves and showcasing our portfolio would lead to more work, but we quickly learned that we were unintentionally stepping on the toes of agency art directors.

We didn't realize that by offering both art direction and design services, we were declaring that we were going to step on their turf. Ad agencies are very territorial and protective. They hire designers to reproduce and execute their ideas, not to contribute their own creative input. As a result, we found ourselves reduced to being production artists.

Moreover, the few jobs we did get from advertising agencies were not much fun to work on. Some art directors were nit-picky and difficult to please, which made the process less enjoyable for us.

Overall, our experience working with ad agencies taught us the importance of understanding the industry and finding clients who value our creative skills and expertise. We learned that success is not just about securing new clients but building long-term relationships based on mutual respect and shared values.

However, instead of servicing ad agencies, our strategy was to target small clients who needed agency-quality work but could not afford agency rates. This allowed us to cater to a niche market and provided us with the opportunity to showcase our creative abilities, which led to many diverse projects and collaborations.

Fortunately, I found a new basement suite that was brighter and larger than the first one; this would be Rachel's and my new home. Thanks to the intensity of starting a new business and setting up the apartment, August and September flew by, and before I knew it, it was time to head down to California for the wedding. I had never felt so assured in my male identity as I did then. I was convinced God was at work in my life and would soon completely fix me, and I didn't want to do anything that would jinx that process.

With all these wonderful things happening around me and

sensing I was enjoying blessing upon blessing, I was oblivious at first, but then I realized my brother Enrique was not doing so great. It was hard for him to admit, but his personal life was unraveling. He had always been the strong one, the one I would look up to and get direction from, but now the roles were reversed, and he was coming to me for guidance, with many questions having to do with spiritual issues.

I remember that soon after he gave me the ultimatum that he didn't want me talking to him and his housemate about religion, I prayed to God to help Enrique see and admit his need. I asked God to do whatever it would take to get his attention, even if it meant something tragic happening to me. I was willing to suffer for Enrique if that is what it would take for him to get serious about God. That's how I saw things in those days.

I thought God answered that prayer because, in a series of events, his heart was broken by the woman he had fallen in love with. He was inconsolable. Enrique called me one night in tears because she had decided she could not marry him. He could not understand why and wondered how this could be happening. Shortly after this, he, too, surrendered his life to God in a new way, and we grew closer than we had ever been before. I was no longer his "little brother" but an equal. Everything was going to be new; everything was going to be different.

For me, marrying Rachel was to mark the beginning of a new life with hope for the future, free of the guilt and confusion I had lived with all my life. The wedding was everything I hoped it would be. Rachel was beautiful, and I was so proud to declare my love for her in front of family and friends, while at the same time, I was so humbled by the fact she loved me. I wanted to believe I could be the best husband possible.

For our honeymoon, we drove up to Vancouver in the van loaded with Rachel's things, but we spent our wedding night in a cabin in Ben Lomond in the Santa Cruz Mountains. Our mutual timidity and bashfulness gradually melted as we embraced for the first time. That night, her love, humility, and gentleness will be forever emblazoned in my memory as the best gift I have ever received, and she caused me to forget all my fears and apprehensions. My insecurity as a man finally seemed like it could be a thing of the past. I was so grateful to God and believed he was answering my prayers, and Rachel's love for me made me believe this all the more. I wanted it to be true for her too.

Sunday morning, we drove to Santa Cruz and had breakfast, and I'll never forget how wonderful it felt to be sitting across from her at the table, holding her hands and gazing into her eyes. I was so grateful to God and hoped this was the beginning of a new me. After breakfast, we drove back to San Jose to load up the van and say goodbye to family and her friends. Then we headed north to San Francisco and across the Golden Gate Bridge. We had booked a room in a cozy motel in Russian River, where we spent Sunday night.

We continued up the coast on U.S. Highway 1 all the way to the mouth of the Columbia River before turning east to connect with I-5 to head north. It was typical autumn weather, sunny with a chill in the air and the trees starting to change color. I felt we were on our own "Magical Mystery Tour," and it was all good. It was all very good!

When we got to the Canadian border, it started to sprinkle, and then rain. We hadn't seen any rain on our whole trip until now. As Rachel remembers, it rained nonstop for her first month in Vancouver. She wondered what she had gotten herself into and felt like she went through withdrawal from California weather.

Though she had been working for several years in an oral surgeon's office, she wasn't sure if that was what she wanted to do again. I had met one of the couples from First Baptist Church who volunteered at the Hobbit House on the weekends. His family owned a food and restaurant supply company and offered Rachel a job in telephone sales. All the orders were pounded onto the four-part NCR forms used before computers, and Rachel had good typing skills, so she accepted the position.

The great thing was that this company was just three blocks away, at the other end of Gastown, so we could drive to work together. More importantly, we were able to meet for lunch every day.

We started going to the church with the college and career group, where I had been attending some Bible studies, but we also assisted the youth pastor with the high school students. They welcomed us as a couple, and for the next few months, we helped out once a week with the group's activities.

My older sister, Carmen, and her husband had their second child that January. I have to admit that being around her baby boy got us thinking seriously about starting our own family. We made some decisions and set some goals for ourselves. We were determined that if and when our children came, Rachel would be a stay-at-home mom. We also decided we would try to stay in one place to give our children a chance to grow up and develop roots in one spot, unlike the two of us, who had moved several times throughout our childhoods.

By this time, my parents had decided to sell their business and home in California and move to Canada. Dad came to Vancouver to scout job prospects, leaving Mom to pack their belongings. He found a job managing a dry cleaner in Vancouver and got the right of first refusal if the owner chose to sell the business. It was a good arrangement and made it possible for my parents to immigrate before the summer.

My younger brother and sister were the only unhappy people who felt they were being pulled away from their friends without much say. John had one year left in high school, and Angela was working as a dental assistant in San Jose, but I'm sure our mom would not have wanted her to stay in California by herself.

By March of 1975, the whole family was reunited again, and permanently, from Colombia to British Columbia by way of California. It had taken 15 years.

7.1: Starting a Family

Our doctor's office called me at work at about ten with the pregnancy test results, and I found out first because Rachel had asked our doctor to call me since she couldn't take the call at work. I immediately called Rachel and arranged to see her during her coffee break. On the way to meet her, I stopped at a gift shop and bought a porcelain Beatrix Potter rabbit nestled in a cozy straw bed with a baby blue blanket. They wrapped it in tissue, put it in its box, and tied a ribbon around it. When Rachel opened it, we both cried tears of joy.

Despite my elation at the news of our impending parent-hood, I couldn't shake my contrary feelings about myself. I felt like I should be overjoyed and fulfilled, yet I was tormented by doubt and confusion. I told myself it was a spiritual attack, that Satan was trying to sabotage me, but it didn't make sense to me. I had hoped that marriage and fatherhood would dispel these feelings, but they persisted.

I was determined to be the best husband and father I could be for Rachel and our baby, but the pressure I felt to be "pure" was overwhelming. Despite my knowledge of scripture and my ability to articulate my faith, I beat myself up over my perceived failure to claim God's promises and defeat the enemy. I felt like a hypocrite, like one of the whitewashed tombs full of dead men's bones that Jesus accused the religious leaders of being.

We began searching for a more suitable home with a baby on the way. We found a perfect two-bedroom house for rent, owned by a man from Hungary who worked as a pipe fitter with the Boil-ermakers' Union. He lived downstairs and maintained a beautifully manicured backyard that we could use whenever we wanted.

We were so happy, and life had all the appearances of normal-cy—and that is how I wanted it for Rachel. Whenever I thought that I needed to share my secret struggles with her, I would be reminded of her disgust when she told me about Mark, the cross-dresser. How could I tell her now? It would crush her and rob her of joy and antic-ipation for the baby inside her. No, it was too late for that. I would have to keep this to myself and never open my mouth.

I don't know how I survived; I was so schizophrenic. In the movie A Beautiful Mind, there is a scene where we look into a room that has all the walls completely covered with notes, magazines, and newspaper clippings. That scene aptly portrays what it was like in my head. I labeled and categorized my identity struggle to death. I had to keep it in the realm of good versus evil and make everything black and white, rules upon rules, disciplines upon disciplines. It was exhausting.

Rachel was due any day, and we invited some friends for dinner. But Rachel's water broke before we could sit down to enjoy the meal. We were all excited, and our friends wished us well and said goodbye as we left for the hospital. When we got to the hospital, her contractions had not yet started, so the nurses prepped her, and we waited. We had attended a prenatal class together, so I got to be in the delivery room when our son was born, just after sunrise. I was so grateful when I saw he was healthy and had ten fingers and ten toes! I had this nagging fear that God would punish me for my "perverted mind" and our baby would not be perfect—how could I expect anything else? I apologized to God, asking for His forgiveness for my lack of faith and for allowing my mind to have such morbid thoughts.

My parents and sisters came to the hospital as soon as I called them with the news, and for a brief moment, I experienced a profound sense of wholeness. I wanted that sense of peace to last forever.

The first time I had slept alone since we got married was the night after our son was born. I am sorry that it is also the first time I finally caved in. I was in the bathroom getting ready for bed, and hanging on the back of the door was one of Rachel's flannel nightgowns. I put my nose to smell her scent, then pressed my face against it with my eyes closed as I thought of her and how beautiful and happy she looked holding our son to her breast. I took the nightgown off the hook and brought it into the bedroom as if it were a safety blanket—and everything would have been okay up to this point.

I don't know what compelled me to slip it over my head, put my arms through the sleeves, and then lay in bed. My mind raced as I tried to sleep; I felt terrible guilt. What would Rachel say and do if she knew? I think I knew the answer, but she wasn't there, and no one would ever know. I finally fell asleep and spent the whole night in her nightgown.

To say that I was remorseful the following morning is an understatement. I felt horrible, and I asked God for forgiveness and cleansing. I also wondered why I had given in after having been so good for so long. How ironic and wrong, I thought, that in less than twenty-four hours after the child I fathered had been born, I was back to where I had been before — unable to make sense of my life, feeling shame, and resorting again to the need for secrecy.

But now there was a new focus in my life. It's amazing how quickly your priorities change when a new little person is in your life. One minute you're free to be spontaneous, and the next, you're no longer a free agent; it's as if your wings get clipped. Every couple I know has gone through this readjustment of schedules as their life suddenly revolves around their baby's needs. The mysterious thing is, though life gets turned upside down, you can't imagine having it any other way. The joy felt and the love that suddenly springs from the heart for the child is like nothing ever experienced before, and it was certainly true in our case.

I'm sure it's universal for parents to pray that their children will not be afflicted with their problems and issues. We ask God to spare them the suffering we have experienced and wish for our children a life free of adversity and sorrow.

As a Christian, I had been taught to believe that we live in a broken world, that we are all wounded, and that Jesus had come to save us from this predicament. I found hope in this, which is why I prayed for our son to be spared from my "affliction."

I was spiritually defeated for the first few months after our son was born. I could not reconcile myself to my internal struggle. Even though I had fathered a child, I still questioned my gender identity. During this time, we stopped attending church and no longer had any obligations or responsibilities with the high school group. Since we had been involved as a couple, I did not want to continue without Rachel, and this was the convenient excuse I used to isolate myself spiritually.

Our friends Peter and Corinne had also made some changes and were no longer working with First Baptist Church. They were now attending a new church that met primarily in homes called "households," and all the households had a joint celebration on Sundays in a rented community center. What was novel about this church was how the real focus of the congregation's life was these small groups. There were no paid ministers or staff. The leadership consisted of lay people with regular jobs , who formed a Deacons' Board. Peter and Corinne invited us to one of the Sunday evening joint celebrations, where we fell in love with the concept and the people. The church was called Dayspring Fellowship.

We transitioned very quickly into the life of this church, and because Peter and I had a history of making music together, I was soon involved in worship during the Sunday celebrations. The format of the weekly household meetings made it easy to come with the baby, and for Rachel to take part since the older children watched the little ones while the adults did "church."

It was a safe and nurturing environment for all, quite different from all the traditional churches we had attended. Things were a little different on Sundays, and the service resembled a more conventional Protestant format. The children who came were taken to another room and usually babysat by the parents with babies since it was much easier for the moms this way.

With my parents' help, we purchased a small eight-hundred-square-foot fixer-upper with two bedrooms, one bath, and a low-ceiling unfinished basement where we could set up the washer and dryer. We gutted the interior, insulated it, and refinished all the surfaces. We also installed double-glazed windows.

We had taken possession of the house in September 1977, and while the renovations were taking place, Rachel went to Texas with our son. I was able to have it ready in time for their return.

From all indications, life was good. No, it was great! My love for Rachel grew daily, as did my love for our son. I rededicated all my efforts to maintaining a "pure" perspective on my life. How could I possibly risk harming these two people who meant more to me than anything else in the world? Tenaciously, I adopted an even harsher set of rules for myself, hating my tendency to feel inadequate as a man. I don't know where it came from, but I had an inordinate fear of something terrible happening to our son as punishment for my "sinfulness." Our little boy used to stand at the front window and blow kisses at me as I drove off to work. I was often reduced to tears as I pulled away, pleading with God to please protect him and not let anything harm him.

A year after moving into our house, we were pregnant again. Our second son was born in the summer of 1979. We accommodated both boys in their small bedroom thanks to a bunk bed from Ikea. We were blessed to have two healthy boys, and our joy knew no bounds.

With the birth of our second son, the tension in my life was reaching a breaking point. All my efforts to suppress and deny my problem had not worked as I had hoped, and I no longer expected God to fix this. If, after getting married and having two sons, I still had this confusion about my gender, how would I survive?

Chapter 8: Full of Beans & Fessing Up

One legacy of our family's life in California was our new appreciation for Mexican food. It was very different from Colombian food, even though we had dishes with the same Spanish names. It's not that we ate Mexican food all the time in California, but when we did, we enjoyed it. One of Mom's alterations customers, Josefina, owned three popular Mexican restaurants with her husband. As Josefina and Mom became good friends, we feasted several times at El Gordo, their flagship location in Los Gatos, California.

Before my parents moved up to Canada, those of us who were already in Vancouver would often reminisce about the great meals we had in Josefina's restaurant. Unfortunately, Mexican food was not readily available in Vancouver. We craved the food so much that we even made junkets across the border to Washington State to buy tortillas and other Mexican ingredients to make the food for ourselves. We called these tortilla runs.

At one point, we even convinced mom to tell Josefina they should consider opening a restaurant in Vancouver. "Well, Honey, Vancouver is so far away. We have our hands full here with these three restaurants, it would be impossible. But you know what? Your family should open a restaurant, and I will give you all the recipes." That was her promise, and when Mom told us what Josefina had said, we could hardly believe our ears! This became our family's little fantasy.

After my parents moved to Vancouver, Dad's arrangement with the dry cleaner's owner fizzled, but he was undeterred. He found another dry-cleaning plant for sale, and the owner was willing to help finance the purchase. Mom and Dad were now operating their own business in Vancouver in an excellent location not far from where we lived. They were also fortunate to find a house in the neighborhood; the design and architecture reminded them of the building style at the country club in Bogotá. They felt at home.

I must stop here to say how much I admire my Father for having the stamina and wherewithal at his age (he was fifty-seven) to start life in a new country again. The one concern that nagged him was getting older and approaching the traditional retirement age of sixty-five in just a few years. He also realized that everything he had was dependent on their business investment.

Dad worried about what would happen if he got ill or, worse yet, died. Then who would take care of the business, and what would happen to Mom? He knew none of us were even remotely interested in taking over the dry-cleaning business or helping him run it. He feared we would have to sell the business in a "fire sale" and not realize its value.

Dad called our bluff one day when we were fantasizing about opening a Mexican restaurant. He told us about his concern with the dry cleaners and said he was prepared to sell it and put the money toward a restaurant. As long as we all promised to help run it, the whole family would have to be involved. It was a preposterous idea, but he had an ace up his sleeve. One of his dry-cleaning customers owned a Spanish restaurant in the west side area of Vancouver known as Kitsilano. This man had the same misgivings about his restaurant that Dad had about the dry cleaners. His children did not want to be part of it, so he was looking for a buyer.

One day the man came into the cleaners, and Dad asked him if he had sold the restaurant. He had. But the new owners had quickly run it into the ground and were now desperate to unload it. He suggested that if we were serious about buying the restaurant, we should contact them and make them an offer.

Talk about a turn of events! Dad's idea was for us to purchase the restaurant at a salvage price and transform it into a Mexican restaurant. With a little effort, it was doable since the Spanish decor was ideal. We discussed this crazy idea and decided we might have a chance if we were going to be the recipients of Josefina's recipes. To make a long story short, this is precisely what our family did. In September 1980, we opened a California-style Mexican restaurant in Vancouver, Las Margaritas. ,.

Since I had worked in a restaurant kitchen when I lived in California, I was designated by the family to go down to San Jose for two weeks to be tutored by Josefina's husband at one of their restaurants. It was hilarious! Josefina's husband said, "We have nothing written down; it's all in the head. You are just going to have to watch and take notes."

And that is what I did. The cooks just opened this and that and scooped, poured, and added ingredients by eye. I would try to ascertain the quantities by volume or weight and took copious notes that I had to re-write along with the procedures. I had a blast—and the best part was that they all worked when we tested the recipes in Vancouver!

Enrique knew a Mexican girl whose Dad was a chef in Los Angeles. We convinced him to come to Vancouver to help us set up the kitchen. His visa was approved quickly because we were able to demonstrate to Immigration Canadian that there were no Mexican chefs in Canada with his skill. That was another lucky break.

While I was in California, the rest of the family was busy cleaning and painting the restaurant. We were closed for two months while we got all our ducks in a row. Enrique and I got busy contacting our clients to tell them we were cutting back on hours for a new venture. It was strange to be doing that, but we had agreed to jump into the restaurant business with both feet.

At about this time, I concluded that God did not answer my prayer because I had not been forthright and honest with my wife. I had squandered the opportunity to disclose to her and be truthful about myself before we married, and I could not change that now. But if we were, as I believed, joined and as one before God, I had an obligation to be completely transparent and honest with her—I shuddered at the thought. However, I could see no other way to expect God to honor my prayers for healing than by disclosing to Rachel the full extent of my brokenness.

I wrote a letter as a confession and shared with her the best I could about my problem, my feelings of inadequacy as a man, the sense of disconnection with my body, and how much I feared she would not want me as a result. I asked for forgiveness for not being completely honest with her that night in San Jose. I could only explain my behavior by saying I was fascinated with women's clothing.

Crossdressing, or the need to feel feminine, was the symptom but not the cause. I didn't understand what made me feel the way I did; I certainly didn't know it was a medical condition. I interpreted it simply as my sinful nature.

I agonized about how I would express all these things, the words I would use, and how I would present them to her. I decided the best and only thing I could do was read it to her in person. One night after the boys were asleep, I finally found the courage to tell her I had something I needed to discuss with her. We sat on the couch, and I read her the letter. It was all so intense; I could not keep myself from choking up. I composed myself and continued. And when I finished, Rachel just sat there in stunned silence.

The first words out of her mouth were, "I knew you were too good to be true." She apologized for placing me on a pedestal and "worshiping" me. She was proud to be my wife and felt secure and loved in our relationship. She was devastated but reminded me she had promised to love and be with me until death. She said she would stand with me, and we would continue to fight this battle together, turning to God more fervently as a couple.

She wanted to know if anybody else knew about this. I told her I had never shared it with anyone. She wondered if my parents had ever suspected anything, so I told her about some of my experiences and the time my sister had found the bra; but no one, I assured her, really knew the depth of my problem. I had kept it to myself, fearing rejection and ridicule and that my life would be over if anyone ever found out.

But there was a fallout from the atomic bomb I dropped on Rachel that night; it was predictable. What other secrets had I kept from her? Could she trust me with our boys? Could she trust me, period? What was this going to mean, and how was our life going to be impacted? What did I want out of all this?

The answer was that I didn't know. I didn't have answers to these questions, but I did have a response to the question of whether she could trust me with our sons—it was an emphatic Yes! I could never do anything to harm them. I loved them more than I loved my own life.

More than these pressing questions, Rachel wondered if what we had was all a lie and a sham. Were all those beautiful memories of our first years together, the birth of our sons, and their birthday parties just an act on my part? These suspicions tore me up because I knew my answers would be met with skepticism and would not be believed. The absolute truth is that I cherish all these beautiful moments to this day. Though I was going through hell on the inside, I was given the ability to be there genuinely for them.

One day I was looking at our family photo albums and remembered this little thought that constantly ran through my head whenever I was aware my picture was about to be taken. I would tell myself, "It's okay, don't worry—the camera can't see the real you."

I was convinced that Rachel's lack of knowledge of my gender issues had been the missing piece of the puzzle. It made sense to me that God would now listen to my prayers, snap His fingers, and voila! I would be healed. That was my wishful thinking.

Soon after this crushing disclosure, Rachel learned one of her sisters in Texas had been diagnosed with breast cancer and was to undergo surgery soon. Rachel wanted to be there for her so she could help take care of the two young daughters. We planned for Rachel to go to Texas for up to one month.

There was more bad news. Enrique was in a motor vehicle accident. He had gone grocery shopping and was one block away from home when he passed out at the wheel of his VW van and crashed into a parked car. Fortunately, he was not traveling very fast and was not injured—just a little banged up. He was taken to the hospital by ambulance and discharged after the doctors concluded that he had not been eating well and his blood sugar was low. A few months later, he began to have seizures, and at this time, he underwent further testing.

They performed a CAT scan, and that's when a brain tumor was discovered. Enrique was banned from driving until the doctors could confirm that his seizures were under control with anti-seizure medication.

During this time, I wondered if one option might not be for me to accommodate somehow my "need" to cross-dress from time to time as a relief valve. But I feared I was walking in a minefield by even contemplating such an idea. I had read an article in a magazine about a man who had been caught wearing his wife's clothes, and she had decided to use this to her advantage. She blackmailed the husband to get her way in the marriage and reduced him to an enslaved person. For example, the husband was expected to clean the house wearing dresses and aprons and was generally demeaned. The story pointed out that the husband feigned protest but didn't resist the treatment.

It was an appalling story against everything I believed constituted a healthy marriage. However, I gleaned a couple of things from this true story. One was that I was not alone—other men had a similar "secret." (The article did not go into the man's history, and he may not have been trans; he could have been only a cross-dresser or a fetishist.) The other thing I learned was that not all wives and this behavior turned off significant others.

Enrique had by now come into his faith with conviction and had joined a church that had a ministry to the gay community. More correctly stated, it had a ministry to help individuals who wanted to leave the gay lifestyle. One of the lay ministers who helped in this particular work of the church operated a janitorial company, and my brother contracted them to do the cleaning at the restaurant. When I found out about the man's involvement in that ministry, I approached him one day and asked him if I could speak to him privately about something. I felt relatively safe.

We made an appointment a few days later, and I confessed everything to him. He was unfazed by my admission and suggested that, if Rachel was agreeable, she might allow me to have some items to wear in the privacy of the bedroom like some couples incorporate sex toys into their love life. He opined that these kinds of aids were morally neutral within the confines of a marriage relationship as long as they were mutually accepted and agreed upon. This was new information to me. I wondered about the wisdom of it since I had spiritualized all facets of this and labeled them sinful. Did other "Christian" couples do stuff like that?

Would our marriage survive if it were possible for me to accommodate my needs? If so, what were my needs? Again, the questions of who I was and what I was needed to be answered—but I was afraid to ask the questions. More importantly, I feared the answers.

There was not much joy the day I drove Rachel and the boys down to Seattle for the flight to Dallas. Once we'd said farewell at the SeaTac airport, Rachel broke my heart with her question. With a pained look, she looked into my eyes and asked if this was goodbye. I looked at her and answered, "I don't know."

I drove back to Vancouver broken, defeated, and unsure whether I could hang in there. I loved my wife and our sons, but I had no hope left in me. Why was I like this? Why couldn't I be normal? What more could I do? I thought that a secret of any kind was, like a cancer, slowly killing me.

8.1: Hitting Rock Bottom

Rachel's haunting question, "Is this goodbye?" left me with doubts about my ability to hold things together. Was I selfish for expecting unconditional love from her, despite my falling apart? What kind of future did we have, and how would our boys be affected? There were many questions, but few answers. Our separation when she went to Texas was supposed to be a trial period. I needed to figure out if I could keep my promise to love and cherish her and to have no one else. We always ended our conversations about these concerns with the phrase, "Divorce is not an option."

Rachel's haunting question, "Is this goodbye?" left me with doubts about my ability to hold things together. Was I selfish for expecting unconditional love from her, despite my falling apart? What kind of future did we have, and how would our boys be affected? There were many questions, but few answers. Our separation when she went to Texas was supposed to be a trial period. I needed to figure out if I could keep my promise to love and cherish her and to have no one else. We always ended our conversations about these concerns with the phrase, "Divorce is not an option."

I questioned whether addressing my needs was unrealistic and would open Pandora's box. But I knew one thing for certain: my problem wouldn't go away, and not telling Rachel about it hadn't made any difference. I was convinced that telling her was the missing piece to the puzzle of why my prayers for healing hadn't been answered. I felt hopeless.

Drinking myself unconscious was never my intention, but during the first week alone in our empty house, I sat down with a bottle of rum and drank two large glasses, one after the other. I refilled the glass, placed it on the side table, and waited for the alcohol to take effect. My low tolerance meant it didn't take long. Trying to stand up and use the bathroom, I was unsteady. I finished the third glass and lay down on the couch, crying myself to sleep or passing out.

Waking up 12 hours later, I was sick with alcohol poisoning. It was no ordinary hangover. While I had been able to turn off my brain for a few hours, I realized the futility of this approach. No amount of drinking or self-medication would ever make things better.

The thought of losing my wife and sons was even more devastating than this realization. I couldn't bear to look inside the small bedroom with the bunk beds, and sleeping in our bed alone was equally difficult, so I slept on the living room couch. I avoided coming home as much as possible because returning to an empty house was horrible.

No one in my family knew what Rachel and I were going through. As far as they were concerned, Rachel had gone to help her sister. The only questions they asked were, "How is her sister?" "How are the boys?" and "Is Rachel okay?" After a lifetime of pretending and putting on a good face, I had no problem maintaining the expected "stable, caring, and mature Jim" façade.

I felt like a hypocrite. How could I allow myself to fantasize about living as a woman and not caring about anyone's opinion? That wasn't me, and I could never do anything that would jeopardize those I loved. I didn't want to hurt anyone.

Rachel had been away for over two weeks, but it felt like an eternity. The thought of life without her and my sons was unbearable, and I knew I had hit rock bottom. We had discussed the possibility of me driving down to Texas to bring them home, but that depended on my answer to her haunting question. I decided to surprise her and drove down in a few days, pleading with God for help during the therapeutic drive.

As I pulled up to my father-in-law's corner house, I saw our two sons playing in the backyard and shouted with joy. Rachel rushed out of the house after seeing me through the kitchen window, and we embraced each other and the boys. Our reunion marked a new beginning for us; I was determined to make things work.

During our time apart, Rachel had time to think, and although she kept her thoughts private, she was prepared to make sacrifices and support me in my brokenness. I was grateful for a second chance but couldn't help but feel like I was on probation. My focus was on being the best dad I could be for our sons, even if I couldn't claim to be the best husband.

After visiting Rachel's grandparents near Paris, Texas, it was time to head home and try to put our lives back together with read-justed expectations. Rachel's willingness to settle for second best humbled me, but I was committed to ensuring our sons would have a normal and happy childhood. They were my motivation. They were a wonderful, beautiful distraction from my struggles, and I was determined to stay in my lane.

Our third son was born in May 1983, precisely nine months after I arrived unexpectedly in Texas, marking our reunion. Living in our 800-square-foot house in Vancouver, we realized it was get-ting cramped for our family. Despite having added a playroom and a second bathroom in the basement, we knew we would eventually need more bedrooms. Our eldest son was already in second grade, and our middle son was attending playschool.

As one of the few stay-at-home moms in our neighborhood, Rachel was invested in our sons' lives, especially as we enrolled our oldest son in a French bilingual school that was not in our immedi-ate catchment area. Rachel became the taxi service for him and his friends whose mothers worked.

Although we were involved in church, our attendance was becoming sporadic, not because of any personal issue but because it was exhausting. Every Sunday, we had to pack many essentials, such as diapers, bottles, and toys. One of us always had to help watch the children in the back room during the service, and it was not enjoyable. Staying home on Sundays became more comfortable for us.

Our restaurant had grown to 150 seats, including a popular deck, and I had trained myself out of a job in the kitchen. It made sense for me to return to graphic design, and I resumed working with previous clients. Enrique was more interested in running the restaurant, but we were approached by Capilano College to teach a course in the graphic design and illustration program. Since we were both busy, we team-taught the course by alternating every other week.

Enrique fell in love with a Canadian woman he met while on vacation in Mexico soon after his diagnosis. They were engaged at about the same time the doctors decided to operate on the tumor.

The surgeons performed a "sub-total" removal of his tumor. Although there was always the risk of physical or mental impairment with brain surgery, Enrique was not affected physically. The only noticeable change was that he became a little passive and was not as enthusiastic as before. He married his fiancée six months after surgery and radiation treatment, and the doctors were confident he would enjoy many more years of life.

The success of our Mexican restaurant drew the attention of one of our original graphic design clients, the Keg Restaurants. I had been doing a lot of design work for their vice president, who oversaw the Washington State region. During our discussions, we explored the possibility of expanding our restaurant, and the Keg was willing to finance a joint venture with our family. As a result, we decided to open a second location in downtown Vancouver, and I became the general manager and president of the new company.

The new restaurant opened in September 1984, and I stopped doing graphic design to focus solely on managing the business. Enrique taught at the college while managing the first restaurant with our father since I was too busy with the new location.

However, I soon realized that my busy schedule had taken a toll on my personal life. Rachel and I were looking at family pictures of our children, and I did not remember some events. Rachel pointed out that I was not there because I was busy managing the restaurant downtown. Although I tried to be at home as much as possible, I missed out on a lot. This realization made me reflect on my priorities and how I wanted to balance my work and family life.

My busy schedule also led to another personal struggle. I coped with it by allowing myself to possess some articles of clothing I could wear under my male clothing without detection. Although Rachel did not support or condone this, she reluctantly accepted it as the price to pay for being married to me. My hope for being free of this "bondage" had become non-existent.

The year ended on a terrible note when Enrique did not show up for class on the last day of the semester. The department dean called me to ask if Enrique was alright, as he had not come to class and failed to turn in the final grades to the office. She explained that the college had been calling his house all day, but there was no answer. I feared he had taken his life, but when we arrived at his house, he had just been sleeping and looked awful. He had been experiencing insomnia for almost a week, and we wondered if he needed his medications adjusted.

The news on Monday was not good: his tumor had grown, and he was given six months to live. The doctor explained that he would become more passive, sleep more often and for longer periods, and eventually slip into a coma due to the location of the tumor.

Enrique died at my parents' home in June 1985, where he had been receiving care from my mom and healthcare nurses. Given our busy schedules, we had all tried to spend as much time with him as possible. However, the restaurant business consumed most of my time, and I felt guilty for not being able to visit him more often. As I drove home in the early morning hours, I would stop in front of my parents' house, look at his bedroom window, and say a prayer. I didn't want him to die.

Enrique's passing was difficult for our family, and his death left a significant void. As time passed, I began to envy him and even resented God. I couldn't help but wonder why Enrique was taken instead of me. It seemed unfair to me that he was the one who had to suffer while I continued to live my life. These thoughts were difficult to admit, but they were a part of the grieving process that I had to work through.

A parent's grief over the loss of a child is beyond measure and comprehension. One particular memory stands out for me:

when my father took Enrique to a neurologist appointment, the receptionist assumed my father was the patient due to his age. My father then explained that the appointment was for his son, and he broke down. This moment revealed the depth of my father's pain, which was similar to mine. We both wished that he would have been the one to die first.

During the six months of Enrique's illness, we witnessed the most beautiful manifestation of our parents' love. They devoted themselves entirely to Enrique, and by extension, to all of us. We could rely on them to be there for us in the same loving manner. Although sudden deaths are unexpected and difficult, Enrique's prolonged illness allowed us to gradually accept his loss. We all wanted his suffering to end. His faith strengthened mine when he told me that he thought about death all the time, but he wasn't afraid because he knew where he was going.

We all mourned in our own way. My mother's sorrow was the most apparent, followed by my father's. As I watched them, I wondered how they would cope if something happened to me. Could they endure such pain?

As the executor of Enrique's estate, I was responsible for informing his ex-wife about the life insurance checks. According to the separation and divorce agreement, that was all she was entitled to receive. When she showed up at my office with her new boyfriend, I found her behavior disrespectful and her giddiness distasteful. I couldn't help but wonder if she had only been with my brother for his money.

Being Enrique's executor was one of the many challenges I faced in 1985. However, I found comfort Jesus' words, that God's grace was sufficient during difficult times; I would have been overwhelmed without it.

Rachel faced her own sorrow that year when her sister died from cancer a few days before Christmas. In addition to our personal struggles, our business was also under pressure. Our second restaurant partners had overextended themselves, and we were left with their liabilities when they sold us their share for $1. Carmen and her husband took over the new restaurant while I returned to full-time graphics.

After Enrique passed away, I resumed teaching the college course by myself in September. I continued for two years before resigning and selling or giving away most of the office furnishings. I bought a Macintosh computer with the introduction of the Laser-Writer by Apple and PageMaker by Aldus and worked from the basement of my family's restaurant.

I remembered how in 1976, Enrique proudly showed me a computer terminal with a tiny green screen in our Gastown office. The case had plywood sides, and the keyboard was in an extruded aluminum enclosure. There was a rubber coupling device next to it where one could place the telephone receiver down after hearing a high-pitched squeal. A resourceful high school teacher developed an accounting program with General Ledger, Accounts Receivable, and Accounts Payable modules. The teacher rented computer time from the University of Alberta's mainframe and leased out terminals to small businesses on a subscription basis to computerize their accounting.

When we got the machine, Enrique was thrilled. We had half an hour of computer time allotted to us each week. Two days later, we received a four-inch-thick stack of large computer paper bound in pale blue cardstock covers held together with plastic spindles. According to Enrique, everything we ever wanted to know about our company was at our fingertips. The only issue was having to sift through the stack of pages to locate the information we needed!

I was a purist and artist, while Enrique handled accounting and administration. Enrique envisioned the day when we would no longer use drafting tables but sit in front of a computer screen to complete our work. By 1985, his prediction about the computer as a graphic design tool was beginning to materialize. Between the two of us, he was always the visionary..

After Enrique's death, I struggled for two years. I felt unhinged and vulnerable, burdened by the responsibilities of being a husband, father, and sole breadwinner. Approaching my 40th birthday in 1990, I recognized the need for professional assistance. I kept my struggles private, fearing a breakdown and the subsequent loss of privacy. I was worried about how this would affect my sons and Rachel, who had endured years of disappointment and resignation.

I wished I could have prevented her from experiencing such pain.

When our oldest son started playing T-ball several years ago, Rachel and I met the two parents who took turns going to the games to see their son play because they were divorced. We learned that the father, a medical doctor, had come out as gay, leading to their marriage's end. One day I decided to call his office.

I desperately needed and wanted to see a psychiatrist. but I needed a referral. I had been too embarrassed to approach our family doctor. Thinking that a gay doctor would likely be sympathetic, I scheduled an appointment to request a referral. Fortunately, he was happy to help and very understanding.

I had three sessions with the psychiatrist; he helped me verbalize my conflicting thoughts, which was a relief after holding them in for so long. These sessions also allowed me to explain things to Rachel. After each session, she would inquire about the discussions and how they went, and I was able to relay everything objectively and candidly. In the final session, the doctor suggested referring me to the Gender Clinic at Vancouver General Hospital, but I declined, grateful for his help in gaining better insight. For the time being, he had defused the time bomb.

With this new knowledge, I felt more equipped to enhance my prayer life and fight with even greater intensity. Although I couldn't imagine considering what the psychiatrist had proposed, with Rachel's support, I was more determined to stay the course. I still saw it as a spiritual battle, and understanding Satan's tactics were crucial in winning the fight.

8.2: Cocoon Time

In 1991, I was invited to be the in-house designer for a group of restaurants that had merged. Many of the people in management had worked at the Keg 'n' Cleaver restaurants in the seventies when my brother Enrique and I were working on that account. To avoid a conflict of interest, I had to curtail my freelance activities for other restaurants, but I was allowed to keep my other clients, which made up a small part of my business.

This arrangement was mutually beneficial for both parties.

The new restaurant group enjoyed having their designer available at all times, and I had a consistent, guaranteed income with benefits, something I hadn't had since I stopped working at our family's restaurant.

Not having to generate so many invoices and manage accounts receivable simplified my life considerably. During the few years that Enrique and I worked together, he had always done the accounting, and I missed him terribly when we parted ways in California. However, we grew closer as adults when I moved to Canada and bonded over our shared faith.I don't know how my brother would have reacted to the news that I was trans. I kept my struggles hidden from him and everyone else, and no one suspected anything. Not family, not friends, not clients. Nobody.

The new restaurant company went public soon after I joined, allowing it to expand rapidly. What started as a group of three restaurant concepts with a total of seven locations soon became seven concepts with over thirty locations. I joined the marketing team, which was made up entirely of attractive women.

Although I loved my work, being around these women was torture. I wasn't attracted to them or "lusted" for them, but working with them every day was a constant reminder of what I physically wasn't.

This new job coincided with our move to a new church with a larger youth group that included children around the same age as our two youngest sons. The church we had been attending had lots of young families with very young children and mostly retired couples. However, couples our age were missing due to their move to the suburbs, where family housing was more affordable.

While our oldest son was no longer interested in attending church with us, our two younger sons still participated. We were concerned that they were often the only ones their age in Sunday school or at church events.

I had become involved in worship and was appreciating many of the new contemporary worship songs from groups like the Vineyard Fellowship churches. These lyrics resonated with me and expressed my yearnings and love for God in a new, fresh, and powerful way. They allowed me to focus on God with an intimacy I had never experienced before.

Before, I had no prayer life to speak of; I could never stay focused long enough to have a meaningful conversation with God. It was like the comic strip Family Circus, where a child's dotted line wandered all over the place. When I tried to pray, I would start on one topic but quickly find my mind wandering to other things, and before long, I wasn't praying anymore. Even in a special place set aside for prayer, I was never able to pray fervently. But worship music helped me focus on God and express my love, pain, and gratitude without losing my train of thought.

The new church we joined also focused on this type of worship, which was another reason we felt at home there. We were introduced to the church by our friends George and Ann, whom we had met at Dayspring Fellowship in the late seventies. Their family was very musical, and both parents were part of the worship team. Since we shared this interest, I naturally joined the worship team with them.

As new members, they also invited us to attend their Bible study group, which met every other week at a couple's house and included about a dozen people of all ages, mostly married but some single. Coincidentally, one of the couples in the group was the retired pastor and his wife from First Baptist Church, whom we had met when we first got married and who was still somewhat involved at the Hobbit House. Their son was the pastor of this new church, making it a small world indeed.

Our life for the next few years was busy and fulfilling. I had a full-time job that I loved, Rachel worked part-time for the Vancouver School Board, and we created healthy memories with our boys. However, my battle with my gender identity had reached a stalemate. Despite my sessions with a psychiatrist, I couldn't admit to myself that I might be trans. It wasn't until years later that I finally accepted this as the only explanation that made sense.

After five years with the restaurant company, I started to see firsthand how a change in management can influence corporate culture. Seeing a long-term future there became harder, so I decided to leave on good terms and continue working with the company from home. While I enjoyed the arrangement, I missed the positive reinforcement of working in-house; and only dealing with people face-to-face a few times a week left me vulnerable to my thoughts and needs.

A few years earlier, the family decided to sell the restaurant so my parents could retire. They offered any of us the option to pay for the business over time, but we felt it would be best to find an outside buyer so they could get all their money out at once. The restaurant had been good to us, and we were proud of what we had accomplished as a family.

By 1998, I had reached another low and feared a break-down. With the help of the Internet, I carried out private research and became convinced that I might be trans. I contacted the Gender clinic at Vancouver General Hospital and learned I needed a referral from my doctor. I didn't think it would be possible for me to ask our family doctor. I was too embarrassed. Instead, I called the clinic and asked for the name of a doctor who was sympathetic to trans people and had previously referred other patients. The receptionist gave me the name of a doctor.

I called immediately and asked if he was accepting new patients; fortunately, he was. It was time for me to have a physical anyway, which gave me a valid excuse to make the appointment. He did the physical and agreed to make the referral to the clinic.

Chapter 9: The Gender Clinic

Since I was twenty years old, I have struggled with a persistent feeling that something was wrong with me. I saw this as a spiritual problem and hoped that becoming a Christian would fix me. However, my fundamentalist and legalistic approach to my faith only made me feel more defeated and worthless. Despite this, my faith has brought blessings into my life, including meeting my wife and finding a sense of kinship with diverse people.

I have always felt a strong intimacy with God, and the words of Jesus have been a guiding force in my life. The Sermon on the Mount, in particular, taught me to value love, humility, and compassion above all else. The Beatitudes, in which Jesus blesses the poor in spirit and those who mourn, gave me hope for a miracle. My faith kept me sober and free from self-destructive behaviors, addictions, and suicidal thoughts, but I still felt unfulfilled and unsure of what to do next.

When I first approached the gender clinic, I felt skeptical and suspicious. As someone who had always seen my issue as spiritual, going to a secular institution felt like a betrayal. However, I came to realize that medicine and the advancement of knowledge could also be gifts from God. In one of my counseling sessions, I expressed thoughts of ending my life, but my counselor helped me see that my family and friends would rather have me live as a woman than not at all. This conversation was a turning point for me, and I began to see the clinic as an opportunity to seek help and support.

After a six-month assessment, the psychiatrist confirmed that I had gender dysphoria, a condition in which a person experiences extreme sadness about their gender. The clinic explained that they could help me make the necessary changes to live successfully as a woman. The choice was mine, but I knew I was not ready and willing to begin the process.

The Harry Benjamin "Standards of Practice for the treatment of transsexuals" protocol ensured that my transition would be carefully monitored and supervised. Though it was a difficult and emotional journey, I found comfort in the support of my family, friends, and the medical professionals at the clinic. As I began to live my life as a woman, I felt a sense of freedom and authenticity that I had never experienced before.

In conclusion, my journey through gender dysphoria was a challenging one that tested my faith and my understanding of myself. I found love, hope, and the strength to seek help through my faith. Though the process was difficult, it was ultimately a way for me to honor my life and the relationships that matter to me. I am grateful for the wisdom of my counselor and the medical professionals who helped me on this journey, and I hope that my story can inspire others who may be struggling with similar issues.

This diagnosis was both a blessing and a curse because, at last, I knew what I was; it explained all the confusion I had lived with all my life. But it was also a curse, as it was a life sentence, and the options open to me were impossible to consider.

I could not begin to entertain what transitioning would do to my marriage and family. I was so fearful of rejection and ridicule—and of being different! I had lived with this fear all my life, but now I was even more frightened. I wondered what would happen when I told my clients. Would they stop using me as their designer? What would my friends think and do? How was my church going to respond? Would I be ostracized, or would I be embraced?

Leaving my last appointment, I was mostly disappointed. I had hoped the doctors would be able to suggest a therapy or medication that would alleviate my burden, yet I knew it was pointless to think so. There was no magic bullet.

Rachel attended one of the sessions with me. It was difficult for her to accept what she was hearing and what I reported to her every time I came home after one of my sessions. She often repeated that the clinic had a cookie-cutter approach and not everything they said was the 'truth.' She pleaded with me to keep trusting in God, that I would get through this with her help, love, and support, and all would be okay. She added that I could dress as I wanted in the privacy of our bedroom—that she understood I had this need—but to never wear anything in front of the boys.

The fear of rejection and scorn from my church was not unfounded. It all started when the couple who invited us to join the church shared a prayer request during one of our home group Bible studies. Ann expressed her disapproval of her older brother's decision to live as a woman, describing him as selfish and self-centered. She was concerned that his actions would jeopardize his marriage and the welfare of his children. To my disappointment, most people in the group shared Ann's view, except for the retired pastor's wife, who showed compassion by wondering what his life had been like.

The home group's reaction did not bode well for me. I could expect them to react the same way if I ever came out. Therefore, I would never come out. That was the only safe conclusion.

As we were grabbing our coats and getting ready to leave the Bible study, Ann turned to me and, with a tongue-in-cheek tone, asked me, "You don't have any trans people in your family, do you?" Ha-ha, how funny, I thought. If she only knew.

During my assessment at the gender clinic, I was given a handout listing various support groups for trans individuals and their significant others. Rachel had no interest in attending, and I was hesitant to join any of them publicly due to the fear of someone recognizing me.

However, one support group in particular caught my attention — a social group for cross-dressers and trans individuals that met once a month. While attendees were free to present as either male or female, the group was not intended for those who were "living full-time." The brochure listed a phone number for inquiries, and calls could be made on Thursday nights to speak with someone directly. Alternatively, one could leave a message, and someone would return the call.

Given my many questions and fears, I decided to call and speak with one of the members to learn more about the group. A friendly woman answered the first time I called, and she explained the group's purpose. She informed me that attendance was reserved for those vetted and approved by the membership committee for confidentiality and security reasons. She suggested I call back the following week to speak with her husband, who was on the committee.

When I did call back, I was surprised to find that he, too, was a Christian, and we bonded over our shared struggles with faith. Despite the connection we made, I never attended any of the group's meetings. I was too afraid to go public, even with individuals who had just as much to lose as I did if there was a breach of confidence.

Interestingly, it was later revealed to me that Ann's brother had been a regular attendee of the same support group before beginning to transition.

Ann and her family became a case study for me. I watched and listened to them closely, paying close attention anytime the trans sibling was mentioned in conversation. I finally got to meet her brother-sister at the wedding of one of their daughters. He presented as male for that occasion, and everyone addressed him by his male name. He looked somewhat androgynous but not over the top. I observed a level of tolerance toward this individual but not genuine acceptance. He was there with his ex-wife, but they were distant with one another.

Then, as each of their daughters married a few years apart, I saw a gradual transformation in this person. I also witnessed how the family treated her and heard what they said about her, which was usually not very complimentary. During one of the weddings, I overheard a group of young people making a joke about finding Aunt Monica, similar to the popular 'Where's Waldo' game. I found the joke to be insensitive and cruel.

I feared I could expect this for myself if I ever came out as trans. Would I be willing to pay that kind of price? "Never!" I said to myself.

9.1: A Disaster and a Wedding

In June of 2006, while finalizing details for our oldest son's wedding in September, an email from our middle son threatened to derail the occasion. He was between apartments and was staying with us for a couple of weeks. He used my computer to write the email that said he was angry with me, accused me of hypocrisy, and questioned my faith as a Christian. He revealed that he had learned disturbing things about me and demanded that I refrain from contacting him.

His anger toward me was devastating, but I also worried about how this would affect his role as the Master of Ceremonies at his brother's wedding. This created a family crisis.

Upon Rachel's return from work, I showed her the email, and she was upset with me for being careless. Despite my repeated attempts to call our son, he didn't answer when he saw it was me in his call display. Rachel used her cell phone to call him, and he answered. She insisted on seeing him immediately and left as soon as she hung up the phone.

For the next three hours, I felt sick to my stomach as I waited for Rachel's return. My suspicion was that he saw my browser history of the web pages I visited when searching for information on trans issues. I am not surprised that he found some of the links disturbing. Unfortunately, when searching the internet for information on trans people, many of the results are pages with highly sexualized or pornographic content. While waiting for Rachel to return home, I examined some of the pages and realized why my son was so upset. Rachel was right; I should have been more careful.

However, the damage had been done. I played out all kinds of possible scenarios in my head. Was it time to disclose my secret to my sons and my family? Would my son boycott the wedding or refuse to attend if I was there? How would we explain this to the rest of the family and the new in-laws? I wished I could roll back the clock to prevent this misunderstanding.

When Rachel returned home, she refused to provide details of their conversation, but she explained to him that I had a coping issue and was always under stress. She spoke highly of me and reminded him of what a good dad I had been to him. She asked him to consider these factors before making any decisions but avoided telling him about my medical condition. She told me he needed time to process things and to wait for him to come to me.

I saw my son for the first time since he cut me off on the wedding rehearsal night. He was polite but not talkative with me. All I could say was that we needed to talk and asked him to come to me when he was ready. However, I was grateful for how he rose to the occasion on the wedding day, putting on a good face and being kind and loving despite his inner turmoil.

As I have previously shared, October was a busy month for our family, with many special days to celebrate. However, our middle son boycotted all those family events and fabricated excuses when others asked him about his absence. The same thing happened in November for my birthday; he arrived late for dinner at Christmas and stayed only a short time. Everyone asked us if something was wrong with him and if he was okay. Were my worst fears being realized? Was this just a taste of things to come, with people judging and ostracizing me as my son had? Things did not look good.

By this time, I had come to accept my diagnosis. You've probably heard this story or a version of it:

A man falls overboard in the middle of the ocean and prays to God for a miracle. First, a fishing boat comes up to the man, and the fishermen try to help him on board. But he refuses to be picked up by them, saying he is expecting a miracle from God. Next, a Coast Guard rescue boat comes to his aid but again refuses help because he expects a miracle. Finally, a helicopter arrives on the scene, but he waves it away. A few hours later, exhausted, he drowns.

When he gets to heaven, he demands to speak to God about his untimely death. The man is ushered into God's presence and asks why God let him drown.

God looks at the man and says, "What do you mean I let you drown? I sent you a fishing boat, the Coast Guard, and a helicopter, but you refused my help! That's why you drowned."

This little parable described me. It dawned on me one day that perhaps God was answering my prayer, but I had been so focused on how I thought it would look that I failed to see He was answering it in a completely different way than I had expected.

The fact I lived at a time and in a place where my condition was understood—was that not an answer to prayer? There were now people trained and available to help me navigate these uncharted waters—was that not an answer to prayer? Wasn't I like the man in the story who failed to see how God had made it possible for him to be rescued?

Now my biggest anxiety was how I was ever going to be able to pass as a female, given I now had a receding hairline and a beard that produced a five o'clock shadow by 3:00 p.m. every day. Though I was an avid jogger and ran three times a week, I was still packing a fair amount of excess weight. How was I ever going to pull it off?

The other obstacle to overcome had nothing to do with my ability to pass in public. It had to do with how my parents would take the news. Dad was already close to ninety, and Mom was a few years younger. Should I hold off on everything and wait until both passed away? Rachel often stressed this was why I should put the idea of transitioning completely out of my mind, an impossible demand.

After much consideration, I began doing things that would not draw much attention to myself. I started doing longer runs whenever I jogged, doing stomach crunches daily, and I started electrolysis to reduce my facial hair gradually. Within six months, I had lost fifteen pounds and gone from a thirty-four to a thirty-one-inch waist. By July 2007, I had lost 25 pounds, and my waist was now under thirty inches.

People noticed there was something different—especially my mother—who asked every time she saw me if I was okay. In her opinion, I was too skinny. None of my clothes fit anymore, and I looked like I was wearing borrowed clothing. I had also endured close to one hundred and fifty hours of electrolysis—and to my disappointment, it looked like I still had as many more hours to go.

I had not yet contacted the Gender Clinic because I wanted to be prepared. You see, when I was diagnosed years earlier, I was told I would have to start living as a woman immediately—even before beginning hormone therapy. Those were the protocols of the day. I remember telling the doctor there was no way I could do that. I told him, "Look at me; I can't pass as a woman; I would be a joke!

If I go out in public, I will be spotted instantly." It was a deal breaker. So, this time I wanted a better chance of pulling it off.

I called Vancouver General Hospital, but I was unable to find the phone number for the Gender Clinic. That's when I learned the Clinic had been closed, and there was now a new arrangement called the Trans-Health Program. The Clinic had fallen victim to politically orchestrated budget cuts.

I called the new office and explained I had been a patient eight years earlier, had been diagnosed, and had decided not to proceed with any changes—but I was ready to do so now. The receptionist entered my name into the computer and informed me that my records had been archived since I had not been at the Clinic for more than three years.

I was instructed to call the General Hospital's records office to request my records be released to the Clinic. The process would take up to three months since it was not an emergency.

I was relieved in some ways about this delay. I was scared to hell and had no idea what they would say to me this time around. I could not bring myself to tell Rachel I had contacted the Clinic. She knew I was up to something, having lost all the weight and facial hair, but she thought I was only doing this to help me cope better.

I did not want or like to do things behind her back, but she didn't like to discuss anything concerning my diagnosis. In this regard, communication was nonexistent.

9.2: What Will People Think?

Hypervigilant and extremely paranoid, that is what I had become. Would I be recognized entering and leaving the Clinic, doctors' offices, and medical labs that I had to visit regularly? Our church had many members who worked in health care, and since I didn't know where any of them worked, I was always on the lookout as I entered and left medical buildings. What would people think? I worried that my discovery would cause controversy within our church if people found out about me. I knew one particular person who was very critical of anything that hinted of acceptance of gays.

One Sunday, during a pastoral prayer, there was a request on behalf of victims of violence due to their race, color, creed, gender, or sexual orientation. That week he railed into the pastor, members of the deacons' board, and anyone who crossed his path. "Since when did we start to look favorably at gays?" he asked. My, oh my, was this individual incensed or what? I was one of the unlucky ones he dumped on. All I could think of at the time was, "Well, brother, you ain't heard nothing yet!"

A few years earlier, some members had left our church because the new assistant minister, who was female, presented too "butch," and they thought this was wrong. They protested with their feet when they lost the vote at the confirmation meeting. Granted, they were only two or three individuals, but they certainly did not like the fact that so many stood up for this young woman and voted for her.

Aware of the potential damage that could result if my disclosure was not handled correctly, I decided it was time to step down from my involvement in the worship team. Toward the end of September 2007, the worship leaders met to discuss and plan the music for the Advent and Christmas seasons. The pastor chaired the meeting, and like all other meetings we'd ever had, this one was sprinkled with laughter and warm camaraderie. We all got along and worked together well; no one had an ego (and I've seen some egos regarding worship leaders.) So, it took the pastor by surprise when I met with him a few weeks later to resign from all my responsibilities on the worship team.

We met one morning, and over coffee, I told him everything. I explained that I was worried about being recognized as entering or leaving a specialist's office by someone from church and about people jumping to conclusions without having all the facts. I did not want to cause a rift in the congregation; neither did I want to become the elephant in the room. I did not want to become the poster child for trans issues or a cause célèbre. I reminded him of how some people had been upset during the hiring of the assistant minister and opined that my issue had a much more significant potential for making things uncomfortable for him and the Deacons' Board.

Admittedly, this is what I said to him, but it wasn't easy for me to get the words out; my heart was in my throat, and I had to stop and compose myself throughout my disclosure. Have you ever been so nervous you can't stop talking? I think that was me that morning. I was terrified that the pastor would judge and exact his Godly wrath on me.

He sat and listened to me as I poured out my heart, offering me tissues and waiting for me to finish. I will never forget the compassion in his first words, telling me that my situation was not a moral issue any more than a physical disability or medical condition.

He thanked me for sharing with him and reassured me that my honesty and integrity made me even more qualified as a worship leader. He correctly guessed that I had been struggling with my self-worth and assured me he did not judge me. He expressed concern for Rachel and her well-being, sympathizing with what she must be going through.

He asked me about my plans to change my appearance and present as a female, and I explained the changes that were already taking place. I told him that I was not planning to present as female for at least a year or two, as long as my parents were alive. He then made a promise that I will never forget: If I ever decided to come to church presenting as female, he would stand with me and affirm me as a member of the congregation.

As we said goodbye, he asked me if I would like him to let the rest of the worship team know about my resignation or if I wanted to do that myself. He promised this information would be confidential between us; he would not say anything to anyone about my reasons for stepping down. I was grateful and accepted his offer.

9.3: My Faith Reconciled, Finally

It must be said I was finally able to reconcile my faith to my condition, thanks to Tim Colborne, who set the tone for his teaching style and theology in his first sermon as our new pastor. He warned us that we would be disappointed if we were looking to him for black-and-white dogmatic answers. He explained, having been a diligent student of the Bible for nearly twenty-five years, that he had concluded that no one had the right to pull one or two verses out of context to formulate a doctrine. By context, he didn't mean the text around the verse only but also its geographic, social, and cultural context.

He told us we needed to approach the Bible with humility, recognizing the Bible itself is ambiguous, if not silent, on most aspects of the human condition. To compound the challenge, he asked how many times Jesus answered His questioners with ambiguity. How many times did He leave His listeners with more questions than they had before? Therefore, the pastor told us, we needed to be open to different points of view as we try to make sense of scripture and how it might apply to life.

His sermon that day made me realize I had been doing exactly what he warned against: I was taking one verse out of context. That verse appears twice in the Bible. Once in Genesis chapter 1, and once in the Gospel of Matthew. In that story, Matthew recounts how the Pharisees came to test Jesus on the issue of divorce. He answers them by quoting from Genesis, how in the beginning "God created them male and female" and proceeds to school them on marriage.

That scene ends with Jesus making a puzzling and what seems like an irrelevant comment to his disciples about eunuchs, which he bookends with two very interesting statements: "Not everyone will be able to accept this, only those to whom the knowledge has been given," and "Let anyone accept this who can."

For years I used the first part of this passage, with its reference to Genesis, to beat myself up. I often criticized myself with this rationale: "It says we are either male or female; there is no other option. Why do you allow yourself to go there in your thinking? Get it out of your mind; you are male! You have fathered three children—what more proof do you need?"

What Jesus said about eunuchs: "some are born eunuchs from their mother's womb, some are made eunuchs by men, and others choose to become eunuchs for the Kingdom of God" flew over my head I never paid attention to it.

Then, gradually, after the pastor's sermon, I saw something in Jesus' comments I had never seen before. First, Jesus re-stated God created us male and female—but, Jesus concedes, it doesn't always work out that way. Some are eunuchs because they are born that way.

Jesus acknowledged that not everyone fit into the binary gender and sex categories of male and female. Some were born as eunuchs or were intersex, and therefore, we should not view gender and sex strictly as one or the other but as being on a continuum with many possible variations.

Jesus did not condemn the eunuch or place any conditions on marriage and divorce. He also did not specify which gender and sex pairings were correct for gender-variant individuals. For example, should eunuchs only be paired with other eunuchs? The Midrash, the collection of Jewish interpretive writings and teachings on the Torah, offers five variations for a eunuch. For example, Rabbis had a word for a female eunuch and a different word for a male eunuch. In the first case, it designated a female person with some male sexual characteristics, and in the other, a male person with some female sexual characteristics. We can conclude that Jesus declared that gender and sex were not always binary—either male or female.

Jesus' comment that not everyone could accept this challenged his listeners to expand their understanding of sexuality. This statement was not meant to be exclusive but rather to challenge his listeners' small thinking and change their paradigm on sexuality. This statement also served to temper my expectation that I would enjoy universal acceptance because not everyone would choose to view things from this much more inclusive perspective.

It was ironic that the passage I had used for years to beat myself into submission was the very one that freed me and gave me permission to be who I am. Unfortunately, the same phrase is often used to oppose LGBTQ+-inclusive doctrines, policies, or laws.

It is also ironic how conservative and right-wing churches and organizations judge and condemn LGBTQ+ persons while insisting they love the person but hate their sin. If the same level of anger condemnation was applied to the issue Jesus addressed in the Matthew chapter nineteen discussion—divorce and infidelity— it would be detrimental to their existence. If they preached against and judged divorced persons in the same way they preach against, reject, and judge LGBTQ+ persons, their churches would be empty, and so would their bank accounts.

Chapter 10: The Genie Is Out of the Bottle

I am not the linguist my older sister Carmen turned out to be, but I am fascinated by the meaning of words. The word "disclose" does not translate into Spanish as directly as the word "disconnect," which in Spanish is desconectar. The closest English synonym to "disclose" with a direct translation might be "divulge," which translates as divulgar. In my simple way of thinking, the combination of the prefix "dis," which means to undo, with the word "close," means to un-close, or better still, to open up or to "unhide."

To unhide is a frightening thing to do after fifty-four years if you discount the first three years of my life when my self-awareness was in its early stages of development. I had never been as terrified as I was in October of 2007. I had to start unhiding, open the door, and let all the secrets out. It felt like I was making my first parachute jump from ten thousand feet: once I stepped off the airplane, there was no turning back; I would be committed to going all the way.

After speaking with my pastor, I went home to work feeling emotionally drained and sick to my stomach. Sharing my personal struggles with just one person was difficult enough, and I couldn't imagine repeating it to ten, twenty, or even thirty people. Therefore, I decided to write everything down so that I could read it to them instead of explaining it every time from memory.

Luckily, I had many projects to work on, which helped me take my mind off of the looming prospect of sharing my personal struggles. I finally had some free time on Friday afternoon to start writing my letter. I had been working on a draft for about two hours when my friend Duncan called to check on the status of a project we were working on. While discussing the project, I nervously mentioned that I was writing "a sort of biographical thing."

However, that was not the best thing to say to a professional writer because he immediately wanted to read it when I finished. I hesitated but eventually agreed on the condition that he read it with his wife and poured himself a stiff drink first. The following Monday, he called again to check on the project and asked how my bio was coming. I told him it was finished, attached the file to an email, and clicked "SEND." About ten minutes later, he called me back to express his and his wife's unconditional love and support. He was hurt that I didn't trust him enough to share my struggles with him sooner.

We had known each other since 1977 and had shared many heart-to-heart conversations about life, death, my brother, and our children. However, I had never revealed anything about my personal struggles until now. He reminded me of how hard he had tried to get me to open up in the past. As we hung up the phone, he promised to be there for me and suggested I tell our mutual clients and several others in our business network as soon as possible.

He offered to review my draft, make minor edits and promised to make me laugh even when things got tough. This conversation triggered a meltdown, and I hung up the phone feeling overwhelmed. The first version of my letter was full of information about the changes that would take place in my life in the future, but the timetable was purposely vague. I asked for confidentiality until I could share my struggles with my aged parents and sons. (Appendix II contains the last version of the letter.)

Duncan was right; I needed to start telling my clients. I picked Linda, who was the marketing manager for a computer company that supplied POS terminals to the hospitality industry. I felt safe with her and thought she would be a good gauge of how my clients might receive the news. Whether you call it luck, divine inspiration, or intuition, she turned out to be the best choice I could have made.

I really should have gone to see her in person. Instead, I called her and asked if she could talk for about fifteen minutes. Fortunately, I called her at a good time. When I told her it was a personal call, she excused herself so she could close the door to her office.

She asked, "What's up? Is everything okay?" I told her I would like to read a letter to her if she didn't mind. She gave me the green light, and I began reading it.

As soon as I reached the part where I talked about being diagnosed with gender dysphoria, she interrupted, "Stop!"

My heart stopped, and I thought, "Oh, no! My life is over."

However, in a very calm and reassuring voice, she said, "I know more about this condition than you may think. My brother is trans. And let me tell you something—you don't have anything to worry about with me nor, I suspect, with any of your clients and friends. You are held in high regard, and people love you! They're not going to throw you away like garbage. You need to give people the benefit of the doubt; they will not judge or reject you. And let me tell you—I think you will have a much easier transition experience than my brother."

She explained that her brother was tall and had extra challenges I would not have to face. She asked me to please finish reading the letter, and when I finished, she asked about Rachel and our sons. Then we talked for a while. As we were saying goodbye, she thanked me for sharing; she knew it must have been very difficult to make the call. She added I could call her anytime I needed to talk.

It had been just over a week since I shared with my pastor. The phone rang one night, and it was our friend Ann from church, whose brother is also trans. She had heard about my resignation from the worship team, but she and her husband were leading the worship that coming Sunday, and she wondered if I was serious about not playing the guitar. She hoped I would still be available to play with them, as I always had when it was their turn to lead the worship. I told her I couldn't and that my resignation was from leading and being part of the worship team.

She was very concerned for my health, assuming it must be the reason for my resignation. She had also seen changes, such as my weight loss, and wondered if everything was all right. I assured her my health was fine and suggested that since Rachel and I were hosting the Bible study the following Tuesday night, if she and George could stay afterward, Rachel and I had something we needed to share with them.

I discussed this with Rachel, and she requested to see my letter. She wanted the right to edit or delete anything she was uncomfortable with. In the end, the changes were minor; we removed a couple of sentences and reworded a few.

After the rest of the group left Tuesday night, the four of us sat around the dining room table facing each other. I unfolded the letter and began to read. When I finished, I could not take my eyes off the paper—I was afraid to look up. Rachel was crying silently, and I heard their chairs move as they stood up to embrace us.

Ann said, "You are going to help me understand my brother so much better."

Then George added, "We love you guys! You have been some of our closest friends, and we've been through a lot together. We are with you."

Although I felt emotionally exhausted, I had only disclosed my gender dysphoria to about eight people. The process of coming out was much more difficult than I had imagined, and I had not even told my family because I feared potential negative consequences.

My tendency to catastrophize situations due to my creative and vivid imagination was exemplified by a quote attributed to Mark Twain: "I've suffered a great many catastrophes in my life. Most of them never happened." After being diagnosed with gender dysphoria, I imagined the worst-case scenario for how my family members, close friends, and clients would react. However, the opposite had been true so far, with no one responding in the negative ways I had always feared, and expected.

Although I wished I could have disclosed my gender dysphoria to everyone at once, I had to take a one-by-one approach due to the emotional toll each disclosure took on me. I needed to tell my sisters, Carmen and Angela, and their husbands, as well as my brother John and his wife, soon to avoid hurting them.

My pastor and I kept in close communication, and he suggested we meet with his friend, a registered psychologist and marriage counselor who had experience with marriage and family issues, to enhance our communication and work through our situation. We met with him seven times.

One of my client restaurants opened a new location and I was allowed to invite another couple for the grand opening dinner. I invited Carmen and her husband, and that night after dinner, Rachel and I shared the news with them as the four of us sat in their van before going home. They responded positively and I was relieved with their response. We discussed whether our parents needed to know but agreed it was not a good idea. Then we shared the news with Angela and her husband at our house after an appointment with the psychologist. Their concern was when to tell their daughters about me. My brother John would face a similar issue with his children. I suggested writing a personal letter to nieces and nephews for the parents to read when they felt it was appropriate. All the significant changes were way off in the future—there was no sense of urgency to share with my nieces and nephew. Sharing with my sons would need to take priority, anyway.

The big question was how and when I would begin the transition. I still did not have the confidence to present as a female when I started to disclose to people. My friend Duncan convinced me one day to visit them as Lisa. He argued that I needed to start presenting, and what better place than in the safety of close friends? He wouldn't take no for an answer, insisting this was something I had to do.

There was a lot of truth to what he was saying, and I concluded he was right about my feeling safe with them. I finally did this one Friday afternoon in early November 2007. I wore a long-sleeved top with a crew neck, a black skirt, clip-on earrings, and a wig I had recently purchased for $45. To complete the outfit, I found some low-heeled mules my size at a shoe discount store.

I will give Duncan and his wife the benefit of the doubt, but they were just being polite as they received me that afternoon. As we chatted and had tea, Duncan took some pictures, but I must admit the adrenaline was pumping, so the experience was more nerve-racking than enjoyable. It bordered more on embarrassing.

My second visit to Duncan would prove even more stressful. It was the morning of Christmas Eve. Again, Duncan had convinced me to visit them as Lisa for Christmas, and we had a lovely visit. Everything was going well until he said he needed to go to Costco to purchase something. Since I was the card-bearer, the implication was I was to go with him.

Costco is about halfway between our homes, so the plan was

to drive our own cars and meet in the parking lot. I thought he was crazy for suggesting such an idea, especially on the year's busiest shopping day. They both assured me no one would know. "You look fine, dear, better than most women there. Just relax, keep your chin up, and walk slowly. You'll do fine." Those were his wife's comments as we went out the door.

I remember very little about that trip to Costco—I had tunnel vision from anxiety. I just wanted to find what he was looking for and make a beeline to the checkout. We were in and out in less than ten minutes—mission accomplished! Back in the parking lot, we wished each other Merry Christmas, hugged, and said goodbye. I don't remember driving home; I felt I was going to puke when I entered the door. It was going to be a long time, a very long time before I transitioned, I said to myself. Going out in public was so stressful. Yet it felt right on a different and more profound level: despite the fear, the guilt was gone.

Rachel would have been very upset if she had known in advance about my excursion that day. Even though the disclosure process was well underway, she would have preferred it if I had postponed any public appearance for as long as possible.

There was no denying that the unburdening was making me feel more optimistic. However, I had mixed emotions because, on the one hand, I wanted to live the rest of my life with integrity and honesty, but on the other hand, I was very aware of how the choices I was making were going to impact the person I loved the most, my wife. At times, I felt as if I had defrauded her. My only defense was that I honestly and sincerely believed I would be "healed" and made normal. I had made my promises in earnest.

Some of the friends to whom I had come out asked plenty of questions and made comments such as, "Don't you wish you'd been able to come out sooner, when you were younger, so you could have avoided all these years of struggle?" My answer was always "No!" If I had understood my condition and had transitioned at an earlier age, I may have avoided the struggle, but I would not have experienced the love from my wife, and the three sons that resulted from our union would not be alive today.

The process of coming out was stressful, but it had to be

done. Every time I told someone, I had to go through the experience of baring my soul, of showing my vulnerability, and of exposing myself to possible rejection. But every time, I felt a sense of relief, of unburdening.

One thing that I learned through this process was that it was essential to have a support system. I was lucky to have friends and family who supported me.

The journey of transition is not an easy one, and it is not something that can be done alone. It takes courage, resilience, and the support of those around us to make it through. But in the end, it is worth it to live a life that is true to who we are.

Except, the sad truth is that my best friend has had to pay an enormous price for my changes. As our psychologist aptly put it, she felt as if the train had left the station, and she was standing on the platform watching it pick up speed, leaving her behind. For Rachel, it was the death of her husband.

10.1: Hormones

As 2007 came to a close, I felt a sense of uncertainty for the new year. Though the direction of my transition was clear, the road ahead seemed perilous. I knew I would have to sit down with my sons sooner or later, but my spouse Rachel and I wanted to postpone this conversation for as long as possible. Rachel wished our children would never know the truth about me.

By the middle of January 2008, my doctor received all the lab results for my blood tests. I was given my first three-month prescription of the testosterone-blocking medication and the female hormones after signing a lengthy release form that outlined all potential dangers and risks of hormone replacement therapy (HRT). From then on, I needed a blood tests every three months to ensure that my liver and kidneys were not showing any signs of distress.

The feminizing effects of female hormones on the male body are slow. I felt the same for almost three months. The first sign that anything was happening was just tenderness in the nipple area. This lasted for a few weeks, and then the tenderness spread as new breast tissue formed. I also noticed my skin was softer, especially on my face. I may have imagined it, but body hair growth had also slowed down. It is too bad hormones don't stop it from growing altogether. Unfortunately, HRT did nothing to improve my receding hairline.

The majority of people in my life still had no idea about my transition, especially at church. The changes to my body were not that noticeable during the winter and early spring since I could layer and hide any noticeable breast growth. However, I found jogging uncomfortable; the only solution was purchasing a sports bra. Thanks to a loose-fitting windbreaker, I could hide the small breast development.

At my appointment in January, my doctor recommended that I attend a peer support group. He explained that I did not have to attend presenting as female if I wasn't comfortable, though most who attended did. Alternatively, I could bring my clothes and change in the washroom so I wouldn't have to be out in public. He told me a little about the format and hoped I would at least try it before my next appointment with him in three months.

I decided to attend my first meeting as my female self. The meetings start promptly at five o'clock and end at 7:30 p.m. I had to leave the house in the middle of rush hour and head downtown on very busy streets. The drive was considerably more frightening than my drive home from Costco, and when I neared the building, I realized I was going to have to park the car on the street and then navigate a couple of busy sidewalks to reach the front door.

An angel must have been looking out for me just then because as I turned the corner and came around the front of the building, I saw an empty parking space directly in front of the door. I parked and waited in the car for the sidewalk to be free of pedestrians before stepping out of the car to feed the parking meter. Duncan's wife's instructions to hold my chin up high and to walk slowly ran through my head as I put my head down and rushed into the building. Though the entrance could not have been more than thirty feet from the car, it felt like I'd run a mile.

I took the elevator to the third floor, where the meetings were held, and met a couple of ladies who had just used the facilities to change into their clothes. We said hello and walked together into the large conference room, where all the tables had been gathered in the middle, with chairs on all four sides. There were enough seats for about forty people. I was surprisingly relaxed as I sat down and hung my coat on the back of the chair.

The moderator entered a couple of minutes later and exclaimed, "Oh good, we have some new people tonight. We're just going to wait a few more minutes to give people a chance to arrive, and then we'll get started about 5:15." A few more people trickled in and sat down. The meeting started at the stated time.

After making a few brief welcoming remarks, the moderator asked who would like to go first. There were about thirty of us present, and as I scanned the group closely, I determined that most attendees were in their twenties and thirties, a few were in their forties, and only a few of us were fifty or older. The format was to introduce yourself by first name, then share a little bit about yourself. Then people could ask a question or make a brief comment. You could take as little or as much time as needed to say whatever was on your mind.

To give a brief summary, I found the meeting very disturbing. As I sat there and listened to people share their pain, I realized how fortunate I was in many ways. A few of the younger trans persons were sex trade workers because that's all they could do to earn a living. Some—not all—had been rejected by their parents, kicked out of the house early, and forced to do whatever they could to survive. A couple of individuals broke my heart, not by what they said, but because I could see how difficult their lives had been just from their physical appearance. Their very big, tall, and masculine bodies would always sabotage their attempts to blend into society. It made me feel guilty that I had it so much easier by comparison.

However, the hardest thing for me that night was listening to Elizabeth, who was sitting next to me, share her story. She began by explaining she had been on hormones for almost a year and her surgery would be within six months if all went well. She had been living in the downtown area for about a year after leaving her home in Chilliwack, a small, rural town ninety kilometers east of Vancouver.

The previous weekend she had gone home for the first time since she transitioned to come out to her family. It did not go well. She told us about her family, how devout they were in their Christian faith, and how involved her parents were in church. With pain in her voice, she told us how her father had kicked her out of the house and told her never to return, that she was an abomination to God and was living in sin. She was rejected and ostracized by her parents.

You should have heard all the negative, pejorative, snide remarks around the table. "Those church people, they're the worst!" Part of me wanted to slam the table and shout, "It doesn't have to be that way! I'm a Christian, and that has not been my experience!" But I didn't out of cowardice. Another part of me wanted to put my arm around Elizabeth and tell her God loved her, and that that was all that mattered—but I stayed quiet. The negative comments around the table saddened me, and I felt guilty for doing nothing to console Elizabeth.

The meeting ended on time, and while some attendees talked about going out for coffee, I was still reeling from all I had heard. I didn't feel strong enough to invest much emotional energy into new relationships. I concluded that if this was what happened at every meeting, I would be better off not going. I needed encouragement instead of so much sadness.

Postscript:
I heard about an empty-closed-casket funeral that was held in Chilliwack by the parents of a trans woman whom the parents declared to be dead to them. Whether those were Elizabeth's parents or not, I do not know. But to think that the church was packed with family and church people. Words fail me.

10.2: The Last Giant Hurdles

As Rachel and I were heading to church a few Sundays after Easter 2008, I was having a conversation with God in my head: "It's been six months since I resigned from worship, and no one has come up to me to say they miss my leading, or they miss my singing and my guitar playing." And just as quickly as I had that thought, I was confessing to God for allowing my ego to get in the way. "Forgive me, Lord, whatever I did in the worship team was not for my glorification—it was to glorify and honor You." Then, just as quickly as I had that thought, I was lamenting to God once again, "But, Lord, it still would have been nice if someone had said something." Another apology followed that. I went back and forth like this several times. I think the conversation ended with yet another apology.

We got to the church a few minutes early because Rachel wanted to set up the tables, chairs, and supplies for her Sunday School class. I made my way up the hallway to the front of the sanctuary to listen to the worship team rehearsing the songs we would all be singing that morning. I couldn't go into the sanctuary because ever since I resigned from the worship team, my heart ached, and my emotions were too close to the surface whenever I heard worship music. I decided to pace the corridor outside the sanctuary instead of walking in.

Out of a side room came Liz, a woman my age fluent in Spanish (I believe she was born in Mexico to Mennonite parents.) When she saw me, she said, "Oh, hi, Jim!" Then, in impeccable Spanish, she said, "I miss your leading, singing, and guitar playing on Sundays. Why aren't you doing it anymore? Were you burned out?"

Her words floored me, and I had an instant meltdown. Liz apologized. She wondered if she had said something wrong and recognized she had touched a very soft spot in my heart. Feeling horrible, Liz came up and hugged me, not knowing what had made me cry. I told her I needed to go outside for some fresh air and that she deserved an explanation. The service wouldn't start for at least fifteen or twenty minutes, so we walked around the block. I told her why I had resigned and what had been going on. She offered her total support and told me she loved us unconditionally. She was concerned for Rachel and wanted to know if there was anything she could do. She was so sweet.

As I recount that little encounter, I am grateful to God for answering my childish and selfish prayer. He didn't hold back. To top it all off, the answer came in my mother tongue.

For several weeks I had been praying for direction, a clear indication of whether or not I should share my truth with my parents. I was trying to weigh my needs to transition against my parents' needs; I didn't want to ruin their remaining years. Indirectly, I got my answer that morning. If God was willing to answer such a small prayer, He could answer the big one about my parents.

I had also been thinking about my sons. One day it occurred to me that it would be so sad if there was something in their lives that, out of a fear of rejection or of hurting me, they felt they couldn't talk to me about it. How sad it would be if they felt that way! It had also occurred to me that if I felt this way about my sons, my parents certainly felt the same way about us. They had already demonstrated their amazing unending love for Enrique, and by extension, for all of us. Thanks to this simple prayer answer, I no longer felt afraid to tell them. Instead, I now saw it as an obligation—they needed to know.

My parents lived about thirty kilometers south of Vancouver, within ten minutes of the U.S. border. One of my clients was close to their house. I had been photographing some food items from their menu and finished a little sooner than expected, shortly after 4 p.m. I had been thinking about my parents all afternoon, rehearsing what I would say to them and how I would say it in Spanish.

I had real peace in my heart when I called them to say I was a few minutes away from their house, had been doing a photo shoot, had just finished packing up, and was hoping to stop by on the way home. Mom and Dad have always loved it when we do things like that. "Of course! How wonderful—do you want to stay for supper?" asked mom. I said no, let's have coffee together—I didn't want to put her to work.

Dad answered the door when I got there. He had just arrived from a trip to the bank. Mom was in the kitchen getting ready to make coffee, and Dad suggested we have some rum and Coke instead of coffee. I said, "Good idea, Dad, make mine a double." I was energized by the beautiful warm spring afternoon and was full of anticipation. We sat around the kitchen table and talked about my day. Mom asked all her usual questions as we sipped our drinks, "How is Rachel? How are the boys?"

After this chitchat, I announced I needed to share something with them. Mom's face went ashen, so before I said anything, I reassured them my health was fine—I had just had a physical and blood work done, and everything was okay. I added I also wanted to make sure they would not blame anyone, or anything, or themselves—that what I was going to discuss with them was a medical condition. Mom's initial reaction stemmed from her concern for my weight loss. Every time she saw me, she asked if everything was okay. They had already lost one son to cancer, and she feared the worst whenever she saw me.

I began by telling them I had had this condition ever since I was a little boy, and only recently had I come to understand what it was and what I could do to overcome it. I recounted some of my childhood memories and events, especially those that were seminal in my thinking and stood out as my vain attempts at understanding what made me feel so different. I asked Dad if he remembered a couple of conversations and Mom if she remembered some questions I had asked her.

They vaguely remembered some of those things, but nothing stood out as significant—there were no red flags. As I suspected, Dad said he thought I was curious about the facts of life and had written it off as a natural curiosity. I explained that through junior and senior high school, I struggled with my image and continued into my college years. I told them this private struggle brought me to the point of coming to Christ, hoping I would be healed and made normal. At this point in the conversation, they still had no idea what I was talking about.

I shared how I had not allowed myself to think romantically about our relationship when I met Rachel because I was leaving for Canada within a year and didn't want to make saying goodbye harder. They already knew the story of our correspondence and how we realized we were in love.

I told them how much I had hoped being a husband would finally make me complete and normal. But being a husband and then becoming a father—not once but three times—still did not make my condition go away. Then when I was forty, I asked to be referred to a psychiatrist, and after three sessions with him, he offered to refer me to a clinic at Vancouver General Hospital, but I refused.

I explained he had helped me enough and that I now felt confident that I would be okay with Rachel's love and support. Fast forwarding to 1998—I was now at the point where I needed to go to the clinic and was willing to admit it; I asked to be referred and underwent a comprehensive assessment. After about six months, I was diagnosed with a condition known as gender dysphoria.

Dad said he wasn't sure what it meant, but Mom had an idea. I explained what it meant and the recommended course of action—with all its ramifications.

At this point, I was holding back the flood of tears that were coming. They were teary-eyed, and Mom said, "I can't believe it has taken you this long to tell us. We are so sorry you have been burdened with this, and we didn't know."

Dad added, "Yes, I am so proud of you—you are so strong to have carried such a heavy load." Then it was time for the meltdown.

After catching our breath, they asked many questions—how were the boys? Did they know? How was Rachel doing? When will you start living as a woman?

Ever since I could remember, I had worried about my parents' reaction if they ever found out about my deep secret. I had feared Dad would either slap my face in rage, accusing me of being a "mariqua" ("queer" or "fag"), or kick me out of the house and tell me I was a disgrace to the family and never come back. I expected Mom to start pounding her chest like a penitent Catholic and cry that it was all her fault. I had always feared this worst-case scenario, and those fears turned out to be completely unfounded.

My parents not only amazed me with their capacity to accept me but to do more than that: they loved me.

When I got home, I told Rachel what had happened. She couldn't believe I had done something so stupid. She thought I had been reckless and selfish and didn't think it would be easy for them.

I would have agreed with her a month earlier. Now I knew better and thanked God for how the day had unfolded and for helping me explain things to my parents—which I did in Spanish.

Having shared with my parents, I felt it was time to share with my sons, and I did. I would have liked to have done it by age, starting with our eldest son, but that wasn't possible because he lived out of town. I tried to schedule a time with our middle son, who had some incomplete, out-of-context knowledge about me, but our schedules didn't align as I would have liked. Therefore, I shared with the youngest first, who was then twenty-five years old. I read him the letter. As I finished, he reached across the table, grabbed my hands, and with tears welling up in his eyes, asked me, "Dad, is there anything I can do for you?"

Oh God, those were the most beautiful words I could have heard. "You just did, son, you just did." That was all I could say.

A couple of days later, our middle son spent the night at our house, arriving after I had gone to bed. I found him asleep on the couch the following day when I came downstairs around 7:00, so I let him sleep a little longer. Then about 9:30 a.m. I started breakfast for the two of us, making enough noise in the kitchen to start waking him up (he is not a morning person.)

He was very pleasant throughout our meal, and when we finished, I said, "You and I have been needing to talk for a long time. Do you think this might be a good time?"

He said, "Yeah, sure."

I took out a letter I had written for him and read it. When I finished, he stood up, came around the table, and lifted me off the floor in his arms. Hugging and kissing me, he apologized for how he had reacted to me almost two years earlier. I apologized for having been so careless and causing him so much anguish. We were finally reconciled, and it was all good. It was very good.

Our oldest son and his wife had been doing some minor renovations on their home, and we had been coming up on the odd weekend to lend a hand. On more than one occasion, I brought the letter I had written to him, but Rachel had insisted it was not the right time each time. But this week began with me sharing with my parents and ended with me sharing with our three sons.

That Sunday, we went up to do some work. In return, they invited us to stay for dinner. On several previous visits, I mentioned something I needed to share with them one of these days. That night, when I again broached that subject, my son, looking worried, said, "You don't have cancer or something else, do you, Dad?"

I looked at Rachel. She was bracing herself for the moment that had finally come. I shared with them for the next few minutes and explained what to expect. Their response was also everything I had prayed and hoped for—not what I had feared.

As I think about that week, one thing that stands out is how I felt when I woke up each morning. Starting the day after I shared with my parents, I would wake up with this sense of complete and total transparency. I had no more need to hide—everything was out in the open. I could breathe. It was as if I had been released from the dungeon and could finally start living. For two weeks, I experienced a sense of awe as I awoke each day. It was a new feeling, I finally felt free, and it was wonderful! It took me a while to get used to it.

Chapter 11: Running Into Transition

My next appointment at the clinic was in May 2008, and I presented as Lisa for the first time. The doctor had seen my photo before, so he didn't notice I wasn't in Jim mode, and it wasn't until I mentioned it to him that he said, "Oh, yes. Congratulations. You look good." If he only knew how rattled I had been as I sat and waited in the crowded, full-service community health clinic. That morning, the waiting room was full of families with little children. I did appreciate his compliment and guessed it was worth the anguish.

He reviewed the lab results, said everything looked good, and asked me how I was doing. I told him I had finally shared with my parents and my sons. At the last appointment, we talked about my concerns for my parents and how reticent I was to tell them. We talked about how not telling them would continue to impede my transition unless I was willing to continuously switch back and forth between presenting as male or female.

We discussed the feasibility of switching back and forth between Jim and Lisa, particularly since I was experiencing breast growth, which would be harder to conceal each month. At the time, I lived as Lisa about 60% of the time, mostly when working alone in my home office. If I knew a client or supplier might drop by for a meeting in advance, I'd stay in Jim mode. From time to time, there were surprises from unannounced visits or deliveries, and I had to switch what I was wearing quickly. Fortunately, I did not wear makeup, so it was possible to do a quick switch. However, I found the constant back-and-forth mentally exhausting.

The doctor asked if I had made any firm plans for when I

would start living as Lisa full-time now that I had brought my parents and my sons into the loop. I replied that I had given it some thought but didn't feel ready to take that step yet. The reason was that I wasn't ready to share with Franco, my Saturday morning running buddy, with whom I had been jogging every week since 1992. We had a tradition of going out for breakfast after our run and became close friends. However, Franco was a second-generation Italian full of bravado and machismo, and I feared he would not want to run with me anymore. Sooner or later, I knew I would have to give him a copy of the letter and let the chips fall where they may.

Smiling knowingly, the doctor predicted that I would be transitioning very soon. He said that his experience was that when the person finally shared their secret with the most important people in their life and was accepted unconditionally, it changed everything. After that, it didn't matter what anybody else thought. I agreed with his assessment and reached a similar conclusion after sharing it with my parents and sons.

A few days later, I was working at home in Lisa mode when Rachel called to say she was thinking of coming home for lunch. We decided to have tuna melts, and she would call me as soon as she left the office. I preheated the oven, prepared the tuna melts, and had them ready to bake. As promised, Rachel called to say she was on her way. I put the sandwiches in the hot oven and went back downstairs to finish an email to a client.

Minutes later, I heard the basement door latch jiggling, and I thought it was Rachel. However, it was my parents! I was surprised and taken aback, but I quickly invited them in and ran upstairs to pull the tuna melts out of the oven before they burned.

I stood behind the kitchen counter and waited for them to climb the stairs. It was too late, I figured—they had seen Lisa, and there was no point running to the bedroom to do the ol' switcheroo.

I stood facing the stairwell as they entered the kitchen. Dad looked at me and said, "Como estás de churra!" which loosely translates as, "You are so cute!"

Then Mom said, "Yes, I'm so proud of you! You present very nicely. You have very good taste."

Imagine that. This momentary crisis lasted all of sixty seconds and was over. That's all they said—and then we got busy figuring out where we would sit and how we would serve the food they brought. Just then, Rachel entered the front door and stepped into the kitchen. Now she was the deer caught in the headlights; she was speechless. Mom, Dad, and I just said hi to her casually as if nothing unusual had occurred.

Poor Rachel. You could have knocked her over with a feather. After composing herself, she said she would feel more comfortable taking her tuna melt back to the office to eat at her desk, adding that it was busy at work.

Rachel returned to work, and the three of us sat down and ate our lunch—nothing more was discussed about this little surprise encounter until they went out the door. Mom reiterated how well I presented and said she felt at ease knowing I would be all right in public and not draw negative attention to myself. Mom complimented me once more for my down-to-earth taste in clothing, gave me a kiss and a big hug, and told me she loved me. My mom was adorable and sensitive; she used feminine pronouns when addressing me. Then I turned to Dad. He hugged and kissed me, second-ed Mom's opinion, adding, "It's like we have a new daughter."

I am grateful they were so accepting and supportive at their age—Mom was 86, and Dad was 91. I still shake my head in disbelief. I was so wrong in my predictions about how they would react.

I waved goodbye and watched as they drove away. I closed the door and ran to the phone to call my sister, Carmen. "You won't believe what happened just now!" I started. I told her everything, and she started laughing hysterically.

"Oh my," she said, "That was probably the best way for them to meet you as Lisa for the first time. Can you imagine how tense all of you would have been if you had planned to meet?"

She was right.

Back to my running buddy Franco; he went to Italy with his parents for a cousin's wedding. They were gone four weeks, spanning late June and early July. We resumed our jogs on his first weekend back. After breakfast that Saturday, I handed him a sealed envelope with the letter. And as I had done with Duncan and several other friends whose wives I knew, I asked him to please read it with his wife when they had a few moments away from their children. He looked at me, puzzled, but agreed.

All weekend I waited for Franco to call, but he never did. I feared the worst. I figured it was over between the two of us. Then, at about 8:30 a.m. on Monday, Franco's wife Sandra called and addressed me as Lisa! She explained they had just had breakfast together and read the letter, which changed nothing for them. Franco had just left for work and asked her to call to let me know he loved me. Then Sandra asked if I had any materials or links on the Internet for educational resources because she wanted to become better informed about what it meant to be a trans person so they could know how to be better friends. She said to call anytime if I needed to talk.

Yet another example of how big people's hearts proved to be toward Rachel and me.

During the weeks Franco was away, I began jogging as Lisa for the first time. Since I wore a wig in public and it was summer, I ran early in the morning while it was still cool. It seemed okay, and I didn't get any strange looks from drivers or people I encountered along my running route. I still had a huge psychological block about running with Franco and going for breakfast afterward. At least I knew running with a wig was not the impediment I thought it might be.

The first week Franco and I jogged together again; I did not run as Lisa—I ran as Jim. We knew he had much to share about his trip to Italy, so we agreed to do that over breakfast. Instead, our conversation as we jogged was about my transition plans. He wanted to know if I had made any progress. I told him I was about eighty percent there. He asked when he was going to get to jog with Lisa finally. I said I didn't know and explained that I didn't want to embarrass him or make him uncomfortable being seen in public with me. He rebuffed that notion. Franco asked if I was worried about him, or if I was worried about me.

"I think you are worried about yourself," he opined.

Then I pointed out we had been going to the same restaurant for more than ten years and were regulars there. Wasn't he going to be uncomfortable? He repeated his question, "Are you worried about yourself or me? Let me ask you something," he continued. "You know the names of some of the staff, but do they know your name, where you live, and what you do for a living? And the regular customers we always wave hello to: do you know their names, and do they know yours?"

I finally admitted I was more worried about myself. Franco then insisted that the following Saturday, he was jogging with Lisa.

That Saturday was the first day of the rest of my life, as the saying goes. Jogging on Saturday mornings with Franco had been my last hold-out. But from that fourth Saturday in July 2008, I never reverted to being Jim again.

You are probably wondering how that first run with Franco went. It was anti-climactic. We met at a park halfway between our houses, and when I got out of my car, he gave me the once-over, head to toe. His only comment was, "Hmm, a ponytail. I was wondering how you would have your hair."

11.1: Navigating Uncharted Waters

In retrospect, I had yet to think through all the consequences of going full-time. For example, I had so many details and questions concerning client meetings. What would I wear? And what would it be like going into a client's office, where I only knew the person I was meeting? Or would that person be embarrassed or awkward introducing me to their colleagues? And should I expect the client to smooth the way for me? Were clients going to feel pressured to do a lot of explaining?

Then there was the issue of church. I handled it by writing a letter to the ministers, telling them I was transitioning full-time and was no longer going to attend. They had been expecting that. Rachel also decided to stop attending church; she had her reasons. She did not want to become everyone's prayer concern suddenly. She would be unable to handle being continually asked how she and I were doing, as well-intentioned people would undoubtedly have done.

There would be other hurdles, such as going through the legal name change and all that entailed. What the process lacked in complexity, it made up for in lack of speed. I had to undergo a criminal record check with the Royal Canadian Mounted Police. I had to be fingerprinted, and the prints scanned to see if they matched prints from unsolved crimes, for example. So much of it was hurry up, then wait. Then there was a delay caused by the constable who took my fingerprints at the Vancouver Police Department and forgot to write his badge number on the card with the prints. The application was delayed until I could get the constable to sign an affidavit confirming that he was the one who took my prints. So much of it was out of my hands—but that's how it was.

About eight weeks later, I received the official Certificate of Name Change from the Department of Vital Statistics. I was now legally Lisa Salazar. A letter instructed me to go to all the government agencies I had dealings with—local, provincial, and federal—to request that my records be updated with the new name. The letter also listed banks, credit card companies, insurance carriers, and any entity with which I had a contractual obligation. Talk about the domino effect!

First, I went to the Driver Services office to update my driver's license. I was given a temporary paper license until the photographic plastic card arrived in the mail. As it happened, I had to renew my car insurance, but I was without a photo driver's license. Great. What new hassles was I going to encounter, I wondered. But before I could renew the insurance, I had to take my car through Air Care, a provincial requirement to ensure my car's tailpipe emissions were within the allowable limits. Fortunately, the car passed, but not the seal on the gas cap. I was given a rejection notice and told to bring a new gas cap for testing. If it passed, I could then insure the car.

Okay, now I was going to finally enter a man's domain, the testosterone den known as an auto parts store. I went twice, not once, because I bought the wrong size. I had to go back to the store and deal face-to-face with a parts-department guy to get the exchange to happen. I had been so happy just going to the aisle with the gas caps and helping myself the first time. Now I had to admit I picked the wrong one for my car. I told the story to a friend, who remarked, "That was a very chick thing to do." Gee, thanks!

My car finally passed, and I could renew my car insurance.

I had made a mountain out of a molehill once again, as the lady at the insurance office didn't even bat an eye; she was professional, which brings me to my following observation of things that I had not anticipated: being addressed as "Ma'am," being helped with groceries, and having the door held open for me. It was all surreal, and my instinct was to say, "Oh, it's quite alright; I can handle it myself."

My sister Angela and her husband were now on the spot;they would have to sit down with their daughters and tell them about me. They had planned to do this at their cabin, where they were planning to spend part of the summer. For one reason or another, it never happened as they had hoped. They were back in town now and didn't want to risk the girls finding out accidentally.

The surprising thing to my sister and her husband was how well their daughters took the news when they finally sat the girls down after dinner one night and read my letter to them. Their oldest daughter, who was in twelfth grade at the time, composed the most beautiful letter on behalf of herself and her younger sisters. She mentioned there were a couple of trans students at their high school and that they had sessions that dealt with accepting gender diversity as part of their curriculum; yet another example of how we always fear the worst.

I got to meet Angela and the girls a couple of days later. They invited me for lunch at their house—we were going to have pizza. My sister didn't tell me the pizza was coming from the hot food counter at the Costco near their home, and we were going to go pick it up. She also wanted to drop off six rolls of film for development—she still owned a film camera. First, we went to the food counter to order the pizza since it would take ten to fifteen minutes to be ready. Then it was to the film counter. That is when it occurred to me that I needed to update my membership card with a new photo and name. I told my sister to do the film thing, and I would go to the customer service counter.

To my dismay, there was only one attendant, and he looked like a real redneck to me: heavy-set and tall. I remembered a tip from a trans handout that said, "a smile will disarm a mighty foe" or something like that. I beamed the biggest smile I could make and walked up to the counter, holding my card up to his face.

"I need to update my card," I said, "because this is what I used to look like—I pointed at my face with my other hand and continued—this is what I look like now."

You should have heard his uproarious laughter as he said, "Oh heck, yes. We gotta change that real quick! Please come around this side of the counter so I can take a new picture." He was the most pleasant person I could have imagined. He was so polite when he asked what name I wanted to use and if I needed to change any other details. It was a great experience and, ironically, a lesson in the importance of not prejudging people by their looks.

Old habits are hard to break. I don't want to sound like I am making excuses for myself; I used prejudice as a defense mechanism all my life to survive. But, most often, I was judging myself.

Transitioning that July (2008) did have one unfortunate consequence: I could not attend my 40th high school reunion as I had intended to. In January, I had indicated to the reunion organizers that I would be coming, and we were all excited about the September reunion.

In early August, I sent an email expressing my regrets that I would not be able to attend. Within a few days, I received several emails pleading with me to rearrange my schedule and not to miss this chance of a lifetime to be with people I may never see again. I had no choice but to write these individuals to explain the reason and ask them to please keep it confidential. Additionally, I did not want to hijack the evening by being the center of attention, even if it was for only five minutes.

One of the most beautiful things that have come out of all this is how people have responded to my disclosure. I've talked about my meltdowns in this book, and there have been many. Mostly there have been tears of joy and gratitude for the overwhelming flood of love and support. I have been impressed by people's eloquence — using the simplest words to say the most profound things. I have collected all these emails and deeply treasure them. I don't read them very often because I know I will not have enough Kleenex in the house for the experience.

When I was diagnosed in 1999, was briefed on what choices were available to me and was explained the "road map" to womanhood, two items made it completely impossible to contemplate. One was that I would have to start living as a woman immediately. The other was if and when I had the surgery, Rachel and I could not remain legally married. We would need to be divorced. These two requirements were, to me, deal breakers.

In 2007, when I returned to the Clinic, one of the first things I said to my doctor was that I needed help because I was going to have an issue with those conditions. However, I discovered a lot had changed in nine years, and the transition protocols had been relaxed. The Clinic respected my concerns and my somewhat nebulous timeline.

The court-mandated divorce was also a moot point since, in 2005, Canada became the fourth country in the world, and the first country in the Americas, to legalize same-sex marriage nationwide. I would not be forced by law to divorce Rachel if I ever decided to undergo gender confirmation surgery.

In my first conversation with the doctor at the Clinic, I explained my concern for my elderly parents and my reticence to disclose to them. I was resigned to the possibility that I would not be able to transition as long as they were alive. My doctor had been understanding about that, too.

Trans Health Services were now considering patients' needs; the protocols were guidelines of care instead of barriers. I was happy to learn about this different approach from how things had been before when patients had to follow the protocol or not be helped at all.

I have shared how much it pains me to see how my choices have impacted my best friend, Rachel. The day after I came out to my parents, Dad wondered if what I was doing to Rachel was too hurtful. Why couldn't I tell myself that I had already fifty-eight years with my condition and that I might as well stay unchanged for however many years I may have left to live? Why not remain as Jim for her? "Yeah, right! If it was only that easy." I thought to myself.

I asked him if he would say the same thing to me if what I had was another "congenital" or lifelong medical condition for which there was now a procedure that could improve the quality of my life. Should I not have such a procedure performed on me, or should I say that I've lived with it this long and might as well take it to the grave?

"That's different," he said.

"How so?" I asked. But his point was well taken. My decision has fundamentally impacted Rachel's self-image since it defined her as someone radically different than my wife. I wish I could have been strong, stayed the course, and remained as Jim for Rachel.

When friends have remarked they are happy for me because I am finally doing something I've wanted to do all my life, I feel compelled to correct them and point out this is the last thing I wanted to do. When others say I am courageous, I correct them for that, too. I told them I was desperate. There is nothing admirable about what I did. I see it simply as basic survival.

I deal in pictures—I make my living doing visual stuff—so it was no great surprise that an image came to mind one day as I was trying to explain to someone how I saw my life: I remembered unraveling a large ball of heavy string or yarn I found in my Mom's or grandmother's knitting supplies when I was a child. I pulled on the end I saw poking out and started pulling on it. I kept this up until the ball lost its critical mass, and what was left collapsed and was formless. Until that moment, the outside shape was intact, and one would not have known its core was slowly disappearing by just looking at it. That was me, and that was my life. I was unraveling from the inside, but no one was the wiser. I knew my "critical mass" would soon be gone, and I would collapse into an unrecognizable heap. For Rachel's sake, I didn't want that to happen to me. I didn't want that to happen for our sons' and the rest of my family's sakes, either.

I knew it was not healthy to dwell on death all the time and to think that death would solve my gender problem. But why hadn't God taken me on any of the many times I had close calls where I've lucked out? "Why didn't you take me then?" I have asked God so many times. Simply saying my time had not yet come is a cop-out. Why hasn't it been my time? Why am I still around?

Despite the fact I have often thought death would solve so many problems, I am grateful I am still around, even if I have to learn to live in a whole new way. As I told the Costco man, "That is what I used to look like; this is what I look like now."

The challenges will continue—how Rachel and I will be able to navigate these waters is still a big question mark. In her own words, we are no longer husband and wife. For now, we remain legally married and dwell together under the same roof, but we live separate and independent lives. The only exception is during family events.

I have a trans friend one year ahead of me in the process. I was encouraged by the fact that she was still with her spouse after the surgery, and it looked as if their marriage would endure. I was sad to learn that it now doesn't look like it will survive.

Though we live in a city, province, and country that is fairly enlightened with regard to trans issues, there is still a stigma for some. An uneasiness remains but is seldom talked about—it is the elephant in the room. I am that elephant, and I know it. It is conjecture on my part, but I believe many trans marriages fail because the spouse cannot withstand this insidious silence.

Rachel once asked me how I would feel if the tables were turned, if she came to me wanting to have her breasts removed, to grow a beard, and become a man: would I still want her if "she" was a "he?" My honest answer was that I could not imagine how I would feel. Therefore, my honest admission is that I do not know the extent of her pain or what she has endured. And she is also not able to live with my pain. The two are different, but they are both very real. One is not easier than the other.

A client of mine recently commented about some events that have impacted their business negatively. They were facing significant losses and possible bankruptcy. She commented, "business is business," and one must be prepared to walk away from it and not let it consume you. That can't be said about marriage—certainly not my marriage.

There will be other challenges that are part of the deal. It's taken me a while to fully appreciate some of these because I have been living, until recently, as a male. For example, as a woman, I can no longer go for jogs late at night like I used to. In the summer, I had been able to go on five-mile runs at midnight. Not anymore.

As a trans person, there are other risks I will face and have already experienced. In the summer of 2009, I had dinner with my friend Duncan, his wife, and a mutual friend at a new restaurant that had just opened downtown. Except for the friend, the rest of us arrived on one of the two rapid transit trains that feed into downtown Vancouver. Duncan and his wife came on the new Canada Line, which connects downtown Vancouver to the international airport. When it was time to go home, I decided to go with them part of the way and get off at the 49th Avenue station—one of the stops along the way—from which I could take a bus, traveling east to my house. The trip would be slightly longer than if I returned on the other train, which was a more direct route. But trying out the new train with some friends was too irresistible.

When we boarded the train, it was already two-thirds full, with only a few empty seats. Duncan's wife sat down in the first seat she saw by the doors. Duncan and I stood beside her, holding onto the pole for support. Across the aisle, in front of the other set of doors, was a man in his late twenties holding onto the pole on his side of the train. Shortly after the train started moving through the tunnel, the guy started muttering something that I couldn't make out.

After the train left the next station, he got a little louder, and I glanced over to see what was going on, and he was making menacing gestures in my direction, so I ignored him. I concluded he might have Tourette's syndrome and leaned forward and commented to that effect to Duncan and his wife. But she looked at me and said, "Oh, no, dear, he's talking about you."

I was terrified, but I couldn't let it show. I tried to stay as calm as possible by ignoring his comments, which I could barely make out above the noise of the train and all the conversations. I started thinking about my options, wondering what I should do. Should I stay on the train and go all the way with Duncan and his wife? I could then take a train back to 49th Avenue and catch a later bus home.

To my relief, he got off at the station before mine. I kept my eye on him to ensure he remained on the platform until the train pulled away. I got out at my station, but now I was rattled, so I left the train with a group of foreign ESL students and stayed close to them until we reached the bus stop at street level. When the bus finally arrived, passengers were packed like sardines; it was standing room only. My heart was still racing from my incident. I took a deep breath, boarded the bus, and crossed my fingers that everything would be okay the rest of the way home.

With so many people on board and the bus making every stop along the way, it would be a long ride. After about six bus stops, more people boarded, among them a tall male in his sixties. He looked like he'd had a few too many and was a bit wobbly on his feet. He looked right at me, smiled broadly, and came and stood next to me, to my dismay. The next thing I knew, he stroked my bare arm with his hand. I pulled it away and gave him a stern look. He continued grinning at me.

A few stops later, the woman sitting next to me got up from her seat. I sat down. Now the man was standing over me. I ignored him until the young fellow who had been sitting in the window seat excused himself to exit the bus. I had no choice but to move into the vacated window seat, knowing the man would most likely sit next to me—and he did. Now I was trapped. He tried to put his arm around me, but I gave him a dirty look, and he withdrew his arm. This little scene ended abruptly when he suddenly jumped to his feet when the bus reached his stop. He wobbled off the bus, and he was gone.

I know I've gone into a lot of detail about this incident—but it was a jolt to my composure. After one year of living as a trans female, I went from being an object of scorn to an object of lust in less than fifteen minutes. I felt vulnerable for the first time as a trans person and as a woman.

I shared my experience that night with Rachel, and she was not surprised by either of the two incidents. She told me, in no uncertain terms, what I should have done and warned me about what I should do in the future if I find myself in similar situations. I felt like a little schoolgirl being admonished and lectured on street safety.

11.2: The Change

The first twelve months of living full-time as a transgender person are known as "the real-life test." This period is significant because, after one year of living full-time and surviving, a person becomes eligible for gender confirmation surgery (GCS), provided they pass a psychological assessment. Initially, I had not planned to undergo GCS, but a conversation with my doctor at the clinic changed my mind. Some of my blood tests showed signs of distress in my kidneys and liver, and the doctors considered taking me off my medications if the next test showed similar results. However, GCS would enable me to go off most medications, whereas not having the surgery would require me to continue taking them for the rest of my life to suppress testosterone, which would put me at risk for complications.

The second reason I decided to have GCS was the legal and safety aspects of living as a woman while still being identified as male in all my official documents, including my passport and driver's license. Depending on the jurisdiction, this situation could potentially cause problems, especially when traveling. There would always be the risk of being delayed, humiliated, or worse if some official were to make a case out of it.

Another reason some people undergo GCS was less important to me; some transgender people view GCS as the ultimate validation of who they are and, therefore, need it. Others undergo GCS to enjoy heterosexual intercourse and function sexually as a woman. Neither of these reasons was of any consequence or significance to me. Therefore, my decision to have surgery was only for medical and legal/safety reasons.

To be eligible for GCS, I needed letters from individuals who could vouch that I had been living full-time as a woman for one year. I asked a couple of clients and friends for such letters since letters from family members were not accepted. My doctor then submitted the letters, his report, and a copy of my file to the provincial Trans Health Services office in Victoria, the provincial capital. The office would contact me in about three months to schedule me for the psychological assessment.

The psychological assessment was done by two of the Trans Health psychiatrists and took about an hour, after which I was approved for surgery. Then I had to wait another three months for the Authorization for Surgery letter from the Ministry of Health. With that letter in hand, I could call the hospital in Montreal to book a date for the GCS. For now, the Province of British Columbia farms out the surgery to the clinic of Dr. Pierre Brassard, a world-renowned GCS specialist. Travel and extended care for recovery are the patient's responsibility.

The authorization letter arrived the week before Christmas, and I called the hospital to book a date. The earliest date available was May 17, 2010—a five-month wait. I wanted to consider whether the other dates might work best for me, but since the hospital was closed for two weeks over Christmas and New Year's, I was asked to call back in January. I chose the first date they had given me, May 17, but then there was a cancellation, and March 30 was now available, so I went for it.

Some friends wondered if I would be attracted to men and if I would consider that possibility if my marriage did not survive. However, I emphatically answered no. I did not wish to have any intimate relationship with a male. The surgery does not change one's sexual orientation. If I were not monogamous and celibate, I would be open to an intimate relationship with a female. I suppose, technically, that would make me lesbian. That is an issue for Rachel as she is one hundred percent heterosexual.

Dr. Cameron Bowman of the University of British Columbia, the only gender surgery specialist in our province, explained the complicated multi-level issue of gender, sex, and orientation in an interview on a local cable community program. According to Dr. Bowman, gender is how we identify ourselves, and it is the brain's imprint. We either identify as male or female, but some identify as neither or a combination of both. Others may identify as more of one than the other, but not one or the other.

Sex, on the other hand, refers to the body's biological, physical characteristics or "plumbing." Most people have either fully developed male or female "plumbing." However, a few may have ambiguous sexual characteristics and cannot be categorized as either male or female. They are intersex.

Finally, sexual orientation refers to who we are attracted to. Again, most people are attracted only to the opposite sex and never to their own. However, some can go either way or are only attracted to their own sex. We have an endless set of possible combinations when we superimpose all three layers. Each of these layers is a spectrum, which further complicates matters. However, it is essential to understand that GCS does not change one's sexual orientation.

In conclusion, the decision to undergo gender confirmation surgery is a personal one and depends on individual circumstances. For me, the medical and legal/safety aspects were the primary reasons for my decision. While GCS is often viewed as the ultimate validation of one's identity, that was not the case for me.

We cannot be so rigid as to say that a person's gender is based solely on their physical body. We need to be open and compassionate toward those who struggle with their gender identity and recognize the incredible diversity in our human family.

In Chapter 9 of my story, I discussed how I came to a new understanding of Jesus' comments about eunuchs. This helped me reconcile my faith with my gender identity and gave me the permission to proceed without fear of judgment. I realized my faith was not at odds with who I was and that God would not judge me for the choices I needed to make.

Despite this, I admit to feeling a touch of doubt lingering in my mind. I wondered if I was only seeing the issue from a selfish point of view. However, my doubts evaporated when I found corroborating evidence in the Bible. I now believe that the disciples came to a new understanding of human sexuality through Jesus' teachings, as evident in St. Luke's account in the Book of Acts about Philip's encounter with the Ethiopian eunuch.

In this passage from the Book of Acts, Luke tells the story of Philip being guided by an angel to a road where he encounters an Ethiopian eunuch, a court official of Queen Candace, who is reading from the prophet Isaiah. Philip asks if he understands what he is reading, and the eunuch responds that he cannot without guidance. Philip then preaches to him about Jesus, and when they come across water, the eunuch asks to be baptized. Philip baptizes him, and they both come out of the water. The Spirit of the Lord then takes Philip away, and the eunuch continues on his way, rejoicing.

There are many lessons to unpack from the story of the Ethiopian eunuch. As a person who has struggled with gender identity, I find his story particularly moving. Despite his devotion to Judaism, the eunuch was excluded from fully participating in the Passover feast because, as a eunuch, he was considered ceremonially unclean. He was an excluded person through no fault of his own.

As a follower of Jesus, what touches me about this story is that it is one of the first acts by one of the apostles, and it involves including sexually and anatomically "other" persons. It declared that none would be excluded for being "different." That Philip did not hesitate to reach out and affirm this sexually-other person as a believer is an equally monumental lesson. I suspect Philip must have been just as surprised as the eunuch by this amazing encounter.

When the eunuch asked Philip if he shouldn't be baptized, it wasn't just a matter of starting out right by following the new rules. His question was packed with so much more importance. It was as if he was saying, "Though I have been a devout Jew all my life and have done everything that is expected and demanded of me, even coming to Jerusalem to celebrate the Passover, I have not been a full participant. As an other-sex person, I have had to stand on the sidelines. Will this also be the case now, or can I be a full participant as an equal?"

I can relate to the eunuch's longing to be a full participant, not just an outsider looking in. For most of my life, I felt like an outsider in my own body. But through my journey of reconciling my faith with my gender identity, I have come to accept myself as a woman. It's a long road ahead, and there will be bumps along the way, but I can rejoice in who I am for the first time in my life.

I realize that not everyone shares my beliefs, and that's okay. I'm not sharing this story to convince anyone one way or another. I want to emphasize the importance of inclusion and compassion toward those who are different, especially when it comes to gender identity. Excluding or stigmatizing someone based on their gender identity is not only hurtful, but it goes against the very teachings of inclusion and compassion that I find so inspiring in the story of the Ethiopian eunuch.

In conclusion, we need to be open and compassionate toward those who struggle with their gender identity and recognize the diversity of human experience. We should not judge or stigmatize others based on their gender identity but instead strive to create a more inclusive and accepting society for all.

　　With that said, I must say goodbye; it's time to finish packing the suitcases. My flight is tomorrow morning, and the surgery is in two days. My surgeon is waiting!

* * *

As the day of my surgery approached, I gave myself the deadline to finish the book on the eve of my departure for Montreal and to end it with "My surgeon is waiting!" But when my friend and instigator in this book writing project read the first draft, she protested that I could not end the book with that sentence; there were too many unanswered questions; what happened next? She was right. I thank Jan Williams for her suggestion to add an epilogue and the appendices that follow. L.S.

Chapter 12: Section 1 An Epilogue

The flight from Vancouver to Montreal via Calgary was uneventful for the seasoned crew of the WestJet 737 that day. But in the mind and reality of a trans person on her way to surgery, this trip was the final destination.

Three months earlier, I had made the final arrangements for my gender confirmation surgery. At that time, the surgery date seemed so far away. I remember sending an email to all my clients, letting them know that I would be out of work for three to four weeks beginning in the last week of March. Although I did not elaborate on the reason, they all knew. The congratulatory replies started coming in within minutes.

As the date drew closer, I was often asked two questions: "Are you excited?" and "Are you nervous?" The truth was, I was neither. Instead, I felt relief that I would no longer be in limbo, straddling the gender divide. I had waited for this moment for so long, and it was finally here.

Six weeks before the surgery, I had to undergo blood work and an electrocardiogram, with the results being sent to Dr. Brassard in Montreal. Three weeks later, I stopped taking all medications as instructed to ensure that my body would be free of anything that might prevent a quick recovery.

I intended to travel to Montreal on my own, which is what most of Dr. Brassard's patients do. However, my two sisters were unhappy that I would be alone and decided to do a tag team. One would come for the first few days, and the other would take her place a few days later. In the end, only Carmen made the trip since her work schedule allowed her more flexibility. She arrived in Montreal on the day of my surgery, Tuesday, March 30. I arrived in Montreal on Sunday, the twenty-eighth, in the early evening. A limousine picked me up at the airport and took me to the "residence of convalescence" next door to the small private hospital.

When I arrived, dinner was on the table. I was welcomed by the nurse on duty and introduced to some other patients before I was escorted to my room, which I shared with a young woman from Ottawa. Her surgery had been earlier that week, and she was resting. I placed my bags on my side of the room and went back downstairs to eat dinner.

I was the last patient to arrive for the upcoming week's surgeries. The hospital and residence were going to be closed for one week to give the doctors, nurses, and staff some well-deserved time off. When I arrived, there were seven of us, four Canadians and three Americans. I was the oldest at fifty-nine; the youngest was twenty-four years old. As I mentioned, three of us were scheduled for surgery; the others were recovering from theirs. It was very moving to be among them all. Our stories were so similar yet so radically different and unique.

On Monday afternoon, I met Dr. Brassard and discussed the surgery. He answered all of my questions. I cannot say enough about him and his staff; my experience was very positive. The most surprising thing was how calm I was before the surgery. I say this because I have always been squeamish when it comes to blood. I can't even look at myself getting poked with needles—and I have been poked with many needles in the last two years. Thanks to Skype and email, I brought my laptop to Montreal to keep in touch with family and friends. It was great to talk to my parents and friends for free. Many friends had asked me to let them know how I was doing, so I sent updates whenever possible. (See Appendix I)

Carmen was so sweet, not only with me but with the other individuals. I am so grateful she came. I was the only one with a family member who came to be by their side. My heart went out to the younger ones, so alone and far from home at such an important moment in their lives. What was beautiful to see and experience was how everyone offered love and support to each other. The hospital and residence staff were also excellent—they made us feel completely safe and cared for, especially since we all seemed highly emotional.

Throughout this journey, I have come to realize that life

is not always easy. We are born into circumstances that we never chose, and we must deal with them as best we can. But we also have a choice in how we react to the situations we find ourselves in. We can choose to hide and be secretive, or we can choose to be open and transparent. We can choose to judge and condemn, or we can choose to love and respect.

I have chosen to be transparent and to live my life openly as the person I truly am. I have also chosen to love and respect those around me and treat them with the same dignity and compassion I would like to be treated with. It is not always easy, and there are times when I still face discrimination and prejudice, but I know that I am not alone in this journey.

There are many people out there who are struggling with their own issues and who are looking for someone to turn to. I hope that my story can inspire and comfort them and that they can find the strength to be true to themselves, just as I have.

As I look back on my journey, I am grateful for the support of my family, friends, and medical professionals who have helped me through this process. I am also grateful for the many people I have met along the way who have shared their own stories with me and helped me see that I am not alone.

In closing, I would like to share the beautiful verses from Micah 6:6-7 that have inspired me throughout this journey: "He has shown you, O mortal, what is good. And what does the LORD require of you? To act justly, love mercy, and walk humbly with your God." These words have reminded me that we are all equal in the eyes of God and should treat each other with the same love and respect that we would like to be treated with.

12.1: The Last Word:

This book must end with a tribute to Rachel, who has had to pay a very high price due to the choices I needed to make. As a friend put it, her story deserves to be told, too—how she has dealt with the hurt, shock, loneliness, love of Jim, loss of Jim, living with Lisa, etc. She is admirable but also very private with an equally strong, private faith. She deserves and has all my love and respect. I wish her peace.

Section 2 Preface

The original name of the book I published in 2011 was "Transparently: Behind the Scenes of a good life." The memoir covered the first 59 years and six months of my life, through the first month after I underwent gender confirmation surgery. I wrote the book in the three months leading up to the surgery; it was a time of ecstasy and hopeful anticipation for me.

As such, the title I picked was descriptive of how I saw my life at that time. I had nothing to hide; I felt open and candid in sharing my life's journey. There was much truth to the subtitle as well; I had lived a good life in the sense that life had been good to me. I acknowledged my gratitude and many privileges. Nothing I said in the original preface was a fabrication or a spin. Those were my honest feelings.

This edition of the book completes the story of my life up through March 30, 2023, exactly 13 years since I underwent gender confirmation surgery (GCS). But I no longer view my life or the world through the same rose-colored glasses.

I considered using "Hellhole" as the title for the second edition of Transparently; It seemed like an apt container for the rage I felt as I wrote. But on reflection, I realized this jaundiced perspective was only apt if I surrendered to the rage.

What is the cause of my rage? It is my response to the persistent and deliberate attacks on trans persons by Christian conservative, right-wing politicians and organizations bent on erasing trans people. As I write this update, a handful of GOP-ruled states have laws in the making that criminalize trans-specific health care to minors and threaten to take the medical licenses away from doctors who treat trans youth and charge parents who support their child's transition with child abuse.

According to Lambda Legal, from January 1 through March 30, 2023, a staggering 435 anti-LGBTQ+ bills have been introduced in 45 States, most of which target transgender youth and adults. And indeed, several states have passed those bills. The Human Rights Campaign (HRC) reports that 23 percent of trans youth in the U.S. have already lost access to gender-affirming care.

These laws go against the best practices of trans-related pediatrics outlined by the American Academy of Pediatrics (AAP), the American Medical Association (AMA), and the American Psychological Association (APA). Numerous studies have shown that a lack of societal acceptance and access to gender-affirming care contribute to high rates of suicidal ideation—and suicide—among trans youth. I personally knew two young people who chose the latter.

The Architects and supporters of these bills are anti-LGBTQ groups include The *Alliance Defending Freedom* and the *Heritage Foundation*, the *American Principles Project*, as well as a more recent group that was formed in 2021, *Moms for Liberty*.

Rather than surrendering to the rage, I considered a more descriptive title for Section 2 of the book. I thought about the narrative process and the question I kept asking myself, "What happened next?" Suddenly I had a new theme—and title!

"Then This Happened:" is a much better container for all the stuff I've experienced and seen in my post-surgery life--most of it unexpected.

Over the years, I'd been asked if I planned to write a sequel to "Transparently." The truth was that I didn't think I would. Then, out of the blue, an author-representative for a publishing company contacted me to ask the same question but from a different angle. They were thinking of a second edition with two parts. Section 1 would remain as my life pre-surgery, and Section 2 would cover my life post-surgery. Not writing a sequel or a separate book sounded interesting, but I was not in the right frame to consider the undertaking. But the seed of an idea was planted.

Coincidentally, this interaction with a publisher happened in 2018, shortly after I completed my training as a multi-faith Spiritual Care Practitioner, also referred to a hospital chaplain. That was also when I began to consider not writing anymore blog posts; call it self-censorship. I had too much rage inside me, and I wanted to lash out at those attacking the trans community; I didn't want to be labeled an *angry tranny*.

I know it makes no sense; on the one hand, I had been training to offer comfort, solace, and spiritual support to total strangers, and on the other, I wanted to lash out. But I'm getting ahead of myself—first, a bit of historical context.

In my original preface, I credited a friend for prying open the story of my life with all her probing questions. Her name was Jan Williams, a retired journalist, and though I never met her in person, we became close friends by email. I gave her credit in the preface to Transparently and at the end of chapter 11. I also credited her for pushing me to write an epilogue (chapter 12) and add an appendix.

Jan was the older sister of one of my brother's closest friends. Just before Christmas 2009, she posted on our high school's Facebook page about her brother Steven, who had been a well-known morning D.J. in Denver, L.A., and Hawaii and had been murdered by a greedy associate. My correspondence with Jan began when I sent her a direct message expressing my condolences. I told her I had tried to let Steven know when my brother passed away in 1985, with no luck. That led to her wanting to learn about my family and me, resulting in Transparently. This all occurred while prosecutors in L.A. were putting together the murder case against the man who conned Steven from his and Jan's inheritance and then killed him. The man was sentenced to life in prison in November 2011. Sadly, Jan passed away penniless a year later.

I am grateful to Jan for the journalistic curiosity that motivated her to ask me all the questions that open me up and got me talking. I trusted her.

Another important person who played a role in telling my story was Duncan Holmes, the friend who wrote the foreword to this book. I am sad to report that Duncan also passed away in May 2021. What saddened me most was that due to the COVID pandemic, I could not spend time with him in the months leading up to his death from pancreatic cancer. He was like an older brother to me; he and his partner were my cheerleading section when I began my transition. Peace to both Jan and Duncan.

Let me touch on how I approached this second edition, Section 2. I first reviewed Part I and corrected typos and punctuation errors. I also looked for ways to improve the word flow and, in some cases, improve the clarity of the text while resisting the urge to revise stories. I reminded myself that though my views have changed with time, including some of my spiritual beliefs, these stories record how I thought and saw things in 2010.

In 2011, I started writing a blog. Even though I hit the pause button and stopped writing in the fall of 2018, the blogpost provided a timeline and archive of experiences and the evolution of my thinking. As such, I include some of the things I wrote during those years, inserting them into the narrative while trying to preserve the chronology. I've included relevant blog posts, published Op-Eds, and summarized essays and papers from my studies. If nothing else, the final product proves that my life today does not look like anything I imagined when I published Transparently in 2011.

* * *

I hope you find Section 2 as interesting as Section 1

— Lisa

Chapter 13: Interesting in Vancouver

The month leading up to my surgery had been hectic. I informed my clients that I would be unavailable from the beginning of April until the middle of May. But I offered to meet their summer promotional needs before I left for Montreal if they sent me project briefs by the first week in March. I was inundated with work but completed every project. Rachel, who did my bookkeeping, joked that I should use the strategy more often; I had doubled my average monthly billings.

By mid-June, I was fully recovered and ready to work. I anticipated phone calls and emails from clients, but there was little work coming in. I consoled myself with the fact that I had been crazy busy in March. I reminded myself that it was the beginning of summer when my business invariably slowed down. But I also wondered if it was time to look for a graphic design position within an organization instead of staying self-employed.

I called Mark Busse, president of the BC Chapter of the Graphic Designers of Canada. We met for coffee and talked about my career prospects and options. He was an excellent sounding board and made me feel less anxious. He promised to call if he heard of any job openings.

Mark emailed me the next day; he said he had a "crazy question" to ask me. Would I be willing to muster the strength to stand in front of a small group of 300 to 400 to give a 15-minute version of my story?

Was he kidding? Me, speaking in front of 300+ people about my life in 15 minutes? It felt impossible, intimidating, and flattering all at once.

As part of the organizing committee for an event called "Interesting Vancouver," Mark needed to recruit fifteen speakers before the end of the month, even though the gig was in October. I'd never heard of Interesting Vancouver, but he included a link to the event's website. I watched most of the presentations from 2008 and 2009.

Interesting Vancouver was an annual community event showcasing regular people and their hobbies, passions, obsessions, quirks, creations and inventions, or occupations. The website described the event as more than another "sage on the stage" lecture series, claiming it was an inclusive celebration of the uncelebrated, expanding the collective vision of exciting stuff happening in the city.

I called Mark. Was he out of his mind? I asked him what had possessed him to think of me as a presenter. His unabashed answer was, "We need to hear stories like yours."

Sigh.

My reluctance and arguments as to why it was not a good idea didn't seem to be landing on him. He asked me to think about it for a few days and let him know within a week. He assured me it would be a warm, receptive, and progressive audience of mostly university graduates and professionals aged 25 to 40. I joked that speaking to millennials would be like speaking to my sons.

Then, as if to twist my arm, he added, "Think how your story might help one struggling person in the audience, or they may know someone who is, and you never know, your story could save a life."

Sigh, again.

I revisited the videos with a more critical eye. Despite the lack of a common theme for the evening, I saw that each presenter had gone through a process, whether it was related to an invention, exploration, discovery, creative endeavor, or social cause. I wondered what process I had gone through, that is, besides my medical gender transition. I was not qualified to explain hormone therapies and surgeries, and I didn't want to pretend to be a spokesperson for the trans community.

Then I had an idea: I could speak about my process to reconcile my Christian faith with being Trans. After all, it had taken me more than 50 years. I could start with my guilt-infused Roman Catholic upbringing in Colombia, then talk about my fundamentalist Evangelical journey through adulthood and conclude with how I finally made sense of my conundrum.

It also dawned on me that the millennial audience would be mostly unfamiliar with the Bible, given that they were the first generation to abandon churches and Sunday schools in large numbers. Perhaps I could do a 15-minute Bible study! I would show them the passages I had used to condemn myself and then talk about how I came to understand these in a new way once I started asking questions differently. Mark liked the idea. "Okay, I have to think about it," I said. "I'll let you know in a few days.

I had never been a public speaker. If I said yes, I would have 100 days to write my talk and produce a PowerPoint presentation.

A few days passed, and I called him a third time to say yes.

After I hung up the phone, I asked myself in panicked disbelief, "What have I done?"

That summer marked the beginning of some significant seismic shifts in my life. What had started as a cry for help to Mark had resulted in a commitment to open up my life in a way that I had never contemplated.

As mentioned above, my career as a freelance graphic designer began to show cracks, but it hadn't crumbled yet. That was why I had reached out to Mark. Ironically, my creative juices were flowing—solutions came fast and easy—if the few projects I was hired to do were any indication. Fortunately, for the time being, the cash flow was enough to meet our monthly living expenses and financial obligations.

The first sign of danger came in early July when my second-largest client, a restaurant chain I had serviced for 15 years, unceremoniously and unexpectedly dumped me. The problem was how I found out. Before my surgery, we had planned a major overhaul of their look. I would re-photograph their complete product catalog since all their internal and external marketing was image-laden. Phase one of the rebranding had a target date of August, when the website would be the first to feature the new imagery.

As promised, as soon as I was ready to work, I contacted their marketing manager to firm up a day to begin the photo shoot, but she did not respond for a few days. In the meantime, I went to their website to reacquaint myself with their website's interface. To my surprise, the website already had all-new photographs boasting the new plating and tableware that had triggered the need to rebrand in the first place.

I called the marketing manager and could barely articulate my bewilderment, disappointment, and shock. She apologized for not letting me know: an executive decision had been made to use another creative service. She emphasized that it had been purely a business decision to get a fresh set of eyes on their branding.

Based on what I saw, I was incredulous, if not astonished, by the explanation. The only difference between the original and the new photography was that the plates, cutlery, and glassware were different. The look had not changed at all. They had replaced round plates with square and rectangular ones, and the wine glasses seemed scaled-up, which made them look trendier. But the new photographer and art director followed the look I had established for the brand years ago; the images' lighting, staging, framing, and mood were the same. I could do nothing; I didn't have a contract with them. All I had to count on was our 15 years of reciprocal goodwill. This client accounted for 30% of my income; losing them was ominous.

While all this was happening, my personal life was also experiencing tremors. Rachel and I still shared a roof, but we no longer ate or even watched TV together; this was out of respect for her wishes. She said she needed time and space to sort things out, which I was more than willing to give her in hopes our marriage would survive.

13.1 The Fork in the Road

While counting the days down to Interesting Vancouver, two things happened that took my life in a direction I never expected or imagined. These two events are serendipitous.

First, in the last week of August, Kaitlyn Bogas called to invite me to a barbecue on the Sunday before Labor Day. (Kaitlyn wrote the second Foreword to this book. How we met is discussed in Kaitlyn's introduction.) The barbecue would be at the home of a mutual friend, Terri, another trans-woman. There would be close to twenty guests, all trans women our age; in other words, all Boomers who had grown up in an unaccepting world.

At the time, I could count the number of trans friends I had on two fingers. Aside from Kaitlyn and Terri, who hosted the barbecue, I did not know any other trans persons. I had been flying solo through my transition and did not socialize with anyone under the LGBTQ+ umbrella. Just because I'd transitioned and had undergone GCS didn't mean I was entirely out of the closet. In retrospect, I can say that my internalized homophobia and transphobia still paralyzed me socially. So naturally, I turned Kaitlyn down.

Kaitlyn was disappointed and said she was doing all the cooking and had planned a great menu, then added she called me because she'd been told she could invite a friend. She wasn't trying to guilt me into going, but it had the same effect; I accepted the invitation and thanked her for thinking of me.

Kaitlyn, a once-famous Vancouver chef and restaurateur before she transitioned, did not disappoint. I have never been to an A-List social event, but I'm sure the food we enjoyed was of that caliber. Terri introduced me to the other women, and among them was the person I had spoken with a decade earlier, when I called a support group for crossdressers. Her name was Tori—not a common name—and I remembered that conversation with a Tori all those years ago. All of the attendees at the barbecue had been active group members.

Once I had put two and two together, I asked her if she remembered a call from a guy who shared how defeated and guilty he felt as a Christian and his struggle to figure out what he was and what to do. Yes, she remembered because she was a Christian herself, and she understood my dilemma and told me a bit about her story. (In Chapter 9, I recount the conversation--and how I never found the courage to attend one of their support meetings or social gatherings.)

Then, Tori asked me if I was attending a church, and when I said no, she insisted I visit her church the following Sunday because they were having a special event. She explained it was an inclusive congregation, where more than 80% of the people were LGBTQ+, called Rainbow Community Church. We exchanged phone numbers and became Facebook friends.

Being invited to the barbecue and meeting Tori was the first of the two important events. The second event was initiated when I clicked on a YouTube video Tori shared on her Facebook wall a week later. The video was titled "Trans People and the Church." I was impressed. The creator was Kathy Baldock, an Evangelical woman and self-described advocate trying to build bridges between the church and the LGBTQ+ community.

I sent Kathy a friend request, spurred on by the fact that she was friends with many of the people I'd met at Rainbow Community Church. I also sent her a brief message explaining who I was and how I had learned about her. She responded almost immediately; she wanted to know more about me. A few days later, she emailed me asking if I could design a professional-looking business card. Her blogs, vlogs, and podcasts were gaining traction, and she was getting invited to speak at churches. She wanted to portray credibility and professionalism.

The highly anticipated and dreaded Interesting Vancouver event eventually took place in October, and a video of it can still be found on Vimeo. I cringe every time I watch the video. I'm embarrassed with my "performance." Truth be told, I have never liked seeing myself in any video. During my talk, I mentioned the increasing number of suicides among young LGBTQ+ individuals that were being reported in the news, and I quoted Kathy's suggestion to become advocates and defenders for these struggling individuals, especially the younger ones.

Being invited to speak that night and my encounters with Tori and Kathy dramatically altered the course of my life in ways I could never have imagined or anticipated. These seemingly minor events set the stage for the rest of my story, and it would not be an exaggeration to say that the trajectory of my life hinges on them. For example, within a week of Interesting Vancouver, two teachers from different high schools who had been in the audience invited me to speak at their respective schools' Gay Straight Alliance (GSA). These were just the start. I was surprised and delighted by the outpouring of positive feedback on Twitter and other platforms from people who had attended that night.

The above-mentioned Vimeo video was not uploaded until July 2011. Maybe that was a good thing because if I'd seen it sooner, I might have convinced myself I was a terrible public speaker and may not have been willing to accept any of the invitations that followed Interesting Vancouver.

I celebrated my 60th birthday that November. I held an open house and invited my sisters and their husbands, my running mate Franco and Duncan, some old friends and clients, Tori, and some of the new friends from Rainbow Community Church. I told people not to bring any gifts; their presence was gift enough, and they could come anytime from 3 until 9 p.m. I don't usually use the word "blessed" to describe how I feel, but that is how I felt that night. I felt supported and affirmed.

When I think about that night, I can't help but smile as I recall how the friends from Rainbow were the last to leave because they wanted to clean up after the party. They gathered all the dirty dishes and glasses, washed and put them away, and left the house looking like it had been staged for a photo shoot. All the jokes were no joke about gay men being fashionistas and home decorators! Their generosity wowed me.

That week, Tori also introduced me to Tami Starlight, the organizer of Vancouver's Transgender Day of Remembrance (TDOR), which is held on the 20th of November. It is an international event that honors trans persons who were killed all over the world that year—for being trans! Tori and other members of Rainbow Community Church attended the event in previous years. Tami asked for my help with graphic design, and I was happy to assist. TDOR was my first LGBTQ+ event with any political and social significance.

We marched half a mile down Hastings Street from the Carnegie Community Centre and Library to the Simon Fraser University downtown campus There, Tami welcomed the crowd and delivered a short speech before the name of each trans person killed in the previous 12 months was read, along with a description of how they died and in what city and country. It was a somber moment as we stood shoulder-to-shoulder with hundreds of trans persons and our allies.

As the crowd approached the entrance of the SFU building, I was randomly approached by a reporter for XTra Vancouver and asked why I was there. I responded that I had never heard of TDOR until that year and came to pay my respects after learning about the event and the number of trans people who were murdered.

That was the truth; it was the reason I was there. She then asked for permission to take my picture. I am embarrassed to say I appeared in their next edition, smiling like an idiot into the camera. I should not have been smiling. There was a glaring disconnect between the somberness and solemnity of the event, which I had just acknowledged, and my cheery expression. Had I been interviewed after the event, my countenance would have better reflected how heartbroken I was as the names of the dead were read.

The year 2010 ended with yet another course-changing event. Kathy Baldock put out a blogpost before Christmas titled "Genocide Brewing in Uganda," in which she described how the Ugandan Parliament was trying to pass the infamous law that the media had dubbed "Kill the Gays Bill." They wanted to execute persons convicted for the third time of a homosexual crime.

This bill was introduced in 2009 but ran the risk of not being passed before the current Parliament's term ended in March. Hence, there was a concerted effort on the part of the Conservative caucus to pass the bill in the remaining days. When I first heard of this inhumane-sounding bill, I remember shaking my head and saying, "I'm glad I don't live in Uganda." But after reading Kathy's blogpost, I was incensed. I called her and said, "What are we going to do? We have to do something!"

Chapter 14: A Whirlwind Introduction to Advocacy

I first became aware of the dire situation facing LGBTQ+ individuals in Uganda after reading the blogpost by Kathy Baldock on December 29, 2010. The reports of widespread discrimination and persecution, fueled by fundamentalist Christian influencers from North America, deeply shocked me.

In her blogpost, Kathy included links to reports from Amnesty International, Time Magazine, the BBC, CNN, and others. As I looked deeper into the situation, the more upset I became. I knew that I could not stay silent. Advocacy became a moral imperative for me, driven by a personal conviction for justice.

However, as a newcomer to this level of advocacy, I felt as if I got sucked into a vortex. I was unsure of where to begin.

14.1: Uganda's Kill the Gays Bill

I called Kathy and said, "What are we going to do? We have to do something!" It turned out that she had recently interviewed Bishop Christopher Senyonjo, who had been excommunicated from the Anglican Church of Uganda for his support of LGBTQ+ people, and Frank Mugisha, a Ugandan LGBTQ+ activist.

They were zig-zagging the U.S. to raise awareness of the issue. Kathy, too, was asking the same question, "What could we do to help?" They explained that the lawmakers promoting of the Kill the Gays Bill (KTGB) viewed all Western interference in Uganda's legislative process as a form of modern colonialism. They were not willing to take orders from anyone outside of Uganda.

The irony of this Ugandan posture was their double standard. On one hand, they viewed Western opposition to the KTGB as a form of modern colonialism. On the other, they were embracing the hateful anti-gay doctrine promoted by American fundamental-ists Scott Lively and Lou Engle. This demonstrated a concerning level of hypocrisy and highlighted the need to call them out on it.

The only threat that seemed effective was economic sanctions. Indeed, the Obama administration, Secretary of State Hillary Clinton, and many E.U. governments were already decrying the KTGB and threatening to cut crucial financial aid.

So, what if, instead of threats, we appealed to reason? That's when the idea to organize an international letter-writing campaign that reached every Member of Parliament came to me. I thought this could be more effective than an international petition drive, which not everyone who needed to get the message was likely to see.

I called my youngest son, who at the time was enrolled in an intensive new media diploma program where he was learning all the tricks of the trade. I asked how we could create a website to promote a letter-writing campaign to reach all the members of the Ugandan government. Could people click a button after entering their name and location and have the website generate all the individual emails?

His immediate response was a resounding NOPE. All those emails would be instantly flagged as spam. Well, I was only trying to think of a quick and easy way to flood the Ugandan lawmakers with letters from all over the world, hoping some of them would change their hearts and their votes. Instead of an automated mail generator, he suggested that all emails should come from the letter writer's own email address and mail server, making it harder for them to be flagged.

It was around noon on the 29th, and I didn't have much time. I called the domain hosting service I used for my work-related website and asked how quickly a new domain could be activated. They said it all depended on web volume and could take from as little as a few hours up to a couple of days. I asked them to register UgandaUrgentAction.com and to let me know as soon as I could upload content.

Next, I called my friend Duncan Holmes, the copywriter and briefed him on my plan. I asked him to write three different versions of the same letter that people could choose from and then cut and paste into an email. I also requested a longer fourth option that people could modify, or to use as an example to write their own letter.

After that, I spent seven hours extracting every single email from the official parliament website, where all the lawmakers were listed alphabetically. I ended up with close to 290 email addresses. The following morning, I created the website, and the home page explained what was going on in Uganda. If you scrolled down, you could see the three boilerplate letters Duncan had written.

Further down the page, all the email addresses were listed in four blocks. This was necessary because some email clients, for example, Gmail, have a limit on how many recipients can be addressed in one email. I appealed to people with the following headline: "Your emails could help make the difference between life and death for LGBTQ+ persons in Uganda," followed by "ACT NOW before it's too late. Please invest a few minutes of your time."

The process required eight steps and took less than five minutes to complete. However, I anticipated that some people would find it onerous. So, I added a disclaimer that explained the reason for the many steps. I said that if all the emails were sent from one mail server, they would quickly be filtered out as spam. Additionally, I reassured people that we were not collecting their name or email address, so they didn't have to worry about their privacy.

The domain host notified me that the site was live in less than 12 hours. I uploaded the content and sent out the link to every person on my contact list in an email that read something like: "Dear (friend), Thank you for your friendship and encouragement during this momentous year, 2010. I wish you a very Happy 2011, a year filled with good things. I have a New Year's wish, and I hope you can make it come true. Please click on the link below and add your voice to oppose the law the Ugandan Government is trying to pass, which you may have heard of. It is called "Kill the Gays Bill." We need to stop it."

While waiting for the site to go live, I also sent an open letter to the Parliament of Uganda, fully disclosing who I was. The letter read as follows:

Dear Sirs and Madames,

I am writing to express my concern for the proposed anti-gay legislation some of you are trying to pass that adds the death penalty to your existing laws that criminalize sexual orientation.

Mr. David Bahati, who introduced the bill, has based his position on discredited sources that erroneously and maliciously blame all dangerous behaviors toward children on gay people and declare that homosexual behavior can be eliminated.

I urge you to distance yourselves from those American fundamentalist Christian Right, anti-gay extremists who have descended on your country and are fanning their homophobic hate. Their agenda, if adopted, could have grave consequences for your country's human rights. They are not doing your country any favors.

I am a Christian myself. I am also a Transgender woman. I live in Canada and am grateful to live in a city and country that has allowed me to live without fear. Additionally, I am thankful to live in a day and age when the medical profession recognizes my condition and that there are medical professionals worldwide who have dedicated themselves to learning everything they can about how to help individuals like me live healthy and productive lives.

Even though gender identity and sexual orientation are two different things that must be understood and discussed separately, they have one thing in common. Neither of them is a choice. One does not choose to be gay or transgender any more than one chooses to be straight. It is, therefore, inhumane to single out those who don't happen to conform to the binary view of sexuality and then criminalize their personhood.

Additionally, to make it a crime not to report a gay person within twenty-four hours is beyond evil. To lay charges against family, friends, counselors, ministers, doctors, landlords, employers, and neighbors will turn your country into

a land full of suspicion, tyranny, and fear. Where can some-
one who is ostracized and persecuted for being deemed dif-
ferent turn for succor? How much more inhumane can laws
become?

In closing, please know that I will continue to uphold
your country in prayer and that the legacy of your tenure
as a Member of Parliament will be how you protected the
human rights, dignity, and diversity of all the citizens of
Uganda. Please repeal and abolish all laws that target any
minority group, including gay, lesbian, bisexual, and trans-
gender Ugandans.

Respectfully yours,
Lisa Salazar
Vancouver, Canada

After I shared the link to the UgandaUrgentAction website with friends on my contact list, Kathy Baldock, who had hundreds of followers, also posted it. It was New Year's weekend, so I didn't expect much action until Monday, January 3. But then I started receiving emails from people saying they had taken action.

The software I used to build the website was called Freeway Pro, and the software company was in the U.K. I sent them the link, which they immediately showcased in their electronic newsletter. This gave the campaign immediate international exposure, and I sensed that it was starting to snowball.

On Monday, I received a dozen replies from some of the recipients. About half were dismissive, but I was heartened to receive a letter from the Leader of the Opposition saying he and his party were fighting the bill's passage. The day's biggest surprise, however, was an email from a young Ugandan lawyer I will call Samuel.

In his email, Samuel confessed his lifelong struggle with his gender identity and expressed his desire to begin a mutually supportive correspondence with me. He also revealed that he worked in the Office of Presidential Affairs and had been asked to investigate the unprecedented number of emails that had been sent to government officials over the weekend.

Over the next few days, Samuel offered to send me notifications of when committees would be meeting to discuss the bill so that I could post the names of parliamentarians for people to send targeted emails. The proponents of the bill were hoping to get it passed before the current session ended, which was nearing its term. If it didn't pass, the bill would re-introduced in the next session.

Between the end of the 8th and the start of the 9th Parliament, Samuel and most government officials in Uganda were given time off work. He planned to spend a week visiting his mother in western Uganda and then driving to neighboring Kenya. We arranged for him to meet up with four Rainbow Community Church members doing humanitarian work in a remote village in western Kenya, about a nine-hour drive. They took precautions and planned to vet Samuel before fully embracing him, as they were also at risk of potential anti-LGBTQ+ sentiments.

14.2: The Unexpected Saga

There was much anticipation and excitement. We were going to make face-to-face contact with Samuel, but then all communications stopped. When my friends in Kenya and I realized we had lost touch with Samuel, I began scouring the online Ugandan news services and death notices, searching for any news of my missing friend. Samuel had told me the roads to his mother's village were dangerous and full of large potholes; I feared he might have had an accident. I even contacted the good Rev. Bishop Senyonjo, who was back in Kampala from his trip to the U.S. He began to make inquiries with his contacts in the police.

In one of my desperate Google searches, I found an obscure short video clip from 2008 in which Samuel is seen standing with two other persons in what appeared to be a photo opportunity.

I emailed the NGO that posted the video, requesting that they forward my contact information to anyone who might know Samuel.

A week later, I received an email from a young woman who had been sent my request. Cheryl (not her real name) wrote that she knew of me because Samuel had told her what we were doing. She said she was happy to make my acquaintance. Samuel had trusted her with his secret struggle with gender identity.

Cheryl referred to Samuel as Angie (pseudonym) and used female pronouns when referring to her friend. (For the rest of this story, I will use Angie instead of Samuel and use 'she' and 'her' pronouns.)

Cheryl told me what had happened to our friend, Angie.

While driving back from her mother's village to Kampala, she got a call on her cell phone; she was 15 minutes from home. An associate from work warned her not to go home because the Ugandan secret police, the State Research Bureau (SRB), were waiting at her apartment to arrest her. She drove to another friend's apartment and hid for several days.

Then her supervisor summoned her to the office. Still puzzled as to what was going on, she went in. She was handcuffed upon arrival and driven to her apartment. The SRB ransacked the apartment and confiscated her computers and passport.

Angie had inadvertently left a flash drive on her desk at work. A co-worker had found the flash drive and plugged it into his computer; he discovered close to 200 emails that Angie had saved. Every one of her emails to me and every email I had sent her was there. Based on those emails, Angie was arrested and charged with treason, promoting homosexuality, sabotaging government programs, leaking classified information to the government's enemies, and collaborating with international forces to destabilize the Government.

Angie was immediately taken to a military prison in Entebbe. She was beaten, tortured, and mercilessly humiliated from the beginning of April to the end of June. On many mornings they would strip her naked, then escort her handcuffed and shackled to the center of a prison yard filled with male prisoners, where she was mocked, "This man thinks he is a girl!"

Coincidentally, all this happened in the aftermath of the Arab Spring. Major riots and pro-democracy uprisings challenged the entrenched authoritarian regimes in North Africa and the Middle East. Riots had broken out in Kampala and other large population centers in Uganda after the election in February; hence, tensions were high in the Presidential suite. Therefore, much of Angie's interrogation centered on what she knew or whether she was part of a conspiracy to topple the government.

Of course, we didn't learn all these details until months later. Not even Cheryl knew any of these details. All she knew then was that Angie was being released to the custody of her uncle, a high-ranking government official. The terms were still being negotiated.

A couple of weeks later, Angie was taken to her mother's house under strict conditions, including reporting weekly to the SRB. Her right kneecap was shattered from being beaten with a metal rod, causing excruciating pain when she walked. While recovering, she received a warning from a friend that extrajudicial action would be taken against her.

Angie's close friends took her to a remote house in the jungle to hide from the agents and goons from the SRB. Cheryl became our communication channel and kept us updated. We suspected that Angie's release to her uncle's custody was a convenient way for the SRB to get rid of the problem without causing an outcry or political fallout.

We knew that the American Embassy in Kampala was aware of Angie's detention, and it would be difficult to explain if she were killed while in custody. It would be easier for them to orchestrate a random car accident or robbery gone wrong.

Those nearest to Angie knew they would not be able to hide her forever and that for her safety, she needed to escape Uganda and seek political and LGBTQ+ asylum. First, she had surgery on her right knee. It was performed by a doctor sympathetic to her plight.

Before learning about Angie's situation, I contacted a human rights advocacy group in San Diego with experience in Uganda to share information about the KTGB's progress. When I learned of Angie's arrest, I contacted the same group again since I knew they had a contact inside the U.S. State Department who could help with her escape and asylum from Uganda.

We formulated a plan for Angie's escape and asylum, which involved getting her to the U.S. Embassy in Nairobi, Kenya. Since her job in the Ugandan government qualified her for diplomatic asylum, we believed it was her best chance for protection.

After communicating the plans through Cheryl, Angie was moved at night to a location on the Uganda-Kenya border to avoid detection. She paid smugglers to take her into Kenya in a truck loaded with agricultural products and supplies.

Once in Kenya, she used her last money to buy a bus ticket to Nairobi. Angie arrived on a Friday at about 7 in the evening, which was morning for me in Vancouver due to the 11-hour time difference. But naturally, the American embassy was closed for the weekend. She had nowhere to stay and no idea where to find a safe place.

Angie called me from an Internet cafe in Nairobi, I was surprised by how quickly she had arrived and caught unprepared since we hadn't discussed contingencies, except that the American Embassy was expecting her at some point.

I wrote down the cafe's phone number and location and immediately went on Facebook to see if any of my Kenyan friends were online. I had made several friends connected to the Rainbow Community Church members who planned to meet Angie in April.

I found a young woman on my Messenger list who lived in Nairobi and had exchanged greetings with me on Facebook a few times. I messaged her, asking if she was available to help, and she replied, "Yes!"

Not wanting to reveal too much too soon, which could endanger Angie (the Kenyan secret police work in full cooperation with their Ugandan counterparts), I asked her if she might be willing to take a risk to help a total stranger; I told her this person was stranded in a Nairobi Internet cafe.

Then, I asked her if she had ever heard of a retired Anglican Chaplain who ran a ministry to help LGBTQ+ persons and organized HIV clinics throughout Kenya. I figured this man might know of safe houses for LGBTQ+ asylum seekers. Imagine my surprise when this Facebook friend said she knew of the man and they were friends. She was ready and willing to help and knew just what to do. Within 15 minutes of Angie calling me, her rescuers had already called the Internet cafe and told her they were on their way. An hour later, Angie was driven to a safe house ten miles outside of Nairobi, where she would remain in hiding for the next six weeks.

It took eleven more months to complete the processing of Angie's application for asylum in America. (And that was fast; she had initially been told the process could take up to three years.)

During those months, she moved from place to place, always in danger of being discovered and under the careful protection of new friends. Angie met with representatives of the U.S. Embassy, the United Nations High Commission for Refugees (UNHCR), and the Hebrew Immigration Aid Society (HIAS). She had to register with the Government of Kenya as a refugee and be certified as a bonafide refugee claimant by UNHCR and HIAS.

Unable to work, Angie was supported by donations from Rainbow Community Church, the human rights advocacy group in San Diego, and a grant from HIAS.

During those sometimes interminable and often frightening days, Angie began daring to hope she could make it safely to America. I promised Angie that I would be there to greet her when she first stepped off the plane onto American soil. This meant a great deal to Angie; she said it was the only thing keeping her going.

Mainly through the support of a couple of international NGOs that help with refugee resettlement, airfare, and safe passage out of Kenya was provided, Angie arrived in New York at noon on Tuesday, June 19. To thwart any possible interference from the Ugandan or Kenyan authorities, all details of her itinerary were kept strictly confidential; no one outside of a few operatives had any idea where in America she was being flown to, or when.

After a brief layover in New York, Angie finally arrived in San Diego, California at 8 p.m. As promised, I was there to greet her. With me was an amazing couple from the LGBTQ+-affirming church who had sponsored her; Linda and Rick offered to house Angie until she was resettled in the U.S. I will end Angie's incredible saga here for ongoing security and privacy reasons.

The number of individuals who took part in this incredible rescue, who need to be thanked for their role, is beyond measure. Many persons must be thanked and acknowledged in the U.S. State Department, the American Embassy in Kenya, the several NGOs, and persons willing to take risks on behalf of a friend and, in many cases, a total stranger.

There are hundreds, if not thousands, more LGBTQ+ persons living in fear worldwide today.

A postscript to this story is that I also contacted the Canadian Government. I sent the same letters of appeal as I had to the U.S. State Department but never received a response. Even though Canadian Prime Minister Stephen Harper had spoken out against the bill and its proposed death penalty for homosexuality, stating that it was a "vicious and hateful law" that had no place in the modern world, I heard crickets. This was very disappointing to me as Canadian.

The Kill the Gays Bill (KTGB) failed to pass before the end of the 8th Parliament. However, the bill's author was re-elected to the 9th Parliament and quickly reintroduced a new version. This new bill was passed with much acrimony and shouting in the chamber as the Madam Speaker celebrated the new law.

However, a few months later, the Bahati Kill the Gays Bill was invalidated by the Ugandan Supreme Court on the grounds of an unconstitutional parliamentary process. The court ruled that the bill was passed without the required quorum of at least one-third of the members of parliament present, violating the country's constitution. As a result, the bill was deemed null and void, and its provisions could not be enforced as law.

This decision was widely seen as a victory for human rights and the LGBTQ+ community in Uganda, who had opposed the bill due to its discriminatory and oppressive provisions.

Unfortunately, the failed KTGB created a climate of fear and violence for the LGBTQ+ community in the country that had already claimed the life of Uganda's foremost LGBTQ+ activist, David Kato, who was murdered at the end of January 2011. The bill gave a green light for vigilantes to commit crimes against people perceived to be LGBTQ+. The mere existence of the bill was used to justify acts of violence, intimidation, and discrimination against individuals based on their sexual orientation or gender identity. In some cases, LGBTQ+ individuals were publicly outed and harassed, leading to loss of employment, eviction from their homes, and, in severe cases, physical assault. The hostile atmosphere created by the proposed legislation contributed to increased human rights abuses against the LGBTQ+ community in Uganda, with many people living in fear for their safety and security today.

14.3: The Power of One

Doubling back to the first week of January 2010, when emails from all over the world filled my inbox as never before, and I was trying desperately to respond to them, my cell phone rang; the call came from an area code I did not recognize. "Hello, is this Ms. Lisa Salazar?" the African-accented caller asked. For security and privacy reasons, I will use a pseudonym again for the person in the story.

Joshua wanted me to meet him and his three friends as soon as possible. Could I come to meet them? When he told me he was calling from Boston, I told him it was highly improbable and explained that I was in Canada, on the other side of the continent, 4,000 kilometers away.

Joshua and his friends were gay men in their twenties. And, like many other Ugandan LGBTQ+ persons, they were trying to find a safe haven. A close friend of Joshua was a closeted lesbian Member of Parliament. In an amazing act of solidarity and kindness, she paid for their flight from Kampala to Boston and gave them my name and phone number. She instructed them to call me when they arrived.

As I was listening to Joshua tell me about their escape, that's when it hit me. I unwittingly included my cell number in the signature block of my Open Letter to Parliament. Yes, I agree — I was an amateur. The four arrived as tourists without any warm winter clothing. The temperature in Boston was hovering around freezing.

The young men only had enough money to buy food and pay for two more nights in a fleabag hotel. He told me that earlier in the day, they went to a church formed by Ugandan diaspora members in Boston, but the pastor damned them when he learned they were gay.

I talked with Joshua for a few minutes, confirmed his phone number and location, and told him I would call back within a half hour. I called Kathy Baldock, who had become my go-to person; she had so many connections. She told me about an online affirming church directory that listed congregations by city. She also gave me the phone number for Frank Mugisha, the Ugandan LGBTQ+ activist who was currently in Washington, D.C.; perhaps the two could connect.

I then called Frank Mugisha to get his permission to pass on his phone number to Joshua. I went online and found the six closest affirming churches to the hotel where Joshua and his friends were staying and called their listed phone numbers. I didn't expect anyone to answer at night, but I left them messages explaining the situation's urgency. Then I searched for the email addresses of all the pastors and sent them a joint email. That was all I could do, given that it was close to 11 p.m. on the East Coast. The earliest I expected any response was Saturday morning.

I called Joshua back within 30 minutes, as promised. He and his friends would need to stay put until further notice.

First one, then another, and eventually, all the pastors responded to my email. It turned out they all knew each other. Many ideas and strategies had been offered. Then, one said they should join forces, work together, and not duplicate efforts. They would take the lead and deal directly with Joshua and his friends.

One of the issues I had talked to Joshua about was their immigration status; they had arrived as tourists but were hoping to seek asylum. One of the churches had a member who worked for an NGO that offered immigration legal services. Before that weekend was over, these four young men had been given shelter and winter clothing and had an appointment with the pro-bono immigration lawyers the following week.

My last communication with the pastors in Boston left me feeling humbled and inspired. At the time, I was relatively new to Facebook and was a novice internet user, despite what you might think. That January was a watershed moment in my life. What would all of this advocacy and connecting with people have looked like without the internet?

Despite the rush I got from advocacy, earning a living was still top on my list. I was still taking on any graphic design project I could find, though the volume was much less than I had enjoyed before my transition. As I have gone back through my blog posts, I am surprised by the volume of words that poured out of me while still trying to keep the wolf from the door. I was also trying to stay on top of Angie's situation.

Do you remember the story I told about the reporter who

interviewed me at the Transgender Day of Remembrance event? She gave me her business card that might. I called her sometime in March 2010 and told her about the Uganda Urgent Action website and everything happening since I started the letter-writing campaign on New Year's Eve. At the time, Angie was still communicating with me and my friends in Kenya, who were anticipating her arrival and meeting her in person.

The reporter was Natasha Basrotti: she interviewed me again for Xtra-Vancouver. I stole her headline for the name of this chapter. Her piece was published on March 23, 2011, and this is what she said:

The Power of One
by Natasha Barsotti—March 23, 2011

It's almost three months since Lisa Salazar's UgandaUrgentAction website went live — New Year's Day 2011. There was no strategy, no "Aha!" moment behind its creation.

Its significance and success aren't easily measured, either, but Salazar's intent is basic: kill the "Kill the gays" bill. Get others involved in its execution.

"I don't have money; I can't go there and fight a battle, but I can raise awareness," she reasons. She's invested $80 to host the site and another 16 to 20 hours to manage it.

UgandaUrgentAction is a model of activism made simple: you visit, find your favorite of four-letter templates condemning the bill and address to all Ugandan MPs, cut and paste into an email, sign and send.

"If it causes one parliamentarian who has been supportive of the bill to question whether or not it's the right thing to do, and that person is able to cast enough doubt so that others begin to question the rationale, how can you put a value on that?" Salazar asks.

Her campaign ruffled the anti-gay feathers of Uganda's former ethics minister James Buturo, who actually replied — along the lines of, Mind your own Western business.

"What is important to us Ugandans," he writes back, "is

that we do something to stem the spread of homosexuality, which to Ugandans is abnormal and an abomination... as well as an affront to our values."

But then there was this, from Ugandan opposition leader Morris W. Ogenga-Latigo:

"I must greatly thank you for taking the initiative to fight for the rights of our own in Uganda," he writes. "There is so much moral pretension in our leaders, and they will sacrifice any life to show how good they are in the eyes of certain people.

"It is only the courage of people such as you that will humble them and shame them into not victimizing our own who never chose to be what they are."

Another opposition MP passed Salazar's cell number on to four gay Ugandans who fled to Boston in anticipation of state persecution, a lifeline that eventually led them to pro-bono immigration lawyers within days of their arrival.

That was the last Salazar heard, but she's convinced they got the help they needed.

"For me to be able to let Ugandans know they have a connection, to put them in touch with people, and ultimately help them in such a horrible situation — it's been a small investment."

Indulging in tired "that's appalling, that's horrible" small talk about Uganda was never an option. Neither was the privileged ugliness of "I'm glad I don't live there."

And then there's the government worker who precariously navigates a sensitive position but harbors the hope of transitioning one day — like Salazar.

"Dearest Lisa, Thank you for everything!" the worker writes. "I am happy you care about me and my safety and most of all you understand me. You are the first close confidant I have had in my whole life who touches the very central part of my being...

"Lately, I started contemplating about resigning my position... in order to concentrate my energies to a cause where I intrinsically feel that I am needed most.

"I am strongly considering that my personal input in trying to pass across the message of LGBT people in Uganda will ultimately make me free and also free those hundreds of thousands of other Ugandans boiling in the same pot with me....

"God bless you. I send you love and hugs."

14.4: Then This Happened

On March 30, 2011, I celebrated the first anniversary of my gender confirmation surgery. A few days later, Rachel left a letter on top of my computer keyboard, listing all the things we needed to do to get the townhouse ready for sale. The list included replacing the carpeting, windows, and door trim and painting the laundry room. That is how I learned that she had decided to leave the marriage, and this was her way of telling me. She left the letter when she left for work earlier that morning, and I was stunned.

I called her at work, but she said we would talk when she got home that night. Looking back, it was good that we didn't talk immediately, as I had time to consider how challenging the situation had been for Rachel. I appreciated how she waited until I was fully healed before telling me her decision. I surmised that her decision had been made much earlier, perhaps even before my surgery. When we finally spoke face to face, she said that I was no longer the person she had married, and it was up to me to divorce her since I was the one who had "nullified" the contract.

British Columbia's relatively straightforward system allowed for a no-lawyer uncontested divorce. I went to the courthouse to initiate the process and learned that if both parties file together, it saves time, as much as a couple of months. We decided to wait until all the work on the townhouse was complete, and we had listed it with a realtor. Fortunately, we sold the house for more than the asking price, and after paying off the mortgage and loans, we split the proceeds in half and went our separate ways.

I moved in with two members of Rainbow Community Church, sharing a house not far from where Rachel and I had lived. It was time to settle into a new life as an older single trans woman.

All this happened days before Kathy Baldock and I took a trip to North Carolina. Going to Charlotte and continuing the efforts to get Angie safely to the United States helped distract me from my own problems, but my woes were not over.

In September, I received a call from the president of the restaurant chain that was my biggest client, accounting for almost half of my income. The stress in his voice was palpable; he had bad news to share.

The chain had more than thirty locations, mostly franchisees, and as they grew, the franchisees wanted to advertise on television. They were jealous of a competing chain that had a heavy presence on TV and wanted to use their marketing dollars to buy airtime.

However, my colleague Duncan and I had already explained that their advertising budget was too low for a comparable television campaign. They could afford one or two weeks of commercials at most, and even then, the frequency would have to be reduced.

We advised them to loosen their purse strings and increase their contributions to the marketing fund, but they were not pleased with our response. The issue had been discussed at every monthly planning meeting, and several advertising agencies had been invited to pitch for the account.

Duncan and I had given them approximate costs for producing one, two, or three different commercials for rotation, but the ad agencies wanted complete creative control over all internal and external marketing. As a result, Duncan and I were made redundant.

The only consolation was that my rent and share of the electricity, gas, cable, and internet were under $800 monthly. And I had opted for early Canada Pension retirement benefits when I turned 60, which covered my rent. The reduced income from graphic design would be enough to buy food, pay for car insurance, and all my other expenses. I didn't want to touch the money from the sale of the house and turned it over to the financial group that managed my parents' investments.

I started searching for new clients and or graphic design jobs on every job search platform I could find; Craigslist, Workopolis, Indeed, Linkedin, Glassdoor, WorkBC, and ZipRecruiter. I also searched in Charity Village for non-profit organizations looking for a graphic designer. I registered with every local government job board and started applying for every new posting I discovered. Sometimes six or more per day, but mostly one or two.

2011 ended with another low blow to my confidence. Someone posted a long and scathing review of my book on Amazon; he would not be the only one. But this review helped me learn a valuable lesson; you never know what lies behind the rhetoric. In a surprising twist, the unsympathetic reviewer came out to me. Here is how it happened.

I don't know if other authors ever attempt to connect with their critics or if they take the good reviews with the bad and go on their way. Is there a protocol for this? As I said, I don't know. Finding this reviewer's email address was relatively easy through his Amazon profile. I believe my email to him was polite, but I expressed disappointment with what he said about the book.

One of the things he said about me was that I used much self-justification for my decisions, to which I countered that it had taken me almost ten years to reconcile my faith with the diagnosis I received at the gender clinic. Admittedly, I said, the last third of the book deals with this process, and it does have 'religious' undertones because, after all, my faith is important to me, and I was not going to gloss over it in my book. Equally important, I was not going to park my brain on the shelf.

He responded the following day, and it took me by surprise. The negativity in his review did not sit well with him either, and even before he received my message, he had already removed his review from Amazon. He was sincerely sorry for having said the things he did and proceeded to say how much he respected my journey and my courage.

The funny thing is that his review threw me into a funk that lasted a couple of days, during which I licked my wounds and did some soul-searching. Who was I in the first place to publish a book and think it would be helpful to anyone? What in the world was I thinking? And now that the deed was done, why was I feeling sorry for myself? All of this questioning prompted me to write him in the first place.

His response to my email left me feeling somewhat vindicated but, more importantly, humbled. It turned out that this person, too, was trans. But instead of transitioning as I had, he swallowed his own medicine of abstention. From the photo in his profile, I surmised we were close in age. He shared that as much as he wanted to transition, he chose instead to devote his attention to helping others by trying to understand gender dysphoria, hence his insatiable interest in the subject. He had become a licensed marriage and family therapist in private practice, so my hat goes off to him. Did he call me courageous? Well, that is what I call him now. I was not strong enough to choose his remedy abstention for myself. Not all trans stories have the same ending, do they?

I learned that rhetoric, at times, can be a smokescreen. My basic instinct was to either run away and sulk or lash out without weighing my words. I needed to learn to consider the possibility that those who attack may themselves be hurting, and I need to remind myself of this more often. Instead of taking a defensive posture, I need to be willing to pray for my 'enemies.'

Chapter 15: Connecting More Dots

Kathy laughs when she recalls my conversation with her and teases me about it. I told her I had this notion that after my surgery at the end of March 2010, I hoped to live a life in quiet anonymity, flying under the radar, a private person who would not have to be talking about where I came from, that I had been a man, etc. Only my family and those who already knew me would know this about me. For everyone else, it was none of their business.

She laughs when she points out that if that is what I envisioned, I had gone about it wrong. One doesn't accept an invitation to address several-hundred people to tell them about their life, and one certainly does not write a biography that reveals all the details.

Ah, yes, this autobiography. I mentioned that I sat on the manuscript for a year before publishing it. During that time, I used the manuscript to answer the numerous questions people were asking me, such as: When did I know I was trans? How did I tell my sons? How long did it take the hormones to work? People were genuinely curious, even if their questions were personal; given that I was the only trans person they knew, I was okay with answering them.

About 18 people read the manuscript with the understanding that it was for their eyes only. And they were to add comments, help catch and correct typos, and send the file back to me. Every time I share the manuscript with a different person, I sent them the latest revised version. The most consistent feedback I received was that I needed to publish it, often followed by "It could save lives."

Having my story in a Word file proved helpful in another way. It was less emotionally draining than answering friends' questions in person and reliving the angst, confusion, and trauma that would inevitably get triggered.

Around the middle of July, I received a call from Brody Levesque, a syndicated veteran journalist who at the time was based in Washington D.C. Earlier that week, I had responded to a comment he made on Facebook to one of Kathy Baldock's posts. Being the curious journalist that he is, he asked his researchers to find out who I was because he had seen my name mentioned several times by Kathy in relation to Uganda.

Brody didn't mince words; it was a sobering conversation. He asked me if I knew the names James Dobson, Tony Perkins, and a few others. I said, "Yes, these men lead various Conservative Right Wing anti-LGBTQ+ Christian organizations." "You are now their enemy," Brody said, adding: "You have three sons, you live on East 58th Ave. in Vancouver, and your phone number is XXX-XXX-XXXX. You were born in Colombia and have been a Canadian citizen since 1977 [Etc...]. My team learned all these things about you in just a few minutes. If we could do it, anybody can. I am calling to warn you that your life could get complicated. These groups used tactics like getting people placed on no-fly lists; they did this in California to the supporters of same-sex marriage. Don't be surprised if you are kept from getting on a flight the next time you want to go somewhere. And let me tell you, once you are on one of those lists, it can take a long time to clear your name."

Brody suggested I write a letter to the Vancouver Chief of Police and the Superintendent of the RCMP in British Columbia and to CC my elected members in Parliament and Canadian Senate documenting who I was, what I have been doing, vis-à-vis Uganda. He said to request that my name be put on the list of people whom extremist groups might target. I didn't know there was such a list. He assured me there was. Brody explained that if I ever needed to dial 911 for help, my name would be flagged, saving a lot of time for the dispatcher. Finally, he insisted I call my sons and warn them that they may also find themselves on a no-fly list; even progeny could be targeted.

That was an ominous and unnerving call. I did everything Brody suggested and crossed my fingers as I boarded my first flight to the U.S. as Lisa a month later when I flew to be with Kathy for the next adventure.

As I shared earlier in chapter 13, Kathy Baldock and I flew to Charlotte, NC, to stand up to the fundamentalist preacher Michael Brown. In the blogpost I wrote shortly after, I connected the dots between what was taking place in Uganda, and in the U.S.

Condensed from Blogpost, August 31, 2011
15.1: Look at Who's to Blame
"Connecting the Dots"

There is something unfortunate that tied Uganda and North Carolina together. What they both had in common, unfortunately, was how a fundamentalist anti-gay preacher from the U.S., Lou Engle, had inspired what took place. Engle was best known for his leadership of The Call, an association with prominent members of the Christian Right. But he was also one of the American fundamentalists responsible for inspiring and fueling the homophobia that gripped Uganda, culminating in the proposed "Kill The Gays Bill," Scott Lively was the other.

Lou Engle's connection with the Charlotte Pride event was one of record. He was buddy-buddy with an equally fundamentalist preacher from Charlotte, Dr. Michael Brown. This preacher was the author of "A Queer Thing Happened to America." His book was a compilation of allegations and accusations of the LGBTQ+ community's purported "Gay Agenda."

It is worth noting that despite the origin of the phrase "Gay Agenda" not being clear, the term gained widespread usage in the 1990s, particularly among conservative and religious groups, to describe what they perceived as a political and social agenda aimed at promoting LGBTQ+ rights and acceptance. The term was often used to criticize efforts to promote LGBTQ+ equality as a threat to traditional values and norms. They honed the art and used it to their political and financial advantage, for there was no gay agenda. Yes, folks, the "Gay Agenda" is a tool used by Evangelical Christians preachers and politicians. Using the term magically generates much cash for their political coffers and support for their political goals.

This Charlotte preacher/author first organized an action

group called "God Has a Better Way" (GHABW) in 2009 to protest that year's Charlotte Pride Event. They aimed to share the "love of 'Jeeesus" with the lost." (Emphasis mine) I don't know much about how effective their efforts were that year, but Brown saw an opportunity to invade that year's Charlotte event since it took place in a public square for the first time. In previous years, Charlotte Pride had been celebrated in a private recreation area, where anyone disrupting the event could be removed for trespassing.

Brown was sad because his friend, Lou Engle, would not be able to join him and the hundreds he hoped to recruit to invade the event. Engle had prior commitments. "Kingdom business" kept Him away, according to Brown. I would rephrase it as it was the Kingdom's business to keep him away. Maybe that is all that needs to be said to give you an idea of this preacher's fundamentalistic perspective and motivations. Lou Engle and he were like two pees in a pod. Back to Kathy. She was incensed when she learned about this planned action in Charlotte and who was behind it. A few months earlier, she had done a thorough, scathing review of this man's homophobic book, guaranteeing her a place as a target in this man's shooting gallery.

Kathy had gone to the Facebook page created by Brown to recruit his army of invaders. They planned to march in wearing red T-shirts emblazoned with big white letters that said: "God Has a Better Way."

After Kathy made several comments to their posts, the page administrator deleted them and blocked her within minutes. Kathy then called or emailed me, I don't remember which, but she said: "Hey, Lisa; you gotta see what 'Brown' is saying about trans persons; it's horrible. I tried commenting, but I'm blocked. But he doesn't know you; go get him!"

I went to their website to read what they stood for and what they were saying, and then to the group's Facebook page. I clicked on the "Like" button to comment on posts. I could not let this man get away with his comments and views on trans persons, which I had read on the GHABW website.

I was polite but critical and expected to see my comment deleted. Instead, the page administrator replied and thus began a lengthy exchange between "them" and me. A few posts into the exchange, this chameleon showed his true color. It was brown. (Pun intended.) He was the page administrator; he and I were communicating.

Our back-and-forth exchange on Facebook went on for four days. Kathy and I created a blogpost where we copied and pasted the comments. It was close to 20,000 words long. I ended my long exchange on Facebook with Brown when I accidentally tapped on send instead of the backspace/delete key on the tiny iPhone keyboard; I was mid-sentence. (I was still learning how to use my new iPhone.) Frustrated, I was about to delete my comment, but then I thought, no. There is nothing more to say; "I'm done!" The back and forth between us had run its course, and there was nothing more to say. I knew Brown would not be swayed, and I had accomplished what Kathy and I had hoped; to go over his shoulder and speak to his audience and devotees.

Had I not accidentally tapped the send key when I was starting to give a lengthy response to his last comment, who knows how much longer this exchange would have gone? He had said that if he was wrong, he would have to humble himself, confess his sin to God, and seek to make right what he had made wrong. However, if I was wrong, not only would I have to do all the above, but I would have to leave "Lisa" behind, go back to my male identity, stop taking hormones, reverse whatever I could surgically (where and if possible) — to mention the most obvious.

He said all this in rebuttal to remarks I made about Jesus' words regarding eunuchs in the Gospel of Matthew. He prefaced the above with, "After all, dealing with LGBT issues does not define who I am, and it is only a facet of the ministry work that God has called me to, whereas these issues, in many key ways, define who you are and why you have done what you have done." My incomplete comment on that thread was, "Many more important passages define me."

The exchange was read by many, and Kathy posted several times telling people to check out what was going on, resulting in even more people reading it. Then, Charlotte Pride organizers, many of them LGBTQ+ Christians, pleased with what was happening on

Facebook, extended a warm welcome to Kathy and me to join them in Charlotte, to stand with them, and present a different Jesus message.

Neither Kathy nor I had the financial resources to hop on a plane, nor could we afford the land transportation and hotel costs. Kathy posted a request for travel points and money donations, and within a few hours, people from Wisconsin to California came through. To Kathy and me, this was confirmation that we needed to be there that weekend.

When I first commented on the GHABW Facebook page, I had 75 friends. A week later, I had over 500, and they were still coming. I received hundreds of heart-warming supportive, and appreciative messages sent worldwide.

Now, do you see why Kathy laughs at my dispelled notion of being a private person after my surgery?

I admit some of my earlier comments and taunts concerning this man are inflammatory and childish, but he pushed too many buttons I didn't know I had. Yep, this advocacy thing was all new to me, and it surprised me as much as anyone who knew me before. I had never been compelled to speak out, never mind do it loudly. I don't know where it comes from, except to say I was stirred to act by how I saw some "Christians" blindly think that the "love of Jeeesus" in them gave them the right to judge and condemn others, especially trans persons. I could not stay silent.

On our flight back to the west coast, Kathy and I spent much of the flight back debriefing each other and comparing notes, studying photos and videos we had taken. Her account jived. What we saw and experienced was very surreal. This is what I remember:

We learned Brown's army had organized a rally for its troops before marching into the Charlotte Pride event decked out in red T-shirts with the "God Has a Better Way" graphics. Kathy and I watched from a block away. The experience was no different than watching a high-school pep rally before a football game or, worse yet, a tribe preparing for a hunting expedition. Getting the sour taste out of my mouth took a while.

The worship leader would call out, "Let me hear you!" "Louder!" etc., as he tried to raise the pitch. I vowed right then and there never to use worship in this way. I had always believed that when we worship, we have an audience of one, God. Here worship was being used to pump up the troops and to get noticed. It was loud, and the worship time ended with the chorus of one particular refrain repeated for close to five minutes, like a broken record, as it got louder and louder.

After the short motivational speech by Brown, he asked the two hundred participants to turn and raise their hands toward the city and shout, "Liberty! Freedom!" It was strange; to whom were they shouting out? The Pride Event was more than four blocks away, and the nearest building was the empty NASCAR Hall of Fame across the street. He then turned the microphone to one of his assistants, who explained the "rules of engagement." I kid you not; in their minds, they were marching into battle. Lovingly, of course.

After invoking God, they marched into the city square carrying bottled water to bless people with, flyers promoting a Christian music concert that night, and a "The Rainbow Promise" handout that 'lovingly" explained how God has a better way.

A bit of backstory: I have mentioned Kathy Baldock a lot; let me tell you more about who she is and what Canyonwalker Connections is all about. I will explain. Kathy is a straight, Evangelical Christian woman who, since about 2005, began to reach out to the LGBTQ+ community, particularly the Christian LGBTQ+ community and affirming churches, to help restore the breach between them and the church at large. She began attending San Francisco Pride wearing a T-shirt that said, "Hurt by Church? Get a Straight Apology." She explains this started a fire in her soul that could not be doused, thanks to the many heart-wrenching stories of judgment and exclusion she heard, and all the tears shed in the process. In 2014, she published "Walking the Bridgeless Canyon: Repairing the Breach Between the Church and the LGBTQ+ Community." It is in its second edition, along with study guides for personal or group use.

At the Charlotte Pride event, Kathy donned her famous T-shirt. She brought enough for several Charlotte straight Christians, who engaged people one-on-one with the message of inclusion and affirmation. She also provided information and links for finding welcoming churches in the area. Since I could not wear the "Straight

Apology" shirt for obvious reasons, I made my own.

We knew they had produced a colorful handout titled "The Rainbow Promise," which they promoted on their website and Facebook page. I drew a facsimile of it on the back of a white T-shirt. On the front: "I Will Be Happy to Recycle the Rainbow Promise Handout" and walked around with a large, black garbage bag. I gave myself the job of collecting the cards that people dropped, littering the street.

When I saw anyone carrying a card, I asked them if they wanted to depart with it. Many hadn't bothered to examine what it said, but when I pointed out the message, they could not dispose of the cards fast enough. The colorful card directed them to a website that preached condemnation to gays, lesbians, bisexuals, and trans persons; so much for sweet talk.

Besides the GHABW group, there was a group of vitriolic street preachers whom Kathy opined were the worst example of how to reach people for God. No doubt the red army was happy these hateful preachers were drawing so much attention and jeering responses, they, the red shirts, could at least say they "were loving" by comparison. I would not be surprised if some were secretly glad these street preachers gave it to the gays.

Kathy was so angry at the language and verbal attacks being spewed out that she decided her place at this event would be to stand in front of these preachers and run interference while simultaneously speaking to anyone she sensed needed to hear her message. Seeing young people break down in tears of joy and gratitude was intense and amazing. Since her return home, in just a few days, she had already received many emails from these people, wanting to engage with her some more.

Another personal note: this event taught me an important lesson. I confess that I had never felt comfortable around drag queens. This was especially true when I began the disclosure process in October 2007. I saw drag queens as a liability as I hoped to blend into society since many people assumed that trans people were nothing more than drag queens or might expect me to look like one of them. The other admission is that I had never attended a pride event for these reasons since the drag queen thing was so high profile and overdone to me.

As I walked around collecting the GHABW garbage, I saw a group of trans ladies that I assumed were drag queens, and this is how I learned my lesson. By the time the red army had retreated to their base, I was under a lot of conviction about my attitude toward these ladies. I finally got the courage to approach them, and I introduced myself. I asked their names and told them I was down from Canada for this event and had come with the "#str8apology" lady playing interference in front of the street preachers.

I asked them if they could each tell me what their life was like living in North Carolina. What they shared with me broke my heart. They not only loved Jesus, but they also had valid reasons for looking the way they did. These women were not dragged queens! They were persons who, due to the discrimination against trans persons, would have everything to lose, their jobs, their homes, their friends—everything. And on top of that, they feared their families would reject them, and so too their churches.

So they would need to continue living as men, not daring to take risks. Social and medical transition was out of the question; coming to the pride event was their only way to feel authentic for a brief moment. Yes, with their undeniably male features, they may have been all too conspicuous, but they were lovely. I realized how wrong I had been for keeping my distance when they were my sisters in this battle.

Blogpost, July 3, 2013
15.2: The Barking Dogma In My Back Yard
"Tucked Inside My Bible I Found This Letter"

I returned to Vancouver, and it took me a long time to process everything I saw and experienced. I must admit that beneath my stoic exterior, I was hurting. Brown posted his views and opinions of how things turned out, boasting about the success of what they had done.

Brown also had a syndicated radio call-in show on a network of fundamentalist radio stations. His show could also be streamed. In his following Monday episode, he said some very demeaning things about me; it was a personal attack. Kathy and I had run into him as he paraded through the crowd with a more petite man at his side. I'm guessing Brown had to be 6'4" tall; he stood out. We exchanged a few pleasantries, but I could see him sizing Kathy and me up; he looked so pompous with his chest out and his Teddy Roosevelt mustache, the "general."

In his fundamentalist way of thinking, I realized he would say that the pain I was experiencing from his attacks on me and all trans people was the "the Holy Spirit of God convicting my heart."

I learned many lessons from my first-ever pride event. Ironically, I didn't need to travel 4,000 kilometers to find myself in a fundamentalist's cross-hairs. In early September, I received a letter from a friend, a retired mechanic with whom I had been part of a men's Bible Study for nearly twenty years. After reading it, I stuck it inside my Bible and forgot about it—until several years later. I discovered it while unpacking after my recent move. At the time, I symbolically shook the dust from my sandals and moved on. All of this man's arguments align with what Brown said in one way or another in that long exchange we had on Facebook.

Note: This old friend didn't use my name in the letter and instead used the initial for my former male name in brackets (J), nor did he begin with a salutation. He also didn't sign the letter or include a return address. I'm sure his heart was in the right place and was thinking of what's best for me, once you strip the paint off, his letter was deeply hurtful and transphobic. While I understand the importance of confronting one another when necessary, it is not an excuse to attack someone's identity and use religion as a weapon. This behavior drives people away from faith and causes deep wounds in the LGBTQ+ community.

Sept 2011
A Little Leaven
Confronting a brother about his lifestyle in a self-righteous spirit is never called for; however, we are told to care for one another, even if it calls for hard love; otherwise, we will be held responsible, We may not get a hearing, but we have done what God required of us according to scripture.

(J) are you sure your feet are still on the right path, or have you been somewhat deceived? I fear for your soul; you have exchanged the Truth for a Lie.

(J) I feel I can talk frankly to you as you and I sat in the same bible study for, is it not 20 years?

Jesus says: "There is a way that seems right to man, but the end thereof is destruction" also"...

(J) fear not, I have redeemed and called you by your name; you are mine."

(J) it still stands; turn back while you still can to embrace your heritage, God's gift, before you are completely taken in and unable to escape.

Jesus also said: "I am the way, the truth, and the life." Perhaps many years ago, your mother read those words to you. (J) stop and consider what you are doing, If you are struggling against the Truth, then it is Jesus Himself you are struggling against, and He is sure to win, so where do you think that lands you? Too terrible to think.

The enemy will seek to lead you into the wilderness, a castaway, forever separated from God. Yes, he can take away our will to even listen to God speaking to us in His Word, and to aid us in misinterpreting The Word, even to give us a sense of peace, all counterfeit, but how terrible the end thereof; for if we don't acknowledge before God that we have sinned, and strayed from His will, until then we are truly lost without Him.

The promise of Jesus is: "Anyone who comes to Me I will in no way cast out."

So let us never categorize sins as great or small, as the little ones may, according to the principle of the way leaven works, at some point exceed the greater ones, anything not laid bare before God, but hidden in the form of sins, will be manipulated by the enemy.

We must never forget we are all sinners and prone to wander, but "He is able to save to the outermost those who came to God through Him" Heb:7:25. Jesus will not let go if we once came to him. So on the journey here, we must be transparent to one another, honest and loving in our concerns, and never hesitate to ask a brother, are you sure you are right with God?

Also, there is a wide road, many walk on it, and a narrow way, and only a few find it... "

It is too dangerous to exercise liberalism regarding God's warnings lest we stray from the narrow way. I believe this is how a little leaven left hidden in our hearth may work in spiritual life. Reluctantly at first, we may half accept something that we know is clearly against God's will. Perhaps we reason; it is accepted by most.

We struggle along at first but eventually tolerate it and soon even defend IT. As we go on, it seems right; however, is that not a spirit of error that has taken root? Soon we even start defending it out of sympathy. Our feelings versus God's judgments literally means we are striving against the Truth. The leaven has now invaded the whole lump, and we are now ready to completely"...exchange the Truth for a lie," at last accepting it as completely normal.

What we hid from God in our hearts when we gave our life to Jesus turned out to be a "baby monster!" To fail and fall into sin is one thing, but to willfully wrestle against Jesus would be the most terrible mistake on our part, as God's wrath is sure to crush such a one, and surety of hell to follow. Stop and consider while it is not too late...anyone who comes to me (J) will never be cast out. " God's Word cannot be compromised by human sympathy.

If this friend had included his return address, this is what I would have liked to have said to him (after counting backwards from 1000 and doing some deep-breathing exercises):

Dear [Friend],

Thank you for taking the time to express your concerns and share your perspective on my life choices. While I understand that your intention is to help me, I respectfully disagree with your interpretation of my journey and your understanding of God's will.

I would also like to address the anonymity of your letter and the use of my pre-transition initials. I kindly ask that you respect my identity and use my chosen name in future communication. Our faith teaches us to love and accept everyone, regardless of their path in life. My journey has led me to deeper self-discovery and connection with the divine, and I am at peace with my choices.

Sincerely,
Lisa

When I received the anonymous letter, I had already shed many of my dogmatic ideas and views. In fact, a previous incident at the "men's" Bible study group contributed to this change. After I came out and began my transition, I said goodbye to the group and didn't plan to return.

However, I received a call from a retired dermatologist who invited me back to the group. During my second visit, a man who attended infrequently reacted negatively to my presence and started to judge and criticize me. He even used Bible verses to admonish and instruct me. He came close to cursing me and calling me an "abomination."

In response, I said, "I'm sorry that I upset you, but none of what you have said even comes close to what I said for years as I cursed and damned myself. I'm free from that now. I am at peace with myself and with God." I don't know if he was more troubled by what I said or that I said it with a grin.

In any case, this experience made me appreciate that some of my previous relationships with people who held dogmatic beliefs needed to be bid farewell. I was committed to living authentically and being true to myself, even if that meant letting go of certain relationships.

Chapter 16: A Different of Focus

The year 2011 was a challenging year for me. It marked the end of my almost thirty-seven-year marriage, making Christmas and the year-end festivities unbearable. I was most grateful to my friends, especially my immediate family, for their sensitivity and love during those difficult days.

Kathy Baldock's blogpost about Uganda had spurred me on to advocacy, a new experience for me. The stories of persecution, beating, and killing of LGBTQ+ persons in Uganda were saddening and heartbreaking.

Though advocating for others did not remove the sting of my own experiences, it helped me see my life in a larger context.

It was the middle of May 2011, and I still knew nothing about Angie's whereabouts. She was missing. About that time, Kathy Baldock invited me to be one of the directors for her recently registered non-profit, Canyonwalker Connections. She told me she had been praying for the right person to represent trans persons and that my name kept coming to her mind.

What did 2012 hold in store? Concerning Uganda's Kill the Gays Bill, as I summarized above, had been ruled unconstitutional by Uganda's Court. A third version of the Bill had been tabled in Parliament, but it was stalled due to international pressure. That was small comfort, given the intensely homophobic mood of the politicians and the country.

Homosexuality had been illegal since colonial times, and Ugandans and other Africans had come to believe that homosexuality was an import from the west. Ugandans had been convinced there was a sinister gay conspiracy to recruit Ugandan children into the homosexual lifestyle with money and expensive toys. They believed their traditional family values were under attack and they had to take action, with or without a law. And Angie was still in asylum limbo, awaiting approval from the U.S. State Department.

These are the thoughts I wrote in a blogpost that captures where I was in my spiritual and social evolution as of January 2012:

The New Year did start on a hopeful note for me. I attended the Gay Christian Network (GCN) conference in Orlando, Florida. Kathy Baldock had participated in the GCN annual conferences for several years and was one of the organization's staunch straight allies. Kathy encouraged me to attend and to propose a workshop. She had opined that folks at GCN needed to learn about trans people. She was right.

Getting Serious About the 't' in 'LGBTQ+

I want to draw attention to the realities of being trans and discuss the challenges and opportunities of being trans-friendly as individuals and as a group, like GCN, which had historically been mostly an enclave of gay, then later, included lesbians.

GCN was not the only gay-friendly organization that described itself as LGBTQ+-welcoming. Unfortunately, the sad fact was that many of those organizations only paid lip service to the "T" in the equation. Trans representation was almost non-existent in their membership and on their boards. Of the four hundred-plus people attending that year's GCN event, I only counted four trans persons. I was one of two trans women, and there were also two trans men. This is not the ratio of trans persons to the general population. I should have seen ten times as many trans persons, given that LGBTQ+ persons are about 5 to 7% of the population in the first place.

It raised the question, why were so few trans persons in attendance, and why were so few trans persons part of LGBTQ+ groups, both secular and religious? The answer was evident to me; I suspected trans persons tended to prefer anonymity for very valid reasons. As I saw it, we fell into one of three sub-groups: those who are closeted out of fear; those who transition but choose the live private and hidden lives; and those who reach a level of social and personal 'congruence' and are free to be themselves. And for those who achieve this third level, the hope is to no longer see and refer to oneself as a trans man or woman but simply as a man or a woman.

Hence, the need to be identified with other trans persons or with the LQBTQ+ community is a low priority or a non-issue for them.

Note: In 2012, Non-Binary (enby) identities and society's understanding had not yet reached widespread social consciousness. At the end of chapter 20, I will share some lessons I've learned about enby identities and the evolving and emerging terminology.

How could an organization like GCN reach out to trans persons if trans persons valued and protected their anonymity? In many respects, most of the fears and needs of lesbians, gays, and bisexuals (LGB) are shared by trans persons. The big difference being an L, G, or B does not require making any external, visible changes to one's appearance, as is the case for trans persons.

Additionally, when one comes out as LGBTQ+ to the world, only the Ts will have to deal with society's impositions and demands if they want to exist in society. You'll need to change your name legally and update birth certificates and all government identification, including passport and driver's license, to name a few. You must request updated diplomas and professional credentials to keep your job or apply for new employment.

After coming out, if you have an emergency requiring hospitalization or you have to go to work or school, if you are LGB, you're not likely to experience any barriers. There won't be any direct ramifications. But if you have come out as T, your gender presentation will be expected to match your gender identity in a way that satisfies the observer, and if there are incongruences, your world could be turned upside down.

As I write this, I recognize that I am privileged. Though I also hoped to go through life in stealth mode as a woman, I am openly trans. That does not mean that when meeting someone, I announce that I used to exist as a man, for that is none of their business. However, I cannot erase my past, nor do I want to. I was a good husband and tried to be a good dad although at times I felt like I was dying slowly on the inside as I struggled with my gender identity.

Like every LGBTQ+ person that I have had the privilege to meet and talk to, I prayed daily for G-d to make me normal, knowing it would take a miracle. The miracle never came; the longer I lived, the more defeated I felt. Was I not praying correctly?

I came to faith in Jesus Christ when I was almost twenty-one. I honestly expected God to heal me somehow. One would think that falling in love with a devoted Christian girl, marrying her, and fathering three children should have done the magic and taken away the dysphoria. My faith kept me from self-destructive stuff, but it produced mountains of guilt. I spiritualized my struggle, which is not a bad thing to do under most circumstances. However, this prevented me from accepting the diagnosis I received after six months of assessment by the gender clinic at Vancouver General Hospital in 1999. It was not until 2006 that I could reconcile my faith to my diagnosis, and now, forty years after my conversion, I find myself living as a woman.

Why did God not "heal" me? And why was the "cure" for such a private and personal struggle so exposed and public? Don't you think I would have preferred it if God had quietly snapped His finger and corrected my gender identity? You bet.

Every LGBTQ+ person I know will echo a similar lament if you ask them. Yet, in God's silence, or call it unwillingness to grant our wishes, perhaps there is an answer. Maybe God views our gender identity and sexual orientation differently from what we have been led to believe by Bible teachers who claim to speak for God and condemn LGBTQ+ persons in the process. May God doesn't see anything that needs fixing.

Condensed from January 14, 2012 Blogpost
16.1: The Exodus Empire Crumbles
"Bump in the Road or a Seismic Event?"

The issue of whether it is possible for people to change their sexual orientation has been a topic of debate for many years. Many organizations, such as Exodus International, claim that they can help people change their sexual orientation. However, the effectiveness of such programs has been called into question by many who have gone through them and not experienced the promised change.

At this year's conference, GCN invited Alan Chambers, the president of Exodus International, to speak. This decision has been controversial, with some members of GCN feeling betrayed or hurt by Exodus and unwilling to accept any apology for their pain. However, Justin Lee, Executive Director of GCN, spoke of the need for reconciliation between Chambers and those who have gone through the Exodus program and not experienced a change in their orientation as promised.

I believe that opening dialogue with Chambers is a step in the right direction, but there needs to be a change in tactics and ideology if not a complete abandoning of false ideas and programs. While Chambers has admitted that 99.9% of people who go through the Exodus program do not experience the promised change, some may still believe that homosexuality is a choice and that change is possible. This is a dangerous belief, as it can lead to discrimination and harm against LGBTQ+ individuals.

Chambers' admission also calls into question the claims made in Uganda by proponents of the "Kill the Gays Bill" that it is possible for people to leave the "homosexual lifestyle" with the help of reparative programs, such as the ones offered by Exodus. This bill, which would impose the death penalty for homosexuality, has rightfully been met with international condemnation.

Ultimately, the truth cannot be hidden forever. I learned this when I admitted to myself that I could not change my gender identity as much as I wanted to and that God did not condemn me. I hope organizations like Exodus International will recognize the harm they have caused and work toward true reconciliation with those they have hurt. I also hope we can continue to have an open and honest dialogue about these issues to create a more inclusive and accepting world for all.

Condensed from Blogpost, June 21, 2013
16.2: My brush with Exodus
"My Brush with Exodus International Left Me Exposed"

Long before I could admit I was trans, I spent twenty-one weeks trying to apply the teachings of Exodus to myself.

In 1991, I was drawn to a ministry that claimed to help gays and lesbians change their sexual orientation. The program director was Marjorie Hopper, who had lived as a man and worked as a custodian before being outed at work. She became an anti-gay advocate and eventually the director of the Living Waters program at Burnaby Christian Fellowship, associated with Exodus International.

At the time, I was struggling with my gender identity, hoping that God would heal me and remove all my feelings of inadequacy as a man. I spiritualized my struggle and didn't dare apply labels to myself for fear of admitting defeat to the devil. But aspects of Marjorie's story resonated with me, and I saw hope in the fact that she had reverted to living as a woman, renounced her lesbianism, and found faith.

I met Marjorie and offered to design brochures and handouts pro-bono for Living Waters. During our meeting, I came out to her about wanting to dress up in women's clothing. She prayed for me and suggested I join her group, which was about to start a 21-week series. My wife learned about it and sponsored me to attend.

Living Waters was an awkward fit from the beginning, as gender identity was not part of the discussion. We spent much time looking at scriptures about being made in God's image, having a healthy image of ourselves, and dealing with abuse and painful experiences. The one positive thing I took away from the sessions was being introduced to a very intimate style of worship. We sang Vineyard songs for close to 30 minutes at the start of each session.

After 21 weeks, my "problem" had not gone away, and I suspected it had to do more with me than God. I wrote a letter to Exodus and received a short reply with photocopied pages on gender identity. The materials suggested that people like me were autogynephiliacs and inordinately in love with the idea of being women, akin to the sin of idolatry and that I had to repent and retrain my mind.

This dashed my hopes and prayers for healing and being a "normal male." I felt exposed and helpless, but ironically, it ultimately caused me to be honest and resign myself to the fact that my struggle was never going to go away.

* * *

It's hard to believe it's been over thirty years since all this occurred. Whenever I think about my timeline, I can't help but wonder what my life would be like today if I had known then what I know now. I wish I could have figured it out sooner; it would have spared me almost fifteen years of additional distress. My only consolation is that the delay spared my wife and our three sons, who ranged in age from 9 to 16 at the time, from what I feared would be the biggest challenge of their lives; it bought us all some time.

16.3: Reuniting with My Cousins in Florida

The Gay Christian Network (GCN) conference was held in Orlando, Florida. I called some of my cousins who lived in Miami and told them I wanted to rent a car after the conference and drive to meet them. I had been Facebook friends with all of them early on; they were the first of my extended family to learn about my transition.

One thing did at the GCN conference was to sell copies of my book at the vendors' tables. I was left with about 30 unsold copies, so I kept ten for my cousins and donated the remainder to GCN to sell on their online store and keep the proceeds.

For the trip, I packed my Garmin GPS for way-finding in Florida. It got me within 1/4 mile of my destination but on the wrong side of a main highway. So much for precise directions. I called my cousin Luz Helena, who re-routed me to their home, where they had planned a surprise welcome party. I had not seen many of these cousins for over twenty years or longer. It was an emotional reunion. We reminisced and talked about our parents; I was the only one whose mom and dad were still alive, and my parents were royalty in my extended family. A few days later, my cousins organized a

Salazar family reunion so that I could meet the rest of the clan and many of their kids. It was overwhelming; our faces were still familiar though we had all aged. My inability to remember names made me wish we had all been wearing name tags with a family tree attached. Those few days in Miami not only allowed me to reconnect with my extended family, but they also felt like a massive and welcome endorsement of my identity and a boost to my confidence in people.

During my visit with Luz Helena, I discovered her son is a gay aspiring actor, singer, and dancer in New York City. And more recently, I learned that her daughter, who lives in Texas, has a child in junior high school who came out as trans. Witnessing my extended family's inclusivity, love, and allyship toward their LGBTQ+ members fills me with pride. It was heartwarming to receive an email from the child's mother, expressing how my story had inspired her to stand up for her child in the face of the anti-trans climate in Texas. Sadly, Texas is among the 45 states that have introduced and passed laws targeting trans youth.

I am worried and saddened by the situation in the U.S. today, which mirrors the hostility toward LGBTQ+ people that inspired the Kill the Gays Bill in Uganda. These policies and provisions have been met with widespread opposition from advocacy groups, medical professionals, and child welfare organizations, who argue that they put trans youth at risk and perpetuate harmful stereotypes about trans people. They also argue that these policies are based on misinformation about gender identity and ignore the importance of affirming and supporting trans children in their identities.

Emboldened by Trumpsim, conservative politicians are embracing the culture war policies targeting trans kids and parents struggling to make the best decisions for their health. I agree with Rafa Pérez of the Texas Freedom Network (TFN), who was quoted in a February 2023 HuffPost piece. Said he, "Are we really going to let Republican values get in the way of best-practice medicine supported by years of science?" and added, "There are just so many better things we could be doing."

* * *

In the Preface to Section 2, I mentioned that I am including Op-Eds and relevant blog posts. These capture moments, thoughts, and responses to things that were going on at the time.

Published on the Opinion Page of
the Vancouver Province February 15, 2012:
16.4: First-ever Op-Ed
"Critics of trans rights need to learn compassion"

Ottawa has passed Bill C-389, prohibiting discrimination based on gender identity and expression. The bill adds transgender/transsexual Canadians as identifiable groups in the Criminal Code's hate crimes law. While this is a bold and positive step forward, there is fear that the Conservative-controlled Senate could vote against the final passage of the private member's bill of Burnaby NDP MP Bill Siksay. This would be devastating for all TG/TS Canadians.

The bill's most vocal opponents are Jim Hughes and Charles McVety from the Campaign Life Coalition, who have dubbed it the "bathroom bill". They say that if it becomes law, it will grant male cross-dressers and drag queens a legal right to use female bathrooms.

How ridiculous and dangerous to use and employ this kind of alarmist language with little regard for their rhetoric's impact on hundreds and perhaps thousands of young people who are aware of their gender difference and are trying to figure out how their future will unfold. Is it any wonder that the attempted suicide rate among TG/TS people is so disproportionately high—as high as 40 percent? I've been there, had those thoughts. I'm grateful to have made it past my 60th birthday.

The fact remains that life for a TG / TS person continues to be fraught with difficulties. Stigmatization, discrimination, and lack of understanding are prevalent, even in Canada, one of the most progressive countries in the world. It must be said that TG/TS persons in Canada fare much better than our American counterparts. We at least get a portion of our medical expenses paid for when we decide it is time to make the difficult changes that allow us to experience congruency as persons finally.

Transitioning two and a half years ago was the scariest thing I have ever done. I am fortunate to have been able to navigate these unknown waters with the support, love, and affirmation from family, friends, and clients.

I am often told that I am the first TG/TS person they have personally known. Many admit that they never gave the issue and its implications any thought until I jarred them with my disclosure.

Ask any of us TG /TS if this was a lifestyle choice, and the answer will always be the same: "Are you crazy? Who would choose to be marginalized and to be in constant fear of rejection and ridicule?"

Sadly, losing jobs, not being hired, or confronting landlords reluctant to rent to a trans person are all realities. Some families even cast their sons and daughters out on the streets.

As long as society holds a view, however subtle or extreme it may be, that TG/TS persons are mentally ill at best or perverts and fetishists at worst, we will continue to face stigmatization and ridicule, if not outright rejection. A recent skit by late-night TV host Craig Ferguson, which was a poor attempt at comedy, was typical of this insensitivity.

Stereotypes and characterizations that make fun of any minority need to end. They are hurtful.

It is a medical condition like no other, and those saddled with it must pay a personal, social, financial, and sometimes a spiritual toll that would not be tolerated if it was exacted, for example, on someone with ALS or cancer.

Those who opposed this bill because they will no longer be able to justify as legitimate their view that TG/TS persons are freaks and undesirable weirdos when refusing them employment or services need to think how they would like it if one of their children found themselves in this predicament.

Blogpost: February 12, 2012
16.5: "Hey, Mr. Tambourine Man"

Do you ever get a song stuck in your head, and no matter what you do, the melody or the lyrics keep playing repeatedly like a broken record?

I just dated myself. How many people still remember broken records? The closest equivalent in today's parlance is when a CD player continuously goes into a digital bleep or a sound file loops.

Mister Tambourine Man has been looping in one part of my brain while in another region. I have been considering a conversation with a new friend, Alexandra Henriques, director of Generations at Qmunity, BC's queer resource center. I met her at a recent workshop at the University of British Columbia. As we were learning about each other, she shared a bit about the sensitivity training workshops she gives at Seniors' residences and care facilities.

Until then, I had never really thought about aging lesbian, gay, bisexual, and transgender seniors and the challenges they may face when they move to one of these homes.

The reality is that there is an aging LGBT population. Contrary to popular opinion, a person's sex drive and need for companionship and affection don't suddenly go dormant when one turns sixty-five. The other reality is that for those who are part of that demographic today, their orientation and gender identity were, in all likelihood, suppressed and kept deep in the closet, thanks to the times in which they grew up and lived when everything was taboo. And now, they find themselves isolated and living in an environment that offers little support and opportunity to be themselves. If loneliness and the sense of abandonment are not already some of the consequences of old age, they are compounded for LGBT persons.

Some facilities have well-meaning rules and policies concerning acceptable behavior, visitation rights, who to call in an emergency, and who is next of kin. Often these policies are biased and prevent same-sex partners from having access to their friends, and the activities offered are based on heterosexist models. Alexandra hopes to change this, one facility at a time, as staff and administrators are educated and enlightened. After all, how else can you deal with the seventy-four-year-old man who insists on wearing nothing but dresses or the senior woman who wants her "best friend" to be allowed to cuddle with her in bed? How else to ensure staff doesn't overstep their authority or jump to conclusions, suspecting diminished mental capacity when they witness "unusual" behavior?

As I said, I had never thought about these issues and the potential complications aging LGBT persons face when it becomes necessary for them to live in a Seniors facility. It made me feel a bit nervous about my future. I suppose what gives me hope is that for the people entering this age group in the next few years, their experience has not been marked by suppression, and they have been living and surviving out of the closet and are comfortable in who they are. Hopefully, as well, the care facilities and residences will have also been infused with staff who, if they are not LGBT themselves, will be attuned to the needs of their residents.

One exciting outcome of meeting Alexandra is the possibility of working with her to provide transgender-specific workshops and exchange information between the two of us so we can make our respective presentations more effective. And that is a good thing.

Yes. Mr. Tambourine Man is still playing in my head!

Blogpost: February 22, 2012
16.6: Witnessing a Rebirth of Sorts

When the moment to start life anew comes, it usually happens in the quietness of one's spirit. Wednesday, February 21, 2012, will mark the moment my friend Tori took that step in the most unassuming way. I have already shared how we met (and I hope you won't mind rehearing some of the details), but I share this story because I want to honor my friend Tori in recognition of her role in my life as I emerged anew. The following is from a blogpost (February 22nd, 2012.)

In 1999, when I was being assessed and diagnosed at the Vancouver Hospital's Gender Clinic, I made a couple of calls to a support group in the area. Their brochure listed a phone number and stated that calls could be made on Thursday nights if you needed to speak to someone. Otherwise, you could leave a message, and someone would reply. The woman who answered was friendly and explained the group's purpose and how one would attend their meetings and other events. Membership was reserved for those vetted and approved by the membership committee. Confidentiality was very high on the group's priority list.

Given that the group's stated purpose was to provide a safe place for heterosexual men to cross-dress and socialize, learn from each other, and support each other, I never did follow through with joining or even attending a meeting as a guest. Though I cross-dressed occasionally, it was not a hobby or a form of socializing, as it seemed to be for those who were part of this group. At least, that was my assumption.

My never venturing to a meeting had more to do with my fears. I was terrified to venture out in public, even to a friendly place where everyone else had as much to lose if anyone was to find out. Many in this group kept this part of their lives closely guarded.

The second time I called the support line, a man answered. It was the woman's husband, one of the group's officers. I don't recall if he was the president or the head of one of the committees. I asked a few more questions and learned more about the group, but by then, I think I had already decided against joining.

As I have already shared, I met Tori in person on Labor Day weekend, 2010. Since then, she told me a few things about our encounter that gave me pause for thought and made me appreciate her sensitive nature.

She struggled to choose between attending the barbecue party or the Sunday evening service at her church. It troubled her so much she spoke to her pastor about it. She told him she had a strong premonition that she was to meet someone new. Who? She didn't know. The pastor told her that if God put that on her heart, she should attend the party.

Perhaps the most significant consequence of our encounter at the barbecue, a few months later, I had the privilege of going to Torl's workplace to do a trans-sensitivity workshop for all the managers and employees at the company, close to 150 persons in all. I left them with the message that at the end of the day, a transition is a group experience, and the group is the context.

You may be wondering how Tori, who has been presenting as herself beautifully at church, was only then transitioning at work. The short answer is she was not alone. Many trans persons find themselves in a similar predicament. You could blame society for making it so difficult for people to be themselves, especially when one is gender non-conforming in one way or another. And she was also not alone in finally coming to the point where living a dual existence—going to work as a male but living outside of work as a female—was no longer tenable. To say it was stressful is putting it mildly.

When trans people must finally live honestly with themselves (and others) and can no longer be delayed, something has to give. Fortunately, more and more trans persons are finding the strength to do what they must. I'm sure Tori would be the first to point out that her decision had nothing to do with bravery and that it was desperation. I can relate to that. But it is bravery, nonetheless.

To anyone who would say being trans is a choice, stop and consider for a moment: who would choose the most public solutions for such a private and deeply personal struggle? The only options are whether you will cave in and kill yourself—and many do—or choose life, even if it means making changes in one's body through medical and surgical means.

On February 21, I had the incredible privilege of seeing my friend leave her workplace as a man for the last time. When she returned to work the following Monday, she was Tori. On that day, her new life began in earnest as she finally shed the remnants of her male persona.

Congratulations, Tori! I love you for who you are and for having listened to your heart more than once.

Blogpost: May 10, 2012
16.7: Even God Makes Compromises

The headline reads: "Tea party radicals paralyzing the U.S., GOP veteran says." The story is about the longest-serving Republican, Richard Lugar, who got bounced for being too moderate. Lugar is critical of the Tea Party's influence in the GOP, which can be summarized as a purge of anyone who would dare compromise with the democrats, further polarizing American politics. For his part, Lugar has a record of working for the best of the country, even if it means making compromises to get things done, which is not an unreasonable and unrealistic position.

I have always been somewhat dismissive of anyone labeling a person or group (political, religious, or otherwise) as "scary." I've heard liberally minded persons call conservatives "scary," and I've listened to conservatively minded call liberals the same. What bothers me about such labels is how they can sabotage intelligent dialog. Saying we fear the "other" is an admission that we don't understand, and as we all know, fear of the unknown is "phobia."

Now, I am experiencing a phobia concerning politics and how North America and perhaps the world are becoming uber-polarized on just about everything political. Whether it is about economics, the environment, education, healthcare, or marriage equality, doesn't it seem as if our ability to compromise is almost non-existent? Yes, we can argue that certain things are not open to negotiation and are uncompromising—child labor and human trafficking, for example. But have we lost our ability to think creatively so that both sides of an issue are unpacked, looked at with unfiltered eyes, and perhaps replaced by a "compromise?"

Even God was willing to compromise when Abraham negotiated with him...look it up; it's in Genesis.

My point is that I am tired of the stalemates I see everywhere. The labeling that goes on in efforts to characterize the opposition as less than; I'm tired of it, and it frightens me. I need to go no further than how this vilification of persons has led to the incredibly untenable situation in Uganda and as many as seventy-five other nations that criminalize and persecute sexual minorities, and this is just one issue.

So what am I doing about it? First, I will refrain from calling myself a Christian since most of the crap being slung comes from those who call themselves "Christians." It's a label that is too tarnished to be salvaged. When Jesus said, "A new command I give you: Love one another. As I have loved you, so you must love one another. By this, everyone will know you are my disciples if you love one another." He didn't say, "By this, everyone will know that you are a Christian."

Imagine what our world would look like if people acted like disciples rather than Christians.

Blogpost: October 11, 2012
16.8: Dear Sir

"Dear Sir" — This had been the greeting in recent letters from the Canadian Revenue Agency (CRA). I called them to complain, but though the person I spoke to was sympathetic, she could not change the gender marker responsible for the misgendering. She could not access this option; it was above her pay grade, and she gave me another 1-800 number to call. After wading through the menu options and waiting in the queue long enough to hear the "due to heavy volumes..." blurb several dozen times, I finally spoke to a real person who listened to my request and politely informed me I had to call another government office.

After another 1-800 routine that lasted another twenty minutes, I learned I had to contact another office. After over one hour of phone calls, I was finally given instructions for what I had to do. This insignificant one-letter change could only be done by going to a Canada Services office in person. I would need to bring my Canadian citizenship card and passport—both of which already showed my gender as female—and my Social Insurance card.

This morning, after a short wait in the reception area of the Canadian Services office in Burnaby, I was finally able to get this gender thing updated in the government's central registry. I asked the representative if this would affect future correspondence with federal agencies. His answer: "It won't be instant. This could take months for all computer accounts to be updated." This young man had not processed this kind of request before and asked for permission to ask me some questions, a detail I greatly appreciated. He wanted to know if I had been required to have surgery before I was given a new citizenship card, which of course, is what I had to do.

Canada had come a long way, but I had already undergone a legal name change. When my citizenship card was reissued, I had met the requirement for getting the M changed to F. How is it that this information did not also affect the central registry? How many hoops does one need to jump through to be recognized officially as the gender of your identity? And what about all those trans persons who chose not to have the surgery, are not allowed to have the surgery for medical reasons, or are waiting to have surgery in the future? Why can't the process be less onerous and demeaning? Such a minor aspect of transition, yet one that seems to cause so much angst.

I can't wait for a letter with "Dear Madame" as the greeting. How long should this take?

(The requirement for gender affirming surgery to change one's gender marker in Canada was removed on August 31, 2017.)

Blogpost: October 18, 2012
16.9: Ask a Transgender Christian

A young woman I greatly admire is Rachel Held Evans. She is an amazing author, blogger, speaker, wife, mother, and a seriously articulate progressive Christian writer and blogger who is not afraid to enter into conversations that would make many others run and hide in their little dogma houses.

Earlier in September of 2012, Rachel contacted me to see if I would be willing to be interviewed as part of her popular blog series "ASK A...." Would I be willing to be in the hot seat for "Ask a Transgender Christian?" My new friend Justin Lee, executive director of the Gay Christian Network (GCN) and author of "Torn: Rescuing the Gospel from the Gays-vs.-Christians Debate," suggested me as the person to ask. (Similarly, Justin is the person Rachel chose for the "Ask a Gay Christian" interview.

Having followed Rachel for only a few months, my initial reaction to her email was disbelief and trepidation, given her blog's intellectual and theological depth and the comments it elicited. "Me? She wants to ask me? Why?" But I also felt safe with her, and from everything I had read in her blogposts, I knew she would not be throwing me to the lions. I agreed to take on the challenge.

The "ASK A..." interviews work as follows: first, she posts a photo and a short bio of the person to be interviewed and invites her readers to pose questions and vote for the questions others have already asked. After about twenty-four hours, she cuts off the input and selects between eight and ten questions; these then become the interview. After you receive the questions, you have four days to respond. Once she gets your answers, she does a quick editorial review and posts your response. Sound simple? Well, let me tell you.

The process is straightforward, but the prospect of facing some hard questions is disquieting. In the back of my mind was the nagging thought that everything I said would be shot full of holes and I would look like an absolute idiot. "What was I thinking?" and "Who did I think I was?" Yes, pride and vanity did get in the way, and so did my sense of vulnerability. I admit it: I care what people think about me, and I always have. And there is the nugget, as it were, that kept me in a constant state of high anxiety and provided the motivation I needed never to let my guard down as I tried to live as a man of good standing in the club for so many years.

But as they say, the proverbial cat has been out of the bag for, let's see, five years. (It was the middle of October 2007 when I began disclosing to family and friends that some seismic changes were about to happen in my life.) So why would a set of questions now, which I had already answered at least a zillion times, suddenly reawaken such deep and gnawing insecurity? The reason is simple; responding to these questions honestly required me to go through a process akin to disrobing in front of people. The process also caused me to relive some harrowing experiences, but it also evoked some beautiful memories of how things were between my ex-wife and me, the life we had together, and how we tried to save our marriage.

In the interview, I did not give her enough credit, not because I forgot, but because my words could not have done justice to how much she gave and how much I appreciated and respected her. From accounts of spouses and significant others of trans persons, there is a sense of betrayal-slash-lack of appreciation that is experienced by them when, despite all their best efforts and sacrifice for their loved one, they transition. "Didn't I do enough for you that you could not remain as my husband?" My ex-wife never said this to me, but she told me I rejected her. That was her way of saying the same thing— that I had rejected all she had done for me; it had not been enough to keep me as a man.

October 19 is our wedding anniversary; this year would have been thirty-eight years. It may not be fair for me to talk about this publicly and pretend to fully understand the pain she has experienced due to my decisions. I try to put myself in her shoes, but it is useless. It is far better for me to say I am sorry that my need to survive eclipsed my ability to say no to transition.

So there you have it. These were the things going on behind the scenes as I answered the questions.

Postscript 1

I was very touched by how sensitively Rachel's readers asked the questions and the many follow-up comments to the interview. I thank them all for being as kind and generous as they have shown themselves to be. (The interview can still be found at www.rachel-heldevans.com/blog/ask-a-transgender-Christian-response.

Postscript 2

I had the privilege of meeting Rachel in person at the 2014 GCN conference in Chicago in the crowded lobby. We were about fifty feet apart when we made eye contact, and we recognized each other immediately from the photos we had seen of each other. She was as excited to meet me as I was to meet her. It was humbling. I thanked her for introducing me to her audience and her incredible openness and sensitivity. I shared how total strangers would come up to me and ask if I were the person she interviewed and would thank me for helping them understand (which still happens today).

Postscript 3

Sadly, Rachel died on Saturday, May 4, 2019, at a hospital in Nashville. She was 37. Her husband, Daniel Evans, said on her website that the cause was extensive brain swelling. During treatment for an infection last month, his wife began experiencing brain seizures and was placed in a medically induced coma from which she didn't recover. R.I.P., Rachel Held Evans; your books and your blog will continue to inspire and teach those who are genuine seekers.

Blogpost: November 12:
16.10: Am I happy? Yes, But.

I was asked if I was happy (about having transitioned, making the change, paying the price, etc.). I wonder how many people who knew me before are equally curious?

One friend admitted that he prayed for me to fail in my efforts so I would change my mind and return to living as a man.

It's been five years since I started to disclose to my family and friends, and I was nearly paralyzed by the fear that my life would end. I was also afraid for my marriage and hoped it would survive. It didn't. So how to answer the question? The truth is that the answer is not a "yes" nor a "no." It is both. I have never been in as much peace inside my skin as I am today, but that does not mean I am happy with life.

The loss of friends did not materialize as I had feared, or I should say, it didn't happen the way I feared it would. What happened with old friends is that after their initial expression of love and support for my decision, I never heard from most of them again. For many, I was and still might be the only trans person they know. I'm okay with that, and if it helps them open up their heart for the next trans person(s) who may enter their circle, then great.

Their silence could have more to do with the fact that I am divorced. Is it denial on their part? It is always awkward for friends when one has been known as one half of a couple, right? There may be another, more straightforward explanation for their silence, "out of sight, out of mind. I'll give them the benefit of the doubt, or am I being too generous by still referring to them as friends?

I am suspicious and worried about how well things are going for trans persons today. Support for marriage equality may be spreading, and more and more companies and organizations are coming out as LGBTQ+-friendly, anti-bullying campaigns to raise awareness about the suicide rate among teens struggling with their sexuality are also on the increase. Yet, despite all this good that is going on, I fear life for trans persons is not much better than it was five years ago when I began my public journey.

A trans friend sent me a link to an article in the Christian Post one morning. I won't dignify the story by giving you the link; why give them unmerited page clicks? It was a vicious transphobic rant by some Christians who lacked compassion or did not attempt to understand. This person judges that being trans is a sin and that all the well-meaning support for trans persons perpetuates fraud and an evil perversion.

Trans people are the new target of conservative Christian Right now that they have lost the gay and lesbian battle. A friend and blogger shared that he gets many letters from pastors telling him his writings have helped them grow in their understanding and acceptance of gays and lesbians but confess they are terrified about the prospect of a trans person entering their church. By the way, this blogger is a straight Christian, yet he has been speaking out on behalf of LGBTQ+ people.

He says little about the T in the LGBTQ+ discussion with these pastors because they are uncomfortable with the idea of body modifications and any discussion regarding gender fluidity. The binary view of gender is too well entrenched in their thinking.

It made me think that if I had known that finally coming out as trans and deciding to transform my body medically and surgically would be so unsavory to so many, would it have made a difference? Though it might have given me more anxiety, the answer is no. I've said this before, but I'll repeat it: I chose to embrace life and not do what 41% of trans persons have tried. Suicide has sometimes seemed like the only other option, and God only knows how many have succeeded if so many have tried but failed. I must admit that the thought often crossed my mind to make a purposefully failed attempt simply so people would take my need to transition as a serious need—to make that proverbial cry for help.

By all indications, most trans persons and specialists in the field would say that my transition has been a success. I, too, believe that I have been fortunate in that regard. But it is of little comfort to me when I see how society is still so unbending and unwilling to let us live in peace and treat us like the elephant in the room. We are far from enjoying equality if people claim that trans people have fallen for an evil lie and that changing our bodies is a sin. Why are pastors terrified about the prospect of someone like me entering their churches? Am I—and by extension all trans persons—really that horrible and scary?

Among some of my new trans friends, there are a few who give a rat's ass about what people think; Kaitlyn Bogas is a great example. The only drum they march to is their own, and they don't allow people's opinions to keep them from living. They are a thousand times more courageous than me in that regard. I have agonized about how well I am accepted and whether or not I can go through life without drawing any attention to myself, especially negative attention. So much of my emotional energy has been consumed dealing with perceptions.

So am I happy? I've already given it away in the title of this blog…. "Yes, but I'm full of rage." I am happy to be alive. I'm happy to be able to share my story, especially with those who don't have the token trans person in their circle of friends. I am happy that my transition has gone off without a hitch, medically speaking. I am happy for new friends who don't have a history of my former self and are not tripped up by that history—that we can write a new one together void of that duality. I am also happy that I can be transparent about my past and have nothing to hide. These are just some of the things that I am happy about. But as I said, I am also full of rage.

My rage stems from the systemic and pervasive discrimination I see toward trans persons and anyone who appears to be gender non-conforming. Negative articles like the one my friend sent me are painful to read but equally painful is when discrimination is silent and when people find it easier to turn a blind eye to our needs and existence than to engage.

That may help explain why the T is so invisible in the LGBTQ+ picture. It also might help explain why my marriage, like many other trans marriages, has failed. As long as society views us with disdain, how can we ever expect that those who matter most will not be affected by the negative perceptions? It is unfair to our spouses when the only possible explanation for why a marriage may survive is because the wife (of the male-to-female trans person) is assumed to be a lesbian or at least bisexual. That notion is cruel, not just because it is homophobic and transphobic, but because it is not anyone's business.

On the other hand, when marriages survive different "devastating" life situations, such as cancer, they are held in high esteem and honored for their courage and proof of their love for one another. Why can't that be society's take for those transitioning after marriage? — I think it might have given my marriage a better chance of survival.

What to do with this newfound rage?

This rage is a new thing for me. I could only put my finger on it a couple of days ago. This realization may have been awakened by the questions from my friend, who wondered if I was honestly happy. I have been in a strange head space. I thought it was depression I was dealing with, but it's rage.

By all outward appearances, the people around me have not been aware of anything because I have mastered the art of internalizing stuff. This ability to bottle things up is not the best form of resiliency, but it allowed me to survive before I transitioned and is kicking in once again. But I am drained pretending all is okay, so I am speaking out today.

It's not okay when "Christians" accuse us of being perverse and write the stuff that makes it difficult, if not impossible, for trans persons and our families. And I worry about the impact those comments may have on anyone— young or old—who, at that moment, is trying to decide whether to choose life or to end the nightmare.

16.11: I Thought So

A few days after posting my above rant, I celebrated my 62nd birthday. I decided to call the marketing manager for the restaurant chain that 'fired' me in 2010 to wish her Happy Birthday; we happened to share the date. After some friendly banter and well-wishes, I asked her if she could be honest with me. I needed to know if my transition had anything to do with their decision to use another creative service. She started to cry and apologized profusely, saying she felt terrible. I thanked her for her honesty and told her I forgave her; she'd been put in a horrible spot.

As I had suspected, the Chief Operating Officer had walked into her office and said, "I don't care who you get to do the photoshoot and re-branding; I don't want Salazar coming into our restaurants or offices again. It makes people feel uncomfortable." This man was someone I had known for more than thirty years; we went way back to the early Keg Restaurants days when he was a manager. I had always sympathized with him because I sensed he also didn't have a positive body image. Over the years, he had put on weight to hide his gynecomastia and was constantly adjusting the front of his shirts to minimize his breasts. I concluded there must have been much projection going on in his head or I triggered his insecurity.

Going from highs to lows best describes my life at this point. Still aching from the worst Christmas ever, when my now ex-wife and sons celebrated without me, we celebrated the New Year with a highlight, my youngest son's wedding. Navigating this significant family event was not as difficult as I had imagined and feared. My daughter-in-law's family, whom we knew from church, were nonplus and utterly unfazed by my presence and were downright affirming and loving, even though they introduced me to the guests as, "This is our son in-law's dad, Lisa," which I found funny. I was used to this introduction; my sons routinely introduced me to their friends as their dad, Lisa.

What would be in store for 2013?

Chapter 17: I Knew it Wouldn't Be a Cakewalk

As I reviewed my emails and blogposts for this chapter, I was reminded of the emotional state I was in at the start of the New Year; it was a conflicting mixture of anger, impatience, agitation, and grieving, combined with deep gratitude, humility, and--yes, even joy--sprinkled with episodes of self-pity.

Case in point: the house I shared with friends from church was in Burnaby, the city immediately east of Vancouver. It was only three miles as the crow flies from the townhouse Rachel and I had sold. I still had things to do and people to see in Vancouver, and to get to my destinations, I would invariably need to drive down streets that took me past previous places we had lived, parks where our sons had played sports, their schools, and random places where memories had been built.

More and more, I was looking for alternate ways of getting to my destinations, often adding unnecessary mileage and time to my travels. Why? Because being the sentimental fool that I was (and still am), I would break into sobs and uncontrollable crying. I would need to pull over and recover before continuing to drive. These episodes were growing in frequency and intensity, and I had to make them stop somehow. I was too proud and embarrassed to talk about this with anyone. I wondered if Rachel was going through the same thing. I missed her. I missed our home. I missed the life we had.

One afternoon, I was running late. My most direct and fastest route was chock-full of triggers, and I knew I was in big trouble. A block from crossing Boundary Road, which runs north-south and is the border between Burnaby and Vancouver, I stopped and turned off the ignition. I closed my eyes and took a deep breath. "I can't go on like this," I thought. Then this idea came to me, and it has become my mantra, which I use to this day: "Don't be sad. No one and nothing can take these beautiful memories away from me. I must celebrate and give thanks for all of them."

I sat in my car and began to list all the memories I would be driving through that day and thanked God for them. I turned on the ignition and was back on the road, smiling and celebrating my good fortune as I drove through Vancouver to my destination.

Still, I was in a funk; I was severely underemployed. My freelance graphic design practice barely generated enough for me to meet the living expenses. I decided to double my efforts to find full-time work because finding new clients proved impossible. I sent out dozens of resumes and applied for every posting I saw, even applying for medium-level positions. After all that effort, I only got one interview for a job I could have done with one hand tied behind my back. I was told I was overqualified, and they would not blame me if I jumped ship when something better came along, and besides, they had a couple of candidates to choose from with the right qualifications.

I didn't particularly like letting my circumstances get the best of me, but there I was, going into 2013, feeling defeated in January.

I attended my second GCN Conference the first week in January. There were 700 attendees that year, an increase of 300. As mentioned earlier, I was introduced to Gay Christian Network (GCN) by Kathy Baldock in 2012 at the Orlando Conference. The 2013 event was held in Phoenix. I was grateful for the opportunity to present another workshop on trans issues together with Kim Pearson, a 'Mama Bear' whose youngest of three kids first came out as lesbian and a few months later as trans. Kim, Executive Director and Co-Founder of TransYouth Family Allies (TYFA), advocates exclusively for trans and gender-variant children.

Despite this opportunity to present, I felt defeated as I prepared for the trip to Phoenix. I did much soul-searching about my motives for attending. Had it not been for the fact that I was granted a scholarship that paid the registration conference cost and the fact that I shared the hotel room with three other women, and had I not maxed out my air points to help with the airfare, I would not have been able to attend. The only three compelling reasons I could think for going were that I was doing a workshop, being with Kathy

Baldock again, and finally seeing Namoli Brennet, the trans-singer-songwriter I introduced to GCN, live for the first time. (A few months before my surgery in 2010, I stumbled on NamolI's music and created a playlist I listened to daily during my recovery.) Was this enough justification? Booking the flight sealed the deal, and there was no backing out. I prayed I would be pleasantly surprised; I wanted a good start to the New Year.

Once in Phoenix, I felt a little better. It was great to reconnect with people I had met the year before. I attended my first-ever women's retreat, held on Thursday before the start of the conference. I volunteered at the registration desk that evening and got to experience the build-up of excitement as more people arrived.

Friday was the big day for me; I did the workshop with Kim in the afternoon, and the concert was in the evening. The Plenary Session on Saturday morning was great, and then it was lunchtime. I was torn between eating lunch with the Cascadia group (people from Oregon, Washington, and British Columbia) or participating in an unofficial question-and-answer session Kathy Baldock had organized with two of her organization's board members. I dropped into the Q&A for a few minutes, but the topics did not apply to me. It was too late to join the Cascadia group, so I went to my room for a snack.

As soon as I closed the door and slipped off my shoes, I was engulfed in a wave of loneliness and self-doubt again. Being alone brought back all my questions about why I was even there in the first place. I laid down for a nap, and it was already 6:30 pm when I awoke. The way I was feeling, I didn't have much interest in doing anything else the rest of the day and was considering staying in the room. But one of the women who shared the suite was in the sitting area reading a book when I got up. We chatted briefly, and this brightened me up. I went to my laptop and checked my emails.

There was a notification about a new email to my book's email account; it was from a man in Reno who had just finished reading Transparently. He wanted to tell me how much the book had helped him to understand trans people. He admitted that though he was straight and had been an ally to LGB people for many years, he had always struggled to make sense of the "T." He was a therapist who worked with LGB persons! Upon reading his email, I had a minor meltdown. Why was I always so hard on myself? I thanked God for this unexpected "love letter" when I needed it most.

I washed up and decided to attend a workshop starting at 7:00. I was more composed but still somewhat emotional. I ran into Kathy there, and after the seminar, I went with her to the Open-Mic Session in the large auditorium. This had been a tradition at GCN for years. People lined up at two microphones and shared, in two minutes or less, how the conference had affected them. I was bowled over as three young people, one after the other, came out as trans men and shared how my workshop had unlocked the door for them to come out. It was a beautiful and humbling moment. I stood up from my seat and huddled with them at the edge of the stage to pray. It had all been worth the effort and expense to be there.

What happened Saturday night was a confidence booster that filled my head with ideas. I felt compelled to write a letter to Justin Lee and the GCN Executive to offer my thoughts on making their organization and its conferences more relevant, affirming, and welcoming to trans people.

I recognized it was essential to offer workshops to help LGB attendees understand trans people. After all, in Orlando, before my workshop, many people had confessed they did not understand trans people and were looking forward to what I had to say. Then, after the seminar, many thanked me for what they had learned. The same thing happened in Phoenix. But given what had occurred on Saturday night, it was clear there needed to be workshops for trans people that addressed the life issues that trans people face. For example, how to come out to family and friends, at their school and church, to name a few. On the spiritual side, there could be sessions dealing with pastoral issues and topics such as integrating one's faith with being trans and developing a supportive network of friends if one's faith community has failed them. There could also be workshops on how to do a legal name change and update personal identification documents.

One nagging issue remained, which had no easy answer; it all came down to numbers. Trans people are much less likely to be part of organized religious groups than non-trans people, according to research. In one study titled "Understanding Spirituality and

Religiosity in the Transgender Community," the authors posited this reason:

"The tendency not to identify with a formal religion may reflect an affirmation of one's dignity that these religions fail to honor, an expression of protest against certain religious tenets, and or a refusal to align oneself with institutions contributing to the marginalization of gender and sexual minorities."

This aligned with the experiences of the trans persons I had met in Vancouver; they had little or no interest in attending any church-related event, even if the gathering was exclusively for trans people. Did this mean GCN would never enjoy more than a token number of trans persons at their conferences? Add to this the issue of affordability; the other trans woman at the Phoenix conference, besides me, said her trans friend had not been able to attend with her because she worked for minimum wage and simply couldn't afford the costs.

Trans people were, and are, more likely to be unemployed or underemployed than other members of the LGBT community. This is a statistical fact. Therefore, it is not enough for event organizers to ensure the inclusion of meaningful content for trans people; they need to reduce the cost of attendance. I am convinced that financial ability will always be the biggest impediment for trans people to participate—it had almost stopped me from attending.

Back in Vancouver, it was time to face the music again. The elation I had felt at the conference evaporated within a few days, and I resumed my job search. This time, the mantra that sustained me was more direct, "I knew it wouldn't be a cakewalk when I started." Repeating it was as necessary as breathing some days.

Blogpost: February 22, 2013
17.1: At What Point Do I Throw In The Towel?

More resumes were sent out today; I've stopped counting how many this makes. Companies have embraced the web for recruiting and refuse to accept resumes and SVs delivered in person. These virtual firewalls around the hiring person(s) have made the process impersonal and unresponsive, perhaps proving that it matters not what you know but whom you know.

Many friends have told me about the importance of networking. Others have suspected that my back story, which is not so secret, could be the reason for not getting any hits on my job applications. After all, in this internet age, little remains a secret for very long. Then, a fellow trans woman suggested turning my trans status into an asset. Will companies see this as a positive, just as hiring visible minorities or disabled persons can earn them valuable bragging rights about diversity and equality?

A few months ago, I listened with great interest to a discussion about age discrimination on CBC Radio. One fact that was discussed was based on a survey of IT managers. They were asked whom they would hire if they had to choose between two candidates with similar experience and qualifications, but one was in their thirties and the other in their fifties. You guessed it; almost all said they would hire the younger candidate. The show discussed how the "baby boomers" were becoming unemployed, falling victim to silent-age discrimination.

I'm no spring chicken—I was born in November 1950 (you do the math). Lucky me, I not only need to put a spin on being trans, but I also have to overcome my age status somehow.

Then a friend on Facebook told me that companies who recruit online have software that vets the hundreds, and perhaps thousands, of resumes they receive. Only those that match specific keywords and phrases get short-listed. So, good luck if your resume lacks those words.

The job I had been trying to find is technical in many ways. Being able to use the latest versions of graphics software is a given.

Specialization in different areas can also be an asset, such as the ability to code things for the internet. But the essential asset is creativity and the ability to execute your ideas; this is imperative. How can this be communicated effectively on a resume that is analyzed by a computer? God knows.

Last week, in a hail Mary, I wrote an open letter to my colleague members of the Society of Graphic Designers of Canada (GDC). I talked about what it has been like since my transition in 2008. How my freelance practice has all but dried up and asked for leads. I attempted to cast a giant net, hoping to get a few nibbles. (I know, mixed metaphors, but you get the point.)

Unfortunately, the graphic design profession is where the waters could stand to be a little less muddy. The GDC tried to regulate the profession for years, as engineers and architects are regulated and licensed. Today's problem with graphic design is that anyone with a computer and the right software can go into business, claiming to be a graphic designer. How often have I been told that a nephew or a cousin can design a logo for fifty bucks, for example, when I have quoted $1,500?

To receive the professional designation of Certified Graphic Designer (CGD), one must go through a peer review. The quality and depth of the work submitted must demonstrate a high degree of professionalism. This designation should convince a potential employer of one's suitability for the job. Could it be that no one outside the GDC knows what it means to have the designation? What to do?

As many of the baby boomers interviewed in that radio program I mentioned above, I now wonder if it is time to throw in the towel. Like all those white-collar workers who are part of the "middle-aged displacement" cohort, I, too, might be applying for a job at Walmart or Home Depot. Or perhaps it's time I run an ad with the following headline(or would that be too hot to handle?:

"If you want your stuff to look sexy,
hire this 62-year-old trans woman. She's a pro!"

Chapter 18: The Redirection

Life is full of twists and turns, and sometimes we find ourselves on unexpected paths. A sudden change in circumstances, a new opportunity, or a newfound passion can lead us down a different road than we ever imagined. While major redirections in life can be disruptive, they also offer the opportunity for self-discovery and growth.

In this chapter, I'll delve into the pivotal moment that changed the course of my life and led me to a new vocation and a renewed sense of purpose. It all began with a simple question on the way to a Saturday brunch.

18.1: If Money Wasn't an Object

The following story begins with an email I received on the 12th of August 2012. It was sent to my book's email address. The writer shared she was a 32-year-old trans woman who hadn't started her transition yet and was hoping to come out to her loved ones. Her best friend was visiting her in a few days, and she planned to tell him about her plans to transition. She thought my book could help him understand, but she couldn't wait four days for it to arrive from Amazon. She wanted to know where she could buy it in Vancouver. She explained that she grew up in a Christian family, and her friend had a master's degree in divinity. She was hoping my book could provide insights on how to reconcile faith and trans identity. Her name was Megan.

I wrote her back and said, unfortunately, there were no bookstores in the Vancouver area selling my book, but I told her I had copies at home. I asked whereabouts she lived, and it turned out we lived less than 1 kilometer from each other. We arranged for her to come to my place that Saturday morning, and we sat and talked for close to three hours. Initially, she was nervous, but it didn't take her long to relax and make eye contact.

Megan was still "Craig", at the time. She worked for a U.S. hi-tech company with offices in Vancouver; she managed a team of 16 software engineers. Her employer's HR department was fully supportive and arranged for her team to undergo trans-sensitivity training the week before she came to work as Megan.

Back to the story and fast forward to April 6, 2013. Megan called to invite me out to brunch and wondered if I'd heard of a new restaurant on the riverfront near my place. She picked me up about 30 minutes later. Then she brought up the topic I had hoped to avoid; she asked me how my job search was going.

I told her I'd rather not talk about work because it was too upsetting and asked if we could change the subject. After all, didn't we want a relaxing time to celebrate how well she was doing, and didn't we have so much to get caught up on?

Megan apologized and was silent as she drove, with the wheels in her head also turning. Then she asked the question that is singularly responsible for who I am and what I do for a living today. It was pivotal. She asked: "Can I ask you, if money wasn't an object, what job description would you like to have?"

"Wow! Good question." I remarked. Then hummed and hawed as I began to think out loud. I went from "I don't know" to listing all my previous job descriptions; teaching graphic design, designing a restaurant, managing it, hiring, training, and firing staff, yet nothing emerged as a dream job. I listed negative reasons for those previous jobs and why I wouldn't want to do them again. I never enjoyed business administration, report writing, or committee meetings. Oh, the irony.

Then I said, "I love to create, I love designing, and I love photography. But if money wasn't an object, I would do it pro-bono for non-profits and NGOs. But I know that's not what you are asking."

I turned and looked at Megan and thought about my relationship with her. I'd become more than her friend. I had become a kind of life coach and mentor, and spiritual director as I encouraged and supported her emotionally when she began her transition. In an attempt to be sarcastic, I said, "Maybe I should become a chaplain to trans people and their families."

Megan almost drove off the road as she exclaimed, "Oh, my God, Lisa! Yes! That's what you are!"

"Keep your eyes on the road!" I told her. Then I said I was only joking, but she responded with, "Well, that's what you have been for me."

Then I listed the reasons why being a chaplain didn't make sense. "I don't know what is involved in becoming a chaplain; I can't start calling myself one. I'd probably need to be ordained or certified somehow. People would want to know my training; I know I would want to know if I was looking for that kind of support."

"Why don't you find out?" asked Megan.

I responded mockingly, "Yeah, right. Google 'Chaplaincy training Vancouver, BC.'"

"Yeah! Give that a try," said Megan.

We changed the subject, didn't discuss the issue anymore, and spent a lovely time together over brunch. Three hours later, Megan dropped me off at home. We hugged goodbye. and as I climbed out of her SUV, she pointed her index finger at me and said, "Don't forget to Google." "Yeah, yeah," I responded and almost help up a middle finger.

After hanging up my coat, I sat before my computer, checked my emails, and googled my query. At the top of the search results was the link to a Vancouver Coastal Health (VCH) website page that talked about their "Clinical Pastoral Education" (CPE) units taught in partnership with the Vancouver School of Theology (VST).

I couldn't believe my eyes; there was such a thing as chaplaincy training in Vancouver! I read everything on that page and learned that the next teaching clinical unit would be in September and would cost $2,250. The application deadline was less than three weeks away. It was Saturday, so there was no point calling the Director of Spiritual Care and Multi-faith Services to only leave a recorded voice message.

The next day, Sunday, April 7, was my Dad's 95th and my

oldest niece's birthday. My oldest son, whose birthday was on the 13th, was also included in our planned celebration. I have a photo of the three of them about to blow out the candles on the cake. That would be Dad's last birthday. More on that a little later.

On Monday at 9:30 a.m., I called the number on the VCH website. The Director answered. I told him who I was and my reason for calling. He was direct. "Why do you want to be a chaplain?" he asked. "I'd like to be a chaplain to work with trans people and their families," I answered. "I can't help you with that," he said bluntly.

"Let me rephrase what I said. I read on your web page how the training prepared students to journey with patients and their families as they face trauma, loss, grief, a different future from what they imagined, and the unknown. These are all the things that trans persons—and their families—go through when they decide to come out and transition. I want to have those competencies."

"Well," he said, "I need to interview you in person. I can see you on Wednesday at 1:00 p.m."

The interview with the Director lasted an hour. He listened to my story and gradually came around. He was initially skeptical, and I sensed that part of it was that he had never spoken to a trans person before, at least not in this capacity. We talked about theological courses I had taken at Regent College between 1990 and 1995, which were too long ago and insufficient. The minimum requirement to be accepted in CPE was a master's degree in theology, Social Work, Counselling, or Health Sciences. I asked if life experience could be taken into consideration. He thought for a moment and said, "possibly."

I was instructed to call three persons at VST, the academic dean, the registrar, and a professor with experience in Urban Missions with the United Church of Canada. The director wanted me to pick their brain to see what courses they would recommend for me to take. He reasoned that the more theological training I had under my belt, the better, and since I would have to register for the CPE unit through VST, I could take advantage of the opportunity to learn.

When I got home that afternoon, I called and set up three appointments, one with each. The next day, the registrar called. She said, "Hey, Lisa, you booked three appointments. We talked amongst ourselves and thought it made more sense for us to see you together. Can you come at 11:30 next Wednesday, April 16?" I looked at my calendar and accepted. I was attending a symposium in Fort Lauderdale but would be returning the night before at 9:30 p.m., and I would have lots of time to prepare the following day.

The blog post below details a bit of that trip:
18.2: You Can Ride on My Lap.

I spent a week in Fort Lauderdale to attend a trans-related medical symposium. One of the event's unexpected highlights was meeting Jazz Jennings and her mother in person. Jazz is a well-known trans girl who became famous when Barbara Walters interviewed her in 2008 when she was only five years old. In her teens, she published a book and starred in her own reality TV series, "I am Jazz," where she has been very open about her experiences and struggles growing up trans. It is unfortunate that Jazz and her family have become targets of anti-trans hate and trolling since I met them.

Another highlight of the trip was staying with my first cousin, Carlos, and his wife, who live in Ft. Lauderdale. Carlos drove me to the airport on Tuesday for my return trip to Vancouver via Chicago. As he pulled away, my phone vibrated. A text message from United Airlines told me my 4:15 flight to Chicago was delayed until after 7:00 p.m. I panicked.

I rushed into the airport and went to the United Airlines ticket counter. I told them I had a problem. I was scheduled to catch a connecting flight from Chicago to Vancouver at about the same time I would be boarding the plane in Ft. Lauderdale. There were no later flights from Chicago to Vancouver on United or any other airline that night.

I had an urgent appointment at 11:30 a.m. at the Vancouver School of Theology the following day, and it looked like I wouldn't make it. Crap!

The United Airlines representative told me that since the delay was not due to the weather but a mechanical problem, they would put me in a hotel in Chicago and then on to a flight to Vancouver that left at 9:00 a.m., but because of the time difference; I would arrive in Vancouver at 10:15 a.m. It would be tight but still give me enough time to get to the meeting, barring any snags. The annoying thing was that I would have to go to the United Airlines customer service counter upon arrival at O'Hare to get them to put me in a hotel.

O'Hare is not a small airport. When I collected my suitcase and made it to the United Airlines counter, there were over 100 people ahead of me. It was 11:150 p.m. when I finally got to speak to an agent. She was visibly overworked that day—it had been a long shift for her. After confirming that my flight's delay was mechanical and not weather related, she gave me a voucher for a night at a Quality Inn and told me where I would find the shuttle to the hotel.

United Airlines would have been off the hook if the delay had been weather-related. I would have had to find a hotel for the night and pay for it and the taxi to and fro myself.

I made my way to the spot where the shuttle was to pick me up. Before long, there were five more passengers who had vouchers for the same hotel, all men, ranging in age from thirty-five to fifty. We had all been told the same thing: a shuttle came by every thirty minutes.

After 45 minutes, we were still waiting for the shuttle. One of the men had a great idea, to call the 1-800 number on the voucher. He spoke to the front desk at our host hotel and learned that their shuttle service had made its last run at 11:00 p.m. and would return to the airport at 7:00 a.m. The other bad news was that the Quality Inn we had been booked into was a thirty-minute drive from O'Hare. The hotel was located next to an executive airport outside of Chicago.

We were screwed. But then I spotted another Quality Inn shuttle stopped about 100 meters away. I told the group I would find out if it could take us to our hotel. We knew every shuttle was from a different hotel, but I reasoned they were the same company, right?

No-go; the van driver told me he could not take us to a different hotel and suggested we take a cab.

I turned around and saw the men loading their bags into a Yellow Cab, a Ford Crown Royal, and then climbing into the cab. I started running, pulling my suitcase on wheels as I watched all four doors close, and then the taxi started to pull away with its rear end loaded low to the ground. I put my right thumb and index finger together to my lips and let out the loudest whistle I could produce. The cab stopped!

Those jerks, I thought. They were going to leave me behind! (But their excuse made sense at the time. They lost sight of me when I half-entered the van's sliding door to speak to the driver. They thought I'd solved my ride situation and was leaving without them.)

The driver managed to find room in the trunk for my suitcase, but there was no seat for me. The man sitting by the back door on the passenger side offered, "You can ride on my lap."

I figured I would be safe in numbers and accepted his offer. Was it awkward? Hell, yes! (I put this incident out of my mind for five years before finally being able to share it in my blog.)

The ride took over thirty minutes, and the six of us split the $120 fare. It was after 1:45 a.m. before I was handed a room key at the front desk. I needed to catch the hotel's first shuttle that left at 6:30 a.m. so I could be at the airport by 7:00. The front desk programmed a wake-up call for 5:30. At least I got a hot shower and three hours of sleep.

My flight from Chicago landed at YVR at 10:45 a.m., and by the time I collected my checked-in suitcase and made it to my car, it was already 11:05. The good news is that I made it to my appointment at VST. And to think I sat on a stranger's lap to get there. I've often wondered what that man, or the rest of them in the cab, would have said if they knew I was trans.

Postscript to the blogpost:

As I typed the words that night, there was a nagging sense there was something else—something important to say about this somewhat humorous, if not awkward, event. Perhaps there is a hint of this in my questions at the end.

Today at work, it hit me. I failed to acknowledge my privilege as a trans person whom society seems to have granted "passing" status. This is a complex topic in the trans community because some would argue that the whole notion of passing is odious; it makes second-class citizens of those who don't get passing status.

Here is where it gets thorny. Who, after all, is the final judge and arbiter for society on who passes and who doesn't? Where do we draw the line as to who "looks" like a "real woman" or a "real man?" A more challenging question might be: why must we make such a distinction?

I hope you can see why this is a troublesome conversation, but I had to acknowledge that the story's outcome could have been very different if I had not looked "woman enough" for this group of men. I don't mean hyperbolically, for example: that I could have been viciously attacked, sexually assaulted, killed, and dumped on the outskirts of Chicago. I'm talking more about not being accepted into the group. That is what we became at that moment; our common struggle made us a group.

I could have been shunned and rejected or made to feel unwelcome. But things worked out okay for me that night. The men saw me as a woman who met their unconscious, socially programmed criteria for a woman's appearance. I passed the test.

Chapter 19: A Passing and a New Beginning

Feeling nervous and winded from the rush of making it to my appointment with the three women at VST, I was instructed by the receptionist on how to find the meeting room. The building that housed VST was referred to as 'the Castle' due to its distinctive castle-like appearance, making it a popular choice for filmmakers. Some of the movies that have been filmed there include "The Changeling" (1980), a horror movie starring George C. Scott, and "Masterminds" (1997), a comedy starring Patrick Stewart and Vincent Kartheiser. The Castle has also been featured in several TV shows, including "The X-Files," "Supernatural," and "Smallville." I didn't know any of this then, but walking through the main entrance that morning was a breathtaking experience.

The three women were already seated in the room when I walked in. Brochures, course syllabi, and several forms were on the table before them. After greetings and introductions, the Academic Dean, Dr. Patricia Dutcher-Walls, said that upon reviewing my stated goals, the three agreed that I should complete a Master's Degree in Public and Pastoral Leadership (MAPPL).

I must have looked like the proverbial deer caught in the headlights. I stammered, "Oh, not just a few courses, but a whole degree?" They all smiled and said, "Yes!"

I had not expected this at all. I asked how much money I would need to come up with and explained that my finances were limited and that I could only pull it off by taking money out of my retirement savings. The Registrar gave me the run-down and added that I could do my first CPE Unit as an elective in my second year. I would still need to pay the $2,250 fee for the Unit because that was not included in my tuition. Then I decided to swallow my pride and ask: Are there any bursaries or scholarships for which I could apply?

Yes, but with a caveat, said the Registrar; the deadline for fall applications was that Friday, the 18th, at 5:00 p.m. I would need to prepare a budget, provide income tax returns for the last two calendar years, my college transcript from San Jose State, three character references, and two essays totaling 5,000 words.. One essay was to be on a theological issue I felt passionate about, and the other, a biographical sketch. I was advised that all financial aid decisions were made by a committee, in which the three of them had no say. I had one more question; I had emailed all three of them a copy of my eBook and a link to my blog before leaving for Ft. Lauderdale, so I asked if I could copy and paste from these sources. As long as they were my words, I could. The meeting ended with their encouragement and well-wishes.

The drive home from VST took 30 minutes, but it was the middle of the day, not rush hour. I was thinking ahead to Friday when I would have to make the delivery of my application package. I wanted to ascertain the latest I could leave my place and still make it to VST by 5:00. The long and short is that I made the deadline, which felt anti-climactic. I walked into the Castle, and there was not a soul around except for the receptionist, who was gathering her coat and purse and getting ready to leave and close the door. My steps echoed on the marble floor as I approached the counter. I handed her the envelope and said it had to be there before 5:00; she took it, wrote the time on the top right corner, and told me she would put it in the Registrar's inbox. She wished me good luck as we said goodbye. I returned to my car and sat there for a few minutes before leaving. There was no marching band or confetti to mark the moment.

I drove home and thought, it's all in God's hands. It will be if it's meant to be.

Two weeks later, on Friday, my Mom called to tell me Dad had fallen and they were waiting for the ambulance. I contacted Carmen and told her to meet us at their community hospital. I made good time from east Burnaby to South Surrey, where they lived. I pulled into the emergency parking lot as the paramedics unloaded my Dad from the ambulance.

The story is that Dad had gone with Mom to Blaine, Washington, five miles from their home, to fill their tank. This was something they often did to save money on gas. Both had their Nexus cards, which made the border crossing much faster. When they pulled up to the border guard, Dad was summarily lectured for having an expired Nexus card; it had expired on his birthday 20 days earlier. They were allowed through but were told they had to report to the Nexus office to deal with it before returning to Canada. Dad filled the tank, drove to Nexus, and dealt with the renewal of his card. He tripped on a speed bump in the parking lot as he returned to the car where Mom was waiting. He landed hard on his left knee, and his face made contact with the ground, giving him a bloody nose. A man came to his aid and helped him up. Dad was embarrassed and assured Mom he was okay to drive home.

Once home, he opened the door to climb out of the car but could not bend his left leg. He had not realized that from the time he got in the car to drive home, less than 20 minutes, including the border crossing, his leg had swollen to almost twice its diameter; it was hemorrhaging.

X-rays showed there was nothing broken; it was all soft tissue damage. Due to his heart condition, Dad had been on a high dose of blood thinners for about five years; this made the fall his demise. Dad passed away on Tuesday morning. His body had not been able to deal with the build-up of so much blood and fluid in his leg. My sisters and I took turns staying with him, sleeping on a cot the hospital provided. I am happy the grandchildren visited him at the hospital on Sunday. I was with him through his last night. My sister Angela stayed at my parents' place to be with Mom. I woke up in the early morning and noticed that the color had gone from his face, and his breathing was different. I pressed the call button, and the nurses came. They confirmed what I had suspected; Dad was dying.

I called Angela and told her to bring Mom as soon as possible, and explained what was happening. It seemed like they took forever to arrive. They walked in as the nurses were monitoring Dad's blood pressure. He had an oxygen mask over his nose and mouth, but he saw them enter the room. In the time it took me to turn to look at Mom and look back to my Dad, he took his last breath. He had waited until Mom arrived. It was very moving to see.

The funeral that weekend was attended by many of the new friends they had made after their move to South Surrey from Vancouver. They were all new faces to the rest of my siblings and me. In Dad's honor, their townhouse subdivision flew the flag at half-mast that weekend. My sisters and I decided I should come to be with Mom in the days that followed. We didn't want her to be alone, and we didn't want her to drive herself to the church every morning, which had become Mom and Dad's routine seven days a week. Whatever little graphic design work I did in those days could be done on my laptop at their house. On the third Saturday after the funeral, I told Mom I needed to go home to check the mail and grab some clothes and that I would return before 6:00.

I didn't expect to find much mail, perhaps some bills and flyers, but amongst the envelopes, there was one from VST. I sat down, took a deep breath, and opened it. I unfolded the letter, and it read: "Congratulations. You have been accepted to the Master of Arts in Public and Pastoral Leadership Program with full financial support." I sat there frozen, re-reading the line over and over again. It was a work-study arrangement in which I would have to do 60 hours of work per term for VST in some capacity. They suggested that I work with the Development Office and do graphic design; for example, brochures and fundraising collateral materials. I was invited to call the Registrar to plan my courses for the first year as soon as possible. It felt as if God had opened the door and drop-kicked me across the threshold!

I met with the Registrar the following week, and she suggested I might want to look at some of the courses being offered during the summer session. The program I was enrolled in, the MAPPL, is a 48-credit degree, 30 credits in required courses, 9 in designated advanced elective courses, and 9 in open electives. Though summer courses only counted for 1.5 credits, I could still learn the ropes, become familiar with the campus, and prime my brain for academic work. The last time I had written an essay for a grade was in 1972, my senior year at San Jose State, 41 years earlier. It was advice.

In conversation with my sisters and Mom later that week, we all agreed that I should move in to live with my Mom. I gave my housemates notice, and before the summer term started, I moved to South Surrey. My commute time to and from campus would be almost tripled, but using the transit system would save $15 in fuel cost per trip. I would only have to make one transfer mid-way, and I could read on the bus for 1.5 hours each way; there would be lots of that to do.

Graduate studies began the first week in July, and I had a couple of months to get used to my new routine of living with my mom as she adjusted to life without my dad. I stopped attending Rainbow Church since the services were held on Sunday evenings; I stayed home to cook dinner for Mom and tried to be in bed by nine. My new routine was to wake by five in the morning, and I needed 8 hours of sleep to survive.

Unpublished blogpost, a tribute to my Dad:

For the last few days, I have been humming the first few lines of the beautiful hymn, "How Deep the Father's Love for Us." I cannot help but make the connection between how much my earthly father, Enrique, loved us and how much our Heavenly Father's love flowed to us through my Dad.

I cannot help but see my Dad's love for me these last five years that I have been Lisa as evidence of just how powerful love is, that it can overcome even what seemed impossible, that a man at the age of 91 would be able to accept his 58-year-old son as his daughter. I am so grateful and blessed—it overwhelms me.

Dad lived 95 years and 23 days.He was the last remaining member of his family to depart. The youngest of seven children, he had no memories of his mother, who passed away when he was only two. Along with my many cousins scattered throughout the United States and Colombia, we have imagined the next amazing family reunion, including my older brother, who pre-deceased my Dad by twenty-eight years.

Dad often said he would be waiting for us. he knew his days were numbered, and he made sure we all knew he was at peace with that reality. He wondered if he would reach 100, yet he accepted each day with gratitude for one more day to spend with the love of his life, my Mom. They were looking forward to their 70th anniversary this October!

It was very moving to see how many people attended the

memorial service for my Dad yesterday, almost one month after his birthday. The service made me realize how we all have spheres of influence—our separate little worlds—which we don't get to see or appreciate until we have moments like these.

Dad had a profound and private faith. He said confidently to the priest who visited him at the hospital that he was unafraid. The priest said, "I'm sure of that, Enrique. You've said that many times before."

He was self-effacing and quiet; he never wanted the spotlight to shine on him. Yesterday he received all the honor and respect that he deserved. His friends who came to offer their condolences and pay their respects made sure of that. Dad would have been embarrassed to receive this much attention, but it was a fitting way to say goodbye to him.

A Dios, Papi. I love you.

Blog Post: May 24, 2013
19.1: Do you have a husband?

As I waited for my sister and Mom to come out to the car so we could be on our way, Mom's next-door neighbor approached me to ask how we were doing.

My Dad had passed away a couple of weeks earlier and this neighbor was the last one to see Dad alive before he was admitted to the hospital; he had waited with Mom for Dad's ambulance to arrive. The neighbor's name is Dave, and on many other occasions, we made small talk as we came and went. As far as neighbors go, he is the best anyone could hope for, always willing to lend my parents a hand. He is the quintessential handyman and Mr. Fixit, friendly, easy-going, and talkative.

From the many years he has been my parent's neighbor, he has been able to piece together a bit of my family's history, that we were born in Colombia, how we ended up in Canada, that we owned a California-style Mexican restaurant, how many children my parents had and how that explained all the grandchildren and the number of cars that showed up for family events, filling all the available visitor parking spaces in their corner of the townhouse complex.

There we were, just the two of us talking. Suddenly, he got quiet and asked me a question as delicately as possible. I am used to this happening and don't take offense when I sense the person is genuine and respectful. I thought he was going to ask me if I was trans, which I have been asked occasionally, but not so much lately, thanks to the fact that no one assumes that I am anything but a woman these days.

It wasn't always like that; in the early days of my transition, perhaps because my voice was lower or I may have carried myself more like a man than a woman, I may have confused some people. Dave's question, however, was not one I had ever been asked before; he asked: "Do you have a husband?"

As far as questions go, this has got to be one of the most innocuous and unthreatening things I have been asked as a trans person. Still, it both delighted me and perplexed me. It pleased and flattered me that he saw me only as a woman. Yet, I was perplexed because I was faced with a decision, should I take the easy route, tell him I am divorced and leave it at that, or explain why I don't have a husband by outing myself to him?

I hesitated and then told him I had been a husband and was the father of some of the young men he often saw coming to visit my parents. I explained how I was one of my parents' three sons but that I was now one of their three daughters. Dave's expression betrayed his thoughts, and the look on his face went from total confusion to epiphany when he had his "A-ha" moment. "That explains it," he said, "I've been doing the math and could not quite figure it out. I knew your parents originally had three sons and two daughters, but the numbers didn't add up. I assumed you were a cousin or a relative who visited from out of town."

Interestingly, Dave was not the only one of my parent's equally confused friends. During the reception that followed my Dad's memorial service, I had to explain the math to some of my parent's friends. (I met most of them when I was still living as one of the sons, but they did not know about my transition to female five years ago.)

My parents never felt the need to tell the whole world about me and only shared the news with a few of their closest friends on a need-to-know basis. In my conversations with their friends that day, I was asked which of the daughters I was or whether I was a niece or a cousin. To all these questions, including Dave's, I could have lied or not told the truth, and I'm sure nobody would have been the wiser.

Transparency has become my motto, especially when transparency helps educate and enlighten people. With my parent's friends, what I hoped would impact them the most was not that I am trans but how my parents loved and supported me. For all they knew about my Mom and Dad and how much they admired and respected them, they now had another cause cèlébre to add to the list of admirable qualities.

Going back to my conversation with Dave, there was one more thing that he said that I could have taken in two ways. He exclaimed, "You're the first one of them [trans person] I meet in person!" I took it as a compliment on behalf of all trans persons. I felt honored to have shed light by helping someone else understand and represent our marginalized community.

There is always a risk one takes when answering these types of questions; there is always the possibility that the answer one gives is more than the person can handle. In many ways, I had no choice but to answer honestly; I will be moving in with my mom, I will be his neighbor, and the last thing I want is to be walking on eggshells and skirting the issue every time I see him.

From his response, I think I (we) have another new ally.

Chapter 20: Still So Much to Learn

Graduate studies are one thing. Life's lessons are another, and I needed to immerse myself in both. I had to confront my biases; I wanted to do better. It was never too late to learn in the milieu that was my life. Here are some of the themes I dealt with during those months; they are from three blogposts, one written before going to Ft. Lauderdale and the other two in the following weeks.

You will note that "Non-Binary" was not yet part of the LGBTQ+ lexicon when I wrote this blogpost. It would be two more years before the term gained traction. Rather than inserting non-binary into stuff I wrote in those days, I will provide a brief description of the term at the end of this chapter.

Blog Post: Apr 6, 2013
20.1: Who Made Me Gender Police?
On Pointing Fingers and Being Out of My Gender
Non-Conforming Comfort Zone (an admission)

The story is titled "About a Boy: Transgender surgery at age sixteen" by Margaret Talbot in the New Yorker Magazine (March 18, 2013). It talks about how many more females are coming out as trans now than in the past. But as I reflected on the amazing progress trans people have made in recent years, it made me aware of my subtle bias about gender-role conformity.

Indeed, my doctors tell me that compared to twenty years ago, when it seemed that twice as many males transitioned to females than females to males, today there is equilibrium in the numbers, with as many females as males identifying as trans. Margaret Talbot says this:

"In the past, females who wished to live as males rarely sought surgery, partly because they could "pass" easily enough in public; today, there is a desire for more thorough transformations."

The subject of her story is a young trans man named Skylar who underwent top surgery at sixteen, a much younger age than would have been possible a decade ago. Though Skylar has transitioned medically and surgically, he is not fixated on conventional masculinity and is entirely comfortable with a certain amount of gender ambiguity. He is quoted as saying he does not feel the need to be a "macho bro."

Skylar is not alone. Many trans persons of his generation have a level of comfort with their gender presentation that is admirable. I admit that I don't possess that kind of self-confidence. Because of my need to avoid drawing negative attention to myself and, by extension and association, with my cisgender* friends and family, I am guilty of a certain degree of gender policing. This means I am guilty of judging based on society's expectations of what is appropriate for males and females.

I don't think I am alone; many trans persons invest time, energy, and finances to retrofit their bodies to achieve congruence between brain and body. One pitfall some fall into is taking these efforts to the extreme of the respective ends of the scale and potentially end up as grotesque caricatures of their identified gender. More disconcerting than this, however, is how for the majority of the trans population, these options are out of their reach, and they must cope with their gender dysphoria one way or another.

This has often caused friction in the trans community because this is where gender policing comes into play. The standards of acceptability, after all, are part of the social construct and, as such, come with a huge emotional, social, and financial price tag. It strikes me as ironic how to pass society's test of what is appropriately male/masculine and female/feminine, we seem to force ourselves back into boxes and judge and discriminate based on how well we express or adhere to the gender binary.

The term "gender-queer" is one that not many people understand but is pertinent to this discussion. Wikipedia has a good primer on all the nuances of this umbrella term; it says in part:

"... gender-queer has been used as an adjective to refer to any people who transgress distinctions of gender, regardless of their self-defined gender identity, i.e., those who "queer" gender, expressing it non-normative ways."

Being part of the baby-boomer generation means that I grew up in a vacuum of information, compared to how language allows younger people to make sense of their sexuality today.

Nevertheless, I must constantly educate myself as our knowledge and experience grow. In the same way, I covet having a support network of well-informed allies; I realize I need to be better informed so I can be an ally to those who express their gender differently and more confidently than I have the guts to do. I also realize I am more insecure than my younger counterparts, who don't need society's approval to be comfortable in their bodies. Perhaps there is even a touch of jealousy on my part.

Simply saying that I admire their courage seems so patronizing and hypocritical; I'm upset at how easy it is to devalue those who bend the rules I have felt compelled to follow. While I hunger for inclusion, equity, and equality, I know how my subconscious biases make me want to deny others a seat at the table.

What's worse is that even though I credit my Christian faith with keeping me from self-harm as I struggled with my gender identity and gave me hope, I quickly shifted to gatekeeping. I have never expressed this publicly or said anything to any gender-nonconforming or gender-queer person, but I have harbored those thoughts at times and sincerely apologize.

I say all of this while at the same time claiming I have never felt as comfortable in my own body as I do today. I am grateful for being able to access the help I needed and live in a time and place that made it all possible. But I am also acutely aware of the role privilege plays in all this.

I celebrate the fact that younger persons can access help and benefit from this early intervention. But this also means that we all need to do a better job of allowing them to find their comfort zone and fight like hell to protect their right to do so.

Unpublished Blog Post: April 30, 2013

20.2: What am I?

The Medical Symposium I attended in Ft. Lauderdale in April was everything I had hoped it would be. It wasn't a large gathering, perhaps 90 attendees, which meant the breakout sessions were more intimate and allowed more audience participation. I attended a presentation by a board-certified physician assistant specializing in psychiatry and trans care. I sat in the front row, as I am prone to do, and the session began with a welcome to the group, and then the speaker pointed the finger at me and asked, "What am I?"

Talk about being put on the spot. I said something to the effect of, "I have never met you. By appearance, you were assigned female at birth but are dressed in a very elegant, perfectly tailored men's Italian suit and shoes. Your face and how you use makeup are very feminine. But your presentation doesn't tell me anything about your gender identity or your sexual orientation."

My observations were accepted as valid. Without apologizing for singling me out, they announced, "I identify as a feminine man, I am attracted to women, and I use they-them pronouns." They then proceeded with their talk , and that is all I remember. I was so rattled by the surprise exchange at the beginning that my mind went blank. Upon reflection, I realized there are no cookie-cutter templates regarding gender identity or gender expression that I should rely on. Each person has the right to self-identify and express however they choose that makes them feel authentic. And I learned that whatever assumptions I may make about someone, it is not up to me to impose those assumptions on them—end of story.

You would think I had eaten enough humble pie and had learned my lesson not to make assumptions or pass judgment on others.

Blog Post: August 13, 2013
20.3: Then, a Retraction and an Apology

I just removed the blogpost I wrote yesterday. Upon reflection, I confess that what I said in it was harsh and judgmental toward the subject of a story that appeared in the New York Post.

My comments were about Don Ennis, a former ABC News assignment editor who came out as trans and changed his name to Dawn. Then a medical event resulted in memory loss and amnesia, so Dawn became Don again.

I was convinced my criticism and skepticism were justified, and the story seemed too fantastic. But as others have pointed out, I didn't know all the details. More importantly, I didn't know the person and what they are going through. I acknowledged that each person's story is their own and reminded myself how I have advocated for understanding and have often said that unless we have walked in someone's shoes, we cannot claim to know what motivates them.

This is my apology for having jumped to conclusions.

I forgot the pain I've seen in the three persons I know who have "detransitioned" and returned to their previous gender expression. One did so because the person she loved made it a condition of the relationship, another because all attempts to embody their true identity would be impossible, given their masculine body, and the other could not live with the rejection. These friends have struggled with depression ever since, and I worry about them. I should have extended the same level of compassion to Dawn Ennis.

The fact that some trans persons find transition impossible to complete says more about society's intolerance than it does about the trans person's character.

Postscript:
A year later, in 2014, she returned proudly as Dawn. As of January 2023, she is an award-winning journalist, Sports Editor at the Los Angeles Blade, university professor, TV news producer, reporter, host, writer, blogger, podcaster, and fellow LGBTQ+ and human rights advocate.

Blogpost: December 14, 2013
20.4: Why I don't look forward to Christmas

Have you ever considered the irony in the Christmas story concerning family?

Luke tells us, "A decree went out from Emperor Augustus that all the world should be registered. All went to their own towns to be registered. Joseph went from the town of Nazareth in Galilee to Judea, to the city of David, called Bethlehem, because he was descended from the house and family of David. He went to be registered with Mary, to whom he was engaged and who was expecting a child."

Whether this census really took place in exactly this way is debatable. It may have been a more localized census, affecting only the Province of Syria, which included Judea.

Assuming there is some truth to Luke's account, can you imagine a homecoming where you cannot connect with any of your family and are forced to find shelter in a stable? If Joseph was returning to his roots because of a decree, one would think his roots would also be aware of this decree and anticipate the arrival of many kinfolks, perhaps meeting them for the first time. Was Joseph's family so fractured that he couldn't connect with a relative? Or was it the fact that they were poor and were being ostracized and made to be unwelcome?

You don't have to be a family-ancestry aficionado to think with wonder and curiosity about your ancestors. Imagine being able to gather with all your kinfolk at your ancestral home. What would it look like? It could explain why you have a receding hairline or large ears. But think of all the stories as you trace the history of the gathering?

Unfortunately, homecomings aren't always joyous events. Families don't always enjoy a happy history. No family is free from some form of dysfunction or brokenness. Most families deal with this with pretense and denial, keeping silent about the taboos. Some families are embarrassed to be seen with some of their members. You know why. A healthy family system must be aware of its failures and successes, whether real or imagined, public or private. I'm not suggesting for a moment that we should be hanging our dirty laundry for all to see. Rather, I suggest that if we cannot be honest about our families, realizing none are perfect, then there will be no possibility for us to be family to each other.

Additionally, families with intergenerational trauma face a difficult reality that cannot be overlooked or minimized. Reunions can retraumatize and re-open wounds. The call for forgiveness and kindness in family relationships cannot be applied universally. Some histories are too difficult to reconcile. Optimally, our focus, then, has to be on how we can create safe spaces for individuals who experience this kind of trauma and brokenness within their families. It is our opportunity to think creatively and act with compassion.

If there is any truth to the saying: "Kindness begins at home," and if our answer to the question in Micah, "...and what does the Lord require of you but to do justice, and to love kindness, and to walk humbly with your God?" and if mercy does not radiate out from family, what hope is there for us to know what it means to do justice and love kindness in the community?

In other words, if we have become selective within our own families so that either collectively or individually, we have come to deem some less deserving of our kindness than others, can we really hope to celebrate the Season that celebrates humanity's liberation with any integrity?

In the last four months of graduate theological studies, I have come to appreciate one reason why the Bible continues to inspire people. The Tanakh (i.e., the Jewish Bible; Hebrew Scriptures formerly referred to as the Old Testament) and the New Testament do not gloss over family dysfunction. They bear testimony to the importance of having this collective memory I've been talking about, where mistakes are admitted, and the consequences for forgetting always have sad results.

The inspiring part has to do with how the opposite is true. When we remember, we are compelled to walk humbly with God, act justly, and love kindness, and then blessings flow out to the community with a cascading effect.

This brings me back to why I don't look forward to Christmas. Actually, I have several reasons. One is that I see how families find it easier to avoid their black sheep and make them invisible. Regardless of how justified they may feel for doing this, they are poorer. Another reason is the ease with which we (I include myself) can treat strangers like family treat family like strangers.

My family is not perfect, and I am not perfect. My divorce two years ago is responsible for much of my difficulty with Christmas. Despite our best effort to minimize the pain, there continues to be sadness that can spiral quickly into a deep funk at this time. I know I am not alone in this. Many experiences deep sadness over broken family relationships. Compounding this sadness is when we are prevented from giving and receiving grace to and from those we have called father, mother, brother, sister, son, daughter, husband, or wife.

Is there any hope? I think so, or I wouldn't waste your time with my thoughts. I really want us who find Christmases difficult to get through this time of the year and come out smiling at the other end. I don't want to minimize the hurt many of us experience by spooning out many greeting card platitudes. Instead, I want to challenge us to do the impossible and perhaps the radical: forgive them and forgive yourself.

Whether you are the protagonist or the antagonist in your Christmas story, remember this time-tested truth: "Whoever sows sparingly will also reap sparingly, and whoever sows bountifully will also reap bountifully."

Our material generosity means nothing in the grand scheme of things. What's important is being generous in kind, even when we feel bankrupt. And what can happen? Our storehouses will be filled to the top.

20.5: As promised: Non-Binary Identities

Non-binary individuals, who do not identify as exclusively male or female, represent a growing and diverse group within the trans community. The term transgender was first adopted in the 1990s to describe individuals who identify with a gender different from the one assigned at birth.

Since then, trans identities have continued to evolve, with the emergence of terms like non-binary, genderqueer, and gender-fluid to describe gender identities outside of the traditional binary.

In a large study conducted by the National Center for Transgender Equality in 2015, close to 29,000 people participated, with 35% of trans respondents identifying as non-binary That is slightly more than one third of the total. Of those who identified as non-binary, the majority were female assigned at birth, and the majority of non-binary respondents were under 25.

These findings highlight the ongoing evolution of gender identities and the importance of recognizing and affirming the diversity of gender experiences. It also underscores the need for more inclusive spaces and policies supporting individuals who may identify outside the traditional binary.

As with many of the terms we hear associated with gender identity, Non-Binary *or Nonbinary,* took a few years to enter the Oxford English Dictionary (OED). This adjective was only added in 2019. Another surprising term that I have been using for several years is "gender-affirming." It only made it into the OED in 2022, along with EnBy, which is short for Non-Binary since the abbreviation "NB" refers to "Non-Black."

20.6: Interlude
The End of Summer 2013: Pflag and Pride

The summer of 2013 held one more first for me: it was the first time I attended Vancouver Pride, which already had a history of 35 years. I had always avoided it and, I confess, frowned upon it. My internalized homophobia and transphobia, which had kept me on a solitary tract all those years, had also kept me far from this event, which drew an estimated crowd of 650,000 in 2013. Pflag Vancouver was being recognized that year, with three moms who had been long-standing members of the Vancouver chapter being named Parade Co-Marshalls. I drove one of the convertible Austin Minis that carried the moms perched above the back seats.

Pflag, which stands for parents, friends of lesbians, and gays, was not an organization I was familiar with until my trip to welcome Angie in San Diego. The couple that sponsored Angie was very involved in their local chapter; they convinced me to get involved in the Vancouver chapter or at least check it out. I had always assumed Pflag was to LGBTQ+ people what Al-Anon was to alcoholics; a peer-support group for loved ones and significant others, and not for the person who is LGBTQ+. So, why would I want to go?

Linda and Rick acknowledged two things about Pflag. As an acronym, it was dated because it left out bisexual, trans, and queer people. It also implied what I had assumed: it was only for family members and friends. What excited Linda and Rick was how the focus had changed, and trans persons were the new thing.

Whereas historically, most people who attended Pflag meetings had gone because of a gay or lesbian family member, they were now coming because a family member had come out as trans. And more and more LGBTQ+ persons were coming to help answer questions and share their life experiences. I started attending Pflag meetings in September 2012. Everything Rick and Linda said was also true in the Vancouver chapter.

Unfortunately, I had to take a break from active participation once I began full-time studies a year later. The deep dive had begun.

Chapter 21: I'm In Over My Head

Vancouver School of Theology is ecumenical; it is not beholden to one particular doctrinal position nor sponsored by any particular denomination. The school prides itself on its Indigenous and Inter-Religious Studies programs, which attract a multicultural, multi-ethnic, multi-faith, and multi-denominational group of students. With an annual enrollment of about 200, class sizes are small, creating an intimate learning environment with a diversity of religious and cultural perspectives.

I pursued the Master of Arts in Public and Pastoral Leadership (MAPPL) with fewer required credit hours than an MDiv, as it is designed for individuals interested in ministry outside of traditional religious contexts.

My experience at VST taught me the importance of self-monitoring and questioning my beliefs to uncover the basis of my core values and perspectives. It also taught me the value of diverse perspectives and how they can enrich the learning environment. While my spiritual beliefs underwent a significant shift during my studies, I ultimately emerged with a deeper understanding of myself and my beliefs. I am grateful for the experience, and I believe it has equipped me with the tools to navigate complex theological questions in the future.

From the beginning of my full-time studies, I was consumed by the amount of reading required. The summer course I took paled in comparison to the four courses I took during my program. As a contemplative reader, I found myself needing to read paragraphs twice and then contemplating what I had read before continuing. However, there was so much reading, it felt like I was trying to get a sip of water from a fire hose.

The themes of the courses overlapped so much that it was

difficult to differentiate which reading material belonged to which course. Dr. Dutcher-Walls, the Academic Dean at VST, taught two required courses on "The Hebrew Bible," parts 1 and 2. Her teaching approach involved weekly reflection journals that invited us to dive deeper and self-monitor our thought processes. Her questions about interpretive principles proved to be a challenge for me, but I eventually learned to weed out essentialist ideas and question my beliefs to uncover the basis of my core values and perspectives.

As I delved deeper into my beliefs, I found that my spirituality and my core beliefs began to shift. Much of what I had been taught no longer sounded as solid, and I began to reconsider and reconstruct my faith. It is not uncommon for depression to arise in graduate studies in theology as the disruption to core beliefs can be unsettling. However, I had already done a substantial amount of sifting related to being trans, so I didn't find myself emotionally exhausted or anxious. It was energizing. It was nothing short of shedding dogma.

While many of my classmates had career goals within a particular denomination, some hoped to work with non-profit and humanitarian organizations. I had no idea what organization would consider hiring me as a chaplain for trans people. While the hospital-based Clinical Pastoral Education (CPE) was responsible for my theological studies and took place in a hospital, I didn't see myself pursuing a job as a hospital chaplain. I also did not envision becoming a chaplain at large with no visible means of support, especially if I hoped to work with trans people and their families; I would never be able to charge for spiritual support. Some professors thought I should formally join the United Church of Canada (UCC), given its official pro-LGBTQ+ inclusion stance; however, I had no denominational affiliation or sponsorship. I put off making any decisions or commitments until I was closer to graduation.

The first fall term was a blur. I surprised myself by completing some of the most grueling mental work I had ever done.

21.1: Coming Up for Air

I took advantage of the two-week winter break from studies to attend the 2014 Gay Christian Network (GCN) conference in Chicago, and, upon return, I attended a short intensive course for aspiring United Church of Canada (UCC) clergy. The latter concentrated on the theology, doctrine, and polity of UCC. This short course surveyed its history and emerging theology, and doctrines. It promoted intellectual quest, theological and personal commitment with an eye toward societal and world issues. This all sounded good to me.

The GCN conference in Chicago was my third time presenting a workshop for them. I went to the assigned meeting room early to set up, hoping I would still have a few minutes to relax before people came in. The audio-visual team got their instructions wrong and had not set up a projector for the PowerPoint presentation. I found one of the conference support volunteers who had a walkie-talkie, and he went to work looking for a projector. A few minutes passed, and he returned with the news that all the projectors were already assigned. With his apologies accepted, I asked if any flip chart was available. That, they were able to provide.

By then, I had already presented workshops on trans inclusion to about 20 groups and organizations. I felt confident that I could do the workshop without the visuals and use the flip chart to write down terms and key points as I went along. I planned to use my laptop as my outline, going from slide to slide. A piece of cake, I thought. But then I had another idea.

What if, instead, I asked the 100 attendees what questions they had about trans issues? So, in my opening remarks, I told them about the goof-up with a projector and explained my plan. Starting with the first person on my left in the front row. They were to say their name and where they were from and tell me what burning question they had about anything trans? Then I said that when it was their turn to introduce themselves, if someone had already asked their question, only to say their name and where they were from. It took ten minutes to go through the whole group. It turned out that after the people in the first row had introduced themselves and asked their questions, we had already identified the six most pertinent questions in people's minds. I wrote the questions on the flipchart, which became my outline.

That I was surprised at how well the workshop had gone is an understatement. Still a novice at presenting workshops, the most obvious difference was how meaningful and powerful it was to have constant eye contact with the audience. In all the times when I used PowerPoint slides, people's attention was on the screen, naturally; it's what I also do when sitting through a presentation. The experience boosted my confidence; I knew my stuff well.

GCN absorbed the cost of my hotel room and waived the conference fee once again, and once again, I was grateful. The person I was to have shared the room with didn't show up, which was too bad. By now, socializing and meeting new people were not fraught with insecurity. And as I shared earlier, I met the wonderful Rachel Held Evans in person. I also met Betsy, an ally from Ottawa, who purchased a copy of my book to give to an old high school friend, Samantha, who had transitioned but was having a rough go. She, too, had gone through a divorce and was also underemployed, but unlike me, she had little family or community support.

Compared to my experience in Tucson a year earlier, I was much more engaged. This may have been partly due to meeting Rachel Held Evans, but also the fact that there were more trans participants, though our numbers still could have been higher.

Sunday is typically a travel day for most attendees who leave after the close of the conference at noon. A few of us who weren't leaving until Monday went to Second City to catch a show that night. Though the comedy troop that night was made up of only apprentices, we had a blast. I had a memorable time in Chicago.

Back in my hotel room, I received an email from Betsy. She was already back in Ottawa. She had just learned that her trans friend, Amanda, had ended her life that afternoon. She was heartbroken, and so was I. On Facebook, I posted the following:

21.2: A Punch in the Gut
A sad postscript to "My highs and lows of advocacy."

In my blogpost a couple of days ago, I touched on some of the things that lift me and those that, well, shoot me down. However, I have been unable to get one thing out of my mind since I received the news on Sunday evening. Let me explain.

At last week's Gay Christian Network (GCN) Conference in Chicago, I met Betsy, a fellow Canadian. She attended as an ally, and we had a long chat about an old high school friend who, like me, transitioned from male to female in her fifties, Amanda. She shared how Amanda had friends who supported her, but these relationships had slowly cooled, and Betsy was concerned for her friend. She thanked me for my work and was looking forward to being a more informed friend to Amanda.

The note I received from Betsy on Sunday night was short; Amanda had ended her life.

This, my friends, is a very low of lows. It is a sad commentary that life is made to be so impossible for some that they cannot envision living another day. That impossibility is often a combination of many small factors, none of which may seem damaging or threatening on their own but can break the camel's back when accumulated through time. Getting the sideways looks, hearing the whispers behind one's back, being addressed with the wrong pronouns or name, feeling like the elephant in the room, or feeling invisible; all these may not seem like much in isolation from each other, but when you cannot go anywhere in your community where you can be free of these life-sapping scenarios, it is easy to slip into quiet despair and hopelessness. It doesn't always have to be a hostile, judgmental comment; those seem to roll off one's back much easier. But all the seemingly benign non-verbal barbs stick like Velcro to one's heart until it is pierced as if with a spear.

Dear Amanda, I am sorry your light was slowly snuffed out. I'm sorry you were not allowed to imagine a better life for yourself, where you could be you and all your talents and all the things that made you special could be celebrated by all.

Dear Betsy, I'm sorry you have lost a friend. I'm sorry that you will mourn instead of cheer for her. Thank you for what you did for Amanda.

Blogpost: January 13, 2014
21.3: The Highs and Lows of Advocacy.

Sometimes I preach to the choir, sometimes to the genuinely curious and sensitive; at other times to hostile skeptics, but often to myself.

I had the honor and privilege to do a workshop at this year's Gay Christian Network Conference (GCN) last weekend. I cannot begin to describe what it is like to be among 700 attendees who have one thing in common, a hunger and a love for God, and for whom faith is not a legalistic dogma but the river of life.

To say that gays, lesbians, bisexual, trans, and gender-queer persons are excluded from the "banquet" of the King is to deny the essential message of the Gospel and comes pretty close to that unforgivable sin, which is to ascribe the work of the Holy Spirit to the devil. One only needs to meet a large number of parents of LGBTQ+ persons who attended this year's conference, listen to their stories, and see the love in their eyes, to appreciate what it means to be affirming.

No one can sit through Linda and Rob Robertson's telling of their story and then accuse them of any heresy. And you better have a good supply of tissue on hand as they recount the process they went through when their son Ryan came out to them as a teenager, a process of transformation from narrow-minded religious judgment to unconditional love and support with a capital "S."

Despite this transformation, their son died tragically from an overdose. Now they want churched parents to open the eyes of their hearts and consider the logs in their own eyes. If you have a box of tissues and an hour to spare, search on YouTube for: "Just Because He Breathes — Learning to Truly Love Our Gay Son."

At GCN, Linda and Rob were gracious enough to recount their painful journey through their son's final moments and the years of struggle that preceded his premature death. Their love for the son and their passion for the church is palpable. They share their story to help us all grow in love for one another.

This was my third GCN conference and the third time I have given a workshop on what it means to be trans as a Christian. I typically cycle from nauseating nervousness to transcendent peace in the days and hours before my workshops. I have identified two reasons I go through this cycle: one, I am an introverted, shy, and insecure person; and two, I am an introverted, shy, and radically transformed person. The difference is that I am aware and cognizant of how God has been at work in my life.

Consequently, when I recount how I reconciled my faith to my medical diagnosis of gender dysphoria, I, like the Robertsons, have the privilege to declare God's unconditional, transforming love and power. The truth is, I need to remind myself that I am truly loved because even after five years, undoing 56+ years, the effects of self-loathing take time.

Chater 22: Blogposts 2013-2014

The kind of stuff that occupied my mind when I didn't have my head buried in my studies, starting with this blogpost from October 29, 2013:

Blogpost: October 29, 2013:
22.1: Do I know you? You look familiar.
Ever wonder what it might be like to change into
a different person?

I've lived in Vancouver for the last forty years of my life. That's about two-thirds of the total trips I've taken around the sun.

I've met hundreds of people during those years, if not thousands. Some were my business clients, a couple were my bosses, dozens were my employees, about three hundred were my students at Capilano College, a crazy number were customers I had the pleasure of serving at my family's restaurant in Kitsilano, Las Margaritas, another five hundred or so were fellow worshippers in the seven different churches we attended as a family, and several dozen were neighbors, the parents of our children's friends, and the many other people I knew only by first name—the grocery store clerks, pharmacists, postal delivery persons, etc. I haven't added all these people up, and I don't know how my list compares to yours—is it larger, smaller, or average in size?

I have no way of knowing how many people this might be, and this uncertainty contributed to one of the biggest fears I entertained for years. It had nothing to do with anthropophobia; it had everything to do with transphobia—in reverse.

I assume that you are familiar with the term. Basically, it is the fear of trans persons. Except, in my case, I was afraid of people who might be transphobic. "Might" is the operative word here; after all, I lived in Vancouver—what better place to be if you plan to jump into the LGBT alphabet soup?

Unfortunately, "might" is a flimsy platform to stand on when it is the only option apart from falling on your own sword after growing weary of one's internal battle. What if all the people in these overlapping circles of my life chose to hate me? In some ways, hate would be preferable to derision and mocking, I thought to myself. For this reason, too, death seemed so utterly convenient and reasonable.

I feared that everywhere I went, the likelihood of running into someone who knew me in my previous life as a guy was pretty high. What would they say to me? How would they react?

At the time, it made sense to me why so many trans persons started life in a new place once they began their life over—presenting as their true selves—with no need to worry that their past would get in their way. But I also saw how lonely this had left many of them, living without the most important people in their lives to accompany them during what must be one of the hardest things anyone could think of doing, to live in the sex other than the one assigned to you at birth.

This is not a plea for pity; I'm only telling you what it was like for me six years ago, at the age of fifty-seven, when I began to disclose to family and friends the changes that were about to take place in my life. Each person I disclosed to was sworn to secrecy, yet the process left me emotionally drained.

After two weeks, I had only disclosed to ten people, but it felt like I had already poured myself out, and there was no more energy to continue. I had cried so much that all the heaving and wailing had left my stomach muscles cramped. That weekend I went to bed after I did my Saturday morning run and did not wake up until mid-afternoon on Sunday. The disclosure was exhausting, and I didn't know how I would survive.

One of the first persons I disclosed to, a client, turned out to be a lifesaver for me; she surprised me by telling me she had a brother who had also come out as trans. She gave me the best piece of advice anyone could have given me; she told me to give people the benefit of the doubt. "People who know you love you. They are not going to throw you away," she said. She was right: those first disclosures—as difficult as they were—afforded me the opportunity to experience a deeper connection than I had ever experienced with each person I told. It gave me hope that my life would not be over.

The need to control how the information went out about my pending plans to live as a woman became less important as time passed. Though it had been important at the beginning to control the flow—neither my aged parents nor our three adult sons knew anything—the news spread throughout my world without me being the messenger. Yet, I would like to have been a fly on the wall each time the information was shared.

I quickly learned that once the most important people in my life affirmed me with their love and support, I couldn't care less what others thought. I'll never forget how it felt waking up the morning after I shared it with my parents. It was a sunny morning in May 2008, the sky was blue, and the birds were chirping. I sat up in bed and took a deep breath—no more secrets to hide. I felt free, like a bird being let out of its cage. Tears of gratitude flowed freely; I had a reason to live now.

I'm not a statistician, so I have no way of knowing what my actual odds were of running into someone I knew on the street who would take one look at me and say, "Do I know you? You look familiar." Nevertheless, I had assumed this would be a regular occurrence for me—isn't Vancouver just a small village?

Five years ago, on the last week of July, I started living full-time as a female, and to this day, I have only run into someone I know perhaps a dozen times. Each time that it happened, my eyes made contact with theirs, I knew immediately who they were, but they—on the other hand—had a puzzled look on their face, their expressions betraying their thoughts..."I think I know you." Generally, I greeted them by name and told them I knew them from a previous life. Their response has mostly been: "Oh. A-ah. Yeah. Wow! How are you?" followed by a loss of words.

No one has run for the exit door—yet. Everyone has been

amazingly mature and supportive once they have recovered their ability to speak intelligently.

It hasn't been a cakewalk in every one of my circles. I want to respect those who, for some religious reason, have not yet been able to wrap their brain around the idea that gender identity is not always linked to the set of gonads, appendages, and orifices one was born with. This does make me a little impatient at times because, even in Vancouver, life for trans persons isn't always easy. We often lose young and old people who cannot imagine a future when all they know in their present is rejection, ridicule, and marginalization.

Do I know you? Do you know me?

I'll be looking for you. Say Hi!

Blogpost: March 10, 2014
22.2: Jesus Set His Face to Jerusalem

Chapter Nine in Luke has got to be one of the most action-packed chapters you may ever encounter in the Bible. In only sixty-two verses, we see thirteen different dramatic scenes flash before us:

1. Jesus sends out the twelve Apostles
2. Herod is perplexed by news about Jesus — Is he Elijah?
3. Jesus feeds the five thousand
4. Peter Confesses Jesus as the Christ
5. Jesus foretells his death
6. Jesus talks about taking up your cross daily to follow him
7. The Transfiguration!
8. Jesus heals a boy with an unclean spirit after his disciples can't
9. Jesus foretells his death again
10. Jesus talks about who is the Greatest
11. Jesus talks about how anyone not against us is for us
12. A Samaritan village rejects Jesus he sets his face on Jerusalem
13. Jesus spells out the cost of following him

Each of these scenes provides a lot to think about and talk about. I've been reflecting on number twelve when the Samaritan village rejected Jesus.

Verse 51 says: "When the days drew near for him to be taken

up, he set his face to go to Jerusalem. And he sent messengers ahead of him. On their way, they entered a village of the Samaritans to prepare for him."

Presumably, to arrange for a short overnight stay?

Verse 53 continues: "but they did not receive him, because his face was set toward Jerusalem." The Samaritans confused Jesus' objective with the historic disdain Jews had for them as inferior or unworthy of respect, an attitude that predated Elijah. This was hardly what Jesus had in mind.

For the disciples, heading to Jerusalem had an entirely different meaning and purpose. In their minds, Jesus' objective was to become King of the Jews. Naturally, James and John bridled at the Samaritans' enmity toward their future king.

There is a kind of irony in all of this: on an earlier occasion, Jesus and his disciples were traveling north, having "abandoned Judea" (Jn.4:3). John will later recount the incident of the Samaritan woman at the well and all the goodwill that resulted from that short stay in Shechem, in Samaria.

Maybe they assumed the Samaritans would receive Jesus enthusiastically on his return south to Judea. Reports about Jesus' earlier visit had no doubt gone out throughout their country by then.

James and John were indignant, and without considering what Jesus would wish to do, the "Sons of Thunder" wanted lightning — "Fire from heaven"— to teach the Samaritans a lesson.

After all, that is the way Elijah replied to the bullying tactics of Samaria. Did he not say, "If I am a man of God, let fire come down from heaven and consume you and your fifty." (2 Kings. 1:10-12)

"Lord, show them that you, too, are a man of God" That's what James and John wanted Jesus to do. Hadn't the Transfiguration proved that their Jesus was greater than Elijah?

While the sons of thunder were proposing what course Jesus should take, Jesus had already turned away, metaphorically speaking, and had wiped the dust off his feet. Instead of rebuking the Samaritans, Jesus turned to rebuke James and John.

The NRSV notes that some ancient authorities read:" Jesus rebuked them, and said, "You do not know what spirit you are of, for the Son of Man has not come to destroy the lives of human beings but to save them."

If he consented to their suggestion and punished these Samaritans with fire from heaven, then the whole of the province of Samaria would have been shut to the Gospel after that, and the Gospel story, as we know it today, would be a very different one.

It was a simple lesson, which the apostles were slow to learn, that once you have used violence or hard words of judgment against anyone, your hope of having any relationship with them may be gone forever.

A few months, or maybe even a couple of years later, the apostle John returned to Samaria with Peter and received an enthusiastic reception. They had come to share the spiritual essence or power with all who had embraced the Gospel of Jesus' resurrection, as preached by Philip. (Acts 8:14)

Indeed, if fire from heaven had consumed the Samaritans on that earlier occasion, would John's return to empower the Samaritans have been possible?

Does this help explain why there has been so much suspicion from the LGBTQ+ community toward those in the church who are piously calling fire down from heaven on the gays since 1980, at the start of the AIDS epidemic?

What rebuke might Jesus have for us today when we wish for the destruction of our enemies? Could it be the same as it was for Peter and John?

"You do not know what spirit you are of, for the Son of Man has not come to destroy the lives of human beings but to save them."

Blogpost: March 6, 2014
22.3: No, I Haven't Seen Dallas Buyer's Club

...And I don't plan to. It's my wallet that decides what I do these days! But in the meantime, I have been reading the ongoing negative commentary about the portrayal of the trans character "Rayon" from the perspective of the trans community.

What needs to be considered is that there is today a generational divide in the trans community that needs to be understood. For us over 55, our experience is vastly different from those in their thirties and forties. And a universe away from those who are in their youth and into their twenties.

I suspect all the clamor comes from the younger sets, which had not lived through the painful years when we did not have the nomenclature to make sense of our lives.

In 1980, I was thirty. I had been married for six years and was terrified. I didn't know what I was. That year, I came out to my wife. All I could tell her was that I felt inadequate as a man and feminine, and I confessed to my secret guilt-ridden cross-dressing episodes and how I needed her to help me fight Satan. Yes, those were my words, and that was my mindset. I saw it as a spiritual attack on me as a person and as an attack on a couple of young parents.

It would be another ten years before I learned that there was a word for this cursed condition. But it would take another ten years for me to be able to apply that label to myself. To have considered myself trans would have been akin to admitting defeat to the devil. I wanted this conundrum, whatever its cause, to go away.

Earlier, I said I was terrified. Let me tell you why: I had no role models, and the only "trans" persons I had seen—from a distance—were the pathetic Rayons. They and the drag queens in the media provided perspective for me, and both of these characterizations offered no hope for me. If I were trans, I would be either a joke and a laughingstock or someone who would be relegated to the margins of society. I preferred death.

I agree with Capelinia Addams, American trans actress, musician, spokesperson and activist for trans rights and issues when she points out that in today's trans community, an "elitist hypocrisy" wants to erase these negative portrayals and reminders of what it was like for our pioneers. I admit, they were braver than me, and it is because of the path they helped to clear that I can exist and speak today from a relatively secure position of privilege. I had access to services and help that were not there even twenty years ago.

While I am uncomfortable with portrayals that depict trans persons as less than. Yet, in this case, the historical perspective needs to be appreciated. Those who led the way need to be honored.

Blogpost: March 24, 2014

22.4: Falling into the hands of God

Let us fall into the hands of the Lord, but not into the hands of mortals; for equal to his majesty is his mercy, and equal to his name are his works. (Sirach 2.18 – NRSV)

In all the reading I've been doing in preparation for my Hebrew Bible class, I've come across several verses that have captured my imagination. The one above made me pause, and the more I reflected on what it describes, I couldn't help but compare it to the admonition in the letter to the Hebrews, where the perspective of falling into the hands of God is described as a frightful experience. (Heb. 10.31)

Because of what I learned during my "Kill the Gay" Bill opposition phase, keep an eye on the key players. These American fundamentalists are recognized as fully responsible for instigating the homophobia that resulted in the infamous legislation.

In an Op-Ed in the Los Angeles Times on March 23, 2014, Kapya Kaoma (an Anglican priest and the senior religion and sexuality researcher at Political Research Associates in Boston) said:

"The vitriol that has fueled U.S. culture wars for so long is now being exported, and some of our most ardent culture warriors are finding a far more receptive audience abroad.

In nations such as Uganda, Russia, Nigeria, and Belize, an insidious homophobia engineered in America is taking root. I have seen this hate being spread with my own eyes."

What does this have to do with the verse in Sirach and Hebrews? A lot. It's a matter of perspective and perhaps experience—the experience of God. I suppose our interpretive principle about the nature and character of God can fall anywhere along the spectrum between a deity consumed with rage and one consumed with compassion. If the idea of falling into this deity's hand is frightful, then you will be motivated to scream out the warning as loudly as possible, like the watchman in the tower who sees danger on the horizon. If, on the other hand, one's concept of falling into the hands of a compassionate and merciful deity, what should the response look like? If those whose God is angry are motivated to frighten people into compliance, what do those whose God is love do to impact their world?

Looking at another event from last week, the death of the homophobic Southern Baptist pastor from Kansas, Fred Phelps, it has been interesting to read the range of opinions his death has generated. From those who despised the man and all he stood for and are glad that he is gone to those who also hated everything about him but are willing to recognize that his hatred and anger brought a different God into focus, a God who is love. That logic helps us understand something by first understanding what it is not.

In a somewhat related way, I stumbled upon a newsfeed on Facebook it pointed out that 34 years ago today, Archbishop Oscar Romero of Sans Salvador was assassinated as he lifted the chalice celebrating the Eucharist. Why? Because he had spoken out against poverty and social injustice. He once said, "There are many things that can only be seen by the eyes that cried." Perspective, there it is again...and experience.

I think we tend to equate evil with horrible people who are in bed with the devil. But as I have listened and read the words of the American fundamentalists that Kaoma accuses in her OpEd, one is struck with their passion and zeal for God. Unfortunately, on that spectrum I described above, they seem to fall on the side of an angry God looking forward to the fiery death of all those who do evil.

And there lies the tension. Acting according to our perception of God can sometimes result in evil and unfortunate consequences. If our perception of God is rooted in our experience of God, we may have entirely different Gods. Even though we may all claim that there is only one God overall, we all describe God very differently based on the part of the elephant we get to feel, as the elephant and blind men parable illustrates. Hence, our reality is the only reality we may claim to know for sure. Can we trust another's person's experience of God if it does not align with ours? I hear myself say what sounds too simplistic...does it first meet the test of LOVE?

May 17, 2014:
22.5: On Belonging and Mattering to God

A friend, Matthias Roberts, recently invited me to write some thoughts on belonging. He said, "Specifically if you could share a story on a time when you felt that you truly belonged — even if it was just for a moment." Here is my response:

I felt like I did not know how to pray for nearly two decades. Oh, I prayed, but I sensed that my prayers were ineffective—like lead balloons—my prayers didn't even reach the ceiling, let alone God, or so I thought.

Maybe the reason I felt this way had more to do with my expectations than my prayers. I wanted to be "normal." I did not want to undergo a social, medical, and surgical transition from male to female.

At times I preferred death to all the potential shame, awkwardness, and embarrassment that transition would heap on the most important people in my life: my wife and three sons.

And my parents.

And my sisters.

And my brother.

And their spouses and kids.

And my friends.

And my clients.

And my church.

And my students.

Do you get the picture? The very public process of transitioning seemed so drastic and unfair. After all, the struggle with my gender identity was a very private matter. Why was the solution—if, in fact, transitioning was the only solution—so damn public?

On top of that, the prospect of rejection loomed large, and it was too scary to consider. I fully expected all of my relationships would end. Who would want to be seen with a freak and a deviant— or as one? I was pretty hard on myself.

I prayed for God to make me a girl when I was young. That didn't happen. As I grew older and the reality set in that my body would not be transformed miraculously, I prayed for God to fix my brain—to keep it from replaying the endless loop that caused so much self-loathing and guilt. But God didn't cooperate. I figured the problem was not with God but with me. Like Paul's diatribe in Romans, I concluded that sin living in me was the problem.

Since I placed my faith in Christ during the Jesus People days, Jesus' invitation to come to him with my burdens stirred my heart the most. I wanted to find rest, which meant, as I stated above, I wanted to be normal. Over the years, I figured it would only be a matter of time before God snapped his fingers and "poof!" I'd be a regular guy; no more wanting to be a girl. I was memorizing Scripture, reading devotional books, reading about how to pray with power, etc. Yet...nothing.

The persistent, pervasive, and insidious nature of gender dysphoria only intensified my guilt and sense of defeat as a follower of Christ. But one surprising thing I discovered, which saved me, was how worship and praise music allowed me to experience a connection with God. I played the guitar well enough to help lead worship services in the churches we attended as a family in Vancouver. These churches had one thing in common, they sang the same style of music, and each had enough talented musicians and singers among their respective members. This meant we would rotate and take turns leading and playing on Sunday mornings.

I discovered I could commune with God through worship and praise songs. What prayer and crying could not do, worship and praise did; I experienced incredible intimacy with God. It transcended my self-loathing and guilt and transported me into God's presence. It provided temporary rest for my weary soul.

The songs I gravitated to were those we sang directly to God, expressing our deep love for Him and the yearnings of our hearts. What I call "marches, witness, and cheerleading songs" did nothing for me. Most of the music we learned came from Maranatha Music, Vineyard, and later Hillsong.

These were the days before iTunes when music CDs were the thing. As with all music, unless you know a band or singer well, much of what I bought collected dust on the shelf after listening to the CD once. One or two songs deserved consideration, but there needed to be better music without simplistic and trite lyrics. But every once in a while, I struck gold.

One such song was The Shepherd Song by Bob Farrell, sung by Kelly Willard in a compilation CD titled Evening Tapestry (1992). When I heard this song, I immediately connected it with Jesus' tender words about how he is the good shepherd. But the one verse that still fills me with joy every time I think about it is found in John's Gospel, chapter ten, verse sixteen. It says this:

"I have other sheep that do not belong to this fold. I must bring them also, and they will listen to my voice. So there will be one flock, one shepherd."

This verse stirs me and fills my heart with gratitude on many levels. Most powerfully, as someone who felt disqualified for being different and felt like the "other," it reminds me of the verse above. The Shepherd song has always made me feel like I belong and matter to God. Despite struggling with my chaos all those years, this song offered me a pasture where I felt safe and gave me hope.

Good Shepherd Song — by Bob Farrell
I can't live without your love
I can't find my way back home
Should I wander far away
You carry me back to the fold
Sing to me and I will follow
the only voice I know
Safe inside the shepherd's care
And comes the time to move along
You gather me to your side
Leading me so carefully
You're changing me all of the time
Sing to me and I will follow
The only voice I know...

I love the second verse with the line, "You're changing me all of the time." Hasn't that proven to be true?! Maybe the simplicity of the words that contain such rich imagery made it possible for me to sing to God. Or perhaps it is because the song helps remind me that I belong. How amazing is that?

Blogpost: May 24, 2014
22.6: Can I trust you with a secret?

Do you have a secret? How big is it? How do you think people will respond if they find out?

Disclosure, revelation, exposure, or whatever word you may have for it is a visceral, frightening process. Especially if the information is so sensitive, some would prefer death by flaying. But in fact, that is what disclosure is all about, peeling away the layers that hide the "body" of truth. Perhaps that is why it can be so traumatic.

On October 2007, I began disclosing to family and friends that I had been diagnosed with acute gender dysphoria—that I was "trans." I had already lived eight years with this verdict; it took me that long to reconcile myself and my faith to my diagnosis. The news shocked everyone; only my wife knew my secret.

Ever since I put my faith in Christ at age twenty, I had prayed to be normal and coped with this secret, ugly, persistent, cursed, and yet unnamed condition by spiritualizing it—maybe it's more accurate to say by "demonizing" it. (I had no name for it until 1990. I was 40 by then.) But not even placing my faith in a savior and doing all the things a Christian "soldier" is supposed to do, like putting on the armor of God and claiming victory over a defeated enemy, doing anything to stop the battles from raging.

Looking back on those years, the amazing thing is that this conflict was so well hidden. It's as if this war occurred on another planet or in a parallel universe. The curtain was drawn, and the wounds were shoved deep down to hide the evidence.

There is this idea among Christians that if you act right, look right, and live right, everything will work out. It's not true. Didn't Jesus accuse some who held this view of being nothing but whitewashed tombs full of dead men's bones? That is how I felt: squeaky clean and spiritual on the outside and chaos and confusion on the inside. Integrity Quotient: zero.

Does this mean no simple black-and-white "Christian Guidelines for Dummies" exist? Well, actually, no, there aren't any simple answers. That is not to say there aren't some radical one-liners with the power to change the course of history. I can think of several, but one will do: "Love your neighbor as yourself." Frederick Buechner, the author of "Telling Secrets," adds: "and love yourself as your neighbor." But I digress. I was talking about disclosure—and secrets.

To make my point, let me bring a more positive note to this conversation. Instead of thinking about a horrible secret, let's talk about a wonderful, beautiful secret. One that gives you goosebumps just thinking about it. Maybe it's how you felt the first time you fell in love with someone and nobody, but nobody, knew—especially the one by whom you had been smitten. (If you've never felt this, let me tell you, it's ga-ga-land amazing!)

Now, think back and try to recall some of the emotions you felt and how the palms of your hands sweated and your heart raced every time you thought about them. Then remember the moment you told them and how that felt. If you are anything like me, you may have felt a combination of nausea and ecstasy—all simultaneously, followed by a moment of surreal transcendence.

Still thinking about emotions, now substitute this secret love with a horrible secret, one that, instead of giving you goosebumps, makes you cringe and gag with shame. Now imagine picking up the phone to tell the person(s) you love the most this explosive truth. What emotions might you experience?

Physiologically, you may experience similar things, such as a pounding heart, nausea, and fear. Not just any fear. I'm talking about the anxiety that may propel a person to jump from the twentieth floor of a burning building. The type of fear that is highly irrational on one level and extremely logical on another — the logic that says, "This will spare you any more pain."

Now imagine repeating this disclosure a dozen or even a hundred times. Could you do it?

Coming out as lesbian, gay, bisexual, and trans (LGBT) can be this traumatic. While disclosure may be one common experience for all LGBT persons, it is several levels more intense for trans persons.

For most, the process has to be done twice; once when you disclose that you are trans, and once when you present yourself for the first time as the gender you identify as. In my case, as a woman.

The sense of vulnerability is akin to disrobing in front of people. Then, just when you think the whole world knows or has seen what you look like, you get a call from an old friend (or distant relative or client) who knows nothing about your new life and needs to meet with you. It doesn't matter how often you've done it before— even if everything turned out okay, it's just as heart-stopping scary every time you do it. It has no thrill; you want the earth to open up and swallow you whole.

In many ways, it's much easier to deal with strangers with whom you have no history. It's counterintuitive. The truth is that our family and friends should be our source of support, who can inflict the most pain.

I have been thinking a lot about this lately, not just because it has happened to me again recently, but because I get several weekly emails from total strangers who bare their souls and tell me their secrets, including pastors and church leaders. These men and women are terrified of what will happen once their secret is out. It's the primal fear of abandonment and rejection.

When their families reject as many as 50% of trans persons, many of them wonderfully squeaky clean on the outside church people, you can understand why 41% of trans persons admit to attempting suicide at least once.

I am therefore profoundly touched by the level of trust these frightened souls place in me — most of all, I admire their courage — for I know their heart was racing, and they felt nauseated as they wrote their email and pressed "SEND."

If you have previously thought being trans is a deviant lifestyle choice, let me ask: Who would choose such a thing, given the gloomy statistics?

If the abandonment, rejection, and judgment of trans persons will ever end, I believe it will be up to people of faith to make that choice. It really is in our power to love and embrace.

That's what the Bible shows us, and it's what I had to do for myself.

Blogpost June 12, 2014

22.7: We're in—We're out
It's a dizzying time for trans people.

Last night, I attended a meeting at the Vancouver School Board (VSB) as it listened to the final presentation from medical experts. The issue being considered is revising a 2004 VSB policy that spells out the district's guidelines for providing a safe, positive environment for trans and gender-variant students in all grades, from kindergarten to grade 12. The associate superintendent said, "The biggest change was about getting some clarity of language."

This simple administrative procedure became the entrée for a well-organized and vocal group of conservative parents who self-described as Chinese Evangelical Christians. They used this as an opportunity to lobby against the adoption of the proposed updated policy, arguing that this policy took away their rights as parents and guardians to decide what was best for their children. Unfortunately, these parents are using both race and religion cards.

They demanded more scientific research and that the BC Medical Association and the College of Physicians and Surgeons of BC weigh in on this issue. While claiming that they care about trans students, they don't want their children to be subjected to having trans and gender-variant students in their classrooms.

What they seem unwilling to recognize is that the original policy has been in place for several years and that the policy aligns with both Federal and Provincial guidelines for the school board's responsibility to provide a safe space for all students, regardless of race, ethnicity, religion, and sex and is in keeping with both the Federal and Provincial human rights codes.

The updated policy adds language to help schools create a more inclusive and safe space for trans students, including calls for schools to provide single-stall, gender-neutral washrooms, to "reduce or eliminate the practice of segregating students by sex," and to respect the rights of transgender students to decide how much information about their gender identity to share and with whom, among other things.

Additionally, the policy has the full support of the Vancouver Coastal Health Authority, designated by the Provincial Health Ministry to oversee these things. In other words, all the demands these parents are making were already met years ago.

This policy not only protects students who are LGBTQ+ but also those who are perceived as such. There have been instances of students who are "straight" but for whatever reason are perceived as gay or lesbian, or some other letter in the "alphabet soup," who have been bullied or made to feel unsafe at school.

In summary, the difference between the policy from 2004 and the updated version from 2014 is how it incorporates a more inclusive and comprehensive approach to supporting LGBTQ+ students, particularly addressing the needs of transgender students. These differences reflect the substantial social, legal, and cultural changes during that decade.

This was the fourth and final public meeting before the proposed updated policy went to a vote the following week. In the previous meetings, the board patiently listened to countless persons who spoke passionately for and against this policy. At the end of the session last night, all the trustees had a chance to make a final comment, and each one, without exception, thanked all who made presentations and shared their stories, including a Chinese mom of a young trans boy who eloquently shared her family's story of acceptance. Except for two of the nine trustees, all said they would vote in favor of the proposed updates to the policy.

What is their fear?

You only have to engage some parents in conversation to realize how much misinformation exists about trans people and issues. The persistent fear is that their children will be turned into trans persons by the school staff.

I was flabbergasted when I asked one of the mothers, whose name tag said "Organizer," if she knew any trans persons. I recognized a slight language barrier, so I asked the question again. She nodded that she did, but still wanting to make sure she understood my question; I asked her if she knew them personally. She said she felt sorry for them and added, "I don't want to become trans, and I don't want my children to be made trans. Schools should be about education." Oh, the irony.

The irony, too, is that within a week of the U.S. Department of Health and Human Services ruling that people receiving Medicare may no longer be automatically rejected for coverage of sex confirmation surgery, the Southern Baptist Convention passed a resolution that opposes attempts to change a person's "bodily identity" through such treatments as gender confirmation surgery and adds "God's good design that gender identity is determined by biological sex and not by one's self-perception" and "we continue to oppose all efforts steadfastly by any court or state legislature to validate trans identity as morally praiseworthy."

Blogpost June 18, 2014
22.8: I Care to Differ on This Occasion
...with a Regent College Professor —

I won't malign this professor, but I did take issue with the WSJ Op-Ed he promoted, which weighs in on the trans debate.

All the discussion concerned the recent debate at the Vancouver School Board regarding their policy on how trans and gender-variant students should be treated. This became a circus when parents self-identifying as conservative Asian evangelical Christians lobbied against it.

Much has been said for and against this policy, including the professor's Facebook wall comment thread.

One perspective missing in this banter is that we are talking about only one trans person out of 166 (.6%) in the general population. Additionally, not all trans persons who experience gender dysphoria may desire social and or, eventually, medical transition. In other words, all the pedagogical anxiety expressed is, for the most part, unfounded. Not every teacher, class, or school risks being blessed by a gender non-conforming student. A school with a student body of 500 will only have three trans students in all the grades combined.

If the numbers are so "insignificant," some would argue, then why force this issue on the 99.4% of the students who don't struggle with their gender identity? The reason is this: in a study of close to seven thousand trans persons published in 2011 by the National Centre for Transgender Equality, 41% responded they had attempted suicide at least once. That number is ten times higher than the general population. Why such high numbers? The simple answer is that they are made to feel unwanted and rejected by 99.4% of the population (now commonly referred to as those who are cisgender).

The fact that younger and younger gender-variant persons are emerging does not mean there are more and more trans persons. All it means is that trans persons, thanks to the availability of information and services, can access help much sooner than ever before. This is germane to the conversation; these ever-younger emerging persons have every right not to postpone their transition until after they are out of the school system. By this time, their bodies will have matured with the 'wrong' secondary sexual characteristics. And it follows that many trans people face difficulty changing their bodies to conform to their gender identity. Transitioning from one gender to another can take many forms but often requires hormone therapy and sometimes surgery on the face, breasts, and or genitals. The financial cost, ranging from $75k to $150k, creates an impossible barrier for many.

All this is to say that accommodating and supporting trans youth during their emergence and social and medical transition is the most compassionate thing that can be done for them. It will not only avoid traumatic, painful, and expensive procedures later in life; their bodies will develop and mature with the desired secondary sexual characteristics. How can this not be considered a wonderful modern-day gift of science?

Most people fail to realize that given the trend for trans persons to transition sooner rather than later, it won't be long before trans persons fade into the woodwork and not be seen. Not because they have disappeared but because, as stated above, their appearance will not give them away to society's obsessed gender watchdogs who freak out when people don't conform to their ideas of acceptable masculine and feminine behavior and presentation.

Yet, there will still be those who, for whatever reason, will choose not to or cannot transition from one gender pole to the other and will be quite comfortable living with a degree of ambiguity. While this may drive many people crazy, it points to the need for society to chill out and learn from these courageous souls that life has more to do with what is on the inside than what is on the outside. I could hit you with a barrage of Bible quotes about this, but I will respect that you are smart enough to know this already.

This is a fact: trans people have existed in every culture, age, group, etc., etc. The fact, too, is that living today there are many trans persons who live stealthily and are successful contributing members of society. If you are reading this comment thread, there is a high chance you are serious about your theological education; perhaps you are a student at Regent? One day, a person or family may come to your church or congregation (or school) who transitioned in their youth.

Today, there are many trans persons in their twenties who transitioned early and have enjoyed the benefits of having a body that only went through the 'correct' puberty. You would never be able to point them out in a crowd. Within probability, you may already have a trans person in your midst, and you don't even know it. Suppose the church cannot open itself to this probability and refuse to welcome and affirm trans persons as equal and full participants. In that case, you will go against the Gospel you preach. You might as well adopt the Southern Baptist Convention's recent resolution on transgenderism.

Consider this possible scenario: a family with teenage children comes to your church, and one is trans, but how will you know unless they volunteer this information? They may decide to keep it to themselves so that this truth will not prevent that person from full participation. The person may be the dad or the mom, both gifted and talented with an expressed desire to get involved in leadership. The same could be true if it is one of the children.

Now consider this same family coming to you and volunteering that one of them is trans. What will be your response to their desire to be full participants? Will you now impose some 'biblical' restrictions and prevent this person from taking part in the life of your church without any objection? Wouldn't this mean that you have a double standard? You will be welcoming as long as you are in the dark, but if you are in the light, you will have issues. Doesn't this seem wrong to you?

I am open about the fact that I am a trans woman. But I am not about to place myself in a situation where I will be made to feel "less-than" or to be the elephant in the room. I know that most churches in this great city of Vancouver would impose restrictions on what I could do should I be interested in joining them. For example, I may be banned from attending a women's retreat or told I can only use the handicapped washroom. That is, if I make it known that I am trans. Fortunately, I 'pass' society's test for femininity and have never been confronted, but that would all change if I walked around with a sign on my forehead that read "TRANSSEXUAL."

The genie is out of the bottle. How will you respond? With compassion and understanding, or with judgment? Let me leave you with two names: Copernicus and Galileo.

Blogpost: June 13, 2104
22.9: Paradox = Father's Day for A Trans Woman

It seems innocent enough to have a day to celebrate fatherhood, paternal bonds, and the influence of fathers in society.

If one's relationship with their father was good, this honored day will seem appropriate and welcome. This yearly reminder could be extremely painful if your dad did not deserve this kind of respect.

Equally, if you're a trans woman who fathered children, this day can either be a good or a bad—if not surreal—experience. It all depends on the kind of relationship you now have with your children. Father's Day is extremely painful when your children have rejected you and want nothing to do with you. As far as they are concerned, you might as well be dead. It hurts. However, if your relationship has survived, you can count yourself lucky.

I was fortunate on two counts: I had a loving dad, and, best of all, despite his relatively old age, when I came out to him (he was 90), he accepted me. When I came out to my sons, they did not reject me either.

I have three adult sons and two young granddaughters. How

does this paradox I find myself in as a trans woman, father, and grandfather work itself out? This is part of the ongoing process of transitioning. Though I am coming up to the sixth anniversary of living full-time as a female, there are still many I's to dot and t's to cross before it's all said and done. In the process, I have learned the journey is full of surprises.

I remember, for example, the day I was helping my middle son in the back room of his art gallery when we heard the front door open. My son went to see who it was, and I could hear him talking to someone; it was a friend of his. I heard them walking in my direction, and when they entered the room, my son said, "Kenton, I'd like you to meet my dad, Lisa. Dad, meet my friend Kenton." There was no sense of awkwardness, embarrassment, or hesitation on my son's part. This struck me. It bowled me over—it was a gift to me.

How else could he have introduced me? His warm and uncontrived introduction showed how comfortable he was with me. Had he been embarrassed about me, he could have dispatched his friend at the front door, and nobody would have been the wiser for it. I have often thought about that incident; it has helped me embrace that I am, above all else, a dad.

For one of my recent courses in pastoral care, I had to write a reflection paper at the end of the term. It talked about my experience providing spiritual care. I commented that I felt very protective of one of my clients—that I experience strong paternal instincts. My supervisor wondered why, if I was a female, I had not said "maternal" rather than "paternal"?

This is part of the paradox. But as I thought about it, I said perhaps it had something to do with the fact that I vowed I would never assume the title of "mother" concerning my sons. It would be presumptuous to equate my parental role to my ex-wife's, who mothered and nurtured my sons. She alone deserves that title and honor, and I get to claim that I am their father.

This helps explain why I may find it more authentic to say I have paternal versus maternal instincts that can be evoked. Perhaps I should consider the gender-neutral alternative and say "parental" instincts. But to me, that is just splitting hairs.

How do other trans women deal with the fact they may have

fathered children? I know one whose children were much younger than mine when she transitioned. She negotiated terms with the whole family, and they referred to her as "Maddy." I've heard of others who have done something similar. It does get complicated, especially with young children.

With my granddaughters, I am referred to as Tia Lisa. This seemed like a fitting moniker since my niece has two young children close in age, and they often spend time with my granddaughters. I still don't know how they will address me when they are older and are finally helped by their parents to understand my relationship with them. Will my grandchildren say to their friends, "Meet my granddad, Lisa"?

Two days ago, I received a text message from the youngest of my three sons; he is thirty-one and married. My middle son, who now lives on Vancouver Island, is coming for the weekend, and the two have invited me out for dinner to celebrate Father's Day. You cannot imagine how thrilled I am. I feel like a kid before Christmas, honestly.

Such a paradox this Father's Day thing is for me. I'm relieved I have not been given a Happy Mother's Day card to date—that wouldn't be paradoxical, but it would be weird.

Blogpost: October 13, 2014
22.10: Come and See

Such a simple invitation, but when acted on, it has the power to change.

One might think it's getting better. After all, how many millions saw Laverne Cox, the trans actor of the popular "Orange is the New Black" Netflix series, on the cover of Time Magazine? And what about all the buzz regarding the Amazon TV series "Transparent"? I'm talking about trans inclusion. But I have my doubts that even such high-profile public relations coups have made that much impact on most of the population.

I hate to sound so pessimistic, but when school boards, city councils, and other elected members continue to debate whether or not to give gender non-conforming persons some basic level of human rights protection, what else can I think?

Even in Canada, with its fair share of progressive people, there is little to no discussion about the Canadian Senate's stonewalling of a proposed bill to amend the Canadian Human Rights Act and the Criminal Code. The bill would add language offering protection based on gender identity (Bill C-279). It's the same kind of protection the law already offers based on sexual orientation. In other words, if you are gay or lesbian, you're covered.

The silence from the cisgender (non-trans) majority of the population is deafening. Especially disappointing is the silence from the cisgender gays and lesbians who, one would think, would be crying out with us. Personally frustrating to me is the silence from people of faith.

As long as there's an attitude of apathy and silence on the issue, no wonder the decision-makers sit on their asses and do nothing.

The only voices that seem to get attention are those of uninformed politicians and pundits who weigh in with the tired (and completely false) myth that if trans rights are enshrined, predatory men pretending to be women will be peeing and showering next to your thirteen-year-old daughters and your wives. They've dubbed these laws "the bathroom bills." They fail to consider the stories of the violence experienced by trans and gender-variant persons when using public restrooms.

When the critical conversation of human rights for trans persons gets reduced to which restroom a person can use, how do you get people's minds out of the toilet?

Come and see!

I'm convinced that the only way minds will be changed is if minds are first opened. And it must be done exactly the same way Jesus began his relationship with two of John the Baptist's disciples. The two walked up to Jesus and asked, "Rabbi, where are you staying?" and Jesus responded, "Come and see." Then we are told they went with Jesus and remained with him that day. (John 1:39)

Please consider the lesson from this simple account: Jesus could have given them an answer that satisfied the question, but he didn't. Instead, he welcomes them into a relationship of discovery. Rather than giving them data, Jesus allowed them to see and experience the answer to their question—and they could not leave—they remained.

Then, the Gospel writer tells what happened the next day when Philip, the latest to be invited by Jesus to follow him, goes to tell Nathanael, "We have found him about whom Moses in the law and also the prophets wrote..." Nathanael, a devout Jew, responded with sarcasm. Instead of debating him and trying to convince him, Philip, said, "Come and see." (John 1:45-46)

Once again, the experience of seeing and experiencing something for yourself is more persuasive than talking points. Come and See. So simple, yet so life-changing.

The invitation to "Come and See" holds the power to inspire change by encouraging individuals to explore new perspectives and experiences. By accepting this invitation, people can develop empathy, compassion, and open-mindedness, fostering personal growth and promoting positive social change. Engaging with the unfamiliar can lead to increased understanding, tolerance, and unity in both individuals and communities.

That is what I am suggesting is the only way this impasse will ever be overcome. I could dump plenty of data on anyone who only wants to engage the brain. But if you're going to engage the heart, you'll need to use your eyes and ears much differently. Come, see, listen, and remain with us...Stand with us. Listen to our stories, and see where we are being forced to stay.

Chapter 23: Mom, don't move!

Mom fell a few weeks before the convocation ceremonies and just days after I presented my capstone project. She was 91 at the time. We were doing some spring gardening together at the entrance when she lost her balance and fell on her right side. She landed on the edge of the cement sidewalk and broke her pelvis. All my training at Vancouver General Hospital on Falls Prevention kicked in. She was moaning in pain and said she felt something break. I told her not to move and to stay still. I called 911 on my cell and then called both Carmen and Angela.

I ran inside and grabbed a bath blanket to cover her and a towel to place under her head; then I crouched beside her, held her hand, and waited. The fire department was there in less than ten minutes, and the ambulance arrived a few minutes later. Mom was admitted to the same hospital where Dad had passed away two years earlier. The X-rays revealed a crack on the right side of the pelvis, for which there is little that can be done except convalescence. The ER doctor was relieved it hadn't been a broken hip or femur because hip replacement or orthopedic surgery would have meant months of rehabilitation at her age. Worse yet for Mom, she could have ended up in a long-term care facility—her worst fear.

23.1: Terror Management Mode
My final reflection for Field Education Placement program

I initially planned to reflect on my role as a "leader." However, recent events with my mother shifted my focus. I am traumatized by her situation and uncertain about my future. I've been suppressing my emotions and confusing resistance with resilience.

Enneagram Type 2 describes me as a Helper, someone who

is empathetic, caring, and nurturing, but also needy. It's not easy for me to give voice to my emotions, and I tend to suppress them instead. This term, with my stint at VGH, showed me that I need to look at how my emotions impact me. I need to be honest with myself and not pat myself on the back for how resilient I am.

The honest feelings are that I am both scared and uncertain about my Mom's situation. I'm afraid I will not be able to focus on the vocation I have been preparing for. How can I possibly expect to start a new career when there is so much uncertainty about what the next few years might hold for her? Then there is the guilt for even thinking this way that I am putting my plans ahead of my Mom and what she may need. And in the meantime, the clock is ticking, and I am growing older.

Whatever windows of opportunity I might hope to have, how long will they stay open? Right now, I want to scream as loud as I can. Of course, I won't; but that is what it feels like.

But I digress. I'm unsure I can fill three pages with well-reasoned and well-thought out plans for the future. Whatever I had initially conceived seemed so shallow in the face of my predicament.

In broad strokes, I reasoned I would first develop a hit list of contacts in secular and faith-based organizations. My ploy was to use the study results judiciously and strategically to draw attention to a need and then follow up with suggestions how I might help them support trans people. But to get to that point, I was going to begin by networking, starting with people who already know me, know about me, or should know about me. I had already started doing this, even before the study was finished; I shared with several persons whom I thought would be interested in the findings. Following up on these leads would be the next step.

I didn't have any grand ideas, but I could see the likelihood of having speaking opportunities and doing workshops. Pursuing public exposure is not what I want to do, but it might be necessary.

What else can I say? I can be more lighthearted about all of this. But I'm afraid it would only sound like self-mocking. When I scored 2 in the Enneagram test, I thought, am I really that predictable? I almost threw up reading the brief description because it was as if someone had read my journal, and that's why I never kept a journal growing up. It's not that I don't like this description; it's just that it makes me feel so damn needy. Actually, yes, I am needy...I hate the fact that indeed I am.

What kind of leader can a needy person make? I know I'm being hard on myself right now. Instead, I will reflect on what my heart tells me about my role as a leader or how I perceive myself as a leader. I want to be both proactive and reactive. Proactively, I want to create a safe, inclusive space...and yes, this can be interpreted as being protective. It can also be misinterpreted as avoidance or denial, perhaps an unwillingness to be confrontational, even when it is needed. However, I think of myself as a peacemaker, intervening when I believe an intervention is necessary. In this regard, I also see myself as a facilitator, advocate, and activist, not just as a spiritual care provider but as, for example, a diversity trainer. I feel most animated when I sense communication is suffering from lack of clarity, how things are said or not said, but also when it seems as though communication is impaired due to cultural and religious differences. And when it comes to trans identities, there are significant cultural differences. I feel motivated to help bring clarity and understanding to the situation.

The TSPS study has given me permission to not feel guilty about drifting away from church. But the guilt I felt was for missing church, because I was not drifting away from God. The only thing that kept me safe and sane all the years I struggled with my identity was my relationship with God, which I can only describe as an ongoing, intimate conversation. The kind of conversation you have with a close companion when you're on a road trip; ebbs and flows, and the topic changes often. There are periods of silence that last until the song on the radio ends, and then it picks up again.

That is what my relationship with God is like. The irony is that when I feel like I should be more intentional and attempt centering prayers and Mertonesque approaches, I experience ADHD., and nothing happens. It's as if God says, "Oh, that's how you want to do this? I'll return after you've played at religion, and then we'll chat some more." So, from a spiritual perspective, mysticism, labyrinth walking, and too much esoteric stuff, is like putting on costumes; it's pretend time, and it doesn't work for me. It's been like this for the last seven years since I began my transition. Once I removed the mask, I didn't need to put it back on again.

In closing, the most important quality of leadership I hope to embody is to be as Christlike as possible, even to the point of not seeking to be recognized, as it was with Jesus on the Road to Emmaus...he was not recognized as he walked alongside the two. They carried on a conversation, and when it got dark, he broke bread and gave thanks. This is the model for my ministry. That is how I hope to experience church—along the way.

23.2: Ironically

I was invited to speak at two denominational clergy-only meetings. The first was at a gathering of pastors from the Korean branch of the Presbyterian Church of Canada (PCC) in British Columbia and Alberta. And the other was the Vancouver Diocese of the Anglican Church of Canada.

One of my classmates was a Korean woman pursuing an MDiv and was the first Korean female candidate for ordination with the PCC. She had wondered if the upcoming gathering of Korean pastors to debate their position on LGBTQ+ inclusion was going to include any voices from LGBTQ+ persons. She asked the pastor of her church in Vancouver since he was the organizer of the conference; he responded, "We don't know any LGBTQ+ people." She told him about me, and I was invited to Harrison Hot Springs, where they held their mini-conference.

There were approximately 50 people, made up of mostly men and a few wives, who accompanied their husbands. It was the first time I spoke through an interpreter. I don't believe they resolved the issue that night, but all I can remember was the greeting line that formed to say good night. I was hugged by several of the pastors as we shook hands.

The next day at VST, my Korean friend asked how it had gone. I said I didn't know Koreans were so affectionate and told her I'd been surprised by the hugs. She was as gob-smacked as I had been the night before. "No!" she said, "They are not; that is amazing. You must have really gotten to them."

The invitation to speak to the Anglican clergy came about through the Rev. Dr. Richard Topping, the principal of VST. He had been in conversation with the Executive Archdeacon, Douglas Fenton, who was organizing an education day for ordained clergy only, titled Clergy professional development: gender identity/gender variance and socio-sexual ethics. Dr. Topping told them about me and my study, and I was invited to spend the whole day with the group. It was a match made in heaven, as they say. Though this event didn't occur until January 2018, I mention it here because of its connection to my studies at VST.

Fenton was the moderator that day. After welcoming nearly 100 men and women, priests, and deacons, he went to a flip chart and wrote down the one burning question each person had about trans inclusion. They had been asked to come prepared with that question. He then posted all the flaps of paper across the front wall of the auditorium. As had happened in Chicago at the GCN conference, if their question was already asked, they said, "Already asked."

Then it was my turn. I thanked them for their questions, and before starting my 2-hour presentation, I went to the posters and crossed out all the questions I would be answering in my talk. The remaining questions would be the fodder for the 90-minute Q&A planned for the afternoon.

Personally, this event meant much to me. It was a validation I would never have imagined. It was made even more special by all the friendly faces I saw in the audience of the clergy; among them were fellow VST students who were now ordained and one or two faculty members from VST.

But my biggest surprise was not the standing ovation I received, which was humbling in itself; it was meeting Megan's best friend, the one she wanted to come out to in 2013 when she emailed me about where she could buy my book in Vancouver. In my talk, I shared the story with the group about Megan's pivotal question and how I ended up at VST; then, James approached me during a break and said, "I'm Megan's friend." We laughed and marveled at how Megan's question about my book and later her question about a job description had come full circle. And there I was, meeting one of the persons who had caused her to reach out to me in the first place.

23.3: Keynote Speech to the BC Camps Association

I was still a board member with Qmunity, BC's Trans, Queer, and Two Spirit Resource Centre, when I was approached by the Director of Education in the fall of 2017. The British Columbia Camps Association called to book workshops and a keynote speaker for their upcoming conference and AGM at the end of January 2018. BC Camps Association decided the conference's theme was going to be Sexual Orientation and Gender Identity (SOGI) because that was the hot topic in schools at the time. I was approached because of my theology related degree since half of the attendees would be from Christian and church-run summer camps.

I was flattered to be representing Qmunity and to co-facilitate a worship and deliver the conference's opening keynote. This is what I said:

Thank you for inviting Qmunity to your conference. I'm honored to speak to you tonight.

When Joel, the DE, spoke to me about this conference and delivering this keynote, I wondered how I might make it relevant? I knew I could not talk from personal experience about summer camps, and I didn't want to rattle off research studies and statistics about SOGI. Instead, I decided to speak to my three sons—I will explain in a minute.

In the last six years, I've had the privilege of speaking and presenting to diverse groups, including corporate, faith groups, denominational leaders, educators, lawyers, high-tech companies, non-profits, community groups, and healthcare providers.

It is ironic that I am invited to talk about secrets I hid and suppressed and never imagined I would be dredging up for others to see. It's always akin to walking on a tightrope because some themes and issues evoke sentimental and emotional triggers.

Admittedly, even preparing for this talk made me feel sentimental and melancholy, mixed with survivor's guilt. Compared to many trans persons whose life is more challenging or who have yet to find a way to live authentically, I am lucky. No, not lucky. I'm privileged.

I no longer dream of a day when I will experience congruence between how I identify internally and how the world sees me. My dream has come true.

This is why I accepted the invitation to speak with you. You are in a special position to contribute to young people's quest for authenticity as they discover things about themselves and grow into who they are.

As mentioned above, in preparation for this talk, I spoke to my three adult sons because I wanted to know what they remembered most about their summer camp experiences some 25 years ago.

Today, they are 42, 38, and 34 years old, so lots of water has passed under the bridge. I've learned that our memories are better at remembering how we felt when we experienced something versus remembering all the facts about the experience. And that is what I hoped my sons could talk about, their emotional memories of summer camp.

I don't have any memories of summer camp because I never went to one. My family is from Colombia. In 1960, we moved to the United States. The first time I heard about summer camps was when Allan Sherman's camp parody song made it to 2nd place in the charts for three weeks during that summer of 1964. I'm sure you've heard his comical depiction of a summer camp.

It starts like this: "Hello, Muddah, hello, Fadduh. — Here I am at Camp Granada. — Camp is very entertaining. — And they say we'll have some fun if it stops raining. —"

The closest I ever came to a camp experience was at an uncle's hacienda in the jungle near Cali. I think I was about seven years old; it was the first time I relieved myself in an actual outhouse or rode a horse—or maybe it was a mule. It was also the first time I came face-to-face with a poisonous snake. I experienced an amygdala moment; I've never run so fast!

Instead of camping, we belonged to a golf and country club. If we got hungry, we went to one of several dining rooms, ate, and signed the tab—hardly a Summer Camp experience.

But I digress.

My oldest son told me about his camp experience when he

was 15. I felt a pang of guilt as I listened to him.

I never stopped to consider how he felt when we signed him up. We didn't even ask him if he wanted to go. If I had known then what I know today about stress and adverse childhood experiences, I don't think I would have put him on the chartered boat to go for a week to Anvil Island.

My wife and I had heard great things about the Camp from church friends who had been on staff for many years. That summer, my son was recovering from knee surgery to repair the damage from a ski accident on his last run of the season at the end of April.

He was wearing a massive leg and knee brace and didn't know a soul at the Camp. He was self-conscious and sat on the sidelines for most physical activities. He hated it! That's what he told me.

If you're from Anvil Island, this is not a criticism of the Camp. It's a criticism of me. I didn't consider his needs; I forced him to go. That is what tainted his experience and what he remembers.

There was a counselor who made a valiant effort. But as parents, we made a mistake; we were wrong for forcing him to go.

The only thing my son remembers about his Summer Camp experience is how he felt self-conscious, uncomfortable, sad, hurt, and ultimately angry.

My second son's summer camp experience was an improvement by comparison. Then again, we didn't think about what he wanted. It wasn't until a few weeks ago that I finally understood his ambivalence on the ferry to Langdale and the drive to YMCA Camp Elphinstone.

The reason? He wanted to play in the Provincial Little League Tournament with the Little Mountain All-star team that same week. That happens when you commit to something, and something else comes up. We registered him for summer camp before the team advanced to the tournament.

The only consolation is that he made it work, thanks to his gift of making friends easily. He is one of those people who has never known a stranger.

Fortunately, his second summer camp experience was much better. He went to Keats Camp with a classmate. And there were other familiar faces; he fit right in.

Son number three feels like he won the lottery in the end. You'll see why in a minute.

In 1994, we started attending a church with a more engaged youth group. The next summer, many of the kids in the group went to Keats Camp. Though he knew a handful of people, he remembers feeling like an outsider at first. There was a camp culture with unfamiliar routines and, as he put it, a clique with a strange lingo.

He went for the first week as a camper and, along with a few other church kids, stayed a few more weeks as one of the volunteers. He washed a lot of pans and dishes.

The next year it was much the same. But went as staff the next two summers. He said that being at Camp taught him valuable leadership skills. Still, more importantly, it is where he met the young woman who became his wife 14 years later.

I wanted to tell you these stories to demonstrate the many intersecting factors and determinants that come into play that can impact a child's camp experience.

Things out of your control. Family dynamics, personality types, personal struggles, cultural and social differences, and the child's sense of belonging and fitting in are thrown into the mix.

And I'm sure you've all welcomed campers who, despite your best efforts, are unable to integrate, who may have disrupted the Camp.

Or you've had someone whose needs you weren't prepared or trained to deal with. Children who, for whatever reason, were not really ready to be in the camp environment.

I don't think I'm wrong in assuming everyone here is committed to making sure kids in an unfamiliar environment with unfamiliar people will feel welcomed and safe.

Suppose a camper arrives with a note of bed wetting. In that case, you waste no time having a quick private talk with them to let them know that if they have an accident, you will help them discreetly.

Or, if a child has a nut allergy, you've ensured all their meals and snacks are nut-free instead of having an exclusion zone, compounding their feeling of being different.

I have tried to imagine what Camp would have been like for me. I am grateful I never had that test. I know enough about myself to say without hesitation that I would not have been a happy camper. I was a bed wetter, always one of the last to be picked for a team, one of the slowest runners, and self-conscious about being shirtless; I preferred swimming with a T-shirt.

That is why, as a dad of three sons, I prayed to God they would not be saddled with gender dysphoria. I was always looking for tell-tale signs from the moment they were born until they were teenagers.

I also couldn't help but compare myself to them; it made me envious to see how, unlike me, they seemed to be comfortable in their own bodies.

I was grateful they were free of my curse.

That is also why I felt so guilty when my oldest son told me how self-conscious and alone he felt when we sent him to Anvil Island. His experience resonated deeply with me. He was dealing with a negative body image. He felt like an outsider and perhaps even abandoned and not heard. It made me think of how I felt being a new kid in school after our move to the US. I remember how incredibly insecure I felt.

Back in Colombia, I had always attended the same boys' school with my older brother, Enrique, who was three years ahead of me. He resented my mom's insistence that he keep an eye on me, but I was grateful I had him in my life. For example, he always ensured I got on the bus at the end of the day for the ride home. He also saved me more than once from a boy named Diego, who bullied me in the playground.

Even in Colombia, I was timid and unsure how to act. I studied my brother—and other boys. I shared a bedroom with Enrique, which made me realize I was somehow different. He didn't appear self-conscious about his body like I was. He wasn't introspective like me. Growing up, I tried to be like him; I liked what he liked + hated what he hated.

There might have been a few exceptions. For example, he didn't like onion rings; I loved onion rings!

But for the most part, I became his mini-me. This is a retrospective view of my life.

As a child, I could not articulate or formulate questions to get the answers that bring clarity to my internal chaos. There was persistent self-doubting, introspection, and unease with all things masculine.

When we arrived in California, my brother and I were split up. We no longer attended the same school. He went to a junior high school, and I went to an elementary school.

This was akin to being thrown into the pool's deep end. It was sink or swim. I could no longer run to Enrique when I felt threatened and didn't have a social role model to copy. There was also the fact none of us kids spoke English, except for my older sister, who went to a girl's Catholic high school.

Like many first-generation immigrant kids, I wanted to fit in; I didn't want to be made fun of, and most of all, I didn't want to stand out or be considered different or odd. I didn't want to get hurt or bullied.

My memory is sharp about the intense feelings I experienced. Many of them were strange, new feelings.

Though I grew up with one sister who was six years older and one who was five years younger, I never spent more than a few hours around girls my age—with a couple of first cousins at each other's birthday parties.

But now I was with girls my age for thirty hours a week and felt unhinged. And why did I feel so drawn to them?

Why did I want to be like them?

There was nothing sexual about these deep feelings. I was too young to know what that meant. I now understand what was happening, but these feelings were very perplexing and confusing at the time.

One night I made the mistake of asking my brother if he ever felt as if he wanted to be a girl. His anger and disgust at my question left no doubt in my mind: this was not what boys were supposed to feel or think about.

Many questions went unanswered.

"Who am I?"

"What am I?" and,

"Am I the only one who feels like this?"

Admittedly, these are universal questions for all kids.

Growing up, these are the questions of survival.

We all yearn for security and acceptance by the group. It is natural to fear rejection, ridicule, and not fitting in.

But as we now know, those who belong to any minority group experience these feelings more acutely and intensely than those who belong to a dominant group.

And suppose one is lucky enough to have membership in more than one minority group. In that case, their life experience will likely be more emotionally complicated.

It is a testament to the resilience of the human spirit that most people survive without imploding or finding maladaptive coping strategies that are self-depleting and damaging.

Here's what I've learned in my role in health care settings... and while the context is different, the lessons and skills are transferable.

Under stress, the brain produces cortisol and modulates adrenalin levels. Together these hormones prepare us for fight or flight, and we experience many physiological effects. Additionally, stress also clouds our thinking; we become hyper-vigilant, while at the same time, we develop tunnel vision.

As a spiritual health practitioner, my job is to come alongside patients and their families to assess their stress and levels of distress and, if possible, help them process all kinds of difficult feelings and emotions. I practice active listening for what matters most to them and their source of inner strength. We also listen for unhealthy attitudes and assumptions about how they view themselves and their situations.

As a transgender advocate who has spent countless hours in conversations with other transgender and non-binary persons as part of my studies and research for my Master's Degree, and more recently, as a hotline operator with the Trans LifeLine, I can attest to the sense of insecurity and stress many of us have lived with all our lives. For this reason, I've sought opportunities to network with various healthcare teams who want to improve patient-centered healthcare for trans and non-binary patients.

The sad truth is trans people continue to experience distressing interactions with healthcare providers.

I could tell you many stories; these stories get around. For example, UTIs are disproportionately high among young trans people who are afraid of using public washrooms, so they hold it in.

That is why healthcare professionals are responding.

The ultimate goal is not just to raise awareness but to change behavior. Head knowledge is one thing; applying that knowledge is another.

That is why school boards are also responding with SOGI123 resources. They are working to create safe spaces that benefit all students.

Indeed, a recent study comparing psychosocial markers between high schools with and without GSAs found that suicidal ideation is several times lower among cis boys who are bullied in schools with a GSA.

Not everyone is happy with this new SOGI initiative in schools. Unfortunately, there is a lot of misinformation out there, and some parents are naturally fearful.

That is why I advocate for inclusion.

I take great comfort that gender identity and gender expression are now protected federally and provincially in the respective human rights codes. The debate will continue as long as people have a problem accepting the mounting medical, psychological, and social body of evidence that informs our current understanding of human sexuality.

Interestingly, the corporate world and the courts have been years ahead in responding to the existence of trans and non-binary persons. Many of North America's largest corporations, Apple, I.B.M., Boeing, Google, Amazon, Netflix, and Microsoft, to name a few, have had trans-inclusive policies for their employees and customers for more than a decade. Courts have also consistently ruled in favor of trans persons in discrimination cases.

In fact, this was one of the arguments the BC government used for stalling the legislation to amend the Human Rights Code— for years; it argued case law already provided all the protection trans persons needed.

But it's helpful we now have explicit language that makes it clear; discriminating against someone based on their gender identity or expression is against the law.

And yet, some wonder, why all the fuss? Don't trans people represent only a very small portion of the population?

.6% of the adult US Population United States equals 1.4 million. In Canada, one-tenth of the population could be 140,000 adult trans people.

BC. South Coast = 10% 4,000 adult trans people.

What about those who are under the age of 18? The percentage could be higher, perhaps 1%.

BC has 634,000 K-grade 12 students enrolled in public and private schools. That is 6,340 young trans people in BC, ages 5 to 18. Fraser Health has the highest youth population in the province and could have 4,500 trans youth.

Admittedly, I've been focusing on trans and nonbinary people. But this does not mean young LGBI2S persons are less important. It can be said that when a safe space is created for the least accepted and understood group, it creates a safe space for all, even straight kids.

I hope this will stimulate you to consider how to create safe, inclusive spaces and programs that will benefit not just LGBTQ+ youth but also benefit straight, heterosexual youth.

I invite you to join the conspiracy with the corporate world, the courts, all levels of government, educators, communities of faith, and medical and mental health professionals, to create a safe space for all. As I suggested earlier, youth are going through an intense period of self-discovery.

They compare and contrast themselves to others as they learn to develop their talents, explore their giftedness and creativity, and develop social skills.

But for those of us who must also juggle self-image issues, the resulting stress can unnecessarily impact us. The solution lies in creating a safe space where stressors can be mitigated if we invest the time to understand and respect our differences and learn to appreciate our remarkable diversity.

I believe this is the role Summer Camps can have in making

a difference in the lives of all campers. Creating a safe space may include making modest physical changes to your facilities. Yes, some capital costs may be associated with some of these changes.

But as we are finding in health care, the most important changes don't cost any money; they are attitudinal and behavioral.

I haven't used the words compassion and empathy, but that is what this talk is about.

May your compassion and empathy stimulate you to find ways to create safe and inclusive spaces for all your future campers. May their camp experiences under your leadership help them connect with the beauty of creation, learn to respect and cherish it, and learn to respect and cherish each other. May this be what they remember most about summer camps for the rest of their lives.

Postscript:

After the keynote speech, attendees were invited to the dining hall for appetizers and refreshments. I made my way to the building and was welcomed by people at the entrance who thanked me for my talk. Then, a man about my age walked up and said enthusiastically, "L-i-s-a Salazar! You completely disarmed me. I was prepared to jump to my feet if you said anything that attacked my faith. Thank you for your words."

I don't know if he is the person who wrote a very concerned letter to Qmunity in December, one month before the conference. The writer wanted the keynote speaker to know that the Christian Camps comprised half of the summer camps in BC and would be deeply offended if the speech maligned them. By the time I saw it, I had already written my address, and I didn't change a word.

Chapter 24: The Personal Became Political

After I graduated in May 2015, I took a break from my Spiritual Care studies. I had only completed the first CPE unit and would have three more to do, but I was still ambivalent because I wasn't sold on working as a hospital chaplain. I also wasn't expecting to land a job providing spiritual care to trans people; who would hire me to do that? Private practice was out of the question; what would that look like, anyway? "Yes, I can meet to discuss your spiritual and transcendental angst. How would you like to pay for that, cash or credit card?"

If I was going to be true to my sarcastic answer to Megan, then money should not be an object. But money was an object. I wouldn't be able to live for free with my Mom. And only God knew what her remaining years would look like.

Doug Longstaffe, the Director of Spiritual Care at Vancouver Coastal Health, had told me that he was designing a CPE unit that would take place in the Vancouver Downtown East Side (DTES). This neighborhood is perhaps Canada's saddest, with hundreds of unhoused people including many LGBTQ+ youth. Doug thought I would make a perfect candidate for the pilot project and asked if I was interested. I said yes, but it would be two years before I got the call. Doug also dangled a carrot in front of me: he said my scores on the unit evaluation demonstrated advanced competencies. He suggested that after completing the second basic unit, I could challenge having to do two advanced units, assuming my scores for the second basic unit were also high.

In the meantime, I volunteered with different groups and reconnected with Pflag Vancouver. Along with a UCC pastor I met at

VST who was on staff in the White Rock First United Church. Bruce and his wife had raised two boys; the eldest had come out as gay and his youngest, who was still in high school came out as trans and was in the early stages of transitioning. Talk about serendipitous. Together, we opened a new Pflag chapter to service all the communities between the Fraser River and the Canada-U.S. Border, including Delta, South Surrey, White Rock, Cloverdale, and Langley. People from these communities who had attended the Vancouver meetings often lamented there wasn't a meeting closer to them.

Qmunity, Vancouver's trans, queer, and Two-Spirit resource center, invited me to sit on the Board of Directors. I had already been co-facilitating Queer Competency workshops with their Director of Education. And because I needed another hole in my head, I applied to be a patient representative in the Peace Arch Hospital's Patient Safety committee.

But I wasn't done. Along with many other advocates and activists, I joined the ad-hoc lobby that went after the BC Liberal Party, which was governing the province. We were calling for the passage of a private member's bill to include gender identity in the BC Human Rights Code.

We marched in rallies but also used every available connection to get the message to the politicians. Unbeknownst to each other, Kaitlyn Bogas and I shared a long-standing relationship with none other than the Attorney General and Minister of Justice, Suzanne Anton. We had known her for a combined 50 years! My wife and I met her and her family when our kids played together in sports, and we had sons who went to play at each other's houses. I had come out to Suzanne in a letter a year or so earlier, and she had responded warmly. Kaitlyn had known her through her restaurants, and after she transitioned, when she did landscaping, she'd done work at her house in Vancouver. Small world.

But now things were ramping up. Acting independently and without knowledge of each other's lobbying efforts, Kaitlyn and I both appealed to Minister Anton in person and via email. She would often try to silence reporters' questions about the proposed bill by saying that trans people already enjoyed all the legal protection they were asking for under the category of sex in the BC Human Rights

Code. Then she would add, "I have friends who are trans," as if to validate her claims and give more force to her rationale.

Morgane Oger, Chair of Trans Alliance Society, and a group of us organized the campaign a letter-writing campaign. We circulated a letter to as many churches and organizations as we could think of with the heading "Urgent personal time-sensitive request and appeal to academics, doctors, CEOs, Managers, and Pastors living in British Columbia." We asked them to send us their letter of support for the bill by Friday, April 22. A week later we delivered 1,253 letters to the Legislature in Victoria. The moment was captured in a documentary titled "1253 Letters: The Fight for Trans Rights in British Columbia" by Christine Lord of Sealord Productions.

Then, in what seemed like out of the blue, Minister Suzanne Anton announced at a press conference that she would be tabling a bill to include gender identity in the BC Human Rights Code. It was almost word-for-word identical to Spencer Chandra Herbert's version. He stood next to Anton at the announcement.

I can't remember how I first heard about the announcement, but I do remember that we were ecstatic! Later that afternoon, Minister Suzanne Anton called me on my cell. "Did you hear the news?" she asked. She called to invite me to be her guest on the following Thursday when she was going to table the bill and call for a vote. I was beside myself with excitement. She said Kaitlyn and I were the two people she wanted most to be there.

About one hundred trans people and their allies were in the Legislative Gallery that day. All but two of us sat in the gallery reserved for guests of the official opposition; Kaitlyn and I sat across from them on the side of the gallery reserved for the guests of the ruling party. We were the only two guests on that side! Hilarious. We smiled and waved at our friends on the other side of the hall and shook our heads in friendly disbelief. Kaitlyn and I were certainly not Liberal party supporters—we had voted for the New Democratic Party (NDP), but there we were.

Interestingly, guests were asked to collect their passes at one of two tables after going through the metal detectors and security clearance. The line for the Liberal table was non-existent, while the 100 or so who were guests of the NDP disappeared around the corner. It's what the man waiting at the table for Kaitlyn and me said as he handed us our passes: "I don't know what the two of you did, but this wouldn't be happening otherwise." Kaitlyn and I looked at each other in absolute puzzlement.

After we took our seats, I asked Kaitlyn what she had done. She asked me the same thing. Whatever it was, we had not acted together. All I could think of was the letter I sent her in April, shortly after the letters had been delivered to the Legislature. I was infuriated when I learned that the Liberal Cabinet had voted to adopt changes to the law governing cat breeders and kennels, as the Canadian Veterinary Association recommended. It was an Order in Council, which meant it would not have to be put to the vote and became law immediately.

Below is the blogpost I wrote, a more extended version of the letter I sent Suzanne Anton to shame her.

Blogpost, April 30, 2016
24.1: Calling Out the Politicians
The Apparent Hypocrisy of British Columbia's
Elected Liberal Government

The same week that trans advocates and allies stood in front of the BC Legislature in support of the introduction of a private member's bill aimed at protecting the rights of trans people, the BC Liberal Government announced an order-in-council that adopts the Canadian Veterinary Medical Association's Codes of Practice for both kennel and cat breeding.

Indeed, this is very good news for dogs and cats in British Columbia.

Yet, this same Government has sat intentionally on its laurels, refusing to pass a "trans rights bill" on three previous occasions. This is the fourth time the Honourable Spencer Chandra Herbert, MLA for Vancouver-West End, will introduce this bill. The bill would amend the BC Human Rights Code (BCHRC) to include "gender identity and gender expression."

Having "gender identity and gender expression" included in the BCHRC will afford increased protection, safety, and equity for trans and gender-variant persons in at least three significant and compelling ways:

It will help educate the public. It will inform the way organizations and companies implement their HR policies by providing an explicit statement of protection. It will clarify the code and hopefully mitigate and help resolve contentious situations—including discrimination—before they escalate to expensive, lengthy, and onerous legal actions for all parties.

This logic has so far failed to influence the Premier, Christy Clark and her Minister of Justice, Suzanne Anton, who refuses to bring this bill to a vote. But when it comes to cats and dogs, this government clearly recognizes the importance of explicit language in the law.

B.C. Agriculture Minister Norm Letnick alluded to the importance of specificity; he is quoted in a CBC story as saying:

"What this will do, is it will provide clarity to breeders of dogs and cats of what the standards of care are in B.C. and will also provide that same clarity to judges and the SPCA as they go about their work to bring people into alignment with that."

The trans community has had to listen to the Government's shallow argument the BCHRC already offers all the protection we need under the category of "sex." That sounds like how it was for cats and dogs until this new order-in-council came to their rescue.

It was noted that BC already relied on the Prevention of Cruelty to Animals Act to help regulate and police breeders. Yet codes will now be added as a new regulation to amend the act. Why can't trans persons be at the receiving end of this kind of humane legal consideration?

Do we not matter at least as much as pets? If it would help our cause, I'm willing to sit on the Liberals' lap and wag my tail—no licking or sniffing, though.

All kidding aside, this is serious business.

Why is the Liberal Government willing to act on pet experts' recommendations, but when it comes to trans people, they disregard their own experts within the Ministry of Health, the World Professional Association for Transgender Health, and more significantly, the United Nations Human Rights Council Resolution on Human

Rights, Sexual Orientation and Gender Identity (adopted 26 September 2014 — A/HRC/RES/27/32)?

BC has fallen behind other Canadian Provinces and Territories, which have already amended their codes to include gender identity and gender expression—and will soon be overtaken by the Federal Government as well. This is especially sad—and disappointing—since BC amended the BCHRC to include sexual orientation in 1992, 24 years ago. Then, in 2003 became the second province to legalize same-sex marriages. Why the delay and outright refusal to include explicit protection for trans and gender non-conforming persons?*

We've tried having a civil conversation, but this has failed. It's time to shame them for their hypocrisy. — End of blogpost.

Kaitlyn Bogas also jumped on our friend, the Attorney General, with a letter condemning her party's hypocrisy.

If what Kaitlyn and I surmised happened is accurate, we both agree that we cannot take credit for the sudden reversal on the part of the Liberal's position. Our part was small. The large boulder had been pushed up the hill by Spencer Chandra Herbert, Morgane Oger, and countless others who began the struggle for trans rights much earlier than Kaitlyn and me. All we did was lean on the boulder as it sat at the top to get it over the hill.

Kaitlyn and I had photo ops with Premier Christy Clark and our friend, Attorney General Suzanne Anton, as we held trans flags on the steps of the BC Parliament Building. Afterward, we were all invited to the Legislature's dining room for a celebration lunch.

What was historic on that day was that the bill was tabled, put to the first vote, and passed. It was put to the second vote and passed, and finally, put to the third vote and passed. Then it was driven to the office of the Lieutenant Governor to have signed and sealed, declaring it law. And it all happened in one day. This had only happened a few times in the history of British Columbia.

It was a "Wow" moment I will never forget.

Time to Call Out the Fundamentalists

I'm going to go back to the summer of 2017. When I completed the unit in the DTES, I had three weeks before the next unit would start at St. Paul's Hospital. I drove down to Reno to visit Kathy Baldock and chill out. One afternoon I saw a message from Colin McKenna, president of Pflag Vancouver, to us on the organizing committee. He was alarmed by a very vocal and militant group railing against the Sexual Orientation and Gender Identity (SOGI) curriculum designed for K-12 students. All I will say about SOGI is that it is a very sensitively produced curriculum that is not only age-appropriate, but educators and parents can also use it to educate themselves. The anti-LGBTQ+ group was planning to hold sessions in various churches and community halls to show a video featuring a PowerPoint presentation by one of the organizers, a fundamentalist pastor. He claimed to be a researcher and an authority on LGBTQ+ issues. Colin sent a link to the video and asked for my opinion as to how to respond.

I spent the rest of the day dissecting the video. The pastor had done a good job of footnoting all the slides that contained data and comments from all the research papers he had used as his sources. I was able to freeze the frames and write down all the studies. I then went online and downloaded them and found the referenced material. I was not surprised. The pastor had cherry-picked the statements and data that seemed to support his narrative but said the opposite when seen and read in their context. Kathy and I found the email addresses for all the authors of the studies, and I sent each an email with the link to the video and the minute and second spot where their research was posted. It was the end of summer, after all...How many would be around to respond in a timely manner?

If memory serves me right, I sent out eight emails. Within a day, half of them had responded.

I wrote a letter to the Editor of the Vancouver Sun, who ran my full letter in the Opinion page on October 10, 2017, as follows:

24.2: Opinion: Parents not getting all the facts... from sexual orientation and gender identity critics

The Langley parents who are afraid of a sexual orientation and gender identity (SOGI) curriculum have been played.

On Sept. 26, a group of about 100 people stood outside the Langley Schools District 35 office in support of the trustees who had recently approved the SOGI 123 curriculum for grades K-12. (See sogieducation.com.)

Among those holding up signs and standing in solidarity with the trustees were students, family members, friends, and allies of LGBTQ students.

I wasn't able to attend, since my current occupation had me stuck in Vancouver. During the two weeks leading up to this peaceful rally, I had been in communication with a few of these supporters who were responding to another group of parents. This first group had voiced strong opposition to SOGI with a well-organized initiative that included a Facebook page and a website to raise money.

The Langley parents who are afraid of SOGI gathered a few weeks earlier to listen to their organizers, who included Kari Simpson, Laura-Lynn Tyler Thompson, and New Westminster pastor Paul Dirks. A video was produced and posted on their Facebook page; it captured pastor Dirks' impressive presentation, complete with slides and transcript. The title of his message was "Gay and Transgender Research."

These concerned parents sat and listened in horror as Dirks cited study after study, which he claimed proved that LGBTQ, and in particular transgender people, suffer from mental illness. This, at least, is what most of those who sat through the presentation would have taken away. The message? SOGI should not be implemented and must be opposed.

Thankfully, Dirks provided the names of the studies and the authors in the slides he projected. I took the time to note at what minute and second mark in the video each study was referenced. I then searched the internet and contacted the authors I could find. I provided the link to the video and approximately when they were quoted; and I asked them these two simple questions: 1) Per his narrative, is he using your work accurately? 2) Do you have any commentary on the use of your research by this and/or similar groups?

Four of the authors quoted by Dirks have responded to my letter. All have basically said the same thing: they were misrepresented.

Though Dirks may have presented some of their findings, he took them out of context conveniently ignoring other facts and the authors' scholarly discussions and conclusions. The implication being their work would actually support initiatives for LGBTQ inclusion.

This raises the question of academic honesty and integrity, and can the rest of the information in the presentation be trusted? (In a trial, a witness who is willfully false in one material part of his or her testimony is usually not trusted in others.)

I sent the Langley Schools trustees an open letter on Sept. 25, with the three responses I had received at the time of the writing. Since then, a fourth study representative has responded this way: "In terms of the quote attributed to our service, selective excerption changes the meaning intended by the original writer in the longer article."

Where does this leave all those concerned parents who sat through the presentation and the countless thousands who have now watched and shared the video? Someone shared the video with this comment: "Paul Dirk shares statistics which need to be known so we can better help those hurting and keep our young children from being led down this path in our public schools."

Obviously, people want the facts, but when someone takes advantage of their sincerity with a calculated attempt to misinform with partial truths and excerptions out of context, then one needs to speak out.

I want to tell the parents who are afraid of SOGI that they've been played. My heart goes out to them. They deserve to be told the truth, the whole truth, and nothing but the truth.

24.3: Calling Out Trans and Age Discrimination

Chapter 11 chronicles how I canceled attending my 40th high school reunion in California and how the small group of friends and organizers who were privy to my situation understood. Moreover, several extended an invitation to stay with them if I ever came down to visit.

These friends were scattered throughout Northern California, including Redding, Sacramento, Lake Tahoe, San Francisco,

Santa Cruz, and San Jose. To celebrate my completion of the MA, I spent 20 days reconnecting with old friends, including my high school art teacher, Judy Lozano, who was living in a ranch in Southern Oregon. Judy was the teacher who cheered for me and encouraged me to study graphic design.

My friend Kathy Baldock lives near Reno, so I planned to stay with her for one week to hike in the canyons behind her house, kayak in Lake Tahoe, and hang out. I only spent one night in a hotel room; my old friends were hospitable and lovely. Those twenty days were invigorating. I would need that bit of recharging because I needed to find a way to earn an income after my return to Vancouver.

About that time, my Mom's doctor refused her request to sign the medical evaluation for her driver's license yearly renewal, given her age. My Mom was more dependent on me driving her to and from daily Mass and whatever errands she wanted to run. My life was very low-key; if I wasn't sitting down to watch television with her, I was cooking our meals, or working on two or three graphic design projects each month.

A part-time graphic design job would have been great in a perfect world, especially if it was close to Mom's townhouse. This would allow me to continue caring for Mom, who was, after all, still fairly independent. I could also continue volunteering and doing workshops since that only accounted for four or five monthly commitments. It was time to revisit the search for a job.

After updating my profile on Linkedin and half a dozen other job banks, I spent the next few months sending out resumes and cover letters again. I could feel my self-worth slowly ebbing away with each passing week.

My morning routine was to pour myself a cup of coffee, sit at my computer to see what new job postings appeared and fill out online application forms attaching cover letters and resumes. My Google search was simple: "graphic design jobs in South Surrey, BC, which was later expanded to include the Vancouver region.

Many of the graphic design job descriptions included technology expertise qualifiers. Cynically, it felt that companies were looking for programmers and engineers who liked to use other fonts besides Arial, Times Roman, and Comic Sans and could use a camera that was not built into their phones.

However, once again, what really frustrated me was how f**k**g impersonal the online job application process was. I hated being in that place again where my application and resume were scrutinized by a bot and not a real person. It made me feel jaded as hell. I don't like feeling this way; it's way too negative. This negativity, unfortunately, came out today in a cover letter I wrote in response to an ad for a Digital Graphic Designer. I had heard many people claim that you won't get a call if you can't grab someone's attention with the first paragraph.

I took that advice to heart. I was ready to throw in the towel; I felt I had nothing to lose. The last question in the online application said, "say something unique about yourself in 150 words or less that will catch our attention and make you stand out." I obliged. I said: "Really? Why don't I turn around and moon you; will that make me stand out in your eyes." I didn't send it.

During those frustrating days, I responded to a story that appeared in the Vancouver Province on Sunday, November 29, 2015, with the headline "There's a Revolution Going On." It painted an optimistic portrayal of how much better things were for trans persons. As I said above, I was jaded about not finding a job, so I wrote a letter to the editor; my letter was featured on the Opinion Page the following Sunday. They gave it the headline, "Lisa Salazar: Despite Caitlyn Jenner, many people still struggle with 'men in women's clothing'" this is what it said:

24.4: Opinion (Letter to the Editor), Dec. 1, 2015

While I am always grateful for positive press regarding trans issues, especially when I happen to know some of the players in the stories, my hopes for greater understanding and acceptance continue to be tempered by the lived realities of most of the trans persons I have come to know. The revolution University of B.C. student Cormac O'dwyer alludes to in Province reporter Glen Schaefer's article on Sunday is, unfortunately, nothing more than a tempest in a teacup.

While it is true that Caitlyn Jenner's coming out caused a

100 percent increase in the number of people who claim to know a trans person (to 16 percent from eight percent), being aware that someone is trans does not necessarily mean you embrace and affirm them. It simply means you know they are trans.

Additionally, for most trans persons who have transitioned and are transitioning later in life — let's say after the age of 30 — dealing with secondary sexual characteristics is not only time-consuming but also extremely expensive. For many trans persons, it means having to deal with physical and emotional discomfort on a daily basis.

Not every trans woman can afford facial hair removal, for example. In my case, it took 300 hours of painful electrolysis and close to $24,000 over a two-year period. Thankfully, I no longer had to shave. I was still employed at the time and was able to afford it. But this — never mind Jenner's financial ability — is not the norm for most trans persons.

Compared to the experience of many trans persons, I have been fortunate in other ways. Not only did my family embrace me, and my three adult sons allow me into their lives, my friends and clients offered their ongoing support. At least, that is how things started out with friends and clients. (Since then, I have experienced being ghosted and have seen most of my previous friendships and business relationships grow cold. I tried to be the one to keep relationships alive, but my efforts were not reciprocated.)

I transitioned fairly late in life, at the age of 57 in 2008. I struggled for many years, not knowing why I felt the way I did. Like many trans persons of my generation, it was not until I was almost 40 that I first heard the word "transgender." This word did not come into use until the late 1980s or early 1990s. Until then, I had "spiritualized" this internal conflict, for which I had no explanation or vocabulary.

In 1999, at the former Gender Clinic at Vancouver General Hospital, I was diagnosed with gender dysphoria and was offered assistance to transition medically and surgically. However, I took almost nine years to act on the recommended treatment.

I first had to reconcile my faith with what the doctors told me. I didn't want to trample over my religious faith, but I also didn't want to park my brain on the shelf by discounting the science. As the devout Christian I had become, in the hope of "being healed" I struggled with incredible guilt and believed that all my internal confusion was simply an attack from the devil.

While it seemed as if my marriage and my freelance graphic-design business were going to survive my transition, my wife asked for a divorce in 2011, and my business gradually dried up. Lamentably, I now find myself severely underemployed; I'm back to living with my 91-year-old mother.

In recent conversations with two of my ex-clients, my worst fears were confirmed — transitioning was the equivalent of committing career suicide.

Though Vancouver's progressive social scene offers one of the safest places for trans persons to transition, the sad truth is that things are seen through a much narrower lens when it comes to employment and business. Employers and clients worry about the optics of associating or working with a trans person. There is the fear that they will drive business away or make co-workers, clients, and customers feel uncomfortable.

If you are a business owner or a recruiter and have a choice between two persons with equal credentials, but one is trans, chances are you will go with the cisgender person. Why risk impacting the bottom line by hiring a trans person? This, sadly, is why so many trans persons continue to be unemployed and underemployed.

North Vancouver counselor Elizabeth Cooke's company Inclusivity — which helps businesses, non-profit groups, and governments accommodate trans people — is a much-needed service. But I suggest it will be long before trans persons are truly included and allowed to be integrated into society's fabric. Too many people, while giving intellectual ascent to what it means to be trans, still are not comfortable with "men in women's clothing," the default perception, never mind the reductionistic and ignorant restroom debate.

Essay published in Medium.com: May 31, 2016

24.5: I'm 65, female, trans. 3 Strikes. I'm out
It makes me feel as if I'm radioactive. What to do?

Since I transitioned from male to female almost eight years ago, I have seen my hireability plummet like a lead balloon.

It's little consolation to read about age and sex discrimination in the workplace, which helps explain strikes 1 and 2. However—mixing metaphors—being trans just puts the proverbial nail in the coffin.

My experience is not so unique. I won't bore you with all the recent studies and statistics that prove the transgender experience, when it comes to employment, is dire.

Every morning, I sit at my computer and scan the virtual job boards (Linkedin, Indeed, Glassdoor, etc.) for any new postings for an in-house graphic designer in the Vancouver area. Somedays there may only be one; but on other days, it could be six or more.

Some companies want you to apply via their own website's career page. Others invite you to send a cover letter and resume to a specific mailbox; sometimes cleverly named "hireme@xxx.com," or "jobs@xxx.com." And others point you to a third-party resume grinding mill.

My resume and cover letter package has been tweaked a hundred times. I've listened to the advice of trusted friends, read interesting how-to articles, and started from scratch many times. But I've always maintained the real proof of my abilities is not going to be found in my words; I believe my portfolio is the best proof of my talents and experience.

The shitty part is that no matter how great I sound, and how amazing my work might be, I've got three strikes against me. It makes me feel as if I'm radioactive. What to do?

I've reached the point where my cover letter now is the equivalent of a "Hail Mary Pass." I'm going for broke. (Painful choice of words.) I'm outing myself as trans.

Dear XXXXXX recruiter,
I am seeking a part-time to full-time position as an
in-house art-director/designer and creative resource with-

in an organization that values diversity.

Knowing XXXXXX is a safe and respectful workplace makes it uniquely approachable; by implication you invite and encourage complete transparency. This is important to me, given that any recruiter worth their pay will most likely vet prospective candidates via sites such as Google, Linkedin and Facebook.

A friend who is a human resources consultant told me not to do what I am about to do. I know I am taking a risk, but it's my way of conceding you are bound to find out I am transgender anyway. Disclosing this to you upfront serves another purpose, it removes the nagging doubt and uncertainty of whether or not you figured it out anyway. In a sense, I'm putting all my cards on the table. Notwithstanding, this is only one facet of who I am.

These are the rest of my cards: I am a multitasking senior graphic designer, art-director, photographer, copy writer, production artist — with over 15 years experience. I have worked with many clients, organizations and firms to develop presentations and create branding, packaging and marketing materials. I am also a trainer and educator with an MA in public and pastoral leadership. But that's another story.

These are my strengths, in no particular order:...

I then have about a dozen bullet points listing my skills and experience and conclude with:

> *I hope you will respond by saying: "Wow, Lisa has an amazing portfolio, depth of experience, and the right skill set. That's what ultimately matters to us. We want her! What's her phone number?"*
> *Here's hoping.*
> *Lisa Salazar, MA*

After four years of trying to find a job where my talents and skills can be put to use, I'm still hopeful despite the odds. Am I crazy?

* * *

The sentiments expressed in the last essay echo the Blogpost from Feb. 22, 2013 "At What Point Do I Throw In The Towel?" Though much in my life had changed, it seemed society was having a hard time keeping up.

Chapter 25: Stepping over Trumpism

S ometimes I wrote things that I never published for fear that my words would engender vitriolic and hateful comments. A case in point is the following unpublished blog post:

Blogpost, November 9, 2016
25.1: Feeling like you've been trumped?

A dear friend, a young trans woman who lives in Oregon, asked for prayers on Facebook last night; she was overcome with dread for her future. I was stunned by how vulnerable she was feeling. My heart broke for her.

How can an election in the world's most powerful democracy reduce any of its citizens, especially those who are marginalized and pushed to the edge of society, to dread their future? This is exactly what the 2016 election has done. And while I sit in relative comfort and safety by virtue of living five miles north of the 49th parallel, where an arbitrary and invisible line divides our two respective societies, I mourn. But I mourn not only for what was lost in the months leading up to the election with all the negativity and mudslinging that infected both campaigns, affecting many friendships on both sides of the border.

I don't want to exaggerate by inflating the numbers, but I was forced to unfriend about a dozen people on Facebook. I did so, not because we disagreed politically but because of the anger and dismissiveness they exhibited in their comments. When these individuals resorted to personal attacks, inappropriate language, or failed to moderate their own comments with civility, I quietly unfriended them. I only told one person what I was about to do and why.

Without getting into the politics of why things turned out the way they did or who's to blame, I want to reflect on where this avalanche of an election has left us all. An avalanche is an apt analogy here. Think of the before and after scenes we have seen in photos or videos; one moment, you see a smooth, still snow-laden slope, and then you see brokenness and devastation. Things no longer look the same; buried somewhere in the icy rubble are its victims.

Is the situation this dire and hopeless? I want to weigh in on the side of hope.

What has given me a certain degree of hope is how those who hoped for a different outcome are responding. Embedded in the words of anger, grief, and mourning, I detect a tone of grace-filled decency. I wonder what we would be hearing from Trump's supporters if he had lost? Would we be hearing of pockets of angry people rising up with arms? Would we be watching in pain as the National Guard began to take precautionary positions around the country? Would it have been the start of a civil war in America? I would hope not. I would hope they, too, would be grace-filled.

Another thought crossed my mind today...it had to do with the obvious irony of the President-Elect's last name. Will there be a collective pause from everyone whenever we use the verb "trump" in a sentence? Will hearing the word always result in a flashback to this moment in history? Not long ago, I overheard someone catch themselves innocently saying, "Well, that trumps everything!" Then quickly followed, "Oh God, I don't want that word in my vocabulary anymore, yuck." and laughed it off. I think the word will take on new significance, and everyone who hears it will nod with a new appreciation for its meaning. Feeling like you've been trumped will have more serious undertones.

A couple of weeks after Trump's Inauguration,
I wrote the following:

Blogpost: February 13, 2017
25.2: Speaking on the Border
The land of the free and the home of the brave?
Is the True North strong and free?

Hundreds gathered at the Peace Arch Border Crossing Sunday afternoon, February 12, 2017, to express concern and opposition to recent American immigration policies and attitudes impacting immigrants and refugees.

This peaceful demonstration was originally planned for February 5th but had to be postponed due to poor weather conditions. I was invited to say a few words. This was the speech I delivered:

I am an immigrant, first to the United States and later to Canada. I am Hispanic, I am Latina... I am white-skinned. I am a citizen of Colombia by birth—and a citizen of Canada by choice. I am a trans woman. I am a lesbian.

Like everyone who has ever lived, I had no choice in which country I'd be born in nor into which religious tradition. I did not get to choose my parents. I had no choice over my mother tongue. I had no choice when it came to the color of my skin. I did not choose my sexual orientation, and I did not choose to be trans.

Of all these things I have listed, only one I chose for myself. I chose to become a Canadian citizen.

I had no choice over anything else on my list.

Isn't it ironic—indeed, isn't it tragic—how the very things none of us got to choose are the things which historically have been used to justify vilification, then discrimination, then persecution, and ultimately—and potentially—annihilation and erasure?

Isn't it immoral how any one of these unchosen things can become a liability when a group needs someone to blame for their woes and needs a convenient scapegoat?

That is what we are witnessing today, and it's not just the immigrant and the refugee who is singled out. The same mentality that has resulted in the Ban and the Wall is casting a wide net. Women's reproductive rights, race relations, and LGBTQ+ rights, to name just three, are threatened.

As a trans person, I am particularly aware of how my trans and non-binary friends in the United States are losing protection from discrimination, medical coverage, and access to public restrooms, to name a few.

The seriousness of the situation cannot be underscored enough. I personally know of one 21-year-old trans girl from Boston who, one week after the new President took office, chose to end her life.

She could no longer envision a hopeful future for herself. Executive orders wiped out her access to trans-related healthcare, and she feared future executive orders would make her life less safe.

Her parents buried her on Monday, January 30th. This was so unnecessary. This is tragic. This is so incredibly sad. Her name was Amber.

It is a travesty how so many people in America are suddenly made to feel: Devalued and Marginalized; Ostracized and Rejected; Hopeless; and the convenient scapegoat!

When I trained to be a multi-faith chaplain, I embraced the radical and downright scandalous teachings of inclusion proclaimed by Jesus, the Nazarene.

He dared to challenge the notion of exclusion on the basis of where someone was from, what they did for a living, their economic or social status, or how they chose to live authentically. He spoke against intolerance. He challenged the gender hierarchy.

He championed the inherent worth of every person: the prostitute, the beggar, the leper, the physically disabled, the tormented by personal demons, the prisoner, children, and the aged.

More importantly, he invited us to seek the face of the Divine in the face of the orphan, the widow, the imprisoned, the hungry, the untouchable, the homeless, and the refugee.

This was good news to me.

But this is not the good news I hear coming these days from those who are consolidating power in the United States. Indeed, this is not the good news coming from those who support these policies yet claim to be Christian.

Shame on them for their hypocrisy!

What happened to "Love your neighbor as yourself" and "Do unto others as you would have them do unto you?"

I am sickened by how some in the United States—and Canada—have been emboldened to spew out their bigotry, homophobia, transphobia, racism, and islamophobia in recent weeks—with tragic consequences.

While we shook our collective heads at the headline: "Hate crimes soar after the election," we were jolted by the senseless shootings in Quebec City!

Our countries are better than this.

The United States' anthem ends with the phrase "The land of the free, and the home of the brave." The Canadian Anthem, "The True North strong and free", "expresses a similar sentiment.

Would that both refrains be true and not just wishful, empty claims in patriotic songs.

There is nothing freeing about banning or rounding up people on the basis of their creed, race, or color. There is nothing brave about building walls or placing handcuffs on grandparents and children.

Let these refrains inspire our two countries to be lands where there is freedom from rejection, marginalization, discrimination, and violence for being different.

Let our countries be known as lands where one's freedom does not come at the expense of another's. This is true freedom.

Let our countries be known as lands where one's bravery is not measured by valor in the battlefield alone but by the resolve that it takes to welcome the refugee and the alien, the courage to protect the marginalized, and the generosity to feed and house the destitute. This is true bravery.

Let our countries demonstrate their strength by how

they lift the burdens off their neighbor's backs. This is true strength.

Let's be:

Truly free,

Truly brave,

And truly Strong!

But more than anything else, let our compassion be what truly defines how we as "Brethren dwell together in Unity," as the monument behind me proclaims.

Chapter 26: Relocation and New Vocation

As I mentioned, one of the committees I joined during those 18 months I spent in limbo after graduation was a Peace Arch Hospital committee on patient care and safety. I got an invitation to attend a professional day with managers from the Fraser Health region. There, I ran into one of the moms who was a regular attendee at GNC conferences.

Her son was gay, and she was his proud ally. She asked if I planned to attend the 2017 conference in Pittsburgh in January. I missed the previous two GCN conferences due to my lack of funds. I told her it was unlikely and explained my situation. She offered to sponsor me without hesitation, including conference fees, travel, and hotel. I was speechless.

She wasted no time. When I got home that night, her son sent me an email with my boarding pass and receipts for the conference. She even ordered the event hoodie for me as a souvenir.

The Pittsburgh conference was my first time attending the annual event without being a presenter. I was pleased to see that in the years since I had last participated, there were more workshops for trans and non-binary persons, including a special time for us to meet each other. I will mention one interaction I had in particular.

As was the tradition, there was always a time for worship before each plenary session. As much as I appreciated the music, I would sit as far from the speakers as possible. This time it meant going out of the hall to the lobby. There was a long line of large whiteboards full of messages. I found the Cascadia group's communiqué and distracted myself as the music played through the doors. Then I heard an excited voice call my name from just a few feet behind me.

I turn and found myself standing face to face, okay, maybe face to shoulders, with Paula Williams.

Who is Paula Williams? She was a pastor and a father of three for 60 years, but then he came out as trans and became Paula. In her best-selling autobiography, she compares her experience as a woman to when she lived as a man. Paula is now an internationally known speaker on gender equity, LGBTQ+ advocacy, and religious tolerance. She has been featured in many media outlets and has given talks worldwide, including TED talks with millions of views.

She is also tall. Paula was standing with her arms wide open, ready to hug me. Though I had never met her, I knew who she was. "Paula!" I said. She said, "I read your book before I came out a few years ago, and it's one of the three books I recommend to people who want to learn more." "Oh? Thank you!" I stammered gratefully. She, too, was waiting for the worship time to end before entering the auditorium; she was the next speaker. And she was the person who moderated the trans meetup.

Paula, unbeknownst to me, was now on the GCN board, and I was thrilled to find out: trans people had a seat at the table!

26.1: Time to Move

About that time, Mom decided to sell the townhouse, wanting to move into a seniors' retirement complex in South Surrey and, a short time later, into an in-law suite at my sister Angela's house in Port Moody, 20 kilometers east of Vancouver. What this meant for me was that I was forced out of the nest.

The rental situation was starting to get ugly in Vancouver. I was content to look for a basement suite, hoping to find something I could afford. April 1 was when I needed to relocate. My search started as soon as Mom listed her place three months earlier, which I learned is too soon to look for rental accommodation since most listings only go up a month before the suites are available. But it gave me a good jolt when I saw what people were charging for veritable dumps. I was alarmed and dismayed. The friends I had lived with from 2010 to 2013 had been forced to move when the house owner notified them that he was moving in with his family, so the option of possibly returning to live with them was gone.

I concluded that social housing might be my only option, given that my income came mostly from my government pension. I was fortunate to find a one-bedroom apartment a block away from a community center with a park in a diverse part of Vancouver called the Drive.

Advocacy always got my blood flowing, but at times seemed to suck me into its black hole; it made me aware of my need to balance. The rage I mentioned earlier was equivalent to a pilot light in a furnace, and my thermostat was too sensitive. The fuel came from the persistent attack from the conservative religious right, and all the people were suddenly emboldened to be horrible toward their fellow man, thanks largely to Trump.

Summer 2017 was a mixture of rage about all of the above and a new horizon opening up. The Director of Spiritual Care for Vancouver Coastal Health had been able to put together the community-based CPE unit, the first ever in Canada, and I was approved to be one of the interns. It was an intensive unit, 16 weeks long, and it ran From May to the middle of August. What was novel or different about this unit was that instead of caring for people in a hospital, we cared for people in the streets of the Vancouver Downtown Eastside—a heartbreaking neighborhood.

Opioid-related deaths from overdose were occurring in record numbers, largely thanks to a tainted supply laced with fentanyl. There was, and still is, a disproportionally high number of Indigenous persons and LGBTQ+ youth who comprise the homeless population. They are drawn to this neighborhood from all parts of Canada. Our job was to develop a relationship with members of this community and offer a friendly, non-judgmental connection and support. When possible, we tried connecting them to social services and developed close relationships with community-based groups and organizations that have boots on the ground.

I was grateful that in preparation for our placement, we received Naloxone training and were issued a kit. On the very day I picked up my kit, two hours later, I saw a young woman looking for a place to plunge the needle into her lower leg. She was leaning against the wall of a building on the corner across the street from the Carnegie Center at the intersection of Main Street and Hastings Street, ground zero for this sad piece of real estate. Community nurses had posted warning notices everywhere telling people to be on the lookout for watermelon-colored heroin, and this young woman was about to inject herself with a syringe full of that color liquid.

From ten steps away, I stood and watched her as people walk past her on the busy sidewalk. After injecting herself, she drew her knees up and leaned her head back against the wall. In no less than 30 seconds after injecting herself, she started to flail her arms and legs. It looked like she was having a grand mal seizure. Then she rolled on her back and now looked like a beetle on its back as she moved her limbs erratically. In the few seconds it took me to run to her, she went limp, and her lips turned blue.

I will say that the training kicked in. I called 911, laid the phone on the sidewalk next to her and put it on speaker. While talking to the dispatcher, I rolled the young woman onto her left side to prevent her tongue from blocking her airway, unsuccessfully tried to rouse her by rubbing her sternum with my knuckles, then I felt for a pulse—it was weak—and prepared the Naloxone syringe. Just then, a good Samaritan ran up. He, too, was on the phone to 911. He had seen her start flailing and saw me bend down to help her. He came to assist. I gave her the first shot.

Emergency responders were everywhere during those days. Two ambulances were a block away, and two paramedics on bicycles were also a short distance away. They arrived in 2 minutes and took over. I was impressed with their non-judgmental approach. The young woman was disoriented and delirious when she jerked from her unconscious state.

While they were tending to her, they found her BC identification card in her bag. They calmed her down using her name, telling her she was safe, that she had overdosed, and were there to help her. You'd expect them to have been jaded and dismissive. I spoke to one who was a supervisor and told him I was impressed with how gently they spoke to her. He told me that all the paramedics working in the DTSE neighborhood had requested to be there. Wow, I thought, what an awesome display of humanity.

Three weeks later, kitty-corner from where a young woman overdosed, I found myself in a similar situation. This time it was a young man who had collapsed in the crosswalk, stopping traffic. People were calling out for someone with a kit. I was on the step of the Carnegie Center when all this happened. I ran across the street, and the training again paid off. As I prepared my kit, I yelled, "Someone call 911" and I heard several people yell back, "They've been called." The young man's friend confirmed that he had just injected heroin. The first to arrive was a police car, and shortly after, the fire department paramedics. By the time they took over, I had already plunged two doses of Naloxone into his thigh. They gave him a third, larger dose and that did the trick.

These and other experiences in the DTES helped me see I had the capacity to think clearly and act in an emergency. After both of those two incidents, my supervisor asked me to reflect on how I was feeling and to process my emotions. One of the operating principles in clinical training was 'action-reflection.' This principle involves regularly reflecting on one's actions, decisions, and interactions with patients and using these reflections to inform future actions and decisions.

26.2: Is This a Calling?

It was this CPE unit, which I signed up for only because of the opportunity to be an outreach worker to marginalized LGBTQ+ persons, that made me reconsider spiritual care in a hospital as a career possibility. It also helped me see that I didn't need to focus only on LGBTQ+ advocacy; I could be there for anyone, regardless of their sexual orientation or gender identity.

My final evaluation for that unit solidified my chance of challenging the requirement to complete two advanced CPE units. I was encouraged by both the director of Spiritual Care and my teaching supervisor to go for it, which I did. I did my third unit at St. Paul's Hospital in downtown Vancouver. Compared to the summer unit, which was an intensive 16 weeks long, this unit ran from September to April of the following year. I went before the assessment committee two months into the unit. I received a high score, which not only gave me equivalency for one advanced unit, but for two advanced; I didn't need to continue training and could proceed with certification.

When the chair of the evaluation committee read out my score, I didn't grasp the significance of what he was saying. I thanked him, thinking I had met my objective of having one less unit to complete. My teaching supervisor was at the meeting as an observer; he said, "Lisa, do you know what that means? It means that you are through. But please finish this unit. I need you in the class; you are a mentor and leader for the others. I don't want to lose you!"

Notwithstanding my supervisor's appeal, there was no way I would stop interning at the hospital. Despite the high score and the equivalency, interacting, caring for, and journeying with patients, plus working side by side with the clinical team could only help to make me better at my job. When I completed the unit in April, the Director offered me a job opportunity, a foot in the door, as he put it. This was the same Director who, in April 2013, interviewed me and pointed me toward what would be my current calling or vocation.

With one of his team on an extended medical leave, he needed someone to cover his shifts until this chaplain returned or retired, in which case there would be an opening. But there is such a thing as seniority. When this chaplain chose to retire, his shifts went to a fellow VST graduate who completed his CPE training before me, and I was offered the part-time position at George Pearson Centre in Vancouver (GPC). This is where I work to this day. A couple of months before COVID-19 hit the fan, I was granted certification from the Canadian Association for Spiritual Care/Association canadienne de soins spirituels (CASC/ CASS). This, I never would have dreamed in a million years!

Unpublished Blogpost: July 5, 2018
26.3: I'm Still Too Raw and White-Hot with Anger
Trigger warning: Death by suicide.

Officiating a friend's Celebration of Life was an honor, but it shouldn't have been necessary. I have been growing increasingly angry, and I want to lash out at the injustice and ignorance that has now claimed the life of someone I was becoming friends with. She was a fellow trans sister.

Katterina was from Nova Scotia and transitioned socially and medically about six years ago. As is the case for many married trans people, she, too, went through a divorce. She was an electrician by trade. After finding her work being sabotaged and her tools disappearing from the work sites, she moved to BC. She spoke to Morgane Oger of Trans Alliance in Vancouver, who assured her that the trade unions in BC had zero tolerance for that kind of crap.

Moving to Vancouver seemed like the only way to find peace of mind, yet she hated being separated from her parents and her adult children. She packed up her belonging into her brand-new Toyota Corolla and drove across the country. Then, tragedy struck on her fourth day in Vancouver when she was in a motor vehicle accident that left her seriously injured and her car totaled.

Dealing with the Insurance Corporation of BC (ICBC) and her out-of-province insurer became the nightmare we all fear. But Katterina was resilient, and despite her brain, back, and knee traumas, she worked hard at rehabilitation. When it became clear that she would not be able to return to the workforce as an electrician, she tried doing gig work in the Vancouver film industry, but this proved impossible to maintain.

She eventually qualified for disability and assistance to retrain herself. She chose Interior Design, where she could use her incredible artistic talent. Katterina enrolled in a private school and was proving that she had what it takes.

Then, in early April 2016, she was dealt a blow that I believe contributed to her deteriorating mental health.

That April afternoon, Katterina made an alarming comment

on Facebook. She had been misgendered in a horrible way by the nurse attempting to insert a stent for an IV line in her arm. She screamed in pain and asked for someone else to insert the line. The nurse was offended and lashed out. This is how Katterina described it later:

"[The nurse] looked at my hospital armband, and when she saw it had an "F" indicating my sex as "Female," she asked if it was a mistake...I was mortified. She then asked if it shouldn't read "T" or "M" instead. There was another patient and her family in the bed adjacent to me on the other side of the curtain, who had to have heard what this nurse was saying to me. To me, this Nurse was telling me that I was fooling no one. Least of all her, and that I was obviously Male despite what my ID said."

In her cryptic post, she talked about the pain, the devastating insult, and how she was crying uncontrollably, but she didn't say which hospital she was at. I read her message within minutes of her posting it and fired off a direct message (DM) asking her where she was so I could come to be with her.

In the meantime, assuming that she was at Vancouver General Hospital's ER, I called Dr. Fleming, whom I knew personally. He was one of the senior teaching doctors in the ER, and I told him about my friend's predicament. He said he would check immediately.

A few minutes later, Katterina answered my DM and said she was at one of the Catholic-run hospitals in Vancouver. I called Dr. Fleming again to tell him my friend was not at VGH. He said he was about to call me back to say the same thing. I thanked him for his quick response.

I asked Katterina to call me. She called sometime later, and I asked her if she wanted me to come, and she said maybe in a couple of days. She expected to be there until her pain was gone. This is how she would go on to describe her ordeal in a post a couple of days later, it was heartbreaking:

"Just spent an evening in ER with another Diverticulitis flair-up. They hopped me up on Morphine and Antibiotics. Worst IV needle I ever had hacked into my arm. And the nurse misgendered me two or three times, and I lost it. I spent my whole evening crying in ER. I thought I was passing very well, but I guess I was deluding myself... "I'm just a freak in women's clothes." Society will never accept me... I'm worn out. I'm tired of fighting to carve out a place in this world... I love you all. Goodnight."

She called me a few days later and asked, "Guess where I am? My doctor's office brought me to the VGH Psychiatric Evaluation Unit by ambulance. He told me I needed to come immediately after I told him I wanted to kill myself." She said she had been allowed to make one last phone call before surrendering her phone, then added she would not be allowed any visitors for 48 hours.

I went to see her two days later, and my heart broke. She was under suicide watch, which meant being in a room with no door and no sheets on the bed. Katterina spent the next five weeks in the Psychiatric ward, where to my horror, she was consistently misgendered by other patients and staff, who should have known better.

By the time she was discharged, her landlord had evicted her from her basement apartment, forcing her to put her belonging in storage. Home became one of the Salvation Army's shelters for women in downtown Vancouver. She spent several months there, during which time she began to put her life back together again.

She filed a formal complaint against Providence Health. She at least got the satisfaction of knowing that the nurse had been reassigned to a different ward and had been ordered to undergo trans-sensitivity training. For added measure, the whole department had been included in the training. She received a formal apology, which seemed sincere. Still, after she posted the contents of the letter on Facebook, many of her trans friends were appalled at the writer's lack of knowledge and sensitivity. She used the word "transgendered" twice.

In the two years and a bit since this life-sucking episode to the day she chose to end her life, Katterina tried to remain optimistic. She posted often on Facebook and shared her ongoing challenges with insurance companies, government agencies, and her financial circumstances. We had one thing in common, we both were women of faith who believed in a God who loves us as we are, but I wish I had been more sensitive to her feelings and thoughts.

In one of her latter posts, she said, "I'm tired of fighting for what's Right! This world is going to Hell in a Hand Basket! And there's nothing any of us can do to stop it...You know. I know TDOR is for those amongst us who have been murdered...But. Isn't Suicide also, Murder by a Thousand Daggers? Each knife wound may not kill you, but given enough painful wounds like this... It can send some of us over the edge...Should we who commit suicide not also be remembered for the pain and suffering we have had to endure? Have we not also been Murdered By An Intolerant Society?"

We were all sleeping on the night Katterina chose to die. Her last few posts were made starting just before midnight, and her final sad note just before 1:00 in the morning.

"Some of you may not know this.
But Katt is a fitting name for me, as I almost drowned
when I was a teen...But two guys saved me."
"Sometimes I still feel overwhelmed and as if I'm drowning..."
"Love you, my sisters! Xoxo"
"We are all both Male and Female because God
is both female and male...we are equals!
Never, forget that."
"It;s over for me. orry"

If you or someone you know has been affected by the story,
please reach out for support. You are not alone.
Trans Lifeline can be reached toll-free
anywhere in Canada at **1 (877)-330-6366,**
or in the U.S. at 1 **(877) 565-8860.**
Talk Suicide Canada can be reached at **1.833.456.4566.**
Please don't hesitate to call if you need help.

Postscript 1:

I shared Katterina's story to immortalize her. She was a kind, thoughtful, creative, passionate, extremely likable, sociable, and spiritual person. This is a prayer she wrote. We recited it together at her memorial service:

Lord God,
I have been so blessed by the valuable lessons
I have learned throughout my life and so truly blessed
to have learned them.
I now live the life of my dreams with wonderful friends
and family who love and understand me....
My cup floweth over, dear Lord,
and I am happy to share and work toward the
greater good of all people.
I enjoy the acceptance of all people, by all peoples,
of each other no matter what their differences.

Amen, Katterina. Amen

Postscript 2:

I never published this blogpost after I wrote it because I was aware of my anger at the world and my possible lack of objectivity. I wasn't sure if it would be triggering to a person in a vulnerable state of mind. This was the worry that caused me to stop blogging a few months later, this was the self-sensoring I mentioned in the Preface.

Blogpost: July 17, 2018
26.4: My Thoughts After 10 Years as Lisa

I took a leap of faith on the third Saturday in July 2008. It was either that or leap to my death. As scared as I was of what lay ahead, it was less frightening than the thought of never having experienced what it felt like to live authentically. I'm happy to still be here, as Lisa.

A topic garnering much attention in social sciences is intersectionality, the categorizations of race, class, and gender as they apply to a given individual or group. It is regarded as creating overlapping and interdependent systems of discrimination or disadvantage.

Add to this idea the questions we ask and the answers we get as we explore our world as children and in our youth. What assumptions, expectations, and conclusions do we draw? Do they set us up for success or failure? Same-sex attracted and trans and non-binary persons navigate and view life through a lens that often makes them imagine a future that is frightening. Fear of rejection, ridicule, and abandonment rank high.

For the last 25 years, we have been in a state of emergency, that is to say, of emergence and coming to light. This emergence is due, in large part, to the internet and the sharing of information. Where once we struggled to figure out who we are in secret, now we can see, hear and read about people asking the same questions, and their stories resonate with ours.

But what are the implications for the rest of society? Indeed, what are the challenges and opportunities?

We can choose to exclude, or we can choose to include. To be inclusive may seem scandalous and radical, but I believe it can make us the best version of who we are as humans.

Dare with me to be scandalous.

A reflection from September 13, 2018
26.5: I Came to Terms
Published in New York Times special feature,
"Transgender Lives"

I came to terms with what seemed like a paradox and contradiction, if not absurd chaos, fairly late in life when I realized the identity I had constructed for myself had to be tossed out, and I needed to start over. I was almost 58 when I began life as Lisa.

Most people don't have a clue of what goes on inside the head of someone who is gender dysphoric; the questioning and the persistent sense that something is wrong and the gender they identify with does not quite align with their body.

The contradictory aspect of all of this is the absolute sense I always had, from the earliest memories of this chaos until today, that I am deeply loved by God. However, this sense of being loved did not stop me from asking the most basic of questions in our human repertoire, "Why this?" and "Why me?"

From childhood, I did the only thing that seemed most logical. But this was a subjective interpretation; it was a logic rooted in the social constructs and expectations about my family, my circle of friends, and the larger social and cultural environment I existed in. My logic was based on what others said; this defined me. But inside me, there was a raging conversation going—a debate of sorts—and at times, a screaming match that lacked words. Without a vocabulary, it meant that this "condition" — or whatever it was —would have to be kept gagged and shackled.

How does one cope or deal with this kind of absurdity? When others were making plans for their future and dreaming of a golden time in their lives, I was ensuring the chains and the locks around this unknown force were holding tight. I grew up envying others who were free to be themselves and who didn't seem to struggle with my kind of questions. At times I felt like a spectator of everyone else's life from behind a chain-linked fence and not part of the action.

What does this have to do with my philosophy of ministry as a spiritual care provider? It is what compels me to want to help others find their voice, if not a language, that will help them begin to make sense of their own chaos. I realize that we all have this burning need to flesh out who we are with words that ring true and authentic, even if those words are frightening and strange at first—before they become marvelous.

Chapter 27: Settling Into the Unknown

Another day that I wake up and see my
reflection in the mirror.
I wipe the sleep from my eyes and splash
cold water on my face.
There is a moment of sadness as my mind reflects on
a much different image—
like a wallpaper that I learned to hate, if not despise...
that of a body that bore no resemblance to the reality
that lay below its surface.
How many years passed as I trusted this ornate wallpaper
to hold up the walls,
to keep them from folding in on themselves?
But this moment of sadness is short-lived,
and the wallpaper is almost forgotten.
It took a long time to peel it away; at times,
it tore into small frustrating pieces,
and at times, it released in large sections.
The surprise was not what was hidden behind it.
The surprise was that the walls were strong
and could stand on their own.
What I see now in the mirror, I can live with.
what I see now is no longer a veneer of pretense;
what I see is what you get...
exposed to the core. And I like what I see.

* * *

When I turned fifty, a friend gave me a birthday card that made me laugh; its message has proven true. On the front, above a cartoony drawing of a little car climbing a hill, it read, "Turning fifty doesn't mean you're over the hill," and on the inside of the card, the little car was speeding down a hill and above it, it said, "You're just picking up speed." Where have the last 12 years gone?

This realization had made me more philosophical, I suppose. The irony is that what my dad often said is true for me as well; I don't feel any older, just not as spunky. Age and the passing of time aside, I know I am not the same person I was 12 years ago, not only from a vocation and career point of view but, as you have seen me state in these pages, from a spiritual and ontological understanding that has finally answered the questions, "Why me?" and "Why this?"

This penultimate chapter of the book spans from the fall of 2018 to the end of winter in 2023. There has been a blur effect in time that has compressed these last 46 months. For a time, the COVID-19 pandemic disrupted the ebb and flow of life as we knew it. But I'm getting ahead of myself.

The part-time position that was offered to me was a perfect fit with all the other irons I had in the fire at the time it was offered to me. But even with a schedule of 18 hours per week, it soon became apparent that I needed to reconsider all my other commitments.

Trans-inclusivity workshops for healthcare professionals was something I wanted to continue doing. What became abundantly clear was that committee and board positions were too much for me to continue with. So, as soon as my terms expired, I withdrew my name from the list of candidates.

When my boss, Doug Longstaffe, the Director of Spiritual Care, first offered the position at GPC, I told him I had to think about it. The reason was that GPC, as far as I knew, was a long-term care facility full of elderly disabled persons that hit too close to home. I had been caring for my Mom, giving respite to my sister Angela two days a week. If I accepted the job, it would mean expending emotional capital six days a week. I wasn't sure I could handle it. Doug said it was a fair consideration and gave me a few days to consider the offer. At the time, I was still covering shifts at VGH for the practitioner who was deciding if he would retire. Later that afternoon,

I followed up on a patient with terminal cancer, but when I went to her ward, her room was empty. I was saddened. A nurse saw me and said, "Hey Lisa, she was transferred to Palliative on the 16th floor this morning." I found her.

There had been many times during my clinical internships when patients would say to me, "When you walk in, I feel at peace inside me," or words to that effect. It always humbled and encouraged me, an endorsement that I was where I needed to be. That afternoon was no different—that is what this kind lady whispered when she saw me walk into her room; she had no more voice.

In previous visits, she always requested I read Psalms 23, 61, and 91, and to sing the hymn Joyful, Joyful We Adore Thee to her; this day was no different. I could see the joy on her face, and it was hard to say goodbye knowing that would likely be the last time I saw her. Before I left, she thanked me for all the time I spent with her and cared for her. Priceless.

Doug was still in his office when I finished my shift. I accepted the job offer. If caring for the folks at GPC would be anything like what I'd experienced with this gentle lady, then I would have been a fool to pass up the offer. Honestly, had never experienced this kind of job satisfaction as a graphic designer, as much as I found it fulfilling. Being a spiritual care practitioner was different.

While I enjoyed helping my clients sell their products and services, nothing compared to connecting with someone on a personal level, be it a friend, loved one, or stranger.

Accepting a role in a dramatic reading of "Trans Scripts," a play based on the narratives of seven trans women, was my first-ever attempt at theater. I knew most of the other trans women whom the director of the production had invited. Someone suggested me for the role of one of the older trans women being portrayed. The characters ranged in age from mid-twenties to mid-seventies. Instead of acting out the parts, we all sat on the stage with the scripts on music stands and microphones in front of us. I read the lines for a woman in her late fifties who had worked in the family business with her father and brothers, a car garage before she came out.

The play featured seven composite lives based on interviews of 75 trans men and women conducted by the playwright,

Paul Lucas, over several years, starting in 2012. The lines in the play could not be altered; we had to read them as written, which was too bad because some of the terms used seemed dated, and some lines were awkward to read. But we did it anyway, in front of an audience of about 200 at the Cultch Theater in east Vancouver.

I only share this embarrassing Theater debut because of what occurred after the play ended. One of the other women in the play was Morgane Oger, whom I mentioned in the retelling of our advocacy to have the BC Human Rights Code updated to include gender identity and gender expression. She was the Chair of Trans Alliance at the time.

Morgane had offered to drive me home after the performance, but we got stalled talking to various audience members in the foyer. Then I saw Morgane motion that she was ready to go, but a woman came up to compliment me and to say how much she appreciated my comments during the question-and-answer session that followed the dramatic reading. I was very flattered.

She reminded me that we had met at a mutual friend's party. Yes, I vaguely remembered meeting a red-headed woman months earlier at after-Pride party. And this woman also had red hair in a similar Peter Pan style.

I asked her if she needed a ride home; I knew Morgane had room in her car. She declined graciously and explained that she only lived two blocks away. She told me her name, which I proceeded to forget, as is my common practice. But the penny dropped as I climbed out of Morgane's car in front of my apartment.

Back in the middle of August, the mutual friend Catherine (who had hosted the party), sent me a curious email. Catherine asked if I was dating anyone and to whom I was attracted. I wrote back and said, no one and women, respectively. "Why?" I asked her. She couldn't tell me—she'd been sworn to secrecy. Then added, "Don't be surprised if you get asked out." Could this be that woman?

Facebook came through one more time. I could not, for the life of me, remember her name. I went to Catherine's mutual friends directory, and there she was; her name was Karen, and we were already friends!

I clicked on Messenger, and I sent Karen, a short message. I did not admit to forgetting her name; my first message to her was: "Hi. Sorry, I couldn't continue chatting last night; I didn't want to delay Morgane, who offered to drive me home. Fortunately, it wasn't too far out of her way since I'm only 1 block past Trout Lake Community Ctr. It's a Rest Day today, I slept in until 9:30. I haven't done that in a long time. I guess the adrenalin from last night needed to be burned off. TTYL"

Karen replied, "Yeah, me too. It was really nice seeing you! I didn't know you lived in the area (I think it's my favorite neighborhood in Vancouver.) You probably needed the rest; I usually sleep in on Sundays myself because my Friday/Saturday schedule is kind of...inhumane. My Sunday so far has consisted of perogy lunch/culture crawling."

And there we were, the beginning of a most timely and welcomed relationship; one I never dreamed of, or allowed myself to entertain as a possibility. I had grieved the end of my marriage to Rachel and had accepted my lot in life as a single person. I was not looking for someone. Instead, and when I least expected it, someone found me. Our love for each other and our times together each week have made me appreciate life all the more; I am grateful for her companionship.

As I shared in the preface, I stopped writing blog posts at about this time. In fact, my very last blogpost was written in San Jose, CA, the week before I started working at GPC. I flew down for the weekend to attend my 50th high school reunion, and when I was down there, the Brett Kavanaugh SCOTUS nomination hearings were playing out. With the exception of the dinner at night, I had all of Saturday to myself, and I made the mistake of watching the proceedings. I was triggered, having been sexually assaulted and raped in San Jose when I was growing up.

I wrote the following blogpost in the hotel room. I didn't know it then, but it was the last blogpost until just a few weeks ago.

Blogpost: September 22, 2018
27.1: Me too
But some of you already knew that

Coincidental with my Class of 68' 50th high school reunion, the reports of Republicans bullying Dr. Christine Blasey Ford, who question her memory of the attempted rape by Supreme Court nominee Brett Kavanaugh, has thrown me into a bit of depression. I've been triggered.

I am here, in a motel room in San Jose, California, where my high school reunion is to take place in an hour.

Earlier this afternoon, I drove to the two locations where I was sexually abused and raped. I remember all the details. I may not know the name of my attackers, but my body and brain remember how it felt to be forced to masturbate a man who was one of my paper route customers. I was 12 years old.

I resist the compulsion to wash my hands for, God only knows, the millionth time.

Then there was the rape when I was 15 years old. Someone who purported to want to help me audition as a rhythm-guitar player in a garage band and had offered to drive me to a house in Willow Glen, a neighborhood in San Jose. But he had other plans. He took me to his apartment, and, well, it happened.

I do not know the names of the two predators. But I remember what they looked like. I could not pick them out in a lineup if my life depended on it, but I can draw you the floor plans of their apartments.

I drove to each crime scene today and took pictures of the outside. The abuse took place in a 2nd story apartment—number 33. And the rape took place two miles away in a downstairs unit, G6.

I will keep the street names secret.

In my book, I've detailed these two events, so I won't get into the details here.

I felt compelled to write this post because the sheer stupidity of those who are suggesting Dr. Ford's memory should not be trusted is beyond words. Anyone who has been a victim of a sexual assault remembers.

I remember with painful detail.   #metoo
Blogpost: August 25, 2018
27.2: Oh, I've heard about that happening!
An unexpected (and unforgettable) end to a story.

A couple of weekends ago, I went to visit my Mom. My sister arrived unexpectedly a short time later with her grandson, who is eight years old. Figuring the last thing the little guy wanted to do on a summer afternoon was to sit indoors with three older women, I said, "Let's walk to the convenience store at the gas station; it's only three blocks away, I'll buy you a candy bar."

We trundled off talking about candy, and as we passed the elementary school a block away, he asked, "How old are you?" Hum, I thought to myself, I wonder why he wants to know my age? "I'm sixty-seven, almost sixty-eight," I replied.

"Oh, then you're older than my dad. He's fifty-one," he remarked.

Then he asked, "Do you have any children?"

At this point, I realized I had never spoken to my niece, his mother, about how much and how soon he should be informed about my 'real' position in the family tree. I concluded I would answer him honestly and hope for the best. (He's only known me as "Auntie" Lisa; he was born after I transitioned.)

"Well, yes, I do. They are your three uncles," and proceeded to name them. He looked puzzled. "But I thought Granny was their mom!" he exclaimed, referring to my ex-wife.

"Yes," I said, "She's their mom, and I'm their dad."

I knew I had crossed a line and was preparing myself for what might happen next, that I would have to go into a carefully worded explanation of what I had just revealed to him.

After a few seconds of silence as he pondered my answer, he shrugged and said, "Oh, I've heard of that happening."

End of story. Next subject.

We went back to talking about his favorite brand of candy bar. My niece's son...He gave me hope for the future.

27.3: Doing Less But Doing More

As this new life situation unfolded in the fall of 2018, I split my emotional capital between Karen, my Mom, and the residents at GPC. It had been a long time since I hadn't been in intense learning and training mode, and I was finding my new rhythm and balance. You could say the year that followed was remarkable for its unremarkableness. In saying that, I know I'm glossing over a whole year. But it was true. I toned down the advocacy quotient, with the exception of my obligations listed above. I didn't have as many irons in the fire, and I found time to go on long walks to unwind as I consumed audiobooks and podcasts.

Living so close to the gym and the community center gave me the idea to see if core strengthening exercises would help reduce the frequency of symptoms I had been experiencing since before my CPE unit in the DTES. Both my feet would fall asleep at the same time, and the sensation moved up my legs until it reached my behind. Have you sat on the toilet too long, and your butt and legs fall asleep? It was sort of like that. Walking seemed to reduce the intensity and frequency of these symptoms. Though I walked close to 10,000 steps inside the hospital each shift, going to all the wards, I mostly stood when talking with residents and staff. The frustrating aspect was that these symptoms were random; they didn't happen daily.

I saw my doctor, and he ordered a C-T scan, which was inconclusive. Then a second one revealed the problem, I had nerve impingement in my lower lumbar. I had four options, surgery with no promises and a lot of risks; cortisone injections, which would last a few months and would need repeating; exercise to build up the back and core muscles; or do nothing and live with the annoyance.

I went to the gym and spoke to one of the trainers. For $400, I could get ten one-hour sessions with a personal trainer, but first, I had to complete a medical history and get my doctor to sign off, given my back's situation. Jogging 10K three times a week for 15 years was to blame. I had already stopped jogging six years earlier because of a problem with my bobblehead and neck. And finally, I was not to do any weight-lifting exercises where the weight would be transferred down my back. The trainer and I started the ten weeks, eleven weeks before COVID-19 restrictions closed all Vancouver community centers and gyms. Fortunately, all the exercises I learned were ones I could do anywhere and didn't require special equipment.

27.4: Bubbles and Deep Sadness

Given our fragile and vulnerable resident-patient population at work, our hospital had some of the strictest protocols of all the hospitals in Vancouver. With my sisters, we also decided to be very careful when caring for Mom. Karen and I became each other's social bubble. Unlike me, she had to work from home, which meant Zoom meetings ad nauseam. Like pretty much everyone I know, all family events, such as birthdays and anniversaries, were canceled. At times, the routineness and monotonous sameness to each day made forgetting which day of the week we were on the new normal.

For the first time since I transitioned, I could finally say that my life was boring. Well, at least on the surface. I was aware of the rage was boiling beneath my calm and boring exterior. I still refuse to acknowledge and talk about all the crap that streamed endlessly everywhere I turned. The anti-vaxxers, the conspiracy theories, the vitriol, the hate, the impatience, the arrogance, the lies, and deceit, and basically, the lack of love, or human compassion and decency. I think I would have been consumed if I had focused my gaze on what I saw. Why? Because in among all the stuff I saw, what stressed me the most was how anti-trans rhetoric was also on the increase, even in Canada. Ideologies respect no borders.

There is no denying that intolerance on all fronts has increased in the last five years, and it can be draining. My job turns my focus away from the ugliness I see increasing against trans people, and we are only being dished a small piece of the vitriol pie. It has been therapeutic for me to be in the moment with people whose life has been reduced to the confines of their hospital bed and wheelchair. One can't help but experience a balancing out of priorities when one's world is larger than a 10 by 10-foot room.

Mom world began to shrink after moving into my sister's house in Port Moody. Her decline was the inevitable result of the vascular dementia she was diagnosed with a few years earlier. The most noticeable symptom was her decreasing capacity to make new memories, but her long-term memory was intact.

The combination of being forced to stay home, thanks to COVID restrictions, which resulted in being shut out from seeing her friends and all of us, except for Angela, Carmen and I being able to be with her, meant she had less social and mental stimulation. I saw the same thing happen at work, especially during those months of isolation, when not even family members could visit their loved ones and had to content themselves with virtual visits.

Summer 2020 marked a significant change in Mom's daily experience. She was staying in bed longer every day, sometimes only getting up to use the washroom. She was also eating less and less, often finding the food less appetizing even though we only prepared her favorite things. She would complain that they had changed the quality. 'they,' meaning the food producers. There was no point trying to dissuade her to explain that her tastebuds were not working. Her need to salt her food was proof.

By the time November rolled around, she had grown frail, and we took her to the hospital when she started to complain of lower back pain. We suspected her kidneys were in distress and this was confirmed. She sent three days connected to the IV. In consultation with her doctors in the geriatric unit, we agreed to bring her home. That is where she wanted to be. The hospital had accommodated our request to let one family member to be always with her since Mom had reverted to speaking Spanish only. She was a very capable bilingual person, but English seemed to fade from her.

The palliative team was summoned and organized what her home care would look like. I cannot say enough about the Eagle Ridge Hospital's team as well as Fraser Health's community palliative support nurses who came three times a day to help us care for her. We celebrated her 96th birthday in October and all knew this would be the last time. November 14th was my birthday. It fell on Saturday; I wondered if she would last that long.

Carmen's daughter, Ana, came from Toronto to say goodbye to Mom and to be with us as we gathered around her that weekend. My brother drove down from Grand Forks, BC, and all the grandchildren took turns spending time with Mom. She was mostly sleeping all the time and we were providing comfort care.

At 1:30 in the afternoon, she opened her eyes and was cheerful and full of energy. Carmen was with her in the bedroom and called out to us. We propped her up in bed and made her comfortable. She asked who was there; she had heard voices and was curious and lucid. I can't remember how many of us were there or who was there besides my two sisters, my niece Ana, and possibly my two brothers-in-law. John had not arrived yet.

We were still trying to maintain some protocols and were masked in the living room. Mom wanted to see everyone, so we took turns going into her room and sitting with her. When it was my turn, I went in and sat on the bed next to her. I removed my mask and kissed her. As I pulled away, she stretched up, cupped my face with both hands, and said, "Oh, Lisa, I love you."

Birthday presents are mostly material things with a temporal value. What my Mom gave me that day was the best birthday present I have ever received; it will last forever. I told her as much. I thanked her then, and I thank her now. I call bullshit on anyone of any age who misgenders or deadnames their trans child, friend, or family member. Both of my parents were elderly when I came out, and I can count the number of times they slipped up and misgendered me on one hand—their love and acceptance knew no bounds. Gracias, Mami, te amo.

Brother John arrived later that day; Mom's window of lucidity had closed by then—it was open only briefly. The last time she had been that lucid was a few days earlier, when her local parish priest, Father Mark, came to administer the Sacraments for the Sick and the Eucharist. it was another special moment for us who were there. She slipped away in her sleep early Monday morning, the 20th of November.

Unlike my Dad's memorial, which was attended by many, Mom's service was limited to ten persons, counting the priest. I wish we could have invited her many friends from the churches they had been part of.

Around the world, the COVID-19 pandemic has forced our hands on many levels. I have seen the negative and positive consequences of every day I work. What my family and I experienced was not unique; we've all been impacted in some way. Life, as we knew it, was disrupted once again, but this time on a larger scale than 9/11.

My mantra now applies to all the good memories from these last twelve years. "Don't be sad. No one and nothing can take these beautiful memories away. I will celebrate and give thanks for all of them."

Chapter 28: Epilogue 2

As I completed this second edition, I was struck by the stark contrast between the title and tone of the original and that of the sequel. "Section 1: Transparently" reflected the hope and anticipation I felt leading up to my gender confirmation surgery, and "Section 2: Then This Happened" captured the tumultuous reality of the events that followed. The new title speaks to my life's unexpected twists and turns of the 13 years post GCS, an acronym you should be familiar with by now. Then This Happened hints at the resilience and determination I have found in the face of the unknown.

I cannot ignore the fact that the world has become more dangerous and hostile for trans people. As I write these words, the rights of trans individuals are under attack across the United States and to a lesser extent in parts of Canada. The rise of antagonism from conservative, right-wing politicians and religious organizations has led to a concerted effort to erase and marginalize our community.

Despite these challenges, I remain hopeful. I am heartened by the growing support and visibility of trans people in mainstream society. I am inspired by the resilience and courage of those who continue to fight for their rights and dignity.

As I bring this second edition of my memoir to a close, I am reminded of the power of storytelling. By sharing our stories, we can break down the barriers that divide us and create a more compassionate and just world. I hope my story can serve as a source of inspiration and encouragement for others, and it can help pave the way for a more inclusive and accepting future.

What happens next?

28.1: What a horrible way to end a book!

I wrote the Epilogue above in the middle of March. But if I am going to be true to my goal for this edition of the book, to cover until the 30th of March 2023, then I must include the following blog post from that day. I had picked that specific date because it marked the 13th anniversary of my gender confirmation surgery. Instead of being in a celebratory mood, I was distracted by the mass-shooting event in Nashville, Tennessee 3 days earlier.

Blogpost: March 30, 2023
America, The Sick Land of Thoughts and Prayers

Even before the bloody Columbine High School massacre in April 1999, mass shootings had been frequent in the US. From schools and churches to shopping malls and city parks, radicalized, politically motivated, and mentally ill persons with easy access to guns continue to shed blood and leave death in their wake.

So, what else is new?

The recent shooting in Nashville, Tennessee, occurred at a Christian school where the killer had once been a student. The shooter happened to be trans, which opened the door for hyper-conservatives to attack the trans community.

The conservative media quickly seized on this fact and is using it to spread more lies and further their agenda to erase trans Americans. They labeled trans people "domestic terrorists" and are now using this unfortunate incident in Tennessee to justify their inaction regarding the gun violence epidemic. This is a pattern that minorities have seen before, with the Black, Muslim, Jewish, and Asian communities facing similar attacks.

What is true is that lawmakers have failed to act despite the frequency of these tragedies, choosing to defend guns instead of lives. The result is that Americans have become numb to these events, with lawmakers blaming mental illness, poverty, people of color, and now, gender identity to avoid accountability.

The trans community is not responsible for the actions of

brutal murderers, nor should they be used as political currency to further a cruel and heartless agenda. Conservatives have a history of instigating hatred and violence toward minorities to protect the interests of stereotypical white, Christian, cisgender, straight, and sexually insecure American men.

When we heard the shooter was trans, there was a collective gasp in the trans community. We knew what was coming next. GOP and far-right representatives would immediately leverage the killer's identity and weaponize it for their agenda. Trans people would make for the perfect deflection to take the attention away from inadequate gun laws.

Conservatives use emotional events and unspeakable trage-dies to create false narratives about marginalized communities; they are experts at laying targets on the backs of minorities. It makes sense that trans people are now being branded as would-be child killers, with politicians using them as an excuse for their inaction, claiming that "it's not guns that are the problem: it's trans people."

Blaming the trans community for the actions of one individ-ual, who happened to be trans, is a strawman argument because it presents a false and exaggerated version of the trans community. Most trans people are not violent and do not support or engage in mass shootings. By blaming the trans community for the actions of one individual, the real issue of gun violence in America is obscured, and the trans community is unfairly targeted and scapegoated (again).

Using this tragedy to further a political agenda is reprehen-sible. Americans should not let the recent deaths be leveraged for political reasons. Americans must look hard at the gun violence epi-demic in their country and enact meaningful change to protect their citizens.

It is time for allies to show up for their transgender loved ones. You can start by educating yourselves on the issues facing the trans community and amplifying their voices. You can support trans-led organizations and donate to their causes. You can call your representatives and demand they take action to address the gun vio-lence epidemic in your country.

In conclusion, the recent shooting in Nashville, Tennessee, is a tragedy that has left many mourning the loss of innocent lives. It is important to remember that the actions of one individual do not represent an entire community. The trans community is not a threat but a vulnerable population that deserves protection and support.

Conservatives and the far-right media will continue to spread lies and false narratives to deflect from the real issue of gun violence in America. You cannot let their propaganda go unchecked. Call out the lies and the propaganda, and demand action from your lawmakers.

Grieve and heal, but take action to prevent further senseless acts of violence as you ponder the question: do you have the courage of your convictions to create a society that values the lives of all its citizens, regardless of their race, religion, skin color, sexual orientation, or gender identity?

28:2 Final Take-Away

You have come to the end of story and I thank you for investing the time to learn about me.

This is not how I hoped to end the book, but I feel that the more you know, the better is our chance of create a social framework that does not single out trans people. I am including below a bit more about the groups that threaten our existence. Remember that international borders are porous to ideologies if you are in Canada. A growing number of mostly far-right and religious factions hope to see these tactics employed here. We all need to be vigilant.

There are three conservative organizations that have played a major role in the deluge of new anti-trans laws in the U.S. in recent months: the Heritage Foundation, the American Principles Project (APP), and the Alliance Defending Freedom (ADF).

The Heritage Foundation is a conservative think tank that promotes limited government, free enterprise, and traditional values. The organization uses various tactics, such as producing research and analysis, mobilizing grassroots support, meeting with lawmakers, testifying before Congress, and building coalitions with other organizations to advance their policy positions.

The American Principles Project (APP) is another conserva-

tive organization that is involved in promoting a socially conservative agenda. APP has been involved in promoting anti-transgender
policies and legislation, particularly in the realm of education.

The Alliance Defending Freedom (ADF) is a legal advocacy
organization that advocates for conservative Christian values. ADF
has actively promoted anti-trans policies through litigation and
lobbying efforts. The organization has been involved in high-profile
cases related to bathroom access and transgender rights in schools
and sports.

All three organizations use research and policy analysis to
advance their positions, as well as mobilize grassroots support and
meet with lawmakers. They have been involved in lobbying efforts
at the state and federal levels, advocating for policies that restrict
transgender rights.

However, when it comes to transgender issues, these groups
are best known for their reductionary approach, which focuses on
emotionally charged issues. This approach has effectively politicized
and weaponized transgender identities, generating political and
financial support for Republican lawmakers at all levels of government. They have honed the craft of creating a sense of urgency at the
cost of the well-being and rights of transgender individuals.

Their positions on transgender issues include advocating
for prohibiting access to public restrooms and locker rooms based
on gender identity, banning transgender individuals from serving
in the military, excluding transgender people from participating
in sports competitions that match their gender identity, and prohibiting access to puberty blockers and gender-affirming medical
treatment for minors who identify as transgender. They have also
called for removing medical licenses from healthcare providers who
provide gender-affirming care to minors and investigating parents
supporting their child's transition.

At the core of their anti-trans ideology is the idea that trans
identities threaten the traditional family and society at large. It is,
therefore, essential to question and challenge the notion that affirming the existence of .6% of the population, who are transgender, puts
society at risk of being destroyed. The idea, that 99.4% of the cisgender population is at risk, is not only unfounded, it ignores the

lived experiences of transgender individuals who face higher levels of discrimination, harassment, and violence. But most importantly, it ignores the reality that when trans people are affirmed by society, loved by their families, and allowed to live authentically, their quality of life improves, and they thrive and become contributing members of society.

The Heritage Foundation, APP, and ADF positions on transgender issues, and their tactics for advancing their cause, need to be exposed for what they are. They are a deliberate and calculated long-term campaign of misinformation and scapegoating.

It is crucial that we recognize and call out the hypocrisy that threatens the right of transgender individuals to exist as their true selves. We must demand equity, equality, and basic human compassion and hold accountable those who seek to erase trans people.

Any politician regardless of political affiliation, who espouses anti-trans rhetoric for political gain must be called out for contributing to harm toward the transgender community.

I conclude this chapter of my life with this:

There will always be individuals in positions of power who promote harmful ideologies. Politically, this has real-life consequences, such as voter suppression and the loss of medical autonomy for women and the LGBTQ+ community. However, we should not feel discouraged because society is becoming more tolerant, diverse, and inclusive. This means that those in power who seek to maintain the status quo from decades ago must constantly create laws and outrage to hold back the tide of progress.

One of the tactics that these individuals use is negative partisanship, where they position themselves as the solution to a perceived threat from the transgender community. However, we must remember that these politicians are often motivated by money and votes, not genuine concern for their constituents.

We must work together to create a society that is accepting and inclusive for all. The consequences of hatred and division can be devastating, and we must recognize that everyone deserves respect and dignity, regardless of their gender identity.

We must be aware that anger requires constant fuel to keep burning, and people are becoming tired of the anti-trans rhetoric. The culture is moving forward, and maintaining the status quo takes a lot of effort by creating controversies and strawmen.

When we look at the situation objectively, it becomes clear that more pressing issues require our attention and effort than going after less than 1% of the population. Such as ensuring that everyone has access to quality education, affordable healthcare, and equal rights regardless of gender identity.

We must remain vigilant and speak out against those who seek to spread hate and division. We have the power to effect change, and we can create a more equitable and just society for all by working together.

And, it's never too late to listen to the experiences of trans people and work toward creating a society that truly values and respects their humanity.

Thank you for the time you've invested in reading
Then This Happened: After Transparently,

Sincerely,
Lisa S. Salazar

Appendix I: Bed Posts

Email: Monday, 29 March 2010 — Montreal

Good morning all,

It's going to take me a few days to adjust to the three-hour difference. I see it is only 7:00 AM in Vancouver. Just wanted to say that I'm all settled in at the hospital. Surgery is tomorrow morning. I will be out of touch for the next three days but will try to give you an update as soon as I can. There are three others from the lower mainland: one from New York, one from Florida, and one from California. I have the distinct privilege of being the oldest present. It is a private hospital and the "residence" is just like a bed and breakfast, very comfortable and nicely appointed.

The weather today in Montreal looks like Vancouver— rainy. I will be prepped for surgery around 4:00 P.M. and then fasting from then on.

How am I doing? The best way to describe it is that I feel as if I'm coasting to the finish line; the hard part of the race is behind me. It is the feeling of relief. It surprises me that I am not nervous or anxious. I figured I would be by now, but I am not. I credit this to the way all of you have allowed me to continue this journey with your friendship and support. Thanks!

Drop me a line when you get a chance. I may not be able to answer you personally and may have to rely on an open letter like this to email to all of you on my list.

Bye for now. Lisa

Email: Wednesday, 31 March 2010 — Montreal

Good morning all.

I took out my laptop about an hour after I got a shot of morphine. I wanted to write an update and save it for sending later. (The Wi-Fi connection does not work inside the hospital; it is only available in the "bed and breakfast") So I composed this witty and funny update saying among other things, how wonderful it was to have the anesthesiologist telling me the anesthesia IV was in, that I'd feel sleepy very fast and a second later, hearing a nurse say to me: "Lisa, Lisa, you are in the recovery room and we'll be taking you down to your room in a couple of hours—your surgery was perfect. Congratulations!"

I then saved the email, and I couldn't feel it when I reached to close the laptop... It wasn't there! I had been hallucinating the whole time. So, it is now about eight hours later, and I'm writing this email for real this time. I think. I will now save it for sending when I return to the recovery house next door on Thursday night. Lisa

PS: I think this is a more interesting email than the Holodeck version, anyway. Just noticed a very weak Wi-Fi signal, will try to send it now.

Lisa

Email: Thursday, 1 April 2010 — Montreal

Good morning all.
April Fool's Day!
Hmm, I will resist the temptation to play a joke.

I left the hospital's primary care unit and am back in the residence for the week of recovery. I am doing much better than I had expected. The only unpleasant and unexpected thing that happened last night: I rolled over in my sleep and pushed the plastic end of the draining tube in further. I woke up with a jolt; it felt like I had been stabbed in the gut. After

I rolled back on my back and repositioned the tube, it helped but for the next few hours it felt like I had a pencil stuck in me. Fortunately, the tube came out this morning.

If that is the worse part of all of this, I will be a very happy camper. For the next few days, it is just rest that is on the agenda. I brought a good book; the only problem is that I feel like I have A.D.D. and nothing holds my interest for more than a few minutes. Even this email is the result of two sessions. Heck, I'm bored already. But I do love you all.

Until later, Lisa

Email: Saturday, 3 April 2010 — Montreal

Good morning!
I was able to take my first post-op shower this morning after breakfast! When the others who were ahead of me talked about their first shower, I thought to myself, "What's the big deal, it's only a shower?" Well, now I know why they were so elated... the truth being that you can only shower once all the gauze padding and dressings—which are sutured on—have been removed and one is finally au naturel! Oh, yes! Now I see why it is cause for celebration! (SORRY to be so specific. I hope I didn't put any disturbing images in your head.)

Today, the weather in Montreal is sunny and will be in the low 20s Celsius (70s Fahrenheit). I've been waking up at 6:00 AM just about every day so I hope to be up for Easter Sunday sunrise tomorrow morning to celebrate Life in earnest. I hope it won't be cloudy because the sunrise is really pretty through my bedroom windows.

I forgot to pack my small digital camera. I've been using my cell phone to take photos, but I haven't got the mental stamina to set up the Bluetooth connection between it and my laptop to download the photos. I'll leave it for a couple of days.

Funny things, those endorphins, even though I won't be in any shape to run for a few weeks, all I have to do is see a jogger run by in the park across the street and I get the craving.

I also have a new craving—shopping! I'm told that comes with the territory. It will have to wait. Attention span is much better. That was weird a few days ago when I could not stay focused on anything for very long. It's still not what I would call all there yet. "Squirrel!" Lisa

Email: Tuesday, 6 April 2010 — Montreal

It's getting better all the time. The end of the long weekend and life will return to its usual volume in the morning.

It was pretty quiet around here the last three days and the only time I got to see the two other patients was at mealtimes. I think I mentioned that only three of us are here for now. One of the other two is leaving on Wednesday and the third one leaves on Thursday with me; she is from California.

The residence and the hospital will then be closed for 7 days to give all the doctors and nurses some time off. The intake of new patients will resume on the following Thursday.

Carmen, my older sister, came to Montreal the day before my surgery to be with me. She goes back to Vancouver on Wednesday. I think the two of us were a little optimistic to think that we would be able to tour the city together. I need to follow a pretty strict regimen post-op stuff that repeats itself three times a day; there is no time to be a tourist. Nevertheless, I am so grateful that she came even though she had the tour of Montreal by herself.

All the other girls who are here came alone. My heart goes out to them, especially for the girl from California, she is only 24 years old. So young in so many ways, but she is a very sweet person.

Thank you for all your emails. I look forward to checking my computer whenever I get a chance. It's been great to stay connected.

I see it is only 1:45 P.M. on the West Coast. I just woke up and took a warm shower. It felt so good—no more tubes and bandages to worry about. I'm going to sneak down for a cup of cranberry tea.

In closing, one of the best medicines has been a 3-minute video on YouTube called Upular. It always puts a smile on my face. Check it out!

Lisa

Email: Thursday, 8 April 2010 — Montreal

Two hours left to go before the limo comes to the residence to drive me to the airport. If this were a regular Bed & Breakfast, I would certainly be singing its praises and telling you all to stay here if you ever visit Montreal, but I have a hunch that none of you will be putting it on your list of things to do.

Though it seemed like time was standing still on the first few days after the surgery, looking at it from this end, time has flown by. It's the weird thing about time—it's all so relative.

I am the last to leave; the girl from California was picked up at 11:30 AM so I've had the place to myself. Wow, if walls could talk. It is pretty emotional sitting here in the living room as I leaf through the "Guest Book," so many stories like mine but uniquely different in so many ways. The head nurse tells me the waiting list keeps getting longer, that all we are seeing is the tip of the iceberg. Who would have thought?!

Thanks again for your emails. I will be lying low for at least the next 10 days but don't hesitate to email, call or visit if you are passing through South Vancouver.

Lisa

Appendix II: The (Coming Out)Letter

First drafted in Oct. 2007, it went through several revisions to keep it current and up to date with the changes that were taking place in my life. The "Coming Out" letter was last updated on March 30, 2010.

Letter To my friends

I'll begin by telling you that I'm not a big risk taker, for fear of my worst fears becoming reality. I have feared rejection, ridicule, humiliation, losing friends, being the object of mockery, not blending in, being different, hurting or embarrassing loved ones, and as a self-employed person, I have feared losing clients.

I need to take the risk of sharing something about myself with you—secrecy is no longer an option and I have come to realize that disclosing to you is the only way our relationship can continue, if it is to have integrity.

About ten years ago, after a lifetime of guilt and confusion, I was diagnosed as having gender dysphoria at Vancouver General Hospital's Gender Clinic—a condition commonly referred to as being trans. This diagnosis was simultaneously a blessing and a curse. It was a blessing because it provided an explanation of my past and a signal of hope for something that might end the guilt, confusion and shame, but it was a curse because the options and choices offered to me not only had a hefty personal price tag, they also confirmed that there were no magic cures that could make me normal. While I accepted the diagnosis, I concluded that I could not possibly begin down the prescribed path, which would potentially end with gender confirmation surgery.

I left there not knowing what to do. I needed time to sort things out. At the time, I was not willing or able to pay the social, economic and emotional price that would be involved, not to mention the incredible impact this would have on my wife and our three sons.

The big part of my ongoing struggle is that I've always felt at odds with my body. But these confusing feelings were always kept private. Growing up, I sought to be what most defined as normal, even as I struggled with my own gender identity. As early as the age of four, I remember becoming aware of this dynamic, I also remember sensing that I had to keep these thoughts to myself. As a child, I would often pray that I could wake up with a new body. Then, as I got older, I prayed for God to correct my brain. What research I did on my own just left me more depressed, confused and totally defeated. I begged God to make me normal, one way or another.

It wasn't until I was almost 40 that I finally sought professional help. Seeing a psychiatrist for the first time in my life was not easy. However, he skillfully helped me to verbalize my conflicting thoughts. He also offered to refer me to the Gender Clinic, but I refused. "Hell, no!" was my response. It would take me almost ten years to finally accept his recommendation and ask my GP to refer me to the clinic. Perhaps they now had a cure—that was my hope for going.

Why am I sharing all of this, and why now?

My hope is that by sharing honestly with you, you will be able to understand that it is time for me to face life honestly and allow the hidden person inside me to emerge. Like a butterfly? Maybe not quite that, but a metamorphosis, nonetheless. And the new person will need to inhabit the place that has been vacated by the person you thought you knew.

As to why now, that is a harder question to answer, you can imagine the struggle I have had in reconciling this to myself and to my family. I just know that I cannot live the rest of my life attempting to maintain the shaky facade I have had to erect all my life. I trained myself to behave and act in certain ways for more than five decades, not only for the sake of others, but as a way to survive. So, there is need for a time of restructuring. Fortunately, caring professionals are helping me to navigate these intimidating waters.

I cannot express how I am feeling these days. On one hand, I have never been so scared and felt as vulnerable. On the other, I felt a very large burden finally lift from my shoulders as I began the process of disclosing. The most difficult of these, second only to disclosing to my wife more than 25 years ago (before I understood my condition), was disclosing to my parents and to each of our sons. This finally took place in the spring of 2008. I had already shared with my sisters and brother and their respective spouses a few months earlier. Though each person has accepted the news in his or her own way, I am grateful that I have not been rejected and ostracized. The complete opposite is true. I have never felt as loved and accepted.

I have also shared with close friends and clients, and that circle has been growing gradually. At first, each disclosure was emotionally exhausting. That helped to slow down the pace, though at times I wished I could have shouted it from the rooftops and gotten it over with—once and for all! Now I find that forwarding this letter to people as the need arises has made the process easier on all. It gives people a chance to absorb things at their own pace, and I am spared from having to retell things over and over again.

All of this has been difficult for my wife, who feels as if she has lost her husband. I have felt at times that I defrauded her when I married her. My only defense is that I honestly believed that marriage was the answer to prayers for a normal gender identity. When this uninvited inner person resurfaced, I prayed and hoped that being a father would finally do the trick. What more proof would I need? On and on, my hopes and prayers were always based on yet another milestone of manhood. In all honesty, it is really to her credit and God's grace we have remained together since I first revealed my gender dysphoria to her.

I am eternally grateful that three sons resulted from our union. Had I been brave enough to come out sooner and not married, I may have avoided years of struggle, but then these three wonderful lives would not be here today, and I would not have known the love that I have experienced from my dear wife and our sons. This I cannot deny, and I would not trade the past—even if it were possible to do so.

I am alive today because my faith enabled me to live a life that is one thing on the outside, and a very different thing on the inside—but I felt as if I had simply become a master of disguise. More importantly, my faith protected me and kept me from harmful and self-destructive behavior, which is not uncommon for person's saddled with my condition.

I am aware that not everyone will accept my trans identity as a genuine medical condition—as something I was born with—but rather as a lifestyle choice. I spiritualized it and tried to deal with it as though it was a matter of the will and something that could be eliminated by the retraining of my mind, by perseverance and dying to myself daily. This is what I desperately prayed for and tried to do as I struggled to reconcile my identity with my beliefs.

After all these years I have finally come to peace about my diagnosis. As my pastor put it, this is not a moral issue any more than being born with a physical disability or any other medical condition.

But I am guilty of a sin, and that 'sin' has been my reliance on the secrecy that has underscored my adult life. It is not that I have been living a lie—but rather living without acknowledging the full truth about myself.

The Changes

In July of 2008 I started living full time as a female. Until then, coping had been possible by a gradual discovery of what allowed me to be at peace with my body. Dressing in an attempt to present realistically as female was a learning experience, yet there were changes I had to make before I felt confident enough to be in public.

For example, I have endured and will continue to endure countless hours of electrolysis to remove my entire beard and fortunately, it is almost all gone. I also needed to lose weight and was able to come close to the weight of an average female of my age and height. Finally, there was the issue of an age-appropriate wardrobe that would allow me to fly under the radar without drawing attention.

Though my physical appearance has gradually changed since I transitioned, I am still the same person inside, but I am no longer a dual person. I am no longer cloaked in silence and motivated by fear and a sense of shame from not being truthful about myself. What is new for me is that now when I am asked how I am doing, I give an honest answer and not one that is complicit with a cover-up. You don't know what a joy it is for me to now be able to answer that question honestly and to be transparent! I have nothing to hide.

The final step in the long process of transformation took place on March 30, 2010. I underwent gender confirmation surgery in Montreal. Friends asked me before the surgery if I was excited or nervous. The truth is that I was neither. What I felt was relief since I would no longer be straddling the gender divide. There is a sense of calmness that I have felt ever since, and it is most welcomed.

In closing, I don't know how much you may already know or understand about trans persons. There are many professional resources on the Internet that I can provide links to. Others may be able to explain what it means to be trans and its ramifications better than I possibly could, but if you have questions of me, please feel free to ask. Let me know if you would like me to forward links to you because simply doing a search on the web can be quite disturbing. Unfortunately, there is much pornography based on this issue.

I have shared with you because I felt it was safe and important to do so. I apologize for not having shared with you directly and for relying on what amounts to be a "form letter." Because I value friendships, I was compelled to include you so that we can continue journeying together in complete openness.

Yours, with all sincerity,
Lisa Salazar

Where did the name "Lisa" come from?

Friends have asked why I chode Lisa as my name. I don't have much of an explanation other than to say that it was a name I was drawn to emotionally. My brother has the following theory: He remembers that our sister Angela's nickname was "Mechilisa." It is a coined word from two Spanish words, mechas, and lisa, "mechas" and "lisa," literally meaning "straight bangs." As a little girl, she had straight bangs, which Dad endearingly called her. Perhaps I yearned for that kind of affection from Dad, and Lisa resonates deeply in my person with that yearning.

Appendix III: From my Studies

Of all the essays, papers and research I produced for my Master's degree and during my clinical spiritual training. I am including four pieces that I have been happy to share in the years since. I am not including the verbatim versions with all the footnotes and citations. Below are their distillations. If you are interested in their complete academic form, you can download them from www.Academia.edu.

Roots of Rejection & Injustice

Graduate-level study was an intimidating proposition. During the 90s, I took a few courses at Regent College, an international graduate school of theology on the University of British Columbia campus. My motivation for enrolling in these courses was for personal edification and spiritual growth. At that time, I was not concerned about my grades and was satisfied with a B or B-minus. However, pursuing a Master's degree program to qualify as a chaplain was different.

To prepare myself for full-time graduate studies at VST, the registrar recommended that I take a half-credit course during the summer before starting the first term with four full-credit courses in September. VST invites scholars from other universities to enhance their course offerings; the course I took was taught by highly regarded Professors Sharon Thornton and Fumitaka Matsuoka, a husband-and-wife team. Even though I knew nothing about them, I was advised that their course would be an excellent elective that aligns with my learning goals and calling.

The course I took was titled "Gender Injustice & Reconciliation: Socio-cultural Constructions from the Perspective of North American Hermeneutics," which already suggested that I would need a dictionary at my side.

The final grade was based on the final assignment, which was a 20-page term paper with a correspondingly long title: "Roots of Rejections & Injustice: Digging Deeper into Society's Negative Response to Trans persons and Gender Nonconformity and Its Intersection with Dogma."

Instead of copying and pasting the paper into this book, below is a summary without all the references, footnotes, and bibliography. I uploaded the paper to Academia.edu and you are welcome to download it from there at no cost.

Introduction to Roots of Rejections & Injustice: Digging Deeper into Society's Negative Response to Trans persons and Gender Nonconformity and Its Intersection with Dogma

As a person of faith who transitioned from male to female at the age of almost fifty-eight to avoid self-inflicted 'termination', I have been disheartened by the extent of society's hostile attitude toward trans individuals like me. The church, in particular, has been unable to accept those who do not conform to binary and traditional views of human sexuality. Although I completed my transition without experiencing discrimination, rejection, hostility, or violence, I have met and heard from many trans persons who have endured countless injustices.

During my transition, I was ignorant of the potential dangers and hostility coming from all directions. It was as if I had taken a long walk through unknown lands and was asked if I had seen the signs warning about the deadly bear attacks or the danger sign on the footbridge that said it was condemned. My naiveté was self-induced, as I avoided anything that could derail me, wanting to reach point B as quickly as possible.

Now, my goal is to provide an accessible narrative, address their fears, and help them find answers to their questions. In this paper, I examined the roots of rejection and injustice trans individuals face, not to address why people may be trans, but to explore the systemic hostility, rejection, and injustice many gender-nonconforming persons face. Medical treatments such as hormone therapy and surgery are necessary for many trans individuals and effectively alleviate gender dysphoria. This paper provides background information to understand society's reluctance to accept trans identities and hopes to inform the conversation to reduce this reluctance and unwillingness to extend equal rights to those who transgress society's binary gender standards.

Background Information:

The Injustice at Every Turn 2010 report, sponsored by the U.S. National Gay and Lesbian Task Force and the National Center for Transgender Equality, uncovered the extensive discrimination experienced by trans and gender-nonconforming individuals. Though the report didn't include Canadian participants, Canadian studies revealed a similar situation. Additionally, people of color fared worse than white participants, with African American trans respondents doing far worse than others. Respondents lived in poverty, and 41% attempted suicide, while many were victims of physical or sexual assault. Worst of all, hundreds of trans individuals are killed each year because of anti-trans hatred or prejudice. The Transgender Day of Remembrance on November 20 was created to memorialize them.

The degree of discrimination uncovered by these studies shocked me, and I felt uninformed and embarrassed for not knowing about TDOR six months after my gender confirmation surgery. In my first term paper for my Master's course at VST, I delved into why people struggle to comprehend and accept trans identities, and why they feel justified in their disapproval.

On the surface, gender nonconformity may put people off, and they may not understand the distress caused by gender identity incongruence. From their position of privilege, it can be hard for people, especially those who profess to be Christian, to appreciate that some individuals experience this incongruence. I wonder if Jesus was alluding to this in Matthew 19 when he spoke to his disciples about eunuchs and warned that not everyone would understand.

The Medical Debate

Transgender and gender-nonconforming individuals often experience a disconnection between their biological sex and the gender they identify with. This sense of being trapped in the wrong body has been an issue that has evolved over the years. The science behind it is relatively new, with words such as "transsexual" and "transgender" only entering the medical lexicon in the early 1950s and 1990s, respectively. The history of gender nonconformity in various cultures reflects how different societies have perceived and treated people who do not conform to binary gender roles.

The American media popularized the word "transsexual" when the story broke out about the American G.I. who underwent a "sex change" in 1952, leading to its subsequent clinical incorporation and acceptance. However, it continues to be a source of great controversy among the different disciplines involved in trans research and among trans persons themselves. The word "transgender" was appropriated by trans activist Virginia Prince, who preferred to present as female and argued that she and others like her were neither transvestites nor transsexual but were transcending gender.

Our understanding of trans identities has been significantly assisted by the corresponding knowledge of intersexuality. Dr. Cameron Bowman of the University of British Columbia explained in an interview that we do not have a scientific explanation for why a person born with a perfect male body would at some point identify as a woman. However, he believes the closest parallel we can draw is with intersex children—the condition of being born with ambiguous parts. The implication is that gender identity is more fluid than society's constructs of only male and female, and it is not determined by one's biological sex or how one's plumbing might be modified surgically.

There is much historical evidence of gender nonconformity in various cultures. It's possible that such evidence reflects the existence of intersexuality or trans identities as we refer to them today.

The story of the first specific reference in North America to an intersex person illustrates the Puritans' deeply religious and temperate dogmas. They viewed intersex birth, like other birth defects, as an omen from God, often blaming the mother's sins or misdoings. This reaction to the intersex person as an outsider to society has fueled an American imperative to know a person's sex and to fit them into or exclude them from society accordingly.

The sudden emergence of trans identities in recent years has been met with skepticism, derision, and dismay, as evidenced by the resistance to laws protecting trans rights in the political arena. Trans care is an evolving science; protocols and best practices are continuously updated and improved. No wonder society lags behind the advances. The ethical, moral, and liability questions that surface become politicized and result in a cultural pushback, even within the medical and psychiatric professions. For example, the reclassification in 2013 by the American Psychiatric Association (APA) from Gender Identity Disorder (GID) to Gender Dysphoria took decades of lobbying by the World Professional Association for Transgender Health (WPATH) and submissions by trans advocates.

Stigmatization still looms within the psycho-medical professions. Some argue that a diagnosis of gender identity disorder (GID) offers certification for a condition and facilitates access to medical and technological means for transitioning. Some insurance companies will only absorb the costs of trans-related surgery if it is first established that the procedure is a medical necessity and not elective in nature. Those who argue against reinstating GID and eliminating it forever say that being trans is not a disorder and should not be perceived as one.

The issue of accessibility to medical and surgical transition is not only determined by financial capacity but also by availability. In many areas, there is a shortage of healthcare professionals who are trained and willing to provide trans-related healthcare. Even in areas where these services are available, there may be long waiting lists for consultations and treatments, causing additional stress for those who are already struggling with their gender dysphoria.

The Theological and Philosophical Roots

In recent years, amidst the debate over same-sex marriage, the phrase "God created us male and female" has been repeatedly used as a simple argument for those who oppose it. However, it is often used by people with little experience or interest in religion, making it a convenient and shallow viewpoint to reinforce societal norms around gender. I also used this argument in my misguided attempt to combat my gender identity struggles.

The rejection of trans individuals is not the result of an official partnership, but rather an unlikely alliance between religious fundamentalists, politically conservative leaders, and radical militant feminists. Despite their differences, they share a common goal of denying trans individuals their rights and equal opportunities. Recognizing the cultural lenses these groups operate with is critical in combating discrimination and advocating for trans rights.

The Fundamentalist, Conservative Patriarchal Camp

You will remember how I engaged Dr. Michael Brown in an online debate leading up the Charlotte Pride 2011 (Chapter 15); his views are representative of the fundamentalist, conservative patriarchal camp.

This camp is known for its rigid, basic, and overly simplified view of sexuality that is not open to alternative interpretations of the Bible. They vehemently reject all medical and psychological arguments that do not align with their understanding of what is Biblical and what they claim is a 'natural' understanding of gender. Their dogmatic views on gender and sexuality, are based on a strict and traditional Judeo-Christian interpretation of Genesis 1, which describe the creation of man and woman.

This stands in contrast to the Jewish Rabbis in the two centuries before and during the beginnings of Christianity, who expounded and interpreted these verses in a very different way.

While there is a rich tradition of interpretation and commentary on human sexuality in Jewish thought, no single perspective can be said to represent the "official" or definitive view of Jewish rabbis as a whole. In fact, Rosemary Radford Ruether, in her book "Women and Redemption: A Theological History," talks about how people who read the Bible in Jewish and early Christian times had difficulty understanding the two stories about how God created humans.

The first story says that God created men and women simultaneously, and they were equal. The second story says that God first created a man named Adam and then made a woman named Eve from one of his ribs. Eve convinces Adam to disobey God, and they are expelled from the Garden of Eden.

Two creation accounts caused problems for people who tried to explain these stories. They wondered if the woman in the first story was the same as the woman in the second and if Eve's creation from Adam's rib meant she was less important or less good than Adam. They also wondered if Eve's actions meant women would always be trouble for men.

Echoes of this debate can be found in the letters of Paul to the Corinthians. Paul had to exercise control over the Corinthian church due to controversies and complaints by those who wanted a more structured patriarchal Christian community, with the role of women being a central point of contention.

Paul's teachings created a dilemma because he appeared to reinforce some of the cultural principles the Corinthians were accustomed to, namely, the Greco-Roman patriarchal system that was backed by legal and social norms. These gave men greater power and status in society while limiting the autonomy and opportunities of women and children within the household. His letters to the Corinthians are evidence of his corrective approach. He praised what they were doing right and scolded them for immaturity, which he believed led to errors in their interpretation of the freedom they enjoyed.

For example, some women interpreted their ability to prophesy as evidence that they were equal to men and acted in ways contrary to the social norms of the time. Paul's instructions reined them in and labeled such behavior as inappropriate. Paul's theology on the role of women galvanized the patriarchal model that we see today in the church.

This patriarchal model insists that women are subordinate to men because that is how God ordained it from the beginning. They also insist that human agency does not play a role in determining one's gender/sex alignment. This, in fact, is the Roman Catholic Church's official position, which condemns the radical and "grotesque mutilation of the body" that occurs during sex confirmation surgery (GCS) except when performed for strictly therapeutic medical reasons.

Pope Benedict XVI emphasized in 2008 that, according to his [in-fallible] beliefs, gender is a valuable present from God and criticized anyone who tries to alter it. The Pope stated that it is a matter of having faith in the Creator and respecting the natural order of creation, which humans' self-destructive tendencies threaten.

The rejection of trans identity is not exclusive to the Roman Catholic Church; many conservative Protestant churches also agree that gender identity is based on the birth sex rather than the person's psychological experience or perception of gender.

The goals and ideology of the fundamentalist, conservative patriarchal camp are to rid society of what they perceive as unnatural and threatening, which is how they view all trans and gender non-conforming people.

The Militant Trans-Exclusionary Radical Feminists

The issue of trans identities has been a source of controversy and debate within feminist circles for many years. On this side, we have the militant Trans-Exclusionary Radical Feminists (TERFS), who would celebrate if the male patriarchal camp were to succeed in stamping out trans identities. They believe that this would mean they would not have to deal with individuals they consider "pretend" women infiltrating their ranks. However, this perspective is profoundly flawed.

Some of the most vitriolic voices in this camp are younger feminist bloggers who deride and mock trans women (and trans men) and hold views espoused by feminists a couple of decades ago, which hold that "real women" have a uterus and two ovaries. Until men can have a uterus and ovaries transplanted into their bodies, they are not considered real women. This perspective is not only exclusionary but also ignores the fact that gender is a complex and multifaceted aspect of identity that cannot be reduced to biology alone.

In 1999, Germaine Greer published The Whole Woman, a sequel to The Female Eunuch (1979), in which she stated her opposition to accepting trans persons who were assigned male at birth as women. She criticized governments for recognizing men who believe they are women and had themselves castrated to prove it, stating that this is the institutional expression of the mistaken conviction that women are defective males. However, her perspective is also flawed as it ignores the fact that gender dysphoria is a recognized medical condition and that individuals have the right to pursue medical treatment that aligns with their gender identity.

Some in the patriarchal camp would likely celebrate Greer's acerbic rhetoric for putting trans people in their place. However, her words have given feminists justification for voicing opposition to the inclusion of trans women and barring them from "real woman" events.

There are many anti-trans feminists, including Gloria Steinem, who has offered many pejorative commentaries on trans people over the years. In her book Outrageous Acts and Everyday Rebellions, she lambasted Dr. Rene Richards, the professional trans woman tennis player who made headlines for competing against other women in 1977, arguing that trans women cannot be genuinely female because they have been socialized as men.

However, Steinem also showed compassion for trans persons when she observed that they cited a deep conviction that their true personalities had been denied or restricted by the sex role assigned to them at birth. She concluded that trans individuals are paying an enormous tribute to the power of sex roles and surgically mutilate their bodies to set their true personalities free.

Janice Raymond, a friend of Gloria Steinem, published a book entitled The Transsexual Empire: The Making of the She-Male in 1979. The book is critical of transsexualism and argues that it perpetuates traditional gender stereotypes by relying on psychological and surgical interventions. Raymond blames the psycho-medical complex for medicalizing gender identity and creating a social and political context that normalizes and promotes transsexual treatment and surgery.

Raymond asserts that transsexualism is based on a patriarchal perception that women's bodies should be available to men and that medical and professional practitioners who institutionalize transsexual treatment and surgery on the medical model become shapers of acceptable gender-related behavior.

However, Raymond's views on transsexuality are criticized by many in the LGBTQ+ and feminist communities as extremely transphobic and hateful toward trans men and women. Her book's views were responsible for the U.S. Federal Government's decision to stop funding trans-health-related services in Federal prisons, as well as causing trans-health medical services to not be covered by many insurance companies. Some of her remarks in her report for the Federal Government were dismissive of trans persons and the issues they face, and her arguments continue to influence government policies.

There have been some corrective policy changes in recent years regarding the treatment of trans individuals. However, it's important to note that discrimination against trans individuals still exists in many areas of society, including healthcare, employment, housing, and education.

Summary

I have explored the unlikely alliance between the two camps that have shaped society's treatment of trans and gender-nonconforming individuals. The patriarchal camp argues from a dogmatic religious standpoint with a strict interpretation of the Genesis account of the creation of man and woman, which informs their critical view of trans identities. The other camp is the militant ultra-feminist camp which seeks to liberate women from systemic oppression and sees trans identities as a threat to that goal.

Post-script: As I composed this chapter, I decided to include an update on the ongoing debate about trans rights. J.K. Rowling has become a controversial figure due to her statements about the trans community, which have sparked controversy and criticism. Her comments show that she fully embraces the "Gender Critical" ideology, a worldview deemed harmful and detrimental to the trans community.

The "Gender Critical" ideology promotes the idea that gender identity is solely based on biological sex, which invalidates the experiences and identities of trans individuals. This viewpoint ignores the fact that gender identity is a complex and multifaceted concept that goes beyond physical characteristics. Additionally, this ideology often promotes harmful stereotypes about trans individuals, portraying them as mentally ill, delusional, or predatory. These stereotypes not only harm trans individuals but also contribute to a culture of fear and misunderstanding.

Furthermore, the "Gender Critical" ideology often advocates for exclusionary policies, such as bathroom bills and policies that restrict access to gender-affirming healthcare. These policies harm trans individuals by denying them basic rights and access to necessary medical care. This ideology contributes to the marginalization and stigmatization of trans individuals, leading to increased mental health issues, violence, and discrimination.

It is crucial to recognize that trans people are not a monolithic group, and our priorities may not always align. Healthcare access, employment discrimination, or violence against trans people might take precedence over the culture war debate for many. However, it is concerning that Rowling's rhetoric has given religious and conservative right politicians more ammunition to use against us, and her wealth along with the reach of her platform give her a degree of invincibility.

In conclusion, as a person of faith, Jesus' message of inclusivity and equality stands out as a beacon of hope. Jesus celebrated the reign of God that broke down divisions between the pure and impure in Jewish society, including women, the poor and uneducated, the sick and disabled, Samaritans, and eunuchs. His message was that all were equal and could partake in celebratory meals, a metaphor for inclusion in the realm of God. To achieve this goal, we must engage in dialogue, challenge harmful stereotypes and misinformation, and work toward dismantling systems of oppression. Only then can we create a world where everyone is treated with respect and dignity, regardless of gender identity or gender expression. We can create a more just and equitable world for all through education, advocacy, and compassionate action.

Mining & Minding Merton

A
As I stated in the Preface to this second part of the book, at any given point in my life, there were several things happening all at once. This paper from deals with essential aspects of my evolving spiritual beliefs and practices.

By now, you know I refrain from calling myself a Christian since the crap being slung at trans persons seems to come mostly from those who call themselves "Christians." I said the label was too tarnished to be salvaged and that when Jesus said, "A new command I give you: Love one another. As I have loved you, so you must love one another. By this, everyone will know you are my disciples if you love one another" and that Jesus didn't say, "By this, everyone will know that you are a Christian."

I have also mentioned my lack of membership in any denomination or community of faith, and I have talked about not feeling at home in any organized religion. That may change, or it might not. What is true is that I have practiced a very private spirituality for the last decade. I would not claim that it is mysticism, at least not in the traditional understanding of what it means to be a mystic. However, my studies and my research into trans spirituality—the interviews with the participants, hearing their stories and analyzing the data, all helped to intensify my sense of inner peace and empowerment.

What I left out of the chronological narrative was a paper I wrote for my second summer course with a visiting scholar in the summer of 2014, Thomas Merton Scholar Dr. Christopher Pramuk of Xavier University. My paper explored in detail an essential aspect of my evolving spiritual beliefs and practices.

Here is a summary of the paper I wrote for Dr. Pramuk; I hope it is not too dry and academic. I hope you will find it helpful. The concepts and themes have not only resonated with me, but they have also aligned with my one experiences as a trans person of faith. I believe, however, that these are universal themes.

Merton's Early Years

The life of Thomas Merton was marked by deep loneliness and sadness from his early years to adulthood. He was enrolled in a residential school for boys and was only a child when he received a letter from his dying mother informing him that he would never see her again. This news left a heavy burden on him, leading to adult-like grief and perplexity. He was left without a home, family, or even a country and felt completely alone. At fourteen, when he learned that his father was seriously ill, he was overwhelmed by his loneliness, feeling isolated from everyone and everything. These events left a profound imprint on him, shaping his future tendencies and desires.

As he grew older, Merton's need for independence became more apparent. He started to resist the authority of others and go his own way, determined to have his own will and do what he wanted. His need for independence was perhaps a defense mechanism to mitigate the pain of his loneliness, but it eventually made him yearn for solitude. He felt the need to separate himself from the world, finding solace in isolation.

In 1940, Merton converted to Catholicism and entered the monastery to become a Franciscan priest. However, doubts started to creep in, and he began to question whether he had a true calling to this vocation. Reading a couple of lines from the ninth chapter of Job disrupted his sense of confidence, and he was left wondering about the meaning of these words. He realized that he had come face to face with his secret self and did not like what he saw. He longed for deeper intimacy with God but was full of self-recrimination and humility.

Merton's doubts and fears were compounded by the realization that none of the trusted men whom he had sought counsel from about the priesthood knew anything about his past. He feared that he would not be allowed to become a priest if they knew the truth about him. This realization left him feeling cast out into a dark solitude, wrestling with his thoughts and trying to find meaning in his life.

This experience led Merton to seriously consider leaving the monastery and seeking a different path in life. However, after spending some time in solitude and prayer, he came to the realization that his vocation to the priesthood was indeed genuine and that he had to confront his past and work through his inner struggles in order to move forward.

Through his faith, he sought to find meaning in his life and deepen his relationship with God. He delved deeply into the contemplative life, seeking to understand the mysteries of God and the human soul. Thankfully, he documented his journey in his writings, which include journals, essays, and poetry, reflect his ongoing spiritual struggles and his efforts to find meaning and purpose.

One of Merton's most famous books, "The Seven Storey Mountain," chronicles his journey toward becoming a monk and his struggles with loneliness, doubt, and spiritual emptiness along the way. The book became a bestseller and helped to popularize the contemplative life among a wider audience.

Despite his deep spiritual insights and his profound influence on contemporary spirituality, Merton remained humble and always open to learning from others. He sought to bridge the gap between religious traditions, engaging in dialogue with Buddhists, Hindus, and non-Christian seekers.

On Loneliness and Solitude

In his later years, Merton became increasingly concerned with social justice issues, particularly the problems of war and poverty. He saw the need for spiritual contemplation to be connected to action in the world, and he worked tirelessly to promote peace and social justice through his writing and activism.

But what interested me were his thoughts on solitude, to which he devoted many pages.

His immersion began with an experience at Gethsemane Abbey during Holy Week, which was transformative. He was struck by the absolute simplicity of the monks and how absorbed and transformed they were in the liturgy. He was impressed by their lack of fuss or display and saw this as a metaphor for the paradoxical reversal of the world's logic, which insists on the aggrandizement of the individual. He saw the Cistercian life as the opposite of worldly logic: "men put themselves forward, so the most excellent is the one that stands out."

Merton believed that in hiding from the world, a monk does not diminish himself, but rather his personality and individuality are perfected in the true order, the spiritual, interior order of union with God. Merton's time at Gethsemane Abbey was marked by a struggle between his desire for solitude and his passion for human connection. He felt drawn to the simple and unvarnished life of the monks, but he also craved the company of others.

Merton's tension is evident in his journal entries from this time, writing that he was not interested in the world or things, not interested in doing things, being important, or being good or bad. He was not interested in history or politics or anything else. All he wanted to do was to be left alone, stay in his cell, or be alone and not be bothered.

And yet, he found himself constantly seeking human companionship, wanting to talk to people, be with people, help people, and do something for somebody else.

Merton believed that the truest solitude was not merely physical separation from others but a state of mind that allowed one to be alone in the midst of others. In other words, one can cultivate a sense of inward detachment and spiritual union with God even amid a busy and noisy world. Solitude is not necessarily a physical state but rather an inner disposition.

Merton's belief in the value of solitude and inwardness was not a rejection of community or the world. He believed that the true hermit had not withdrawn from the world but from the false self, the self that is defined by its relationships to others and the world. In Merton's view, the true hermit had found the true self, the self that is defined by its relationship to God. This inward detachment, which allows one to be in the world but not of it, can also lead to a greater sense of compassion and love for others.

Despite his love for solitude, Merton also struggled with the idea of living a cloistered life. He was torn between his desire for solitude and to engage with the world and make a difference. He found himself drawn to social justice issues and began exploring the intersection between his contemplative life and his desire to effect change in the world.

Merton's journey toward a deeper understanding of solitude and contemplation was not easy. He struggled with doubts and fears, constantly questioning his calling.

Our times of loneliness are opportunities for sober recollection. We can shed our disguises and allow ourselves into our personal secret space during these times. No one can enter that secret space except God and us. God is the only one who can penetrate that region of our being and make sense of it, even when we find ourselves incapable of coherent language. This is the groaning of our spirit that Paul talks about. God meets us in those moments, which are the moments of Latin's solus, of solitude.

It is important to note that Merton did not equate or claim that solitude was as becoming God. Rather, it is a spiritual and mystical communion where we become one with God. He understood God is not a being of domination. Instead, God becomes available to us in kenotic generosity. As unbalanced as the equation may seem, God creates a space where we are granted everything pertaining to life and God-likeness so that we may become partakers of His divine nature (2 Peter 1).

Here is what dawned on him: If we allow God to transform us this way, His compassionate, divine nature transforms all our human relationships. How can it not? The lens of compassion will be a palette of color that lets us see everyone in a new God-given light. It is this compassion that has the power to redeem our collective humanity.

The God-awareness we experience in our state of solitude compels and enables us to be compassionate and respectful of others. As we recognize how unconditionally God has entered into our secrecy and loneliness, we can love unconditionally and extend the milk of human kindness to those around us. It starts with us, as Merton suggests: "If a man does not know the value of his own loneliness, how can he respect another's solitude?"

In conclusion, Thomas Merton's life was characterized by a profound sense of loneliness and sadness from his early childhood to adulthood. These experiences shaped his tendencies toward independence and his desire for solitude.

Despite his struggles, he found solace in his faith, delving deeply into the contemplative life and seeking to understand the mysteries of God and the human soul. Merton's beliefs about solitude and inwardness were not a rejection of community or the world but rather a way to cultivate a sense of detachment and spiritual union with God, even in the midst of a busy and noisy world.

His journey toward a deeper understanding of solitude was not easy, but it ultimately led him to a greater sense of compassion and love for others.

As Merton suggests, recognizing the value of our own loneliness can enable us to respect and love the solitude of others, ultimately leading to the transformation of our collective humanity.

The Transgender Spirituality Pulse Survey

The Master of Arts in Public and Pastoral Leadership degree has one requirement that put me in a bind: during the second year of studies, there is a Theological Field Education (TFE) component. It's a chance for students to think about how they practice doing ministry, improve their leadership skills in ministry, figure out what their calling is, connect with others in their field, and grow as individuals. At the same time, they put what they're learning into practice. It's a way for them to bring together what they learn about ministry and use it in real-world settings.

What that looks like depends on the student, but at the end of the day, it is similar to doing a Co-op, where students integrate classroom work with practical work experience. Before the end of the first spring term, we were required to propose what we planned to do and with which organization. For example, one might want to design a program for single pregnant women to complete their General Education. If your proposal is approved, you use the summer break to design the program.

During the following fall term, you implement the program under the supervision of the organization that partnered with you for the pilot. You analyze the results in the last spring term and present the results as your capstone project. You discuss what worked, what didn't, and what you would do differently next time and ponder its future. All of this is to help you develop your leadership skills.

It goes without saying that whatever you design and execute must have a theological basis. Why? You are in a seminary! What that basis looks like is for you to decide and your professors to approve.

I failed to have a proposal for my TFE in on time. The summer started, and I still had no idea what I could do to align with my goals to work with trans persons in some spiritual support capacity. I had so many questions that needed answers. Without those answers, it would have been arrogant and presumptuous for me to design a field education project for trans people. It would be like putting the cart before the horse. I asked if I could do a study instead, one specially designed to get the pulse of the trans community when it came to their spirituality.

I met with my professors to discuss my idea. In the six years since VST introduced the MAPPL, this was the first time someone had proposed to do empirical research. I argued that based on available research on the issue, it was impossible to know what the spiritual needs of the trans community were, that is unless I asked them. The few published studies I found offered little information.

Fortunately, I stumbled upon several studies that offered an approach I could use. These were studies of spirituality in a healthcare context. And in particular, I found a research tool called the Daily Spiritual Experience Scale (DSE), a measure used to assess an individual's perception of spiritual experiences in daily life. The scale was developed by Lynn Underwood, a research scientist who conducted extensive research on spirituality and health. The DSE scale has been used in various research studies investigating the relationship between spirituality and health outcomes, such as depression, anxiety, and quality of life.

The DSE is based on 16 questions asking participants to rate their daily spiritual experience in different areas. I only wanted to use a set of 6 of the questions, but this required written permission from Underwood. She signed off on my application and was pleased to know which population group I was using it with. In her response, she wrote, "This is important information for us to know." The second requirement was that a final copy of the study had to be sent to her.

With this feather in my cap, my proposal was approved. I could proceed with a quantitative and qualitative study titled the "Transgender Spirituality Pulse Survey (TSPS) 2015." I planned to design the study during the remaining summer months and recruit participants for September, interview a cohort of 18 for the qualitative portion and conduct a quantitative study using Google Forms through the middle of November, transcribe the interviews by Christmas, encode the data in January, analyze the data in February, write the final paper and capstone report in March and present my findings to the review committee at the end of the month. When all was said and done, the final printed report with graphs and a bibliography was over 65 pages long. My head hurts thinking about it.

If you want to read the complete study, download it from Academia.edu. Below is the conclusion to the study (if you feel like nerding out): The Transgender Spirituality Pulse Survey (TSPS)

Summary

The Transgender Spirituality Pulse Survey (TSPS) tapped only half of the transgender (trans) community, those who have transitioned socially and live full-time in their identified gender. This study sometimes refers to them as the "emerged" or "visible" portion.

This visible portion of the trans community has been getting much attention lately, with the growing public awareness of trans people in pop culture and mainstream media. Yet there is still much misunderstanding and, as a result, fear.

The apparent growing momentum of the emergence of trans people has given society and its stalwart defenders of morality a severe case of cognitive dissonance. Trans persons are challenging long-held views of what it means to be a man or a woman, boy or girl. This has resulted in a growing pushback, which has also intensified lately—to the point where many religious conservatives in the U.S. and Canada are speaking out against the passage of trans-inclusive policies and laws and lobbying to have any existing ones rescinded.

The message to the trans community is evident. Religious people are not their friends. This is not new. This study found that trans people have little regard for anything related to organized religion. In the qualitative portion of this study, many participants talked about how the homophobic and transphobic messages created a repressive and suppressive environment that lacked love but offered up judgment and the threat of rejection. Despite this negative experience, the TSPS found that trans persons have not stopped being spiritual. Conversely, their struggle to survive has been a crucible for their spirituality, intensifying it and making embraceable.

While it would be arrogant to project the findings of this study on those who either choose or are forced to remain invisible, it must be remembered that all the TSTS participants were also once invisible to society. This was not only due to the repressive environment described above but mainly due to how little was understood about what it meant to be trans. It was not until just a few decades ago that medical science found effective ways of helping trans people deal with internal disconnection from their bodies. While not all trans people may need, want or be able to transition, all endure the negative messages coming at them—that they are psychologically confused.

One underlying assumption of this study is that being trans is a biomedical reality and not a psychological gender identity disorder. Another underlying assumption is that spirituality is universal to all humans, that a person's spirituality is linked to health by promoting expectations of positive outcomes, and that spirituality provides a framework for the interpretation of human suffering.

Therefore, it is important to acknowledge that not all trans people's experiences are the same; some suffer more than others. Trans women of color are disproportionally more at risk of violence and STDs than white trans women. Many layers of privilege and systemic oppression intersect with being trans. This study had some limitations in this regard. For example, only those privileged with Internet access were able to participate in the study. The study also did not attempt to track marital status, employment, income, race, or sexual orientation, which could impact a person's experience of spirituality.

The study found that though most trans people have shed religious conditioning and dogma, their spirituality has become more authentic and honest, making them more compassionate.

Their spirituality has intensified and become transformative, making them feel more connected to God/Higher Power, others, and life.

It also found that on a daily basis, trans people are more than twice as likely to be spiritually touched by the beauty of creation, seven times more likely to be thankful for blessings, two and a half times more likely to feel selfless caring for others, almost three times more likely to accept others even when they do things they think are wrong, and 25% more likely to desire to be closer to, or in union with God/Higher Power, and in general, feel closer to God/ Higher Power than the general population.

The Qualitative Study participants offered a comprehensive list of intentional spiritual practices which are, for lack of a better word, in the public domain—outside the walls or brokerage of institutionalized religion/spirituality. At the same time, the TSPS participants who identify as Christians only make up 39% of the total, compared to almost 78% in the general population. The exodus from Christianity is a result of the negative experiences discussed above. The study found that many have moved to more affirming spiritual traditions and practices, such as Buddhism and earth-based spiritualism, while a few have declared themselves agnostic or atheist. What is telling is that of those still identifying as Christian, only 17% may attend church.

Implications of the TSPS ...for the Communities of Faith:

It's important to recognize that not all trans individuals view the church as distant and irrelevant. It's also important to note that trans individuals are not necessarily seeking acceptance within the church. According to the TSPS, only 17% of transgender people are interested in attending church. However, this does not mean that a church's efforts to become inclusive and affirming are a waste of time and resources.

The goal should not be to fill seats or attract trans individuals to the church but rather to shape the attitudes of the members of the congregation toward trans individuals in the community. How will they treat a neighbor who is trans or the clerk at the market? Will a trans classmate ever be invited to play with their child? If they own a business, will they hire a trans person? If they own rental property, will they rent to a trans person? If a qualified trans person is running for an elected position, will they vote for them?

While people of faith have been unfairly generalized, it is also true that allies within the church, those who consistently support the transgender community, are often in the minority. To become relevant allies, people of faith should not stand silently on the sidelines. They need to speak out against harmful policies and attitudes. They need to call out discrimination and, at times, place themselves between trans people and those who want to harm them. Trans people should not have to do battle alone.

Additionally, the church can play a vital role in supporting the mental health needs of trans individuals. According to the American Foundation for Suicide Prevention, trans individuals attempt suicide at ten times the rate of the general population. Instead of trying to change trans persons, the church could offer resources and counseling services and advocate for policies and attitudes that promote mental health and well-being while abandoning the notion that trans people can be fixed through conversion or reparative therapy.

Lastly, it's essential to understand that supporting trans individuals is a matter of social justice. Trans individuals face significant barriers to accessing healthcare, housing, employment, and other basic human rights. According to the National Center for Transgender Equality, 29% of trans individuals live in poverty, and 30% report experiencing homelessness at some point. The church can help to address these injustices by advocating for policies that uphold equity and justice for all, regardless of gender identity or expression.

In conclusion, the church can become a relevant and supportive ally to trans individuals. This includes speaking out against harmful policies and attitudes and creating safe spaces for trans individuals within and outside the church.

Implications of the TSPS ...for the the Transgender Community:

If you are a trans person, you must be intentional about your spirituality, if only for health reasons. Stress will mess with your body. To what extent you choose to transition is not as relevant as the importance of being self-compassionate and authentic to who you are.

Being able to forgive yourself is crucial, and being able to forgive others will become easier. Rejection from family and friends who have known you for a while is possible initially, but there is some truth to the statement "it gets better." If you don't burn your bridges with family and friends, there is a good chance that, given time, they will come to accept and embrace you.

You will notice how differently you treat others after you come out or transition. Many trans people find they are more caring of others—more compassionate. It stands to reason that once you can be happy with who you are, you can focus on others. Your experience of being trans is transformational in many ways, not least in how you view and appreciate the beauty of life and nature.

The crucible that has been your life has refined you from the inside out. Appreciate it and celebrate it with those you can intimately connect with. It's okay to be very private about your spirituality, but don't be surprised by how good you will feel when you can share it and talk about it with others.

* * *

I'll give the last word on the TSPS to one of the study participants, who sent this lovely note after I emailed the final study to her. This is what she wrote:

> "It is a beautiful thing for members of our community to read about ourselves. Lovely as it is, though, I don't believe it's really surprising. People who embark upon the soul-searching that "our journey" often entails, who endure the suffering and experience the pure joy that "our journey" inevitably produces, no matter the specific details, probably had accepting, caring and spiritual natures to begin with, even if those natures were sometimes buried very deeply. But even if they didn't, going through these experiences would tend to make them that way. I refer, of course, to how we, in our community, share and bear witness to our own suffering and joy and that of others on the journey with us. This cannot help but make each of us "more spiritually touched by the beauty

of creation" and more accepting of and caring toward others. All others."

Template for a Celebration of Life

One of the things I always feared having to do was officiate a memorial service for a total stranger. I don't know about you, but I've attended some memorial services where the person had no personal connection to the deceased, and their comments sounded like hearsay because they were hearsay. I felt sorry for the poor sucker who had that job. Those services stood in stark contrast to when the officiant had enjoyed a personal connection to the person.

When I was an intern at St. Paul's Hospital, I got a call from my teaching supervisor one morning. He told me to go to the safe-injection clinic operated by the hospital in the DTES instead of going to the hospital. One of the clinic's clients had died unexpectedly from a fall, and the staff and fellow clients had organized a celebration of life for the man, but they wanted a chaplain to officiate. I was instructed to call the social worker who was expecting my call and to get there as quickly as possible. It was my turn to enter the twilight zone of trepidation.

I had an hour to prepare a reflection. I interviewed the staff and some of the friends who were already at the clinic. Though I carried a small inter-denominational prayer book, I was never comfortable using it. It wasn't my style. I used my iPad to find an answer to a question that popped into my head; how many words or phrases do we have for feelings and emotions? It was a question I had considered when I was designing the qualitative portion of the TSPS research for my MA.

I know this is a weird thing to include in a memoir. You might wonder if this means I have a morbid obsession with death. Actually, the opposite is true. I share this as a tool to inspire and encourage you to celebrate and connect with life more fully.

Since then, I have shared this template with several colleagues and a pastor who twitted that he was at a loss and asked for help on how to officiate a celebration the life of a total stranger.

In my role as a Spiritual Care Practitioner, I have found versions of the questions below very useful for getting to know a new patient, or resident, and it has led to some wonderful conversations and the person has felt valued and seen. (I've left the name blank and used gender-neutral pronouns.)

Welcome
(Land Acknowledgment)
We acknowledge the sacredness of the space and of the moment, a place and a time set aside to:
- Remember **(name)**,
- Reflect on what they meant to us,
- Celebrate and give thanks for their life.

I would like to take a few minutes to allow us to acknowledge each other with this simple yet profound greeting:
PEACE BE WITH YOU.

*I am privileged to stand with all of you today who knew and remembered **(name)**. But honestly, I am at a huge disadvantage.*

*I never met **(name)**.*

*I didn't know **them** as you did.*

*It would be arrogant and presumptuous of me to talk about **(name)** as if I knew them intimately.*

*And I suspect that even if I had the opportunity to talk to each of you to learn everything I could about **(name)**, we would still have a lot of big gaps in our collective knowledge about them.*

*It is impossible for anyone to know everything about **(name)**, just like it is impossible anyone to know everything about us.*

Think about your own life and all the people who know you. Could they answer three hundred questions about you?

Did you know that we have over three hundred words and phrases in English for different feelings and emotions?

And there are many feelings and emotions for which we don't have a word that other languages describe. For example, Spanish has a word that conveys the embarrassment we feel watching someone else's humiliation; it's "Pena-ajena" (Peh-nah-ah-henna). There are many, many more.

We could try to use that list of three hundred words to help us paint a picture of who **(name)** *was and what made them unique and special. But we would need to allow many hours, if not days, for this project, and we might still not have the total and accurate picture.*

I've been trained to come alongside patients and their families who are experiencing all kinds of deep emotions and feelings. Sometimes there are so many conflicting feelings it is difficult to sort them out in one visit. This process can extend over several visits.

I often ask them, "What are you feeling right now?"

I will then ask about specific feelings and emotions. It is so helpful to name and connect with our feelings.

Connecting—it's a very spiritual process, our sense of connection—with our own feelings and emotions, to other people, and with God, or the Divine, or however we under-stand the Love force in our lives.

As I was preparing my thoughts this morning, I began asking myself some of these questions about **(name)**.

I would like to read some of these questions to you now, and I invite you to think of **(name)** *and how they might have answered. Afterward, as a memorial, I invite you to share your memories about* **(name)***, what they meant to you, or what it might be you will always hold close to your heart about* **them**.

Here are the questions: (in Ying-Yang pairings). Some of your answers may break your heart, but others will warm your heart and put a smile on your face as you think about **(name)**:

*What made **them** peaceful?*
    *What disrupted **them**?*
*What inspired **them**?*
    *What stifled **them**?*
*What made **them** proud?*
    *What brought **them** shame?*
*What were **their** dreams?*
    *What were **their** terrors?*
*What gave **them** strength?*
    *What weakened **them**?*
*What made **them** laugh?*
    *What made **them** cry?*
*What turned **them** on?*
    *What turned **them** off?*
*What toughened **them**?*
    *What **softened** them?*
What made them fearful?
    *What made **them** feel safe?*
*What caused **them** to withdraw?*
    *What drew **them** out?*
*What was **(name)** closed about?*
    *What were **they** open or candid about?*
*What caused **them** to isolate?*
    *What caused **them** to engage with others?*
*What made **them** fragile?*
    *What made **them** unbreakable?*
*What gave **them** dread?*
    *What gave **them** hope?*
And finally,
    *What filled **them** with joy?*
        *What filled **them** with awe?*

*These are only 10% of the possible questions we could ask about **(name)**, or anyone, for that matter, if we went through the long list of emotions and feelings. (Imagine, we have three hundred topics of conversation!)*

I'm sure all of us would cringe at some answers to some of these questions if they were about us. The thought that anyone could know us so intimately is unimaginable, and for some of us threatening. Perhaps, in awe of this idea, the Psalmist was inspired to declare these powerful words:

¹ O Lord, you have searched me and known me.
² You know when I sit down and when I rise up;
* you discern my thoughts from far away.*
³ You search out my path and my lying down,
* and are acquainted with all my ways.*
⁴ Even before a word is on my tongue,
* O Lord, you know it completely.*
⁵ You hem me in, behind and before,
* and lay your hand upon me*
⁶ Such knowledge is too wonderful for me;
* it is so high that I cannot attain it.*
⁷ Where can I go from your spirit?
* Or where can I flee from your presence?*

The Psalmist passed this idea on to us: that the Creator knows us intimately—warts and all—yet loves us unconditionally. Maybe that is why we think this connection is a mystery. How is it possible?

*In small measure, we are declaring a very similar truth here today. If even the little we know about **(name)** is enough to unite us and bring us together, imagine how much more connected to each other we would feel if we knew more about **(name)** and each other.*

*I would like to suggest this is **(name's)** parting gift to you.*

I read an interesting article about a psychological phenomenon called "the Overview Effect." It is the cognitive shift in the mind of astronauts and cosmonauts when they first look down on our planet from space. Seeing the Earth suspended in the vastness of space causes them to see life and human existence differently.

These men and women were all scientists, one way or another. There were Chemists, Physicists, Biologists, Mathematicians, Geologists, Meteorologists, Medical Doctors, Psy-

chologists, etc. We usually think of scientists as atheists and agnostics; that's the stereotype we have. But almost without exception, they return to earth with a transformed sense of spirituality and connectedness. It's a very personal and profound religious experience for many of them, and they are never the same.

While not on the same scale, we experience the Overview Effect when we pause to reflect and remember the life of someone we knew and love. The process helps us reconnect and sharpen our perspective.

As I said, this is (name's) parting gift to you!

They have allowed us to pause and consider life and our human existence together. And for that, we are grateful.

I invite you now to share and celebrate your memories of (name) as you are ready.

Closing prayer — Amen

* * *

As the sentient beings that we are, I believe that reflecting on someone's life, even if we don't know everything about them, can bring us closer together and help us appreciate our own existence. In a memorial service, this can be the gift we receive from the departed. We shouldn't wait until grieving a loss. We need to take the time to reflect on these kinds of questions and use our capacity for empathy and understanding to connect with others.

Let this be an exercise in empathy building. It will evoke compassion. I think it is what Jesus had in mind when he said, "Love the Lord your God with all your heart and with all your soul and with all your mind. This is the first and greatest commandment. And the second is like it: Love your neighbor as yourself. All the Law and the Prophets hang on these two commandments."

Bye for now. Go in Peace, Lisa

I was there.

(The illustration on the front cover is based on photo taken on that day by Vancouver photographer, Leada Stray.)

White supremacists exist in Canada, as proven by the 2017 rally held outside Vancouver City Hall by anti-immigrant groups, the Worldwide Coalition Against Islam's Canadian Chapter (WCAI Canada) and the Cultural Action Party (CAP). The rally sparked concern among political leaders that white supremacists may attend, similar to those present at the Charlottesville rally one week earlier. However, despite fears of violence, civil liberties experts and activists supported the rally's continuation, believing that shutting it down would not address the root causes of racist ideologies.

Vancouver police were present to monitor the event. Thousands of people showed up at Vancouver City Hall for a counter-protest to the far-right rally, with the aim of outnumbering the anti-immigrant contingent. While tensions rose briefly, there were no reported assaults or injuries, as Vancouver police quickly escorted several far-right demonstrators away from the crowd.

The plans for the far-right demonstration were circulated on social media in the same week as the deadly white nationalist march in Charlottesville, Virginia. The rally was protesting Islam and the Canadian government's immigration policies, as stated on the event's Facebook page.

Despite the concern over the far-right rally, political leaders, including Vancouver Mayor Gregor Robertson and the Premier of the Province, John Horgan, condemned the rally, stating that "hatred and racism have no place" in the city, and that the province rejects "all forms of racism, discrimination, intolerance, and bigotry."

The photo used for the book cover illustration was taken on that day. I was proud of how my city responded to the far-right rally. I commends the decision to let the rally proceed, and the successful counter-protest, stating. It was an example of how a community can come together to combat hatred and bigotry, outnumbering the ralliers by more than 20 to 1.